You Can Program in C++

A Programmer's Introduction

COMPACT
DISC

Francis Glassborow

You Can Program in C++
A Programmer's Introduction

John Wiley & Sons, Ltd

Other Wiley Editorial Offices

John Wiley & Sons Inc., 111 River Street, Hoboken, NJ 07030, USA

Jossey-Bass, 989 Market Street, San Francisco, CA 94103-1741, USA

Wiley-VCH Verlag GmbH, Boschstr. 12, D-69469 Weinheim, Germany

John Wiley & Sons Australia Ltd, 42 McDougall Street, Milton, Queensland 4064, Australia

John Wiley & Sons (Asia) Pte Ltd, 2 Clementi Loop #02-01, Jin Xing Distripark, Singapore 129809

John Wiley & Sons Canada Ltd, 22 Worcester Road, Etobicoke, Ontario, Canada M9W 1L1

Wiley also publishes its books in a variety of electronic formats. Some content that appears in print may not be available in electronic books.

Library of Congress Cataloging-in-Publication Data

Glassborow, Francis.
You can program in C++ : a programmer's introduction / Francis Glassborow.
    p. cm.
Includes bibliographical references and index.
ISBN-13: 978-0-470-01468-4 (pbk. : alk. paper)
ISBN-10: 0-470-01468-7 (pbk. : alk. paper)
1. C++ (Computer program language) I. Title.

QA76.73.C153G59 2006
005.13′3 – dc22

2005026864

British Library Cataloguing in Publication Data

A catalogue record for this book is available from the British Library

ISBN-13: 978-0-470-01468-4 (PB)
ISBN-10: 0-470-01468-7 (PB)

Typeset in 10/11 JoannaMT by Laserwords Private Limited, Chennai, India
Printed and bound in Great Britain by Bell & Bain, Glasgow
This book is printed on acid-free paper responsibly manufactured from sustainable forestry
in which at least two trees are planted for each one used for paper production.

Dedication

This book is dedicated to the numerous people who have helped me to master the art of writing simple programs in C++. I appreciate their gentle correction of programming so that it has reached a standard that I feel able to share with others.

Contents

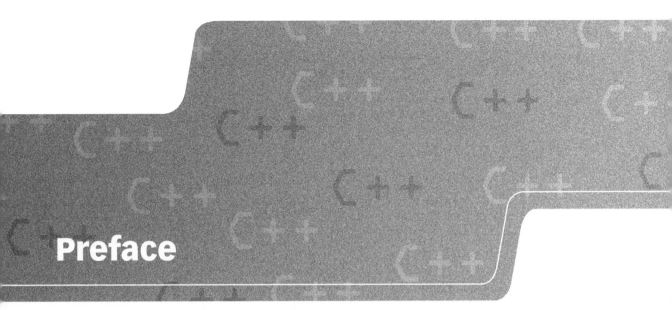

Preface

My previous book, *You Can Do It!*, was written for the complete newcomer to programming. I made no assumptions about the reader's prior knowledge and skills other than that they were capable of using a Microsoft Windows–based machine at the general level of accessing the Internet. It should not matter to such people what language is used for their practical experience of programming. I chose C++ because I felt certain that it was well up to the task, as long as I used a carefully chosen subset and augmented the Standard Library with a library of my own design that would support writing programs that newcomers would find interesting. The priority of that book was learning sound programming.

This book is intended for a very different readership: you should already be comfortable with the basics of programming. Exactly how you have acquired those basics will result in different expectations and problems with learning C++. One of the delights of C++ is its ability to handle the programming paradigms of most of the principal language groups. If your first language is Lisp and you are fluent in expressing problems in that language, then C++ is going to cause you a lot of mental readjustment, but most other languages will provide a good basis for moving to C++, as long as you have an open mind about how the solutions to problems should be expressed in source code.

I do not intend to provide comprehensive coverage of the whole of C++: it is far too big a language to do that. I am not going to attempt to show you all the ways in which C++ can be used: C++ is far too rich a language to attempt that in a single book. Indeed, I doubt that any single author knows enough to provide adequate coverage of all the ways C++ can be used.

My aim is to provide my readers with a sound introduction to a reasonably large working subset of C++. Along the way, I will demonstrate how C++ can be used to handle a variety of programming problems.

You will get as much from this book as you put into reading it, or, more correctly, studying it. I do not believe in trivial, make-work exercises. You should be able to provide yourself with those without any help from me. That means that the exercises in this book, along with the experiments and actively trying the code in the body of the text is part and parcel of reading this book successfully.

If you want to try C++ and have a basic knowledge of programming fundamentals, this book was written for you. I hope you enjoy the journey and feel motivated at the end to continue onwards, because C++ is the most challenging programming language available. It does not seek to constrain what you can do or how you do it. That is one of the ways in which it differs from all the other popular computer-programming languages.

If you can master C++ you will be mistress of programming and able, should the need arise, to adapt to other languages quickly.

Francis Glassborow
July 29th, 2005

Acknowledgements

Like any book, many people have contributed to this one in addition to the named author. Some, such as the staff of Wiley & Sons Ltd, do so because it is their job to do so. However I appreciate the extra effort that each of these people have put in that distinguishes them from the mere time-server or wage slave.

Then there are the countless numbers of people who have added their ideas, sometimes unwittingly, to mine. These include many members of ACCU as well as all those experts who attend meetings concerned with Standardizing C++. Bjarne Stroustrup must take pride of place among these because he is not only the original creator of C++ but has also spent many hours over the last fifteen years patiently helping me to understand his creation.

However there are three people without whom this book would not be what it is. Garry Lancaster was the original implementor of the Playpen Library for Windows. Jean-Marc Bouquet adapted Garry's implementation for machines that use X11 (initially Linux, but also other Unix and MacOS X machines). Finally, Mick Brooks who has spent many hours of his valuable time checking that my text worked on a Linux machine. Each of those people contributed their efforts free, to the benefit of the C++ community.

Elsewhere, I give credit to those responsible for the two IDEs that are shipped on the CD for this book. However, I hope you will show your appreciation for the work of Parinya Thipchart (thipchart@gmail.com) who is the designer and implementor of MinGW Developer Studio. jGrasp, G++ and MinGW are examples of the excellent tools that are made available free by their developers. MinGW Developer Studio is the work of a single person and is distributed as user-supported software. In simple terms, it means that Parinya trusts users to make a contribution based on their use of the product and their personal circumstances.

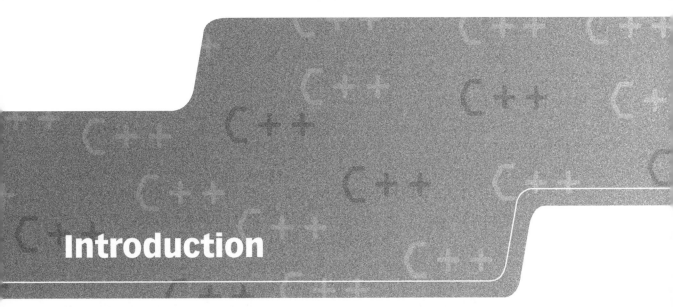

Introduction

If you are reading this, you are most likely to be trying to decide whether this is the book that will help you learn C++. To make your choice, you need to know what this book sets out to do and how it is different from the many other alternatives that litter booksellers' shelves. I am not going to claim that this book is uniquely better than all the alternatives, but I do claim that it is distinctly different as well as being technically accurate.

The first question is: "Can you already program in some computing language?" If your answer to that question is no, then this book is almost certainly not the one for you to start with. You will need some other book such as my own *You Can Do It!* [Glassborow 2004]. However, if you already know about such things as loops, decision statements, and functions, then read on.

I make as few assumptions as I can about what you know about programming. In particular, I do not assume that you know anything about the C programming language. Indeed, if you already know C, be prepared to learn to do things differently. Though the name 'C++' is supposed to suggest the next step beyond C, and almost all of C is also C++, good C is often not good C++. The languages share a common core, but the differences lead to very different programming styles.

I will introduce you to programming in C++ using all the modern idioms and tools that have evolved over the past two decades. For that reason, this book introduces C++ by using high-level features and only covers low-level features as and when they become necessary for further progress.

The purpose of this book is to give you a firm grasp of the foundations of Standard C++. To gain understanding, you need to write programs. So that you can try more adventurous programs, I have supplemented the Standard C++ library with a library of my own that supplies four basic extras:

- A few simple utility functions to make it easier to write correct programs right from the start. They are written in pure Standard C++ and so are portable to all Standard C++ implementations.
- A very primitive graphics window that can be managed from a pure console program (a program that runs as pure text). This works identically on Windows- and Linux-based PCs (and also on OS X versions of the Apple Mac).
- A one-button mouse (i.e. mouse support that treats all mouse buttons as equivalent). This gives the major benefits of having a mouse without the complexity of having to deal with multiple buttons, wheels, etc.
- Direct reading of the keyboard, so that your programs can directly observe the keys you press on a keyboard. That little feature dramatically extends the kinds of program you can write.

Note that I have provided these four elements to make the process of learning C++ a more enjoyable one, during which you can write a much wider range of programs than you would otherwise have been able to. (If you want to, you could even write one of the classic console games such as Space Invaders.) I avoid explicit use of my library throughout most of the book, but you should feel free to use it both to enhance your solutions to the provided exercises and to add other exercises for yourself.

In addition to my own library of tools, this book comes with a full C++ compiler (MinGW) and a choice of two IDEs. The first, MinGW Developer Studio, is a user-supported product. If this is a strange term to you, it means that if you like the product and wish to continue using it, you are invited and encouraged to make a donation (whatever you think it is worth to you) to the writer of the product. It is not shareware, because there is no restrictive licence limiting how much use you can legitimately make without paying a fixed registration fee. Nor is it freeware, in which you are never expected to pay anyone. (MinGW itself is an example of an outstanding freeware product.) So please show your appreciation of a well-constructed tool by going to the product's website and making a contribution.

The second choice of IDE is a more complicated but highly portable one from Auburn University called JGrasp™. It is written in Java, so you will need to acquire a suitable Java Runtime Environment. This IDE was written explicitly for the purposes of teaching and learning. It has a number of outstanding features to help newcomers explore the code they write. It is free to individuals but must not be distributed as part of a commercial product. The licence under which it has been placed on the CD is one specifically for educational books. JGrasp accepts many C++ compilers, including MinGW, as plug-ins.

These IDEs run on both Microsoft Windows and Linux systems. Indeed, JGrasp runs on any system that supports Java, but for the purposes of this book you are limited to systems for which my library has been implemented. At the time of writing, that includes all versions of Windows post 95 and Linux (and, I am told, OS X on an Apple Mac).

The main text of this book will assume that you are using MinGW Developer Studio with MinGW as the compiler. The tools that are available free and supplied on the CD are full-weight professional tools that are often used by professional programmers. You may wish to use some other toolset, but you will need to check the book's website (`http://www.spellen.org/youcandoit/`) to see whether I have supplied a copy of my library for that set of tools. Unfortunately, one of the restrictions of C++ is that library distributions are often specific to compilers and have to be recompiled if used with a different compiler.

This book is also designed for you to use as a reference. For example, when I introduce the built-in types of C++, the study text will use only a subset of the available types. At the end of that chapter, you will find a complete summary of all the built-in types and their derivatives. That provides a single point of reference close to the point where you first learn about the C++ type system. When you first study that chapter, you will probably want to skip the reference part, but at a later stage you may want to read deeper into a subject, or look something up easily.

To summarize: this book teaches you to program in Standard C++ using a modern idiomatic style. To make the process of learning more enjoyable, I have provided some extensions to the C++ library that are, at a minimum, portable between Microsoft Windows (98 and after) and Linux. The book comes with everything you need to read and study it apart from a computer and operating system – those you must provide for yourself. Apart from the extensions (graphics, sound, mouse, and direct keyboard read), everything else in this book is portable to any computer with a Standard C++ compiler installed.

Studying C++

Sometimes circumstances compel us to acquire a new skill by ourselves. It is often much harder that way and sometimes blocks our progress. If you want to learn to play a musical instrument, you need to practice by yourself, but it is also essential to spend time playing with someone else. If you do not, you will acquire bad habits that will very seriously hinder your future progress towards making music with others. To a lesser extent, the same applies in learning to program in a computer language. It will be easy to force the idioms of your first language onto the new one that you are studying (C++). Without the discipline of working with others, this weakness in your use of C++ can go unchecked. This is particularly true if your first language is a close relation of C++ (such as C, C#, or Java). It is not enough to learn the syntax of a language: you also need to learn how that syntax is intended to be used.

When I was at school, I learned the Japanese game of Go from a book. I taught a couple of fellow pupils the rules and played on a homemade board. Many years later, I met someone who had learned to play from an experienced player. Our first few games were interesting for both of us, because my understanding of tactics and strategy was so completely haphazard. There were places where my play was relatively sound and others where I would make a novice mistake. Do not let your C++ become like that.

Ideally, find both a study partner and a mentor. The former will provide an alternative view on the language; the latter will help you to develop a sound understanding. Make sure that you know how things work by checking with someone who already knows. Be wary of the self-proclaimed local expert; like my early Go knowledge, their knowledge may be very patchy. Good places to visit to read and ask questions are:

```
comp.lang.c++.moderated
alt.comp.lang.learn.c-c++
```

Those Usenet newsgroups have resident experts who know more about C++ than all but a tiny minority. There you will find genuine experts. Make use of them.

Learning C++ is an interactive exercise. You cannot learn C++ without actually writing programs. You already know that from whichever other languages you have learned, but I have repeated it here by way of emphasis. If you skip the practice work presented in this book, you will be selling yourself short. You may finish reading the book more quickly, but your C++ will be the poorer for it. This is not a book about learning C++ in some set period; you will need to take as long as it takes in order to master each bit. Sometimes it may be worth moving past a sticking point and coming back to it a little later. But if you permanently skip something because you do not understand it or you think it is not much use, it will come back to haunt you.

Using This Book

Please use this book in conjunction with a computer! Try the code and do the exercises. I hope the exercises are helpful – I did not provide them to fill an expected slot in a textbook. It is sometimes a temptation to look at an exercise and decide that you can see how to do it and move on without actually doing the work. However, practice makes perfect, and it will help your acquisition of fluency with C++. Quite often, doing an exercise will reveal subtleties that you miss at first glance.

At other times, you might get this great idea either for a new program or for developing one from the book. In such cases give in to temptation and spend some time following the idea. If you write up the problem and email it to me (initially via the submissions form on the book's website), I will post it on the site to inspire others.

You will find some source code on the CD, both that for my library and code from elsewhere. Some is good; some is not but is included because I used it as a stepping-stone. For example, the code that supports the Portable Network Graphics part of my library was written in very old C. Its greatest merit is that it works and works correctly, but it is far from the kind of clear, maintainable code I would encourage you to write. Other source code on the CD requires a great deal of knowledge of the specifics of Windows or Linux. It will be far from clear even to programmers who have a good background in the system concerned. Even my own code on the CD is a less-than-perfect example of good code. As time goes by and other experts comment, it improves, but all code is subject to, or at least should be subject to, progressive improvement. One test to apply to code is whether it is structured so that such progressive improvement is relatively easy.

To understand the code in **playpen.cpp**, you will need considerable experience of both C++ and graphical-user-interface code for the OS you are using. That is the file that had to be reworked to provide my library for Linux and other systems that support the X Window System (not to be confused with Microsoft Windows, which is something very different).

You can obtain other source code from the site for my books (**http://www.spellen.org/ youcandoit/**). You should also visit that site for anything else that might have missed this book's CD. Additionally, you can contact me through that site, or directly by e-mailing **ycpcpp@robinton.demon.co.uk**.

If you choose to e-mail me directly, please make sure that you include a subject line, because I usually assume that e-mails without subjects are spam.

This book is not 'C++ in x time units'. You must set your own pace. If it takes you only six months to grasp all that I provide, you are doing well. However, long before you finish, you will have enough knowledge of C++ to do many useful things. On the other hand, even after you have finished, there will be much more to learn. Every one of the leading C++ experts tells me the same thing: they never stop learning and discovering new aspects of programming in general and programming with C++ in particular. Perhaps that continued process of learning and discovery is what has made them into world-class experts.

A Comment on Comments

Some people feel that source code should be extensively commented, and you will find books where the displayed source code is densely populated with comments. I believe that the best documentation of code is the code itself. Comments should be used to express those things that cannot be easily expressed in source code. An introduction to C++ needs to provide a lot of explanation, but comments are not, in my opinion, the place for that.

There are useful things that are not expressible in source code. For example, every file of source code should include both the date of its origin and the name of its author. Somewhere there needs to be documentation that describes what a piece of source code does. However, if there is a comment on every line of code, that coding style has a serious problem. A few well-placed comments can be very useful. However, if those comments are surrounded by repetitious ones that add no value, the valuable ones may be missed.

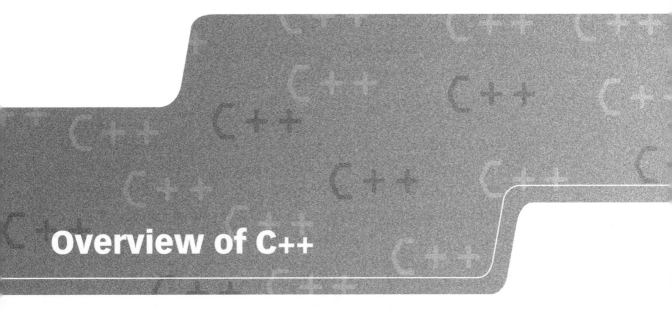

Overview of C++

I very nearly numbered this as chapter -1 on the basis that it precedes your actual learning to use C++. You can skip this chapter if you are anxious to get on with the process of learning. You can always come back to it later. However, I think that a quick read through, even the parts that address languages that you do not know will help you with your study of C++.

What is in a Name

You may already know that C++ (pronounced 'see plus plus') is so named because it was designed by Bjarne Stroustrup as a successor to an earlier (and still widely used) language called C. In C, ++ means 'increment' and, in mathematical terms, to increment means to obtain something's successor. Therefore, you could interpret the name as meaning 'the successor of C'. Like the concept of a successor in mathematics, that does not imply replacement. If you already know C, you need to recognize that C++ is a new and different language, even though much C source code will compile as C++. Usually the result of a successful compilation of C source code with a C++ compiler will be a program that behaves exactly like the one produced by a C compiler. However, that is not always true.

In the early 1980s, Bjarne Stroustrup designed an extension to C that he called 'C with classes'. If you are interested in the history of how that personal tool grew up to become the most widely used programming language in the world and one that has fired the imaginations of many people you will have to look elsewhere. (A good place to start would be with *The Design and Evolution of C++* [Stroustrup 1994].) This book is about programming in C++ as the ISO/IEC 14882:2003 Standard defines it, that is, Standard C++ as it was specified in 2003 (which is the first official standard, with various corrections that were made between 1998 and 2003).

What is in C++

C++ is one of the most widely used programming languages in the world. It is also one of the largest programming languages ever designed. Bjarne Stroustrup specified that one of the design criteria of the language is that there should be no room for a lower-level language between C++ and native machine code. Very few programmers ever use C++'s lowest level, and many do not even know that it has an **asm** keyword, which allows support for writing code in assembler.

The incorporation of C into C++ was an important design decision. On the positive side, it made it easy for C programmers to transfer to C++. Having made the transfer they could, at least in theory, incrementally add to their C++ skills and understanding. On the negative side, it has tied C++ to a number of features of C's design that experience has shown to be, at best, problematical. It has also caused problems to many who have moved from C to C++, because they have made the transition from a C to a C++ compiler without actually making the mental transition from C to C++. They are still C programmers at heart. There is nothing wrong with that, but it does provide a roadblock to their becoming fluent C++ programmers. If you are a C programmer you may find studying modern C++ tougher than you would if your first language were something else.

At the high end of C++ we find tools that allow innovators to do metaprogramming, that is, source code that generates source code. We will not be exploring that in this book, but it is worth noting that in learning C++ you are learning a language that supports the most innovative development of programming currently around.

In between assembler support and support for metaprogramming, C++ provides tools for procedural programming, object-based programming, object-oriented programming (I will explain the difference later when you know enough C++ to appreciate the differences), and generic programming. With care, you can even do some functional programming.

Alongside the raw power of the core of the C++ language, the Standard C++ Library supports a wide range of things that programmers commonly want to do. We have learnt a great deal over the last few years, and were we to start writing a library today we might produce a substantially different one. However, what we have is better than anything provided previously in any widely used programming language. In addition, much of the library has been designed for extension: it is designed so that new components can easily be added and work correctly with standard components. On the other hand the Standard Library currently lacks many of the components that users of more recent languages such as Java, C#, and Python have come to expect.

It is both one of the strengths and one of the weaknesses of C++ that it does not dictate a methodology or paradigm. When people first learn C++ this can be a problem, because the range of choice requires understanding of the implications of those choices. If the newcomer already knows another programming language, they will naturally try to discover how to write their first language in C++ terms. They will think in their first language and try to translate into C++. Such is the range of C++ that they can often get a close approximation, but that usually does not lead to good C++.

C++ can be viewed as everyone's second language. Mastery of C++ requires that you leave behind the crutch of your first language. That is hard and you will make many mistakes along the way. However, the result will be that you are a much better programmer both in C++ and in any other programming language you already know or choose to learn later.

C++ has a wide range of operators. Most of them can be extended to include user-defined types. With the potential for redefinition comes the responsibility to use such a facility wisely. The intention was that it should be possible to add types such as complex numbers, matrices, quaternions, etc. and provide the operators that a domain specialist would expect and find intuitive. Unfortunately, some programmers take the availability of a mechanism as a challenge to find creative ways of using it. The result is that their code becomes ever more obscure.

C++ is a living language. By this I mean two things. The first is that the very best users continue to develop new idioms and other ways to use it. The entire growth of metaprogramming in C++ started one evening when a group of experts realized that the template technology of C++ (designed to support generic programming) was a Turing-complete programming language in its own right, one that was implemented at compile time. C++ was not designed for metaprogramming, so using it is often ugly, but it has enabled experts to explore the potential of metaprogramming.

The second way in which C++ is a living language is that it is subject to periodic change. Even as I write, those responsible for the definition of C++ (WG21, an ISO standards committee) are working on changes that will eventually come into effect at the end of this decade. Some of those changes are to make C++ easier to write and to learn, some are aimed at cleaning up inconsistencies, and some will be aimed at further extending the power of the language. At the time of writing it is impossible to predict exactly what will be added and what changes will be introduced. I know that providing better support for metaprogramming is one of the potential additions to C++.

I am only sharing this with you so that you can see that C++ is alive and well and continuing to develop in a controlled and measured way. What you learn from the rest of this book will be valid for a number of years, and even after the next release of the C++ Standard, almost everything you have learned will still be true, but there may be some easier ways to achieve the same objectives. One of the guidelines for growth and development of ISO programming languages is that every effort should be made to preserve existing source code. This is in marked contrast to some non-ISO programming languages that change on much shorter cycles and often in ways that break existing code.

Different Backgrounds

In the rest of this chapter I am going to attempt to make some helpful comments based on the most likely languages that you might already have learned. Every language has strengths. Every language has its own special properties, and those using them will have learned various idioms. Some of those idioms will not easily transfer to C++.

If your first language uses a syntax that is like that of C++ (for example C, Java, or C#) you are going to have to overcome the tendency to think that what looks the same behaves the same.

In general you are going to have to fight the natural tendency to think the way that your first language works is the way that programming languages should work. There are wide differences in languages. Most computer languages have been designed by highly intelligent people. The differences are not accidental, and the differences do not make one language better than another. Sometimes we can capitalize on the way one language works to write a program in another one.

Many years ago the warden of the Oxford Schools Sailing Centre asked me to write a race-analysis program for him to use on his Acorn BBC Microcomputer (an old British desktop computer built around the 8-bit 6502 processor). The native language for that machine was a version of BASIC. Now in those days my language of choice for problem solving was Forth (check `http://www.forth.org/` if you want to know more). I spent a Saturday morning at the warden's house being fed coffee and biscuits while I wrote the program for him, superficially, in BBC BASIC. When the job was done, he looked at it and said, "That does not look anything like BBC BASIC." He was spot on: the program was designed in Forth and implemented in BBC BASIC. Every program statement was a correct BBC BASIC statement, but no BBC BASIC programmer would have written that source code. Another Forth programmer would have recognized it despite the use of a different programming language.

Sometimes, as a once-off task, you can do something like that. The result was neither good Forth nor good BBC BASIC. It had only one merit: it met the client's needs and worked correctly. If a student learning BBC BASIC had produced that program, they would have lost marks from me for inappropriate use of the language. Mastering a language includes mastering its idioms.

Fundamental C++ for C++ Programmers

No, I have not lost the thread. Quite a few readers may already have done some preliminary programming with C++. Some of them will have had a good experience and a good introduction, while others will have had a less sound introduction.

My book *You Can Do It!* [Glassborow 2004] is specifically a book about programming, and all the focus of that book was on how to program. It uses C++ as the language for writing programs, but it was not written as a book about C++ and so left out a great deal of the language. (I estimate that the book covers only about 10% of C++.) While there is some overlap between that book and this one, those who acquired their basic programming skills through my first book can learn much more about C++ from this one.

There are many other books that introduce C++ as a first language. Some of these do a good job and some a rather mediocre one. You might also have learned C++ at school or from a web-based tutorial. In any of those cases, you might reasonably want a more complete introduction to C++ fundamentals. Like all those who come to this book having gained their programming basics from some other language, you will possibly need to unlearn some things and change the focus of others. If what you read in the rest of this book seems to conflict with what you learned previously, you will need to think hard. Perhaps your earlier learning led you to too specific an interpretation of the way something worked. Perhaps the original source was plain wrong. It is even possible that this text is plain wrong (though I sincerely hope not).

One definite area of potential conflict is that the C++ I am writing about here is very different from the C++ of the early '90s, which many other books introduce. The syntax of the language has not changed (though there have been some additions), but the way that the best modern programmers use that syntax to express solutions to problems has changed out of all recognition.

Try to use any tension resulting from conflicts between what you have previously learned about C++ and what this book says. In trying to resolve those conflicts, you will come to a much better understanding of the way C++ works. While I have given a good deal of thought to the way I write and teach C++, that does not mean that I own 'the one true way'. There is no such thing. There are many bad ways to write C++ and several good ways. One hallmark of a good way is consistency. If I choose to express an idea with a different idiom it is, I hope, because there is a difference. I try not to do something one way on weekdays and a different way at weekends.

However, there is a caveat. One of the ways that programs differ is in their purpose. For example, much of the code in this book is designed to help you learn C++. That is quite different from code written as part of a large application. When you are working as a member of a team, you should conform to the presentational and coding standards of the team. However, you should also take pride in every line of code you write. I do not go for the concept of 'egoless programming'; we should be proud of our contributions, but we should not seek to make those contributions irritate by being in a different style from that of the rest of the team.

The step from good personal code to industrial-strength code is considerable. When we write code for ourselves, we can often ignore the fact that what we write will only work on the machine we are using, or that it depends on the development tools we have. On the other hand, when learning C++ you should have a clear division between what is Standard C++ and any extras. I think you will find it in this book.

Fundamental C++ for C Programmers

The traditional route to C++ was through learning C. Unfortunately, many excellent aspects of C are no longer so sound in the context of C++. In C++ we have to consider issues such as exception safety (be patient, we will get there!), polymorphism, **const** correctness, and overloading of functions and operators. These issues lead us to a very different programming style.

One small example is the issue of using pointers. Good C often relies heavily on correct and extensive use of pointers; good C++ frequently avoids pointers or uses a C++ mechanism for encapsulating pointers (called smart pointers) to control their potential for damage.

Another example is that in C++ we rarely, if ever, use a dynamic array (the kind of object that a C programmer creates with **malloc( )** and manages with **realloc( )**). C++ provides a vector container (**std::vector<>**) that automates most of the resource handling.

C++ provides real types to handle both strings of **char** and wide strings of **wchar_t** (which is a full built-in type in C++ rather than an alias for some integer type as it is in C). It also provides a convenient mechanism for creating other string types such as those we might want for Japanese.

C++ input and output mechanisms are designed to be type safe, unlike those in C, where it is the responsibility of the programmer to ensure that the type the programmer says will be provided is the type actually provided.

A C programmer learning C++ needs to focus on understanding why C++ does some things differently. Contrary to what you may read elsewhere C++ is not better than C; despite the deliberate compatibility of syntax, C++ is a distinctly different language. Unless you come to understand that, your C++ will remain C in disguise. That would be to sell both yourself and C++ short.

There is nothing in C++ that prevents you from using C dynamic arrays, arrays of **char** and **wchar_t**, or members of the **printf** and **scanf** families of I/O functions. It is just that C++ provides alternative mechanisms whose use is less demanding of programmer time.

Sometimes I may write that C++ has a better mechanism for doing something than C. Such statements should be taken in the broader context of programming rather than as an implication that C++ is better than

C. C is fundamentally a language for programming close to the metal. That makes it an excellent language for writing for small, embedded systems such as the dozens of micro-controllers that permeate modern life. C++ was designed for writing very big suites of code where millions of lines of source code is not unusual.

Fundamental C++ for Java Programmers

One of the problems you are going to have is that much of Java syntax is also valid C++ syntax but it does something slightly different. The underlying object models of the two languages are subtly (some would say radically) different.

In some ways, you are going to have more difficulty than anyone else does in learning C++. You are going to be constantly writing code that you expect to work. It will compile and then do something bizarrely unexpected. You will have to resist the natural temptation to think either that your compiler is broken or that C++ must be a broken language. Java has many strengths, and I am certainly not going to denigrate it (I do not do language wars). But learning Java as a first language causes considerable problems when you then try to learn C++.

Major issues concern such things as order of evaluation: Java strictly defines this; C++ states that it can be in any order. Another issue is the concept of references: C++ references simply do not behave the same way that Java ones do. For example, every C++ reference is required to refer to an actual object and refers to the same object throughout its lifetime.

You will also find that there are issues with constructors: superficially, C++ and Java constructors seem to do the same thing, but when we look under the hood, we find that they work differently. At the other end we have the concept of destructors to end the lifetime of an object, but C++ does not have garbage collection (though there is nothing in the language to prevent it being added as long as the programmer avoids some C++ mechanisms). The lack of garbage collection was a deliberate design decision; it can always be added but it cannot be taken away. Java source code expects a garbage collector and will be badly flawed without one. C++ written on the assumption that there is no garbage collection will usually work correctly even if there is.

All these issues and many others are going to make things difficult, because you will need to relearn your code-reading skills.

I am reminded of an episode from my school days, when I was a reasonable chess player. We had the then (1956) British Chess Champion, C.H.O'D. Alexander, visiting the school to give us some instruction and to play the school in a simultaneous match. At the end, we were discussing the subject of fairy chess (chess played with various modified rules). One variation he suggested was to simply swap the values of the pieces so that, for example, the one that looked like a bishop was actually used as a knight.

If you play chess, try it. I think you will understand the problem of things not being all that they appear to be. That is the major problem that Java programmers have when learning C++.

Fundamental C++ for C# Programmers

C# is superficially even closer to C++ (the similarity of the sharp sign to overlapping plus signs is not accidental) and so is going to add to code-reading problems.

Like the Java programmer you are going to have to learn the concept of global functions and data. That can be a hard step. Unlike the Java programmer your first language does incorporate the ideas of destructors and user-defined value types. However, the C# concept of a destructor is very different from the C++ one, so you will have to do some careful thought getting those differences clear in your mind.

C# has garbage collection and is heavily constrained by the requirement that it function under a CLI (Common Language Infrastructure) based virtual machine such as .NET or Mono. For example, types are more strictly defined; they have to be because all languages running on a CLI VM have to agree about the size and layout of the fundamental types.

Again, as for Java, C# references are not exactly the equivalent of C++ references, so be careful when I write about references—they may not be what the word leads you to expect.

In C++, the keywords struct and class, which are used to define a user type, are very close to being synonymous. So close that the only reason why good C++ programmers ever use struct is to emphasize that what they are writing is basically a simple C-style aggregate type. This is not the place to explain why C++ has two words without a substantive difference, though some of us think that this was one place where Bjarne Stroustrup made a less-than-ideal decision.

In C++, the difference between value types (those that C# defines as structs) and object types (close to the C# concept of a class type) is entirely in the way the programmer designs the type. There is no semantic content in the choice of struct or class in C++.

Fundamental C++ for COBOL Programmers

C++ comes as a nasty shock to long-term COBOL programmers. I can remember sitting in the back of an introductory C++ course (I was assessing the instructor). One of the students had programmed in COBOL for 25 years. He was finding great difficulty with the concept of a pointer, because he had never needed such a mechanism in all the years that he had programmed in COBOL. The instructor was having quite a bit of difficulty in trying to get the student to see that C++ needed something that COBOL did not. At the end of the week-long course, the student assessed the course as a waste of time. In a sense, it was, for him. As it happens, I knew his manager, who told me the rest of the story. He had been sent on the course as a last attempt to break him out of a very narrow and specific view of programming. It had not worked, with the consequence that his employer could no longer use him as a programmer, and his rigid thinking made him ill-suited to other work in the company.

I relate this sad tale as a warning to others. A rigid view of how programming works makes professional development difficult and ultimately impossible. If you come to C++ from a radically different language you will need to get down to fundamentals such as decisions (if–else), looping (for and do–while), and functions or procedures. Those basics are shared by all languages, but the exact way they are implemented can vary considerably. Think of natural languages. English, Chinese, Arabic, and Hindi are all powerful human languages, but if you think an alphabet is fundamental to writing, you will have a great deal of difficulty with Chinese.

I was brought up in Sudan, and I can remember my mother's struggle with teaching one of our servants to read English (at his request). In Arabic the basic meaning is carried by the consonants, and the difference between verbs, nouns, adjectives, etc. is largely conveyed by the vowels. Now Abdul knew that English was different, but knowing and believing are different things. One day he sat there struggling to see the logic behind 'hat', 'hot', 'hate', 'heat', 'hut', 'hit', and 'hoot'. From his perspective, there was an obvious relationship between a hut and a hat, and you wore a hat when it was hot, and 'hate' sort of fitted, being a hot emotion. Just possibly, 'hit' could be worked in, because you wore a hat to protect yourself both from the sun's heat and from being hit on the head. However, how did 'hoot' get into the mix?

Beware of trying to force your view of a topic into some preconceived framework. Just as 'ht' does not label a fundamental concept in English, you must avoid trying to force C++ into the mould of your first language.

Fundamental C++ for Python Programmers

Python is a very interesting language. However, those that learn programming using Python must be careful to distinguish programming fundamentals from the way that Python implements them. One of the interesting features of Python is that the program structure is communicated by the program layout. Levels of indentation matter in Python, whereas they do not in C++. C++ uses braces, { and }, to block statements together. We encourage C++ programmers to use indentation to make their code more readable for human beings, but indentation has no significance to the compiler.

Another important feature of Python is something it shares with a few other languages: names are just names. A name in Python takes on the characteristics of whatever was last assigned to it. This is an immensely powerful programming concept, but one that does not work well in the case of a compiled language. C++ source code can be interpreted (I know of one reasonable interpreter for C++) but is generally compiled to machine code for the platform on which the program will run. That is why a compiled C++ program for a Linux machine will not run on a Microsoft Windows machine.

Python gets around the problem by supplying a Python program (effectively a virtual machine) that takes Python source code as data and executes it. In this, it is a little like Java: Java programs only run in the context of special programs called Java Virtual Machines. However, Python goes further than Java by making a great deal more use of the immediacy of code.

I am not going to attempt to explain the gains and losses of each mechanism. All I can do is to warn you that they are very different; each language has its advantages and each has its costs.

Fundamental C++ for (Visual) Basic Programmers

Many years ago BASIC (computer languages were spelled in all uppercase in those days) was designed as a language for teaching programming. It has come in for a good deal of criticism from academics over the years, some of it justified and some of it not. The biggest problem was not in BASIC but in the way that it was often taught. It trapped many teachers into teaching bad programming.

Visual Basic is a Microsoft proprietary language that is a refinement and extension of the original BASIC. It is a powerful language that has been damaged by its owner's propensity for releasing incompatible dialects. One of the better features of Visual Basic is the provision of visual-programming tools that allow you to generate code for complicated components from a palette of more basic ones. One surprise to VB programmers is that Visual C++ (simply Microsoft's toolkit for C++ programming) does not supply any kind of visual-programming tools for C++. There are tools around for visual programming with C++ but they are largely of limited use, because the strengths of C++ are not with visualization but in the exact expression of computation and in data management.

C++ is much more to do with the underlying programming than it is to do with constructing applications from available components. This makes it a more powerful tool when you want to do something different, i.e. something for which there are no pre-designed components.

When you learn C++ you are going to be concerned with expressing solutions to computational problems rather than being focused on data capture and data display. When you have a firm grasp of the C++ fundamentals you will be able to use libraries of pre-built components to handle some input and output problems, but that is not the focus of C++. You may even find one of the visual-programming tools useful (though they are not cheap).

Fundamental C++ for Pascal and Delphi Programmers

Pascal was a language that set out with the grandiose intention of providing a computing language that was hard to abuse. Unfortunately, the consequence was that it created a generation of programmers with one of two bad mindsets. Highly talented programmers knew that Pascal was getting in the way and preventing them from doing things that they knew could both be done and be done safely. This led them to that form of creative programming that used to be called 'hacking'. In other words, they found ways round the well-intentioned obstructiveness of the compiler. The rest of those learning Pascal tended to have a view that if the compiler would compile it, then the code was OK. That created a mindset that what a compiler would compile was safe.

A Pascal programmer reading this book is unlikely to have such a mindset, but be warned: C++ expects users to be responsible, to understand what they are doing, and to avoid doing dangerous things. A C++

compiler will not try to second-guess you and refuse to compile code simply because the result might be dangerous.

One of the more famous problems that C++ has inherited from C is the concept of a buffer overrun (a problem that is by no means exclusive to these languages). C++ expects that when you provide storage for input you will make sure that you provide sufficient storage or add a mechanism to prevent excessive input overwriting other data. If you program carelessly you produce programs that are vulnerable to being overloaded with data. In these days of the Internet, many of us have discovered the bad consequences of such carelessness. Pascal would probably have died out many years ago were it not for the efforts of a single company, Borland. Borland created a version of Pascal with a considerable number of extensions. Those extensions provided a safe and correct way to do many of the things programmers wanted but which were prevented by Standard Pascal.

More recently Borland further enhanced Pascal with features to support object-oriented programming. That extended dialect of Pascal is called Delphi. In addition, they then enhanced their C++ development tools to support mixing of C++ and Delphi. The result is that if you are a Delphi programmer you must be very careful that you do not fall into the trap of believing that C++ is what you get when you use Borland C++ Builder (their implementation of C++) in its Delphi compatibility mode (which is very tempting because you then have the use of an extensive third-party library, written in Delphi but accessible from Borland's extended C++).

In general, Pascal programmers have to learn to trust themselves to get code correct and not trust the compiler to reject dangerous constructs.

Fundamental C++ for Functional Programmers

If you come from a background of functional programming (perhaps having learned Haskell, Scheme, or ML) you will likely be shocked by what C++ so cavalierly calls a function. In C++, not only are functions allowed to have side effects, but they usually do. Perhaps one day we will have a mechanism to tell a C++ compiler that something really is a function in the mathematical/functional-programming sense but that day is not here yet.

By default, C++ variables are indeed variable. Like other programming languages, C++ allows and even encourages assignment. If you are a functional programmer, you are first going to have to master the instinctive revulsion you may feel for such an 'ill-disciplined' language.

For the purpose of this book, you are going to have to put much that you have learned to one side. But do not discard it, because when you move on to less fundamental C++ (not in this book but perhaps the next one) you will find that many of those ideas and idioms that you are familiar with allow you to become a fluent user of some of the advanced aspects of generic programming and metaprogramming. Indeed the very best C++ programmers often deliberately choose to learn a language such as Haskell in order to enhance their C++ skills.

Fundamental C++ for Lisp and Logo Programmers

It is hard to know where to start if you have mastered Lisp. First, you must have been lucky to have been taught by someone who understood how Lisp works. I say that because far too much Lisp is taught by instructors for whom it is a third or fourth language. The problem is that they often do not think in Lisp; they know its syntax but for them it is like an English speaker writing Japanese by using a dictionary and a grammar to translate from English.

The same problem applies to those who have truly learnt Logo (usually by trial and error). If your knowledge of Logo stopped with Turtle Graphics then you may not have too big a struggle with learning C++ but if you went much further then you will need to focus on the fundamental ideas of functions, repetition and decisions. The semantics of those are common to all computer languages but the syntax is significantly different.

Just as those that learn Lisp or Logo as a third or fourth language struggle because they keep trying to impose the structures of procedural languages onto the new language they are learning, those going the other way will have to abandon the thinking they have developed to handle list processing and imperative languages. At least you will have to suspend those ways of thought until you have mastered the fundamentals of C++.

Fundamental C++ for Object-Oriented Programmers

From time to time people describe C++ as an object-oriented programming language (OOPL). It is not; it is a language in which you can do some forms of object-oriented programming (OOP). If you want to do pure OOP, try a language such as Smalltalk. However, if you come from such a background be very careful, because the C++ form of OO is significantly different from what you will have learned. There is enough similarity to lull you into a sense of security and enough difference to make that a false one.

By default, methods (well, we call them member functions in C++) are statically bound. That is, implementation code is selected at compile time, not at execution time. C++ provides a mechanism for delaying binding until execution time (so-called dynamic binding), but the programmer has to make a positive decision that that is what they want.

In C++, not everything is an object in the sense usually meant by an OOPL. When we talk about objects in C++, we do not mean exactly what a Smalltalk programmer would mean by an object. The concept is near but not an exact duplicate.

Fundamental C++ for Every Programmer

There are many other languages that you might have learned. Fortran, Modula 2 or 3, Forth, and Prolog are just a few that I know to a greater or (usually) lesser extent. If you are old enough you might be fluent in PL/1, and if you are a mathematician you might use APL (an outstanding interpreted language for those who think mathematically—and almost impossible for the rest to grasp). You might also have learned Ada. If you really dig into the odder corners you might have learned SNOBOL. I just throw that last one in because it was a great language that did not catch on. However, I believe Andy Koenig has a set of libraries and other tools to enable SNOBOL mechanisms and idioms to be used in C++.

Whatever language or languages you already know, C++ has something to offer you, and your prior knowledge and skills have something to offer your study of C++. The most important thing is that you do not try to make C++ just another way to write the language you already know. This is particularly important if you are learning C++ because you want to broaden your job opportunities. Knowing enough C++ to get through a job interview will not help you if you then try to write Xlang in C++ clothes.

Good programmers write fluently in many computer languages; bad programmers write the same bad code in many computer languages. I hope that by the time you finish your study of C++, you are both a better programmer and a good C++ one.

CHAPTER ①

Getting Started

This chapter introduces you to the tools that I have provided on the CD for your use as you read this book. You may prefer to use some that you already have, or you may prefer to use the IDE provided on the CD. Whatever choice you make, it will be to your advantage to work through this chapter and check that each step behaves correctly (or that you can achieve the equivalent with the tools of your choice). If you use MinGW Developer Studio (which I will refer to as MDS), you will be able to check that you are doing the right thing by comparing what you see on your screen with the screenshots in this chapter. If you are using JGrasp™ from the CD, you will be able to check the alternative version of this chapter that is on the CD. If you are using some other tools, you should still work through this chapter to make sure that you understand how to use them to produce a simple program. Most importantly, you will need to check that you can use my library with your choice of tools.

Before you go any further, read the file **Read_First.txt** in the root directory of the CD. That will tell you what is on the CD and where to find the instructions for installing the software for the operating system used by your computer (Microsoft Windows or a UNIX derivative such as Linux or Mac OS X). When you have done that, or have installed some other development tools of your choice, continue from here.

It may be that you are familiar with the kind of tools used with a compiled language because one of the languages you already use has similar tools. If so, please excuse me for taking time explaining things for the benefit of other readers.

In this book, I assume that you are using an Integrated Development Environment (IDE), which is the programmer's equivalent of a carpenter's workbench. Some programmers are used to using the command line; that is fine if you understand how to write your own makefiles. If you do not (or even have no idea what those are), you would probably be better off using an IDE that will automate much of the interaction between the stages of writing, compiling, linking and debugging your code.

I am now going to walk through the process of producing two simple programs from scratch. The first program is the traditional 'Hello World'. The second one is to check that everything has been correctly set up to use my graphics library. These programs are deliberately simple so that we can focus on the process of creating a program from source code and libraries. As I go, I will add information that may be new to you if you are used to a language that is substantially different from C++.

Creating a 'Hello World' Program

The first step is to launch, or start, the IDE. I always have the IDE icon on my desktop. If you accepted that option when you installed the software from the CD, you will find this icon somewhere on your desktop:

If you chose otherwise, you will have to launch MDS differently. When you have launched MDS, you should see this window on your screen:

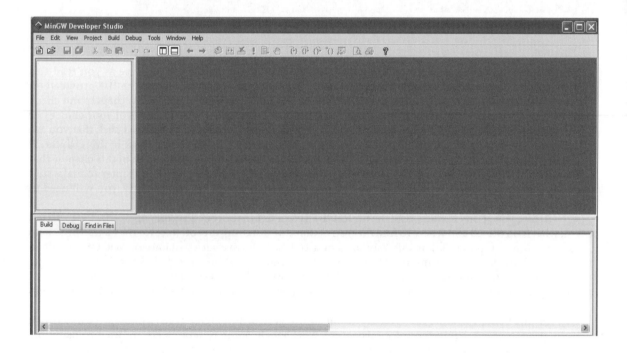

The various panes are adjustable and we will see what each is for as we go. If you are familiar with using an IDE, you will probably recognize most of what is on the screen. If you start pulling down menus, you will notice that most of the entries are 'grayed out'. Most of the icons are grayed out too, but unless you have disabled the feature, you will get a tool-tip if you let the mouse cursor hover over an icon. These tips are minimal, but I find the inclusion of the default hotkey in the tip a useful feature.

Your next step is to go to the Project menu and select New Project (Ctrl+N if you prefer to use hotkeys).

When you do this, you will see a data-capture window that looks like this:

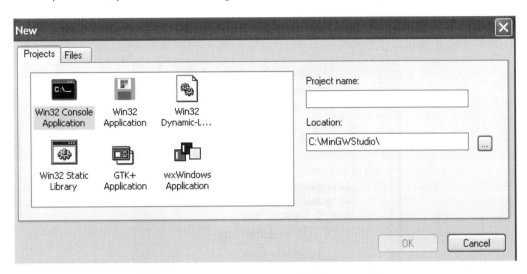

The default project type is a console application, and that is what you will want through most of this book. You need to tell the IDE the name of the project and the location of your files for this project. You are less likely to make a mistake if you identify the location first. If you look at the lower text box, you will see a small gray button on the right. Click on it and then navigate to the appropriate subdirectory. If you installed MDS, by default that will be `C:\tutorial\chapter_1`. Now go to the upper box and give your project a name. Type in `hello_world` (note that MDS does not correctly handle file names that contain spaces) and click on the OK button.

Next you need to create a file for the source code (the correct term for what we write; the compiler turns that into object code). Select New from the File menu and you will see:

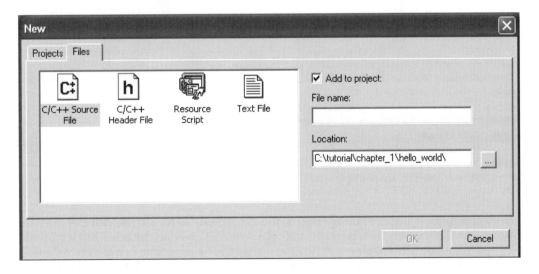

The defaults are correct (or they should be). You are creating a C/C++ source file and adding it to the project; the location of the file is the same place that you placed the project itself. All you need to do is give the file a name. Type **hellomain** into the File name box. After I have opened the FileView tree (in the left-hand pane), the top left of my work window looks like this:

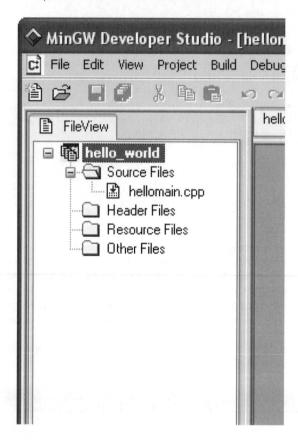

Type the following into the file pane (the right-hand one, which has a '1' in the dark-gray margin zone):

```
// First program written on 21/07/04
#include <iostream>

int main(){
  std::cout << "Hello World";
}
```

Make sure you press Enter after the closing brace, so that the file ends with a newline character.

As you type, MDS tries to give help by its use of color. When you type an unmatched bracket (parenthesis, brace, or square bracket) it first displays it in red. You can use Ctrl+B to go from one bracket to the matching one (if there is one). The MDS editor also supports code folding (the ability to hide code leaving only a header element); try clicking on the minus sign to the left of '**int main**' and you will see what I mean. It is not very useful here, but can be helpful when you want to hide extraneous details while you focus on some other section of code.

When you have typed in the code, select Compile from the Build menu. If you have done everything correctly, you should see

```
hellomain.o - 0 error(s), 0 warning(s)
```

in the bottom pane. If you forgot to press Enter after the closing brace of the source code, you will get a warning. The compiler issues a warning because C++ files can include other files; a missing empty line at the end of a file could cause a problem because the compiler might append the next line of code to that line. If you are used to using an interpreted language such as Python, you may be wondering what you have achieved so far. A tool called a compiler has converted your text (source code) into a form (object code) that the linker can use to produce an executable program. We will look at the rest of the source code shortly, but for now I want you to produce an executable program and run it. You can do that step by step, by selecting Build from the Build menu and then Execute from the same menu; or you can just select Build and execute. The choice is entirely yours. You can even select Execute directly, and MDS will ask if you want to build the executable.

However you execute the program, you should finish up with the following console window:

MDS inserts a closing message (after your program has finished) so that the window will stay open until you are finished looking at the results. 'Terminated with return code 0' means that the program finished satisfactorily.

I want you to try several things before we go on. First, I want you to change the project settings. Select Settings from the Project menu. Now select the Compile tab and check all the warning boxes except for the last one (making all warnings into errors is usually overkill). For now, leave everything else as it is.

The settings can be separately set for a debug version and for a release version. While we are developing a program, we are usually willing to accept slower performance and a much larger program file in exchange for more help if the program encounters some problem while it is running.

However, when we are ready to share our work with others, we probably do not want to have a very big, slow program, so we produce a release version. The release version is normally much smaller and possibly appreciably faster, because the compiler has worked hard to strip out all unnecessary details.

Do not worry about the other tabs in the Project Settings dialog box. We will only be using the Compile and Link panes.

Next I would like you to take some time experimenting with the source code (try adding extra lines of output, leaving out a semicolon, and introducing other typos) until you are confident with compiling, building, and executing it. You are going to spend a lot of time with these tools, so it is worthwhile spending a little time gaining some fluency with them. That is one reason for starting with such a silly little program: it allows us to focus on the basics of our tools before we use them to write programs with more substance.

What the Code Means

Let us look briefly at the six lines that made up the 'Hello World' program.

The first line is a comment. Whenever the compiler meets a `//`, it ignores everything from there to the end of the line. Comments are for humans and sometimes for special code-analysis tools; they are not for compilers. In this case, the comment is almost redundant, and I have included it only as an example.

The second line tells the compiler that the following code may use names from the part of the Standard C++ Library concerned with streaming data in and out through the console. We call the part in the angle brackets a 'header'; it tells the compiler to get relevant information from wherever it keeps such details. Different compilers may obtain the information in different ways. In practice, a header is usually a text file in one of the compiler's subdirectories. (If you are interested, you will find the corresponding `iostream` file in `MinGWStudio\MinGW\include\c++\3.4.2`, but I doubt that it will make much sense to you yet.)

The blank line has no significance and is there purely to separate the introductory part of the source code from the rest. The next line (`int main( ){`) must exist exactly once in every program. Effectively it determines where a program starts. There are some variants that allow the provision of data at program start-up, but that is all.

The fifth line is the substance of the program. `std::cout` is the name of a console output object. In other words, it is the name we use to designate an object that represents the console on the computer where the program will run; the console is usually a window on the monitor screen. The part of the name before the double colon tells us that we are dealing with a name from the C++ Standard Library.

> Language Note: C programmers will recognize << as being the left-shift operator. In the context of an output object or destination, C++ reuses that operator as a streaming operator, to insert data into an output stream.

The text in quotation marks tells the compiler that you want this text displayed. We call such quoted text a string literal. The final element of the statement is the semicolon. That ends the statement and is the C++ equivalent of a period in English. Try leaving it out and then attempting to compile the code; you will see the kind of error message that results.

The last line of the program is a simple closing brace to match the opening brace at the end of the line with `main` in it. In general, we refer to code between an opening and closing brace as a 'block'. In this context, the code between the opening brace and the closing brace is the definition of this version of main and specifies what will happen when the program executes. We call a block that defines a function the 'function body'. So

```
{
   std::cout << "Hello World";
}
```

is the body of the function main( ).

Our Second Program – An Empty Playpen

From time to time, we are going to use a very special graphics window that I designed and several of my colleagues helped to implement. It is called the Playpen. (As you use it, I think you will come to appreciate the choice of name.) This is a fixed size (512 by 512) graphics window, with each pixel limited to one of 256 colors. Modern computers are usually capable of displaying many more colors than that, but I wanted something that was very portable as well as something that would allow you to learn about simple graphics systems. For now, we are going to use the Playpen with its default palette. (Later we will discover that we can choose different sets of 256 colors.)

Start up MDS and select New from the Project menu. Make sure that the location is correct (you are probably going to have to add 'chapter_1' to what it offers you – at least that is what I have to do on my machine). Now enter 'playpen' as the project name and press Enter.

Next, using the File menu or Ctrl+N, create a new C/C++ source file called emptyplaypen, and type in the following short program:

```
// written on 21/07/04
#include "playpen.h"
#include <iostream>

int main( ){
   fgw::playpen blank;
   std::cout << "Please press the 'ENTER' key";
   std::cin.get( );
}
```

Try to compile the source-code file (Ctrl+F7). It will fail with four or more error messages. The only useful one is the first, where it says it cannot find playpen.h. The reason for that is that we need to tell it where to look for header files. (Headers are part of the C++ Standard, but header files are a bit different: they are provided by third-party programmers and relate to third-party code in much the same way that headers relate to the Standard C++ Library.)

Choose Settings from the Project menu and select the Compile tab. In the box labeled 'Additional include directories', at the bottom of the Compile pane, enter 'C:\tutorial\fgw_headers' (or a variant of that if you installed the CD to some other drive or directory). In other words, tell the compiler to look in a subdirectory called fgw_headers that is in the tutorial directory on drive C. While you are dealing with the location of this header file, check that the same warnings are selected as for the first project.

The data-capture window should look like this when you have finished:

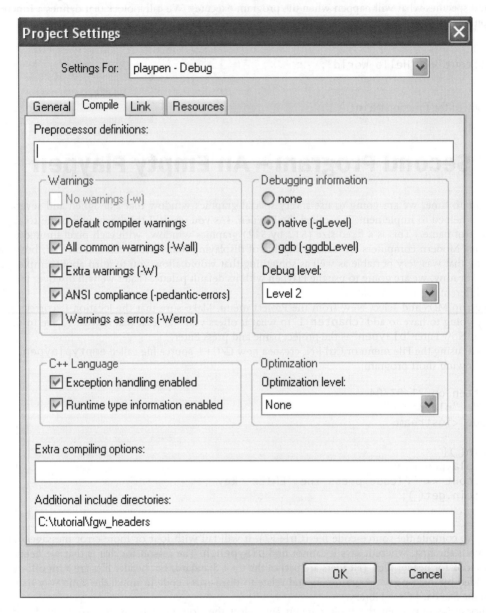

As long as you typed it in correctly, `emptyplaypen.cpp` should compile without errors or warnings. Now try to build it (F7). You get link-time error messages referring to things that you have not written. The problem is that `playpen.h` made some promises to the compiler about what the linker would be able to find, but we never told the linker which library files provide the necessary pre-compiled (object) code. The linker will need two library files: one for the `fgw` library (my library) and one for the `gdi32` library (a system-dependent library providing some basic graphics facilities used by my library).

Open the Project Settings dialog box again and select the Link tab. If you are working on a Microsoft Windows machine, enter '`fgw;gdi32`' in the Libraries box.

This is what you should see on the screen:

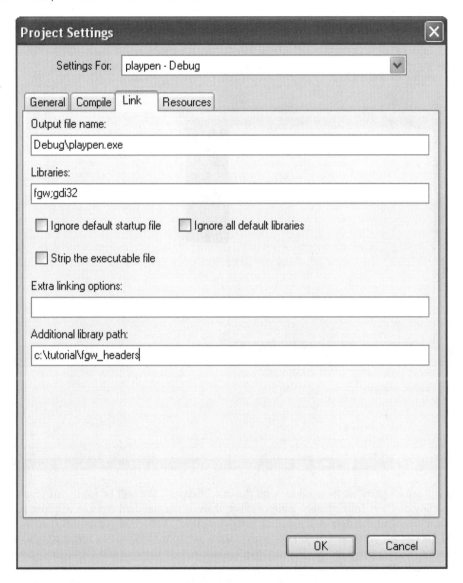

Return to the project and build it. Everything should work.

If you are using a system that can support graphics using the X Window System (Linux, Mac OS X, etc.) you will need to insert 'fgw;X11;pthread' into the libraries box instead of the 'fgw;gdi 32' that you would use on a Microsoft Windows system. You will also need something like 'C:/tutorial/fgw_headers;/usr/X11R6/lib', where those two paths take you to the headers directory for my library and the location of the X11R6 library directory respectively. You may need help from someone else if you are not familiar with the location of X11 support files on your computer.

If you are using a different set of development tools, you may need to know the names of the library files rather than just the names of the libraries. MDS (along with GCC, the GNU Compiler Collection, on which MDS is based) uses a naming convention that libraries are kept in files prefixed with 'lib' and followed by '.a.' Therefore, the library files `libfgw.a` and `libgdi32.a` provide the two libraries for Windows, and `linfgw.a`, `libX11.a`, and `libpthread.a` provide them on systems that use X11 for graphics support.

Finally execute the program and you will see:

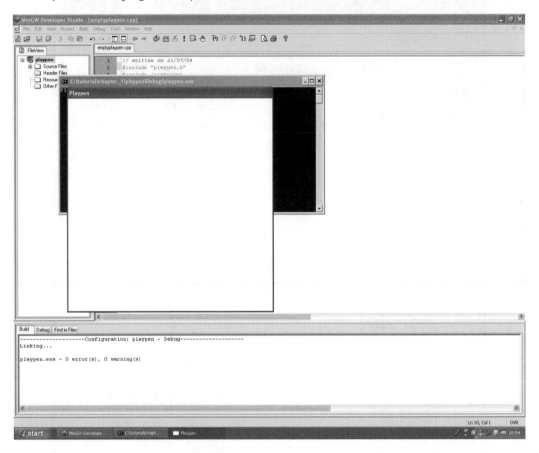

On top you will see a square white window with the title 'Playpen'. We will be using this graphics window during your study of C++. Immediately underneath it, there is the standard console window (usually black unless you have changed the default settings of your computer). On some computers, you will also see a white area at the top left of the screen. Do not worry: some versions of Windows forget to update the screen when they create the Playpen window. If you move a window over the area and then away again, Windows will correctly update the screen.

Use the taskbar to select the console window (or just click on a bit that you can see on the screen to bring it to the top). Follow the displayed instructions.

What the Code Means

The first line after the comment is a different form of **#include**. The use of quotation marks tells the compiler that this is a header file (as opposed to a system or language header) and that it should look for it in the places designated for such files. By default, the compiler looks in the same directory as the current file. As we want it to look for the header file in another directory, we amend the Project Settings by adding **fgw_headers** to the include path. Using the wrong syntax for a **#include** directive is a common error; it matters whether we use angle brackets (headers and system header files) or double quotes (user and third-party header files).

The next three lines are the same as for our first program, with the same significance. The line `fgw::playpen blank;` tells the compiler that at this stage in the program you want a Playpen and that you are naming the object representing it `blank`. If you are familiar with the concept of declarations and types, `fgw::playpen` is a type and the whole statement is a declaration of `blank`. I will be covering the details of declarations in the next chapter.

I hope that the meaning of `std::cout << "Please press the 'ENTER' key";` is obvious. The last statement of the program, `std::cin.get();` may seem strange to some readers. `std::cin` is the standard C++ console input object (the input equivalent of `std::cout`). We largely use it to obtain information from the keyboard. The remainder of the statement tells the compiler that you want to get a single character from the keyboard. C++ only extracts data from the keyboard when signaled that input is complete (usually by the user of the program pressing the Enter key).

We have to use some way to keep the program running until we have finished with the Playpen, because the window will close automatically when the program ends. Try removing the `std::cin` statement (or commenting it out by inserting // at the beginning of the line) and then running the revised program. The Playpen just flashes on the screen. The `std::cin.get()` causes the program to wait until the user provides some input by pressing Enter.

Something to Play With

Neither of the programs you have tried does anything even vaguely interesting, but if you would like to try something a little more exciting you can read Chapter 1 of *You Can Do It!* [Glassborow 2004], which will provide you with more information about what can be done in a Playpen window.

Summary

MinGW Development Studio supplies various tools for software development with the MinGW suite of development tools.

When starting a new project you may need to change the Project Settings. In particular, you may need to tell the compiler where to find some header files, and you may need to tell the linker about any special libraries your program uses. The mechanism may not be the same for other IDEs but the substance will be. Any IDE will need to know where to look for header files and which libraries are used. In addition, the search order of libraries usually matters. In other words, the order of the library list matters. A library name is specified on the command line with the `-l` (minus el) prefix. A library is conventionally stored in a file that prefixes the library name with `lib`.

Every C++ program includes a function called `main()`, which is used as the entry point for the program.

C++ includes a pair of objects, `std::cout` and `std::cin`, which represent the console output device (defaulting to a window on the monitor) and console input device (defaulting to the keyboard). The `iostream` header makes these objects available.

We can send (shift out) data to `std::cout` by using << and we can extract a single character from `std::cin` by using the `get()` function.

CHAPTER ②

Fundamental Types, Operators, and Simple Variables

The main objective of this chapter is to introduce you to some of the most fundamental elements of C++. You may already have a clear idea about the meaning of the terms 'type', 'operator', and 'variable' or 'object' in programming, but even so you should do a quick pass through this chapter to check that your understanding of these things concurs with the way C++ uses those terms.

I am going to cover some simple theory and terminology to start with. You may find it indigestible at first, or it may be telling you what you already know. By putting it up front in this chapter, you will be able to come back to it when you need to, as you work through the rest of the chapter.

If you have a background in a language that provides strict ranges of values for its fundamental types (such as Java), you will need to pay particular attention to the details of C++'s types: C++ has more liberal requirements for most of its fundamental types. If you are coming from a non-procedural language (such as Lisp or Scheme), you may find some aspects of coding in C++ strange. You may even have a gut reaction that they illustrate bad programming. Mainstream procedural languages such as C++ rely heavily on assignment operators and explicit loops.

A Simple Program

Those without a great deal of experience of programming often find understanding the programming concept of type difficult to grasp. This will be particularly true for those whose prior experience has been with languages such as Python, where a great deal of type information is implicit. With that in mind, here is a simple C++ program. Please create a project (as you did for the 'Hello World' program in the last chapter) and then enter the following source code. When you have done that, compile and link it, and then execute the result.

```
1  // written by FGw 06/08/2004
2  #include <iostream>
3
4  int main( ){
5     int count(0);
6     double total(0.0);
7     while(true){
8        std::cout << "Next value please: ";
9        double value;
```

```
10      std::cin >> value;
11      if(value > 9999.0) break;
12      ++count;
13      total += value;
14   }
15   std::cout << "\nYou input " << count << " values. \n";
16   std::cout << "Their total is " << total << ".\n";
17   std::cout << "The arithmetic mean (average) of those values is "
18        << total/count << ".\n";
19   return 0;
20 }
```

Now I will use this source code in the following discussion of type, operators, and variables.

What Is a Type?

Types are specifications for entities that have specified behavior. As well as behavior, most types also specify data that can vary from one instance to another. We roughly divide types into two categories: value types and object types. A value type is one where it makes sense to treat instances with the same data as being interchangeable. In other words, instances do not have any special significance beyond their data. We can reasonably ask whether two instances of a value type are equal. An object type is one where the identity of an instance is significant and it makes sense to ask if two potentially different instances are actually the same object, rather than just having the same characteristics.

For example, such concepts as integer, word, color, and time are all examples of value types. However, such things as programmatic representations of cars, pictures, and diaries are examples of objects. A copy of a picture is distinctly different from the original (try selling a copy as an original masterpiece and see how long a jail sentence you get).

Another characteristic of value types is that they can exist as pure values (usually described as 'literals') that do not have some explicit place where they are stored. In the above program, 0 (line 5) is an example of a numeric literal (whose type, we will discover, is int); "Next value please: "(line 8) is an example of a string literal. String literals actually do need to be stored somewhere, but they do not have a unique identity. If a program uses an identical string literal in several places, it only needs to store a single copy.

We will be mainly concerned with value types in this chapter. However, we have already made use of several examples of object types. The fgw::playpen objects we used in the last chapter to handle the Playpen window do not allow the existence of pure values (i.e. there are no fgw::playpen literals). std::cout and std::cin are also examples of object types (ones designed to handle output and input). Such objects have state, which represents their condition, but we cannot isolate that information from an object that stores the information. For example, an fgw::playpen object remembers what scale it is using for plotting pixels, and we can even ask an fgw::playpen object what scale it is currently using, but scale is an attribute of an fgw::playpen object and has no independent existence. If the concept of 'state' as opposed to that of 'value' is unclear or confusing, put it to one side for now. Eventually, to master use of C++ for object-oriented programming, you will need to understand the difference, but that requirement is still some time in the future.

Most programming languages have some form of integer type. Such a type consists of a range of allowed values together with operations that can be performed on those values. Typical operations for an integer type are addition, subtraction, multiplication, and division. In C++ (as in C), such behavior is normally provided by the use of operators. The addition and subtraction operators are those normally used in handwritten arithmetic (+ and -), but the division operator in C++ is the slash, or solidus (/), which is less frequently used in elementary arithmetic than '÷'. The programming choice was made because '÷' was easily confused with + when handwritten code was being input by professional key-punch operators in the early days of computing. The traditional symbols for multiplication ('×' and '·' – a vertically centered dot) are too easily confused with other uses of those symbols, so the programming sign for multiplication in C++ (and many other computer languages) is *. The juxtaposition of variables to mean implicit multiplication (e.g. $xy = x \times y$) does not work in programming languages, because xy (for instance) is a legitimate name for a single variable.

C++ (and C) provide many other arithmetic operators, such as the += (add the value on the right into the value stored in the object on the left) used in line 13 above. You will find a complete listing of the operators for integral and floating-point types in the reference section of this chapter.

Language Note: If you come from a background of functional languages such as Haskell, you may be surprised by the extensive use of assignment in C++. This is one of the major visible differences between functional languages and procedural ones.

An instance of a value type will need some memory in which to store the value. This is even true for pure values, though we then leave the mechanism entirely up to the compiler. (For those interested in such things, values are often held in CPU registers or in some other form of scratch memory.) For the purpose of this book, I am going to use the terms *value* and *object*. An object provides storage for a value (as well as storage for the state of an instance of an object type).

Lines 5 and 6 of the above program are examples of creating objects (of two different types) and initializing them with values. In line 5 we tell the compiler that we intend to use an object called count. We tell the compiler that the type of count is int and that we want it to start with the int value 0. Line 6 tells the compiler that we want another object called total, with type double and initial value 0.0. Note that 0 and 0.0 are literals (pure values) of types int and double respectively.

If we do not provide an initial value, the compiler will create a default object of the specified type. In the case of types int and double, a default object will have an indeterminate value (i.e. it can be anything, and it can even change from moment to moment). There are very few ways to use such objects until you have stored a value in them. Line 9 gives an example of creating a default object, named value, of type double. At line 10 we extract a value from the console, which is then stored in value. One of the few things that you can do with an object with an indeterminate value is assign a value to it, after which the value is whatever was assigned.

Line 11 provides another example of a double value (literal) rather than an object of that type. The 9999.0 is a value of type double. I know that it is a double value because the rules of C++ say that a numeric literal with a decimal point included has type double (unless explicitly stated to be of some other type, but we will get to that much later.)

Note that we can have a value without an object if we do not need to store it. Such 'naked' values come in two forms: literals (which are provided within the code) and temporaries (which result from evaluating expressions). 17 is a literal and value + 2.2 is a temporary. 17 + 21 is strictly a temporary that results from evaluating that expression (though the compiler usually evaluates simple integer arithmetic on literal values, rather than leave the task to the program).

In addition to having a range of allowed values, a type also has behavior. Loosely, for value types, that means ways in which the values can be transformed into other values, accessed by other objects, or used to create some external (to the program) result. A value of one type can sometimes be transformed into a value of a different type; that is also part of the behavior of a type. I could replace line 6 of the above program with:

```
double total(0);
```

The literal 0 has type int (no decimal point so it isn't a floating-point value). However, in the context, the compiler recognizes that a double value is required. It will silently convert the 0 into 0.0. As this is entirely safe in the context, a compiler would not normally trouble the programmer with any form of warning message.

What Are Fundamental Types?

C++ provides a number of elementary types that are part of the language. These come in two major flavors, integral types and floating-point types. All other types are built by using these. At a minimum, we need four types for simple programming. These are `bool`, `char`, `int` and `double`. The first three are integral types and the last one is the most frequently used floating-point type. You will find a complete list of all the fundamental types in the reference section of this chapter, together with some guidance as to their designed usage, but here are some details of the essential four.

`bool` is a type that has only two values, `true` and `false`. In simple terms, it can represent a single bit of information – the answer to a question that has only two possible answers, such as a simple 'yes' or 'no'. `bool`, `true` and `false` are all *keywords* (words with language-defined meanings) of the C++ language. We cannot use keywords for anything else. In the above code '`(value > 9999.0)`' is an example of an expression of type `bool`. When the program comes to execute the code that the compiler produces for line 11, it generates a temporary `bool` value that is either `true` or `false` depending on whether `value` is or is not greater than `9999.0`.

`char` is the type that is intended for values that represent characters. For historical reasons it is an integral type. C++ requires that it can represent at least 256 distinct values, which can either be −127 to 127 (together with either −128 or −0) inclusive or 0 to 255 inclusive. C++ does not specify that `char` cannot represent a wider range, but on most common desktop machines, the range is either −128 to 127 or 0 to 255.

`int` is an integral type that is required to be able to represent all values in the range −32767 to 32767 (together with either −32768 or −0). The curious alternative of −0 is because C++ allows an implementation to use any one of three binary representations for negative integers: two's complement, one's complement, or sign and magnitude. Most modern desktop computers use two's complement. Two's complement does not have a negative zero.

Representing Negative Integers

C++, along with many other programming languages, uses a binary representation for natural numbers (zero upwards). This matches well with all the generally available computing hardware (hardware that uses non-binary representations is sometimes developed for experimental purposes but cannot be used efficiently by the majority of programming languages, which assume the hardware will use binary representations).

The problem arises with the representation of negative numbers. There are three different ways to handle negative integers with an essentially binary representation. There is hardware around that uses each of the three possibilities, though most hardware uses two's complement. As a general-purpose language, C++ provides rules for integers that allow the use of any of the three representations. The highest bit determines the sign in all three representations. A zero for the highest bit designates a positive value that is determined by the remaining bits. A one as the highest bit signifies that the rest of the bits represent a negative value in some way or other. At that stage, we need to know which representation is used, because the value represented by those bits will depend on the choice. The three options are called 'sign and magnitude', 'one's complement' and 'two's complement'.

Consider the 8-bit pattern 10000111 (I am using just eight bits to keep the arithmetic simple). As the left-hand (highest) bit is one, the remaining seven bits (0000111) represent a negative value. The value depends on the representation used for negative values.

Sign and magnitude is the easiest representation for humans to understand, but very few computers use it. The remaining bits are the magnitude and are a normal binary representation of a value. The value of the example pattern will be negative 0000111, that is, $-(4 + 2 + 1)$. Therefore, the eight bits 10000111 represent −7 when we use sign and magnitude.

One's complement treats the remaining bits by inverting them (swapping one for zero and vice versa). In this case, 10000111 represents negative 1111000, that is, $-(64 + 32 + 16 + 8)$. Therefore, 10000111 in one's complement represents −120.

Two's complement is by far the most common representation used by computing hardware while also being the hardest for many humans to understand. It is like one's complement except that we add 1 to the result of flipping the value bits. Now 10000111 represents negative $(1111000 + 1)$ which evaluates to −121. The reason is the curious mathematical property of this representation that ensures correct answers to arithmetic without having to provide any special support for negative numbers. Well that is true as long as all the values remain within the range provided by the type. If you try adding 10000111 (**−121**) to 10000001 (**−127**) you will get the wrong answer, because the result of adding together those two negative numbers is too large a negative value (**−248**) to fit into 8 bits. Most systems will produce **8** as the answer (though according to the strict letter of the C++ Standard such overflow has undefined behavior).

One curiosity of both sign-and-magnitude and one's complement representations is that they have representations for both **−0** (10000000 in the 8-bit sign-and-magnitude case; 11111111 in the 8-bit one's complement case) and **0** (00000000 in both cases). Effectively they have two representations for zero.

Two's complement has its own curiosity in that the most negative value has no matching positive value. In the 8-bit representations we have been using, 10000000 represents **−128**, i.e. $-((64 + 32 + 16 + 8 + 4 + 2 + 1) + 1)$. If we try to negate that by flipping all the bits and adding 1 we find ourselves back where we started. (Actually there is a final carry but that is lost because we have a limited number of bits at our disposal.) Mathematically that leads to the odd feature that negative 10000000 equals itself.

The above curiosities show that in terms of computer representation of signed integral values all choices have their surprises. Fortunately, most of the time, we do not need to concern ourselves with the underlying representation. The exception to this is when we are actually making use of bit patterns rather than the values they would represent as some kind of integer. For example, the shift-left operation common to most hardware does not consistently multiply a negative value by 2. On the other hand, shift-right does divide by 2 for one's and two's complement representations, but the treatment of negative odd numbers may not be what you expect.

Most recent machines provide a far wider range for **int** (**−2147483648** to **2147483647**) but you should not rely on this if you are writing programs that may be used on older or more limited equipment.

> Language Note: If you come from languages such as Java or C#, you should take special note that C++ only provides minimum ranges for its fundamental types. You must not assume that an integral type will have the same range of values for all compilers. Some compilers even allow the programmer to choose whether an *int* uses a 16-bit range or a 32-bit range. In addition, some systems use other ranges. The only rules are that the range must be symmetric (except for the extra negative value) and that it must be at least 16 bits for an *int*.

Derivative Types

The types I am now going to write about are called derived types by C; however, I want to keep that term for later use when we start working with user-defined types.

There are various ways that we can create new types from existing types. We can qualify any type as **const** and/or **volatile**. A **const**-qualified type is the type for an object whose value (state) must not be changed from within the program. **const** can be used to limit the kind of access provided to an object. Accessing an object through a **const**-qualified reference or pointer (I will be dealing with exactly what those are later on, but for now it is sufficient to know that they are ways of providing access to an existing object) prohibits changes to the underlying object. Think of **const** as a way to specify that a name provides read-only access to an object. It can also be used to tell a compiler that an object is immutable (think of the difference between protecting a file from being changed and placing a file in ROM). In C++, a **const** object cannot be changed. However, a **const** reference or pointer to **const** type cannot be used to change the object referred or pointed to even if that object is not declared as being **const**. **volatile** types are highly specialized; they are types whose values can be changed by events outside the program. We use C++ objects of **volatile** type for things such as memory-mapped ports. This area is too specialized for this book, and little more will be said about the use of **volatile** types.

There are two other forms of derivative type, references and pointers. Any type that is not already a reference type has a corresponding reference type as a derivative. That is the end of the line; you cannot have a derivative type from a reference type.

Any non-reference type has a corresponding pointer type as a derivative type. This includes pointer types themselves: we can have pointers to pointers to ... (Fortunately, we usually manage to avoid these.) **const** (and **volatile**, in theory) can be used to create derivatives from pointer types. Therefore, for example, we can have a **const** pointer to a **volatile** pointer to ... to some type. We will not make much use of pointers, and we will generally avoid pointers to pointers.

In simple terms, a reference type provides a mechanism for accessing an already existing object, and a pointer type allows us to use the addresses of existing objects. Pointers are powerful tools but also dangerous ones, because they allow programmers to deal with very low-level (close to the hardware) details of program objects.

At this stage that is all we need to know about pointer and reference types. We will go into further details when we have a context in which they make sense.

Declaration and Definition

The purpose of a declaration in C++ is to introduce a name to the compiler. A definition tells the compiler how to create an entity to go with a name. Definitions are always declarations but not vice versa. We will not need pure declarations (ones that are not also definitions) in this chapter, because variables (names for objects) are usually defined at the same time they are declared. In other words, we usually create an object and name it at the same time. That will not be true for other program entities such as functions.

> *Language Note: Unlike languages such as Java and Python, names used for objects in C++ are always bound (initialized) to a suitable object at the point of definition. Such names are often referred to as variables. The exception to this rule is that the parameters of a function are bound to their arguments at the point at which the function is called. The concept of binding a name to an object or program entity is fundamental to programming. The important issue is that in C++, once a name has been bound to a suitable object, that object stays bound to that name as long as both exist. C++ does not allow a name to designate different objects during its lifetime.*

Names in C++

Names in C++ consist of one or more characters from the set composed of the digits (0 –9), the underscore (_) and the 26 letters of the Roman alphabet (in uppercase and lowercase forms: A –Z and a –z). A compiler is allowed to accept a wider range of letters (for example, accented letters) but is not required to do so.

A name must start with a letter or an underscore. In other words the first symbol of a name must not be a digit. All the following are legitimate names in C++:

```
acorn c c_ _c c9x _1 a9bc push_back find total01
```

The following are not legitimate names (they either include an unsupported symbol or start with a digit):

```
@abc 0abc ?first #last $debt £symbol first&last
```

The use of consecutive underscores is reserved for the implementation and so should never be used by a programmer (i.e. the compiler can apply a special significance to a double underscore and may create names that contain double underscores for internal uses). Therefore, the following are valid names but not ones that the ordinary programmer should declare:

```
__start First__ not__equal __8 unsigned __int
```

Using names like those can result in bizarre consequences, because you might, for example, accidentally declare a name that matched one that was being used for communication between the compiler and the linker.

The use of an initial underscore is also largely limited to implementers, and so other programmers should avoid using leading underscores. Those implementing Standard Libraries or extended libraries for a specific compiler may be using names that start with a single underscore, so declaring such names in your own code risks unnecessary name clashes. For example, _1 is listed as a legal name above but you would be very unwise to declare it yourself (it is actually used by a specialist library that will probably become part of the C++ Standard at some time in the future).

C++ places no upper limit on the number of characters used for a name. In general, you should choose names that are meaningful in context. That means that short names are often satisfactory for local use (for example as variable names within a function) but longer names may be more helpful in wider scopes. I am quite happy to use `i` as the name of a variable to control a loop, but would be unhappy with its use as a parameter name, and would never consider using it as a function name.

C++ also has the concept of a fully elaborated name, where the name is prefixed with one or more other names that identify the context (scope) in which the name has been declared – for example, `fgw::playpen` (the `playpen` declared in the context of `fgw`) and `std::cout` (the `cout` declared in the context of `std`).

Naming styles

This is a religious issue for many programmers. By that, I mean that they advocate a specific style as being the 'one true way' and then try to demonstrate that it is superior to all others. There are three commonly used basic naming styles:

- all lowercase, no word separators (direct concatenation), as in `firstvalue`, `dothis`, and `getval`
- starting each new word with an uppercase letter ('camel case'), as in `firstValue`, `doThis`, and `getVal`
- separating words with a single underscore, as in `first_value`, `do_this`, and `get_val`

There are numerous added conventions such as starting type names with an uppercase letter. When using such a convention, `Card` would be a type name but `Card` would be an object name.

The most important element for a naming style is consistency. The names in the Standard C++ Library are an example of the results of the inconsistencies that arise when different programmers work on different parts of a piece of source code and ignore each other's naming conventions. The Library uses a direct-concatenation style in some places. Function names such as `getline` are an example of this. In other places, it uses the style that uses the underscore to separate words making up a name. `push_back` is an example of this usage. Both styles are perfectly readable, but mixing them means that the user has to remember which style applies to the function they want to use. Experience shows that that is a time-waster.

If you are maintaining someone else's source code, adopt the naming style the code uses, **even if you hate it**. The alternatives either make poor use of your time (renaming everything to match your preferred style) or generate future problems (by mixing your style with the existing style).

Operators

C++ has inherited a rich range of operators from C and then added a few more of its own. Most operators in C++ are symbols, though a few are words. In addition, some of the symbols have alternative word forms. An operator is something that is applied to a value or values in order to produce another value. The + in (3 + 4) is an operator, as is the - in (5-7). As in many other computing languages, C++ uses * as a multiplication operator and / for division. Some operators come as a surprise. For example, = is an operator in C++ and results in a (reference) value. We are usually more interested in the side effect of evaluating the = operator (i.e. storing a value in an object).

Operators may also be applied to instances of object types. The results depend on how the operator has been defined for such usage. For example the left-shift operator (<<) in the context of an output stream object (such as `std::cout`) sends data to the output object.

We cannot make much progress without at least one comparison operator, that is, an operator that returns a **true** or **false** value depending on the comparison of two values of the same type. One of the more useful comparison operators is == (two consecutive equality signs), which returns **true** if and only if the two values are equivalent. (Exactly what equivalence means depends on the type. In the case of arithmetic types, equivalence means that the values are the same.) We will also be using <, which results in **true** if and only if the left-hand value is strictly less than the right-hand one.

The reference section of this chapter includes a complete list of all the arithmetic, comparison, and logical operators. There are also some other operators that I will introduce when we have a use for them.

A Simple Program

Enough theory. It is time for some practical programming. Create a new project called `using_int` in the `chapter_2` directory. (Do not forget to change the project settings: check all the warning boxes, except the one that forces warnings to be treated as errors.) Type the following code into a new source-code file called `biggest`. Note that the numbers on the left are purely for reference purposes and should not be typed in. MDS provides line numbers by default, to help you locate errors and warnings. You will also find that double-clicking on an error or warning message takes you to the relevant line (the line where the compiler realized that something was wrong – though the actual error may be in an earlier line).

```
1  // created on 24/07/04
2  #include <iostream>
3
4  int main( ){
5     int i(0);
6     int biggest(0);
7     do{
8        std::cout << "Type in a positive number ";
9        std::cout << "(zero or a negative number ends the program): ";
10       std::cin >> i;
11       if(i < 1) break;
12       if(biggest < i) biggest = i;
13    } while(true);
14    std::cout << "The largest number input was " << biggest << '\n';
15 }
```

Now compile, build, and execute this program (you can do all those with a single press of Ctrl+5). Correct any typos that you may have made. When the program runs successfully come back here so that we can have a look at the important aspects of the source code.

WALKTHROUGH

Lines 5 and 6 are often called declarations, though in this context they are definitions (which, you will recall, includes being a declaration). They declare `i` and **biggest** to be the names of `int` objects that are initially set to the value 0. We usually call such names *variables*. The syntax for declaring/defining a variable is to start with the type and then append a comma-separated list of names (variables) and conclude with a semicolon. I could have combined lines 5 and 6 into a single line:

```
int i(0), biggest(0);
```

However, it is considered good programming practice to declare only one variable at a time. I will follow that practice throughout this book.

The (0) after each of the names is an initializer and sets the initial value stored in the variable to the value in the parentheses. For compatibility with C, C++ allows an alternative, assignment-like syntax for initializers; so I could have written lines 5 and 6 as:

```
int i = 0;
```

```
int biggest = 0;
```

I prefer to keep to the more general function-style initialization syntax except in the few cases where the C++ language does not currently allow it. However, many programmers and authors of books on C++ prefer the assignment style for variables of fundamental types.

C++ allows the definition of a simple variable of a fundamental type without an initializer. But there is a potential problem with that: attempting to use a value from an uninitialized variable takes you outside the language's guarantees, and your program can then do wild and sometimes unpleasant things. (Doing things that take you outside the language's guarantees is called using undefined behavior and should be rigorously avoided.) For example, line 12 assumes that **biggest** contains a value, i.e. that it will have been initialized before the first time this line is executed. In this case, it does contain a value, because when I defined **biggest** I initialized it with **0**.

The combination of lines 7 and 13 causes repeated execution of the intervening code (called looping). Note line 13 in particular: the **true** in **while(true)** is an indication that a way out of the repetition (if there is one) must be provided by some internal test. In this case, line 11 provides the exit test. That line tests **i** to see if its current stored value is less than **1** (i.e. **0** or negative). If it is then it 'breaks' out of the repetition and continues from line 14. Otherwise, the program continues with line 12, which is also a test, this time to see whether we need to update **biggest** because the new value of **i**, obtained from the console at line 10, is larger than the previous largest input value.

Line 14 displays the result. We can chain together quoted text (which we already know will be displayed on the console) with other output. The **<< biggest** causes the value stored in **biggest** to be sent to the output stream. The **\n** at the end is the way we tell the output system to go to the start of the next output line.

> Language Note: If you have a Java, C#, or C background, you may be surprised by the way **<<** is used here. You are likely to be familiar with its use as a left-shift operator. It has that meaning in C++ too, but C++ overloads it (provides extra meanings) so that it and the right-shift (**>>**) 'shift' data out to and in from a stream. If the left-hand operand of the shift operator is a stream object (a source or sink for data), it will have the relevant alternative meaning. C++ programmers get so used to these operators shifting data in and out of stream objects that they sometimes forget that they are also bit-shift operators.

Now let us spend a few moments on line 10. This line tells us to try to extract a value for **i** from the console input object. The problem here is that the attempt might fail because the next item (other than whitespace – spaces, tabs, and newline characters) in the input buffer is not part of a valid integer. The code above assumes that you are your own best user and will only input valid data. Good programmers want to protect themselves from bad things happening, even if all they can do is force the program to give up gracefully. So let me show you how to do that.

Exceptions – Handling Bad Input

Eventually we will be looking at exceptions in more detail, but for the first part of this book I am going to use them as a way to give up when a program goes off track (for example, because of inappropriate input). Add the highlighted lines to the above program to get:

```
1 // created on 24/07/04
A #include <exception>
2 #include <iostream>
```

```
 3
 4 int main( ){
 B try {
 5   int i(0);
 6   int biggest(0);
 7   do{
 8    std::cout << "Type in a positive integer ";
 9    std::cout << "(zero or a negative integer ends the program): ";
10    std::cin >> i;
 C      if(not std::cin) throw std::exception( );
11     if(i < 1) break;
12     if(biggest < i) biggest = i;
13   } while(true);
14   std::cout << "The largest number input was " << biggest << '\n';
 D }
E0  catch(...){
E1    std::cerr << "***An exception was thrown.***\n";
E2 }
15 }
```

Line A tells the compiler what it needs to know to compile line C. Without the #include <exception> the compiler will not recognize std::exception( ) as the basic C++ exception object.

Line B warns the compiler that the code between there and the corresponding closing brace (line D) may fail to complete because an exception occurs during the execution of that code.

Line C tests std::cin, and if it is not working (presumably because of an input failure), it raises an exception (in this case the most primitive one available in C++, a default std::exception object created directly at the point where it is needed.)

If the user always types in integer values, the program will run exactly as it did before. However, if the input is not appropriate it breaks out of the repetition and executes the code starting at line E0. The significance of the catch(...) is to state to the compiler that this is the code to run for any type of exception that gets thrown as a result of running the code between the opening and closing brace of the try block (a block is any code enclosed in braces.)

std::cerr is a second standard output object; conventionally we use it to report errors from a program. Like std::cout it defaults to the monitor for PCs. Having distinct objects allows us to overrule the defaults for one or other of the console output objects so that, for example, some output goes to the screen and some to a file. You do not know how to do this yet. Nonetheless, it is good to develop habits that will allow benefits later on; so check for problems, do something about them, if only to raise an exception, and report problems to an object designed for that purpose.

Writing Correct Code

Perhaps you are wondering why I have tackled the problem of bad input at such an early stage. The C++ mechanism for providing minimal handling for this kind of problem is simple. The only excuse for not dealing with program failures in other languages is that it is too complicated and will get in the way of learning. Lines A, B, D, E0, E1, and E2 are simple to add and can be used to wrap the code for any C++ program. You will want finer-tuned exception-handling eventually, but that should not prevent you from developing sensitivity to where a program can fail and taking emergency action to handle such failure before it can do damage.

For the time being, get into the habit of doing at least the minimum of testing for failures and throwing an exception if your code detects one that is not immediately correctable.

Getting Output Before Handling an Exception

One small problem with the code above is that if bad input happens you do not get to see the value stored in `biggest`. You might think to try adding this line inside the `catch` block:

```
std::cout << "The largest value so far was " << biggest << '\n';
```

That will not work (do not just take my word for it; try it!), because `biggest` was declared inside the `try` block and is not a valid name outside that block (i.e. the name is local to the block).

That line of source code is certainly a suitable one, but it needs to go into our source code at a point where `biggest` is still a valid name. The obvious place is just before we throw the exception. We need to modify the `if` statement so that it controls a compound statement (i.e. a block containing one or more program statements). Here is how we do that. Replace line C with:

```
if(not std::cin){
  std::cout << "The largest value so far was " << biggest << '\n';
  throw std::exception();
}
```

Now if `std::cin` fails you first get the result so far, and then it throws the `std::exception()` that results in the program closing down with a minimal error report.

EXERCISES

Note that there are no absolute solutions to these exercises. The specifications are not tight enough to limit you to a single solution.

1. Modify the above program so that it outputs the smallest positive integer input to it. You are limited to the operators I have already introduced, so using > (greater than) is cheating! You will also need to address a hidden programming problem. Initializing the variable used to hold the interim answer to zero would not work because zero is smaller than all the positive integers. You will need to tackle this issue.

2. Modify the program in the text so that it can handle negative values as well as positive ones. You will have to think about what to use to end input. There are several possible solutions, including designating a specific value as one that will only occur as the final input.

3. Modify the program in the text so that it outputs both the smallest and the largest value provided by the input.

4. Modify the program in the text so that it outputs both the largest and the second-largest values input. Note that this version should also handle the case where two inputs are identical and the case where only one value is input.

5. Write a program that totals the input values and counts how many there are. The output should include the total, the number of inputs, and the arithmetic mean (total divided by count). You may notice that some answers are not strictly correct from a mathematical viewpoint. That is an example of integer-only calculations. (For example, the arithmetic mean of 1 and 2 is 1.5, but this program will output 1.)

A Little More About Playpen

fgw::playpen is an (object) type from my library. Objects of this type are used to manage the display provided by the Playpen window. There is only a single Playpen window but many objects can manage it. For now, we will only have a single fgw::playpen object in our programs. Allowing many objects to share a single resource may seem unusual but it is actually quite common. For example, all the programs currently running on your computer are sharing such things as the CPU, the keyboard, the mouse, and the monitor. In a sense, fgw::playpen objects are less constrained, because there is a single Playpen window per program rather than per computer.

The following short program will allow me to introduce you to some of the basic behavior associated with fgw::playpen objects. Please create a new project, adjust the project settings (you will need to add something such as 'C:\tutorial\fgw_headers' to the include path for the compiler and 'fgw;gdi32' to the libraries for the linker – see Chapter 1, Our Second Program). Choose suitable names for the project and the file. Now compile, link, and execute this program.

```
1 // created on 27/07/04 by FWG
2 #include "playpen.h"
3 #include <exception>
4 #include <iostream>
5
6 int main( ){
7 try{
8    fgw::playpen paper;
9    paper.scale(10);
10   paper.origin(50, 50);
11   paper.plot(0, 0, 7);
12   paper.display( );
13   std::cout << "Press ENTER to end program.\n";
14   std::cin.get( )
15 }
16  catch(...){
17    std::cerr << "***An exception was thrown.***\n";
18 }
19 }
```

The result of executing this program should be a small, bright blue square in the upper-left quadrant of the Playpen window.

WALKTHROUGH

It may save time if you note that lines 1 to 7 and lines 15 to 19 are pretty much boilerplate code. Sometimes we will need some extra headers and header files, and line 1 will vary as regards the detail, but otherwise all your C++ programs will contain code such as this. The program-specific code is in lines 8 to 14. Even there, lines 13 and 14 (or something equivalent) are going to be present in any program that uses the Playpen window, to prevent the window closing until we are ready to finish.

The definition in line 8 creates an fgw::playpen object called **paper** and initializes it to the default Playpen window. User-defined types such as fgw::playpen are usually provided with default initialization, which is used if the programmer does not provide an explicit initialization with starting values in parentheses (that is, we do not normally leave a user-defined type exposed to the problems of indeterminate values or states). This is one of the ways in which they differ from the fundamental types, which nearly always remain in an indeterminate state until they are explicitly given a state either by initialization at the point of definition or by having a value assigned to them. We can explicitly initialize `fgw::playpen` objects with a background color. Try changing line 8 to:

```
fgw::playpen paper(224);
```

You should now see the same blue square but on a bright red background. Please see the section on Default Playpen Color Names (on page 36) for an explanation of the default palette for the Playpen window.

We could also write that line as:

```
fgw::playpen paper(red1 + red2 + red4);
```

and if you `#include "colournames.h"` (my library uses British spelling), you could write:

```
fgw::playpen paper(red7);
```

As long as you do not change the palette settings (I will deal with how that can be done much later), the names built into Playpen and those provided by the header file `colournames.h` give you a good idea of what to expect. As an experienced programmer, you probably already know that we try to avoid literal integer values and replace them with names. This is just an example of following that guideline.

Line 9 is an example of some `fgw::playpen` behavior. Things called member functions provide much of the behavior for these user-provided types. For now, all you need to know about member functions is that you call them by placing a dot after the object whose state is being used or modified. `paper.scale(10)` changes the size of the logical pixels used by **paper** to a 10-by-10 square of screen pixels. You can experiment with changing to other sizes. `fgw::playpen` is a robust type and traps any attempts to go outside the Playpen (by replacing any such actions by doing nothing).

Line 10 is an example of another small piece of behavior for `fgw::playpen` objects. Human beings are usually accustomed to using a graphical representation with positions measured from an origin. We usually treat movement to the right and upwards as positive. The Playpen is just such a graphical representation, and by default, the origin is the center of the window. However, positions in a graphical window are usually measured from the top left of the window or screen. Right and down are positive. `paper.origin(50, 50)` sets the Playpen origin to the window coordinates. In other words, it moves the origin of the Playpen to the pixel that is 50 pixels from the left-hand edge and 50 pixels from the top. Note that these measurements are in screen pixels and are not affected by the current scale.

Line 11 demonstrates the basic plotting operation of `fgw::playpen` objects. The first two values give the graphical coordinates (scaled by the current scale) of the pixel to be plotted, and the third value gives the color it will be plotted in.

Line 12 may be a surprise, but the program does not update the Playpen until the `display` behavior is invoked. `paper.display()` updates the Playpen to show the results of all the actions since it was last called.

TASK 2.1 ➡ Please experiment with this program until you are comfortable with it and with changing values in it. Then try these exercises. They will require some programming skill from you. The basic tool for repetition at this stage in your study of C++ is the `do-while(true)` loop.

EXERCISES

6. Write a program that will prompt for a scale, a position, and a color. It should then display the resulting pixel in the Playpen. Remember to trap invalid input and abort the program by throwing a `std::exception` if that happens.

7. Write a program that will allow you to explore, to discover the largest scale that `fgw::playpen` objects can use. When you use a scale outside the permitted range, the last valid scale will remain in operation. I suggest that you use an input of zero as a way to stop the program.

8. Write a program that allows you to build up a 'modern art' picture from different-sized squares of different colors. By moving the origin around, you can get squares to overlap in various ways. You have several choices, which you might explore. For example, you could write a program that prompts the user for scale, origin, coordinates, and color. Alternatively, you could write a program with all the data included statically as fixed values in the program.

Default Playpen Color Names

Each pixel of the Playpen has its color encoded in a single 8-bit byte. The value of the byte is used to index a lookup table of the actual palette of 256 colors selected from all those that your computer can display. The default lookup table encodes the colors by using the bits of the index byte according to the following table:

Bit	Value	Color	fgw::hue
0	1	low-intensity cyan	fgw::blue1, fgw::green1
1	2	dark blue	fgw::blue2
2	4	medium blue	fgw::blue4
3	8	dark green	fgw::green2
4	16	medium green	fgw::green4
5	32	very dark red	fgw::red1
6	64	dark red	fgw::red2
7	128	medium red	fgw::red4
	0	black	fgw::black
	255	white	fgw::white

The fourth column gives the names for the values. `fgw::hue` is a type designed to represent colored light and has some unusual properties when it comes to addition and subtraction: those work on a bit-by-bit basis. You can find more details in the appendix on the Playpen.

Because there are three primary colors for light (red, green, and blue) but only 8 bits in a byte, I had to come to some compromise. The one that worked best for me was to make bit 0 represent a tiny amount of blue and green. If all three bits representing a primary color are on, the result is the maximum possible intensity of that color on your monitor. So 7 (`fgw::blue1` + `fgw::blue2` + `fgw::blue4`) is bright blue, 25 (`fgw::green1` + `fgw::green2` + `fgw::green4`) is bright green, and 224 (`fgw::red1` + `fgw::red2` + `fgw::red4`) is bright red. The first two contain an unnoticeable amount of either green or blue respectively. I chose the intensities so that, for example, `fgw::red1` + `fgw::red2` is less bright than `fgw::red4`.

Characters and Text

As we are mainly concerned with the fundamental types in this chapter, I will leave consideration of the extensive support provided for text objects until a later chapter. However, we do need to look at the fundamental support provided by C++.

C++ provides two types for storing individual characters or symbols: `char` and `wchar_t`. (C programmers should note that the latter is a full type in C++ despite the name.) At this stage, we do not need `wchar_t`. The reference section of this chapter gives the basic details.

A single `char` will hold any value from the basic C++ character set. The range of values is often wider and can include support for accented letters and graphical symbols, but it is not required to do so. C++ specifies two character sets. The characters that are required for writing source code are provided by the basic character set. The basic execution character set is a superset of the basic source-code one. You will find listings of these two character sets in the reference section of this chapter.

A symbol enclosed in single quotes is a literal value of type `char`. For example, `'A'` is the literal value for an uppercase letter 'A', and `'\n'` is the literal value that represents a newline character. (C programmers should note that literal character values have type `char` in C++ rather than the `int` type they have in C.) Double quotes are used around zero or more characters to represent a string literal. Such a literal always includes one more `char` than the visible count – the null terminator, i.e. `'\0'`. So `"Francis"` is a sequence of eight `char`s: `'F'`, `'r'`, `'a'`, `'n'`, `'c'`, `'i'`, `'s'`, and a terminating `'\0'`. The empty string, `""`, consists of the single `char` `'\0'`.

If you place single quotes around more than a single symbol, the result is implementation-defined. (In other words, you will have to look at the compiler documentation to discover how it will be treated.)

Create a suitable project and enter the following code, then compile, build, and execute it.

```
1  //Created on 29/07/04 by FWG
2  #include <exception>
3  #include <iostream>
4
5  int main(){
6    try {
7      char c(0);
8      int count(0);
9      std::cout << "Please type in a line of text.\n";
10     do{
11       c = std::cin.get();
12       if(not std::cin) throw std::exception();
13       if(c == '\n') break;
14       ++count;
15       std::cout << c;
16     } while(true);
```

```
17      std::cout << "You typed in" << count << " characters.\n'
18    }
19    catch(...){
20    std::cerr << "***An exception was thrown.***\n";
21    }
22 }
```

WALKTHROUGH

The framework for this program is much like that for the earlier programs, so I am going to focus on the critical differences.

Line 7 provides an object called **c** that will store a single **char** value. I have initialized it to zero because I always initialize my objects, and good practice requires me to make the initialization explicit for fundamental types. Though we think of **char** as a character, the internal representation is for a small integer. Line 7 results in the creation of a **char** object with the value zero stored in it (equivalent to the null character, **'\0'**).

Did you notice that I moved the prompt for data input outside the processing loop? If my reason for doing so is unclear, try moving it back inside and see what happens when you try to compile and execute the program.

Line 11 is important because it handles some special properties of **char** input. If you replace that line (**but do not do so yet**) by

```
std::cin >> c;
```

the program will still compile, build, and execute, but you will get one minor problem and one major one. The minor one is that it will skip over any whitespace in the input. The major problem is that the newline character that we check for at line 13 will never be found, because newline is a whitespace character in C++ and so is skipped. **std::cin.get( )** reads the next character regardless and does not skip anything.

I want you to be able to try both forms of the program, but you will need to know how to stop a runaway program. Pressing Ctrl+Z on a Windows machine or Ctrl+D on a Linux one forces console input into an end-of-file condition. Trying to read input when the console is in that state is an error; doing so will send **std::cin** into a fail state. Line 12 of the program will detect that and throw an exception. Your program will now end with an error message (the one we provide at line 20). Notice how the use of exceptions has allowed us this escape mechanism.

TASK 2.2 → Now try this program with both versions of line 11 and see the difference.

EXERCISES

9. Write a program that counts the occurrences of the letter 'a' in a line of input. Note that it should count both uppercase and lowercase versions, so given "A cat eats its supper.", it should output 3.

10. Modify the previous program to count the number of letters (not digits, punctuation marks, or other symbols) in the input line. Writing 52 `if` statements (one for each of the 26 uppercase and 26 lowercase letters) cannot be a good solution. For the purposes of this exercise you may assume that the letters `'A'` to `'Z'` are consecutive, and likewise for `'a'` to `'z'`. If you know about some C functions that might help, do not use them. A correct solution to this exercise relies only on what you have read so far together with the assumption I have specified. You may use the `<=` (less than or equal to) and `>=` (greater than or equal to) operators.

Floating-Point Numbers

We need a floating-point type for many of the things we might want to program. The default C++ floating-point type is **double**. That name comes from the old Fortran double-precision floats. C++ requires that an object of type **double** must be able to represent a floating-point value in the range 10^{37} to 10^{-37} to an accuracy of at least 10 decimal significant figures. That range is more than large enough for most purposes, though mathematicians, scientists, and sometimes engineers need vastly larger or smaller values. Though the C++ Standard does not require it, most modern C++ implementations use a binary representation (however, binary representation **is required** for integral types). This sometimes causes surprises to newcomers, because fractional values that can be represented exactly in decimal often cannot be represented exactly in binary. For example, while $1/2$ has an exact binary floating-point representation, $1/5$ does not (just as $1/3$ cannot be represented exactly using decimals). The problem is aggravated when using binary representations, because small changes in the way the program obtains or computes a floating-point value can result in differences in the final bits of the representation. For that reason, we should be careful about comparing floating-point values for equality.

The **double** type in C++ is widely used, particularly for arithmetic computations. If you look back at Exercise 5, you should notice that the output answers were integers; however, the mathematically correct answers would often need a fractional part. For example, the arithmetic mean of 2 and 3 is 2.5, but the result of $(2 + 3)/2$ in integer arithmetic is 2 (integer division for positive numbers in C++ always rounds down, i.e. it discards any fractional part). It could be even worse if you were dealing with negative numbers, because C++ does not specify whether $-5/2$ should be -3 or -2. C++ only requires that the documentation of your compiler must tell you what the compiler will do with negative floating-point values when converted to integers. Fortunately, this problem does not normally concern us. I only mention it because experienced programmers often want, and sometimes need, to know about such details.

First Floating-Point Program

Here is the code for a simple program to calculate the arithmetic mean of a set of numbers input from the keyboard. After you have it working (i.e. you have produced a project, typed in the code, compiled, linked, and executed it at least once), I will walk you through it, touching on the main points. Before you start, I should warn you that this code has an error in it. It is a simple one, but I want you to start recognizing some of the error messages that result from common errors. You should be able to correct it; indeed you might even notice the error before the compiler does.

```
1 //Created on 28/07/04 by FWG
2 #include <iostream>
3
4 int main( ){
5    try {
6       double total(0.0);
7       double value(0.0);
```

```
 8      int count(0);
 9      do{
10        std::cout << "Type in a number. ";
11        std::cout << "(A value greater than 9999 ends the program) ";
12        std::cin >> value;
13        if(not std::cin) throw std::exception( );
14        if(9999 < value) break;
15        ++count;
16        total += value;
17      } while(true);
18      std::cout << "The arithmetic mean of the number input is "
19          << total/count << '\n';
20 }
21 catch(...){
22    std::cerr << "***An exception was thrown.***\n";
23 }
24}
```

WALKTHROUGH

Lines 6 to 8 define the variables we will use. As line 18 (after we have exited from the main processing loop) uses both **total** and **count**, we must define them outside the loop. This is because variables and the objects they refer to only last until the closing brace of the block in which they are declared. We only use **value** inside the loop, so we could move its definition to just before its first use at line 12. Many coding guidelines for C++ would advocate such a change to the above code. It is a good principle to declare variables close to their point of first use.

I have deliberately used both 'declare' and 'define' in the preceding paragraph. Names are declared; the objects to which they are attached (often referred to as 'bound') are defined. When you read other texts the terms may be used with a certain lack of precision. However, we can never use a name until it has been declared, and we can only sometimes use a name before its corresponding object has been defined. In the case of local variables (ones declared as part of a function), a declaration is always a definition.

Line 15 gives an example of a common form of usage of the C++ pre-increment operator. For fundamental types, it does whatever adding one to the variable would do. In this case, the variable **count** just tracks the number of values read from **std::cin**.

Line 16 is an example of a C++ compound assignment operator. This one (+=) adds the value of the expression on the right to the object referenced by the variable on the left. You will find more information about the compound assignment operators in the reference section of this chapter. They are the preferred option in C++ when we want to modify a variable with the result of an expression. Straight assignment overwrites the previous stored value; compound assignment modifies the stored value. So **total = value** would replace the current content of **total** by that of **value**. However, **total += value** replaces the content of **total** by **total + value**, i.e. the sum of the current contents of **total** and **value**.

C++ provides a number of implicit conversions between its fundamental types. At line 14, we compare an integer literal value (9999) with **value**, whose type is **double**. C++ just quietly converts 9999 to 9999.0. Mostly these quiet implicit conversions do the right thing, but we should be aware that they are happening and intervene if they might do the wrong thing. For example assigning a **double** value to an **int** involves an implicit conversion (from **double** to **int**). The potential problem is that **int** objects have insufficient range to cover the possible range of values resulting from simply ignoring the fractional part of a **double**. Such conversions are called narrowing conversions, and good compilers warn you when they detect them in your code. Implicitly converting an **int** to a **double** is generally fine, because we are unlikely to lose any information by going in that direction. Even so, good compilers will issue a warning given sufficiently high settings for diagnostics.

Finally, there is that missing statement. I hope you quickly noticed that I 'forgot' to **#include <exception>**. The result of that omission is that the compiler complains about line 13. Please note the form of the complaint. Next time you see a similar one your first check should be that you have included all the necessary headers and header files.

EXERCISES

11. There is a nasty assumption in the last program. It assumes that the user inputs at least one value less than 9999. If they do not, line 19 will result in a divide-by-zero error. Please modify the program to handle this possibility.

12. A harmonic mean is the reciprocal of the arithmetic mean of the reciprocals of the values. For example, the harmonic mean of 2, 4, and 8 is $1/((\frac{1}{2} + \frac{1}{4} + \frac{1}{8})/3)$, which is $1/(\frac{7}{8}/3)$, i.e. $1/\frac{7}{24}$. That evaluates to $\frac{24}{7}$, which is roughly 3.428571.

   Write a program that computes the harmonic mean of the values input. You can use my program for an arithmetic mean as the basis.

13. The root mean square (an important measure in statistics) is the square root of the arithmetic mean of the squares of a set of values. The Standard C++ Library has a function for computing square roots called **std::sqrt( )**. To use it you must include the **<cmath>** header.

   Write a program to output the root mean square of a set of values.

STRETCHING EXERCISES

Most of the exercises in this chapter have not been very demanding of programming expertise, so here are a couple to stretch your programming a bit.

14. Using only what you have learned about C++ from this book, write a program that asks the user for an upper bound for the numbers they are going to input. The main processing loop then acquires values from **std::cin** until an input exceeds the specified upper bound. Then the program asks the user which of an arithmetic mean, a harmonic mean, or a root mean square they want, and responds by outputting the requested value.

15. Write a program that prompts for two times (each given as three integer values: hours, minutes, and seconds) and outputs the difference between them in hours, minutes, and seconds.

   (Hint: convert the input values to seconds, and then convert the answer back to hours, minutes, and seconds. Make sure you take account of the sign of the result.)

REFERENCE SECTION

Some of the things referred to in this reference section will not be covered until later chapters. This will generally be the case for reference sections. My intention is to provide a single, reasonably comprehensive point of reference for each major topic.

Fundamental Types

C++ provides the following types. I have added a note about the intended usage of each type. However, as all the types are arithmetic types it is very easy to abuse them. Sometimes the abuse might even be justified.

Boolean

C++ provides a single Boolean type called **bool**. Though it has only two values, **true** and **false**, it occupies at least one (8-bit or larger) byte of memory. Sometimes, for compatibility with older C requirements, implementers use more than the minimum required storage. The Standard C++ Library provides a mechanism (**std::bitset**) for packing multiple **bool** values into memory. If it is used in a numerical context **false** is converted to zero and **true** is converted to one. In addition, zero as a numerical value is converted to **false**; all other numerical values are converted to **true**.

Character

C++ supplies four 'character' types. I have placed quotes around the word 'character' because conceptually only two of them are actually for storing characters.

    char is a small type that takes the minimum amount of storage available to the implementation (at least 8 bits – C++ does not allow single objects to occupy less space than 8 bits). It is designed to store characters from the basic source-code and basic execution character sets. The former consists of control characters representing horizontal and vertical tab, form feed, and newline, the 10 digits (0–9), the 26 uppercase letters of the Roman alphabet, the corresponding 26 lowercase letters, and the following symbols:

    `_ { } [ ] # ( ) < > % : ; . ? * + - / ^ & | ~ ! = , \ " '`

    The basic execution character set adds control characters for alert, backspace, carriage return, and a null character (with all bits zero).

    wchar_t is the other conceptual character type. It is a type that is suitable for storing values for wide characters. The commonest set of wide characters is the Unicode character set. However, C++ does not require that the execution wide character set be Unicode (or ISO/IEC 10646).

    C programmers should note that in C++, **wchar_t** is a fundamental type and not an alias for some other integer type.

    signed char is effectively the smallest integer type and should be used for cases where memory is at a premium and you only need integer values in the range **-127** to **+127**. That range only uses 255 of the 256 available 8-bit values; the meaning of the 256th value depends on the implementation. Most commonly, it represents **-128**, but could represent **-0** (for implementations using either one's complement or sign and magnitude).

    unsigned char is effectively the way to handle raw memory. Its values represent all the possible bit patterns for a byte. Whenever you want to deal with the underlying state of memory, **unsigned char** comes into its own. This includes times when you want to apply bit masks and other forms of bit manipulation that are common when handling memory used for graphics.

The C++ Standard requires that char, unsigned char and signed char are all the same size. It also requires that they use the smallest addressable amount of memory being supported. This must be at least 8 bits but can be more; indeed there are systems (such as some digital signal processors) that use 32-bit types. As all three types can store the range of values that represent the source and execution character sets they can all be used to store single characters. Unfortunately, C++ does not specify whether the format for a char behaves as signed or unsigned and leaves it to the implementation to specify that. Avoid using char in situations where it matters whether the numerical value will be treated as signed or unsigned.

The C++ Standard makes no requirement on whether char and wchar_t behave as signed or unsigned integer types. The only restriction is that all members of the basic execution set have a positive representation. There is also a requirement that the representations of the ten digits be in a contiguous ascending order. That is, if x represents '0' then $x + 1$ necessarily represents '1'. There is a subtle problem that only manifests on some systems: there is no requirement that a value represents the same letter when used as a wchar_t as it does when used as a char. It is possible for char to use an EBCDIC encoding while wchar_t uses Unicode. For example 'A' is 193 in EBCDIC but is 65 in both ASCII and Unicode.

Use char for simple characters and wchar_t for international character sets. Use signed char as a tiny integer type. Use unsigned char to handle raw bytes of memory.

Special Representations of Characters

Some of the required symbols (#, }, ^, [,], |, {, and ~) were (historically) problematic because they were not found on some keyboards. C++ has inherited a solution provided by the original C Standard. The solution involves giving a special meaning to nine three-character sequences called 'trigraphs', all of which start with ??. These need not concern us here except in so far as you need to be wary of using multiple consecutive question marks anywhere in your source code; the result will not always be what you expect.

C++ provides an alternative, arguably better, solution called 'alternative tokens'. For example <% in source code is treated as equivalent to {. These, in general, should not concern us. The alternative tokens are less invasive because they do not apply within string literals (where trigraphs can be significant). I will return to this in the section on operators.

More importantly, we need to be able to represent control characters such as newline (\n, which we have already used), characters whose interpretation might be ambiguous in context, and characters where we wish to supply the actual numerical value. The following table lists the representations (called escape sequences):

Text name	Symbolic name	Source-code representation
newline	NL (LF)	\n
horizontal tab	HT	\t
vertical tab	VT	\v
backspace	BS	\b
carriage return	CR	\r
form feed	FF	\f

Text name	Symbolic name	Source-code representation
alert	BEL	\a
backslash	\	\\
question mark	?	\?
single quote	'	\'
double quote	"	\"
octal number	*ooo*	*ooo*
hex number	*hhh*	\x*hhh*

Note that we need the backslash case because a backslash is being given special significance. When you want a \ in a string you have to write \\ in your source code. This is a common cause of errors when giving directory paths in source code. For example, `C:\tutorial` must be written as `"C:\\tutorial"` if it is used in source code.

We need the escape sequence for a question mark because of the special significance given to ?? for trigraphs. If we want to include '??=' in a string literal we have to write \?\?=. Such cases are rare, and it is probably better to avoid repeated question marks altogether.

Integer types

C++ provides six other integer types in two groups of three, `signed` and `unsigned`. Unlike `char` and `wchar_t`, which are neither explicitly signed nor unsigned, the other integer types are signed by default and it is not normal to use the `signed` keyword in conjunction with them.

Signed

The three signed types are `short int`, `int` and `long int`.

The default integer type for a system is `int` and it is intended to be the natural integer type for the underlying hardware. That is, it should be the most efficient type for the machine for which the code is being compiled. The C++ Standard requires that the range of values for an `int` is at least −32767 to 32767. On most modern hardware, it has a much larger range.

Use `short int` if you need to keep memory usage low. Like `int`, `short int` is required to support a minimum range of −32767 to 32767, but on systems where `int` supports a wider range, `short int` will normally stay with the minimum requirement (but it is not required to).

If you require a larger range of values than that guaranteed for `int` then use `long int`, which is required to support at least all values in the range −2147483647 to 2147483647 (i.e. 32-bit integers).

Unsigned

The three signed integer types have corresponding unsigned types: `unsigned short int`, `unsigned int` and `unsigned long int`. Each is required to have the same storage requirements as the corresponding signed type and must use an identical representation for positive values in the range of the corresponding signed type. They must also be able to represent all values in the range 0 to 65535 (for `unsigned short` and `unsigned int`) and 0 to 4294967295 (for `unsigned long`). There is a great deal of argument about the use of these types. However, one major advantage they have is that the C++ Standard specifies how they behave for values outside the range they can represent. It specifies that the maximum representable value plus one be repeatedly added or subtracted from the given value until the result is within the supported range of values. That is, unsigned integer types in C++ use modular (or remainder) arithmetic for addition, subtraction, and multiplication. Division is always based on the values without any adjustment.

The important issue is that great care must be taken when comparing integer values: either compare unsigned ones with unsigned ones or signed ones with signed ones. Do **not** mix signed and unsigned.

The unsigned integer types are useful when you are operating at bit level. For example, a 32-bit unsigned integer type is useful for dealing with graphical material for modern 32-bit color systems.

Floating-point types

C++ provides three floating-point types: `float`, `double`, and `long double`. In general on most common desktop machines there is little point in using anything other than `double`. All three types are required to provide a positive range from 10^{-37} to 10^{37} and a corresponding range of negative values. In practice many support wider, even much wider, ranges for `double` and `long double`.

`float` is often implemented in 32 bits. It is required to provide at least six significant decimal digits of precision. There are two reasons for using `float`: when space is at a premium; and in some circumstances when speed matters. `float` expressions are not always evaluated faster, but where you have a math library that includes math functions for `float` as well as those for `double`, you can sometimes get significant performance improvement at the cost of a considerable potential loss of precision by using `float` instead of `double`. One problem is that in the kind of computationally intensive program where the speed gain is important, the loss of precision is frequently significant. Another is that given hardware that directly uses `double`, the cost of conversions to and from `float` can exceed any notional gains from using a `float`. The upshot these days is that using `float` is nearly always a mistake.

`double` is usually a 64-bit type and is required to support at least 10 decimal digits of precision. It is the default floating-point type for C++. It should always be used for floating-point values unless there are special reasons to choose one of the others.

`long double` is no more constrained than `double`. However, if the hardware can support higher precision and larger ranges, the implementation can take advantage by supplying a `long double` that uses that capacity. Sadly many current commercial C++ implementations for Intel- and AMD-based hardware use the same 64-bit format for both `double` and `long double`, even though the FPUs can support the IEEE 80-bit format. In order to benefit from using `long double` you need a math library that uses `long double`. Without such a library, there is little benefit in using `long double` even where this provides more precision than `double`.

Derivative Types

Pointers

A pointer type in C++ is a type whose values are the addresses of objects of another type. We create a pointer type by placing an * (asterisk) to the right of a type. For example `int *` (or simply `int*`; the whitespace is not significant) is a 'pointer to `int`'. A variable of type `int*` can store the address of an `int` object. With a single exception that we will come to in a moment, any type can be used as the base for a pointer type. For example we can write `int***` to create a type that will store the address of an `int**`, which in turn is a type that represents the addresses of `int*`. This is a type whose values are the addresses of `int` storage.

In practice in C++, it is rare to use more than one level of pointer. C programmers make extensive use of pointers, but C++ programmers make much less use of them. This is because C++ provides a range of alternative mechanisms that either obviate the need for using pointers or encapsulate their use so that the high-level programmer need not bother with them.

Using pointers means that you need to know how to find the address of an object. This happens in one of two ways. Some mechanisms for creating dynamic objects produce an appropriate pointer value (address). Alternatively, placing **&** (the address-of operator) before a variable evaluates the address of the object bound to the variable. For example:

```
int i(0);  // create an int object initialized to zero and bind it to i
int * i_ptr(&i);  // create an int* object initialized to the address of i
```

Note that we can also create pointers to functions. I will go further into that topic at a later stage.

References

One of the ways C uses pointers is to allow functions access to the local objects of other functions. This will work in C++ as well, but C++ provides a better mechanism, *references*. A reference type is created by appending an **&** (ampersand) to a type name (e.g. **double&**). Any non-reference type can be converted to a reference type by adding a terminal **&** (with optional whitespace before the **&**). However, reference types are special in that they are the end of the line. We cannot have a pointer to a reference or a reference to a reference (contrast that with pointers: we can have a pointer to a pointer). We can have references to pointers (e.g. **int*&**), and they are sometimes useful.

The special property of reference types is that there are no objects of reference type. The objects are always of the type being referenced. The major use of reference types is to provide alternative (usually local) names for objects that have been created somewhere else. For example:

```
int i(0);  // create an int object initialized to zero and bind it to i
int & i_ref(i); // make i_ref an alternative name for i
int & other_ref(i_ref); // make other_ref another name for i
```

const and volatile qualification

Appending **const** to a type creates a new C++ type. This new type has the non-mutating properties of the original type. In other words, access to a **const**-qualified object or through a reference to a **const**-qualified type allows reading the value of the object but does not allow its modification. **const** is used in two main ways in C++. The first is to create constants. These can be very useful when we want to create named values. For example,

```
double const pi(3.14159265);
```

allows us to use **pi** wherever we want its value. That is both simpler and clearer. We do not have to comment on the numerical value because the name we have given it is usually documentation enough.

The second main use is to include **const** as part of a pointer or reference type when we want to limit access to an existing object just to reading its value. This is particularly useful when we want to allow a function to access the value of a local variable belonging to another function. Example:

```
int i(0);  // create an int object initialized to zero and bind it to i
int const & i_cref(i);   // make i_cref an alternative name for i, but one
                         // that cannot be used for changing the value
                         // stored in the object designated by i
```

One of the major style debates in C++ is over the placement of **const** in a type name. Unless it is the first token in a declaration/definition, **const** qualifies the type designated by the type to its left. The special case is when it is the first token. In that case it qualifies the type up to the first ***** (pointer modifier) or the **&** (of a reference type) if there is one. Traditionalists prefer placing **const** at the beginning if it can be placed there. The modernists prefer a simple universal rule: always place **const** after the type being qualified. So **int const *** is a pointer to a read-only **int**, while **int ***

`const` is an immutable pointer to a mutable `int` object; `int const int * ptr` would make `ptr` a fixed pointer to a read-only `int` object.

The `volatile` keyword is used to warn the compiler that the value of an object may change through some mechanism external to the program. This may seem bizarre until you realize that there are things such as memory-mapped input ports where the process of reading a value may consume a value that will be replaced by the next input value.

The concept of `volatile` is hardware-dependent. It is useful to low-level programmers but is of little practical use to application-level programmers. The rules for creating derivative types with `volatile` are identical to those for `const`. I will not be dealing with `volatile` in this book because the topic is highly specialized and of little use in general programming.

Operators

The following is not an exhaustive list of C++ operators, but it covers all the ones that have special significance in the context of the fundamental types. Some operators require an *lvalue* (i.e. a designator of an actual object) for one operand, and some work directly on values, which may be provided by an object or a literal, or as the result of an evaluation. All the assignment operators together with the pre- and post-increment/decrement operators require the destination operand (i.e. the left-hand operand of assignments and the only operand of the increment/decrement operators) to be an lvalue. The address-of operator is the only other operator that requires an lvalue as its operand. In other words, if you are going to write information you need somewhere to write it, and if you are going to take an address you need something whose address you are taking.

Standard promotions and conversions

For the purposes of evaluation, `((un)signed) char` values and `(unsigned) short` values are converted to `int` values unless `int` cannot represent all the values of the type, in which case the values are converted to `unsigned int`. (For example, on a system where `short` and `int` are both 16-bit, `int` cannot represent all the values of `unsigned short`.)

In the case where the operands of an operator are of different types after the above rule has been applied, the value of the 'smaller' type is promoted to that of the other.

If one operand is of a floating-point type and the other is of an integral type, the latter is converted to the floating-point type.

The full set of rules is more complicated but I will leave that to Standard experts (see Clause 4 of the C++ Standard for a complete specification).

Arithmetic

The four normal arithmetic operators, `+`, `-`, `*` (for multiplication) and `/` (for division), can be applied to any pair of arithmetic values. The standard promotions and conversions must be applied first. Unless at least one of the operands is of a floating-point type, division will be integer division. For example `5/2` is `2`, but `5.0/2` and `5/2.0` are both `2.5`.

There is a remainder operator that can be applied between two integer values. The `%` symbol is used for this operator. The result is the remainder when the right-hand value divides the left-hand value. Therefore, `5%3` is `2`.

When `-` is used as a unary operator (i.e. there is only a right-hand value) it negates the value. Therefore `-number` is 'minus the value' stored in the object referenced by `number`. There is a corresponding unary `+` operator, which is effectively a no-op and is largely included for completeness. `+number` means the same as `number` in any context where a value is required and is an error in any context where an lvalue (object) is needed.

The `++` symbol is used to designate increment. Its operand must be an lvalue. If placed before the variable it results in the variable being incremented before its value is used, i.e. `++number` evaluates as the incremented value. If placed after the variable it represents post-increment, i.e. the original value is used and the stored value is incremented. So:

```
int main(){
  int number(0);
  std::cout << number++ << '\n';   // outputs 0 but changes number to 1
  std::cout << ++number << '\n';   // further increments number to 2 and
                                   // outputs 2
}
```

The symbol `--` is used to represent pre- or post-decrement in the same way as `++` represents pre- or post-increment.

It is normal in C++ to prefer the use of pre-increment and pre-decrement to the post forms. It is usual (and safer) to avoid using these operators as part of more extensive expressions.

Logical

C++ provides six comparison operators:

Symbol	Alternative token	Meaning
==		true if the operands compare equal; otherwise false
!=	not_eq	false if the operands compare equal; otherwise true
<		true if the lhs is strictly less than the rhs; otherwise false
<=		true if the lhs is not more than the rhs; otherwise false
>		true if the lhs is strictly greater than the rhs; otherwise false
>=		true if the lhs is not less than the rhs; otherwise false

There are also three Boolean operators whose use forces their operands to be treated as bool values. (Arithmetic and pointer values convert to bool on the basis that zero is false and all other values are true.)

Symbol	Alternative token	Meaning
&&	and	true if both operands are true; false if either is false
||	or	true if either operand is true; false if both are false
!	not	true if operand is false; false if operand is true

In this book I will use the alternative tokens for the Boolean operators, because I find them clearer and less subject to confusion with the bitwise operators (see below)

The two binary Boolean operators use lazy evaluation. This means that the left-hand operand will always be evaluated first and the right-hand one will only be evaluated if necessary.

 # WARNING!

Lazy evaluation may lead to unexpected behavior. For example, if the left operand of **and** evaluates as **false**, the right operand will not be evaluated (and no side-effects of such possible evaluation will happen).

Bitwise

C++ provides six bitwise operators, i.e. operators that work on the individual bits of storage:

Operator	Alternative token	Meaning
&	`bitand`	Sets a bit in the result to 1 if and only if both the corresponding bits in the operands are 1
|	`bitor`	Sets a bit in the result to 1 if and only if one or both of the corresponding bits in the operands are 1
^	`xor`	Sets a bits in the result to 1 if exactly one of the corresponding bits in the operands is 1
<<		Shifts the bits of the left operand left by the number of places given by the right operand (as an unsigned integer value)
>>		Shifts the bits of the left operand right by the number of places given by the right operand (as an unsigned integer value)
~	`compl`	Inverts the values of all the bits in the single operand that follows

WARNING!

Bitwise operators can be applied to any integer type, but applying them to signed integer types is usually a mistake and will frequently result in unexpected behavior. The shift operators are particularly vulnerable to inappropriate use of signed values for the left operand.

C++ reuses the shift operators as data-streaming operators when the left operand is some kind of data stream. That is by far the most common usage for the 'shift' operators in C++. Think of it as shifting data in and out.

The **&**, **|** and **^** operators are useful for doing masking operations for such things as graphics manipulations.

Compound assignment

In addition to the straightforward assignment operator (=) that stores the value of the right-hand operand in the object designated by the left-hand one, C++ provides ten compound operators. Each of the bitwise and arithmetic operators that take two operands (**&**, **|**, **^**, **<<**, **>>**, **+**, **−**, *****, **/**, and **%**) can be combined with an = to create a compound assignment.

The general rule for a compound assignment is that

obj op= expr;

is equivalent in behavior to:

obj = *obj op expr*;

Three of the compound assignment operators have alternative tokens (**&=** can be written as `and_eq`, **|=** as `or_eq`, and **^=** as `xor_eq`)

Historically the compound assignment operators allowed programmers to tell primitive compilers that they wanted to use a hardware facility available on some machines to operate directly on memory. They are still widely used even though modern compilers do not need that kind of support. They allow the programmer to emphasize the direct modification of an object as opposed to the overwriting of one.

More on pointers

C++ not only allows programmers to access the machine addresses of objects (and functions), but also allows a certain number of operators to work with pointer values.

An integer value can be added to or subtracted from a data pointer. That will adjust the address by the amount necessary for locating a similar object that number of steps away from the base address. If `ptr` contains the address of an `int` then the value of `ptr+2` will be the address of the second `int` on. It is up to the programmer to ensure that such an address is a valid address, of an object that belongs to the program. The increment and decrement operators (both pre- and post-) can be applied to pointers to adjust the values (addresses) they contain up or down to the next object of the relevant type.

You can also subtract a pointer from another of the same type. The answer will be the number of objects of that type from one to the other.

Preceding a variable by the **&** operator results in the address of the object that the variable refers to.

Preceding a pointer value by the * operator provides direct access to the object whose address (pointer value) you have. So if `i_ptr` contains the address of an object referred to by the variable `i`, `*i_ptr` is another way to access the `i` object.

Any two pointers (either object or function pointers) of the same type can be compared for equality (==) or inequality (!=). Any two pointers whose values are addresses within the same object (such as an array) can be compared for order with <, <=, > and >=.

Note that idiomatic C++ source code makes much less use of pointer arithmetic than does C. Pointers are rare in high-level or application-level C++ code. Indeed pointers are never explicitly used or referred to in my earlier book, *You Can Do It!*, which demonstrates that much high-level programming can be done in C++ without them.

More on references

C++ provides a special mechanism for binding new names to existing objects. As names have types in C++ (unlike names in languages such as Python) and are always bound to a specific object (unlike the situation in Java, where a name has a type but can be used to refer to several different objects during the lifetime of the name), we need an extra type for names that do not have their own objects but use one provided from somewhere else.

Because reference-type names do not have their own objects there is no sense in allowing further derivation of types from a reference type. There are no objects of a reference type, only names. These names include an 'empty' temporary name used for returning objects from functions (called *return by reference*) as opposed to returning copies (called *return by value*).

Other operators

There are a number of other operators that we will come to later. Some of these are very specialized (such as `sizeof`, to determine the amount of memory that an object of a given type will occupy), and some are only appropriate to user-defined types (such as the dot and arrow operators). Some, such as the index and function operators, are surprising but have powerful uses in C++.

CHAPTER ③

Looping and Making Decisions

Looping (repeating some code several times, usually with some variable changing value) and decision-making are two of the most fundamental mechanisms of programming. We have used both in the earlier chapters, but we will look at the details and the alternatives in this chapter. I will also introduce you to the preferred C++ mechanisms for dealing with (text) strings and with contiguous arrays of objects of the same type. These mechanisms are different from those used in C and they are different to a greater or lesser extent from those used in many other popular languages.

A few readers whose previous experience of programming has been with pure functional languages may find the C++ mechanism for looping strange. They will have been used to using recursion to handle many of the places where repetition is desirable. Those who come from other procedural languages such as Visual Basic and Pascal will need to pay careful attention to the syntax used by C++ for both repetition and decision-making; it will be similar to what they are used to, but there will be important differences in the detail.

Some Library Types

std::string – a Library Type

In addition to the fundamental types that we looked at in the last chapter, C++ provides a number of types via the C++ Standard Library. We call these 'user-defined types', and I will eventually show you how to design and implement your own types. The important difference between using a fundamental type and using a Standard Library type (one of the major categories of user-defined type) is that the latter requires the inclusion of an appropriate header before we use it in source code.

`std::string` is one of these types and is the C++ way to handle a string – contiguous sequence – of characters used to represent some text. The Library (I will use 'Library' to mean 'C++ Standard Library') provides a lot of functionality for `std::string`. One of the most important aspects is that objects of type `std::string` adjust the size of the storage they use to meet the requirements of the text they are currently storing as a sequence of `char`. The growth (or reduction) in storage accommodates to the size of the text string.

> Language Note: Code that uses *std::string* is more secure than the C use of an array of *char*, as it is less open to buffer-overrun exploits. This feature relieves the programmer of much of the work that the more primitive C mechanism requires. For those who come from other programming backgrounds there may be other surprises. For example, unlike the string mechanisms found in some other languages, C++ strings are mutable – that is, their contents can be changed (unless they have been declared as *const*).

For the time being, we are going to limit ourselves to four properties of **std::string** objects:

1. They can be created in various ways, one of which is from a string literal. So we can write

```
std::string greeting("Hello World");
```

to create a **std::string** object with the value **"Hello World"** for the variable **greeting**.

2. We can assign one string to another:

```
std::string message;   // create an empty string
message = greeting;
```

This results in **message** now containing its own copy of **"Hello World"**.

3. We can extract a string from an input stream such as **std::cin** and store it in the object specified by a suitable variable:

```
std::cin >> message;
```

This will result in the object bound to **message** containing the next sequence of characters extracted from the console, starting with the first non-whitespace character and ending immediately before the next instance of whitespace. It leaves the terminal whitespace (remember, that includes newline characters) in **std::cin**'s input buffer. We will later see how to extract text that includes whitespace.

4. We can send a string to an output stream such as **std::cout**:

```
std::cout << greeting << '\n';
```

This will result in "Hello World" being displayed on the console (and the output then moving to a new line).

std::vector<> – a Half Type

C++ has an interesting and very powerful mechanism for creating new types from existing ones: *class templates*. Writing useful templates takes a lot of experience, knowledge, and skill; using class templates designed by experts can make our lives much easier and is relatively trouble-free. **std::vector<>** is an example of a class template. It provides a way to create a sequence (or array) of objects. One important feature of **std::vector<>** objects is that they adjust to accommodate the number of objects currently contained. It also provides other useful functionality. C++ provides mechanisms for users to extend that functionality if they ever decide that there is something else that would be generally helpful.

I have called **std::vector** a half type because it needs something else before the result is a full C++ type. To create (instantiate) a type from a template we must provide other information such as, in the case of **std::vector<>**, the type of object it will contain.

 TRY THIS

A well-chosen program is worth many pages of explanation; here is a small program for you to type in and try:

```
1 // numbers program created on 07/08/04 by FWG
2 #include <algorithm>
3 #include <exception>
4 #include <iostream>
5 #include <vector>
6
```

```
 7 int main(){
 8   try{
 9     std::vector<int> numbers;
10     do {
11       std::cout << "Next whole number (-999 to stop): ";
12       int next;
13       std::cin >> next;
14       if(next == -999) break;
15       numbers.push_back(next);
16     } while(true);
17     if(numbers.size() == 0){
18       std::cout << "There were no numbers input.\n";
19       return 0;  // exit program
20     }
21     std::sort(numbers.begin(), numbers.end());
22     std::cout << "Here are the " << numbers.size()
23         << " numbers you typed in ascending numerical order:\n";
24     for(int i(0); i != numbers.size(); ++i){
25       std::cout << numbers[i] << ", ";
26     }
27     std::cout << '\n';
28   }
29   catch(...){
30     std::cerr << "***An exception was thrown.***\n";
31   }
32 }
```

I am going to delay the walkthrough of this program until after I have tackled the issues of looping and decisions in C++. You may feel that there are places where we could improve this program. For example, the program makes assumptions about the correctness of the input. Please be alert to such assumptions and get in the habit of dealing with them. I deliberately leave some of these problems in my code because I want you to check code rather than just taking my word for it. The above code together with the earlier programs supplies some context for the following.

Making Decisions

C++ provides three primary mechanisms for making decisions: if-else, switch, and a special operator that is usually referred to as the conditional or ternary operator (because it is the only C++ operator that takes three operands).

The if-else Statement

Not only do all major computer languages have a construct like this, but they also almost universally use the same words. However, please read on carefully, because there may be differences between C++ and the language you currently use.

> Language Note: Python programmers need to be especially careful, because C++ does not use indentation as a syntactic element. Those used to languages such as Pascal will need to note that C++ restricts both if and else to controlling a single statement. This statement will often be a compound one created by placing one or more simple statements in a block defined by a matching pair of braces.

The form of an if-else statement in C++ is:

if(*Boolean-expression*) *action-one*
else *action-two*

In pseudocode, the **if-else** statement has this effect:

if *Boolean-expression* *evaluates as true*
then *action-one*
else *action-two*

The Boolean expression can be anything that evaluates to a value that is implicitly convertible to a bool. That includes all the fundamental types and all pointer types. The value zero for any fundamental type is treated as false; all other values are treated as true. In the case of pointers, all values are treated as true except for a special value called the null pointer (a pointer that does not point to anything), which is treated as false (more about that when we deal with the details of pointers).

The actions have to be single statements. However, in C++, any group of statements enclosed in a pair of curly braces is a single compound statement. Simple statements in C++ are terminated with a ; (semicolon); however, a compound statement is terminated by the closing brace. Be careful that you do not add a semicolon after the closing brace of a compound statement (sometimes called a block statement), because that would constitute an empty simple statement, whose presence may be significant; for example,

```
{
  a = 3;
  b = 4;
  c = 0;
};
```

comprises two statements at the outer level: a compound one, which itself consists of three statements, followed by an empty simple statement.

The else clause of if-else is optional (we have not used it in any program so far). However, it **must** be the next statement after the one controlled by the if. For example,

```
if(numbers.size() == 0) std::cout << "There were none.\n";
else std::cout << "There were " << numbers.size() << ".\n";
```

is fine, as is

```
if(numbers.size() == 0){
   std::cout << "There were none.\n";
}
else std::cout << "There were " << numbers.size() << ".\n";
```

where I have written the single statement controlled by the if as a compound one. The following if-else statement is also OK:

```
if(numbers.size() == 0){
   std::cout << "There were none.\n";
}
else {
   std::cout << "There were " << numbers.size() << ".\n";
}
```

However, this one is not (see if you can spot the critical difference):

```
if(numbers.size() == 0){
   std::cout << "There were none.\n";
};
else std::cout << "There were " << numbers.size() << ".\n";
```

In this case the compiler may be able to diagnose the problem (the extra semicolon at the end of the compound statement), but in more complicated cases where there are `if`s nested inside `if`s, it may not be able to do so; instead it will misconstrue your intentions and the `else` part will not be considered as related to the immediately preceding `if`.

TRY THIS

Write a simple program that asks for an integer value and then outputs the simple message 'zero' if the value given was 0; otherwise it should output 'not zero'.

The *switch* Statement

The `if-else` statement is for making two-way decisions, but sometimes we want to make a multi-way decision. By that, I mean that there are sometimes logically more than two choices. C++ provides the `switch` statement for this case. Here is the form of the `switch` statement:

```
switch(controlling-integer-expression){
    case integer-value-one:  action-one
    case integer-value-two:  action-two
    etc.
    default:    default-action
}
```

In pseudocode, the `switch` statement has this effect:

if controlling-integer-expression **evaluates as** integer-value-one
then action-one, action-two, . . . , default-action (or until `break` or `return` is encountered)
else if controlling-integer-expression **evaluates as** integer-value-two
then action-two, . . . , default-action (or until `break` or `return` is encountered)
else if etc.
else default-action

There are a number of important details that need attention when using a C++ `switch` statement.

The controlling expression must evaluate either to a value for some integer type or to a value that is implicitly convertible to such a type. All the fundamental types conform to that requirement. However, pointers do not, as there is no automatic conversion from any pointer type to an integer type.

The `case` values must be fixed values known to the compiler. In general, that means that they should be literals for one of the fundamental integer types. Later we will see that there are a few other options.

The final `default` clause (actually, if you want to be eccentric, you can put it anywhere in the selection list) is optional, and if it is missing, the compiler will treat your code as if the default action is to do nothing.

The program will start executing the code from the corresponding `case` and continue until it encounters a `return` statement, a `break` statement, or the closing brace of the `switch` statement. It is important to understand this, because other languages with similar constructs treat the next `case` as terminating the current one.

> Language Note: *Pascal is an example of a language that uses a different design for its multi-way choice construct. The C++ feature (shared by other languages in the C family, such as Java) of allowing a case to fall through, i.e. executing the code for subsequent cases until something explicitly stops the sequential execution, is a cause of bugs in programs, so you need to be careful when using a* switch *statement and avoid simply treating it as the C++ equivalent of a mechanism you already use in some other language.*

Here is a short code fragment to demonstrate the use of a **switch** statement:

```
int i(0);
std::cin >> i;
switch(i) {
  case 0:
    std::cout << "Cannot divide by zero.\n";
    break;
  case 1:
    std::cout << "Dividing by 1 does not change anything.\n";
    break;
  default:
    std::cout << 100/i << '\n';
}
```

 TRY THIS

Write a short program to use the above fragment, and check the consequences of leaving out one of the **break** statements. Do not forget to add input validation to your program.

switch Continued

Here is a second code fragment that uses a **switch** statement:

```
char c(0);
std::cin >> c;
switch(c) {
  case 'a':
  case 'e':
  case 'i':
  case 'o':
  case 'u':
    std::cout << c << " is a vowel.\n";
    break;
  case 'y':
    std::cout << "'y' is a vowel in some contexts.\n";
    break;
  default:
    std::cout << c << " is not a vowel.\n";
}
```

Note how the C++ **case** mechanism allows a piece of code to deal with several cases. Some languages deal with this in a different way, but C++ uses the C mechanism (so that more C code will compile as C++).

 TRY THIS

Write a program using the above code. Now improve it to deal with uppercase letters. We need to do more work to sort out the consonants from the other possible inputs. Accented letters add even more work. If you want to experiment further, the `<cctype>` header provides a number of functions from the Standard C Library that allow you to classify `char`s. These include `std::isdigit( )`, `std::ispunct( )`, and `std::isalpha( )`. Those functions return `true` if the character represents a digit, a punctuation symbol, or a letter respectively. For more details and for details of locale-dependent alternatives (taking account of national character sets), see a good library reference such as *The C++ Standard Library* by Nicolai Josuttis [Josuttis 1999].

The Conditional Operator

C++ provides an operator that allows you to select which of two alternative expressions to evaluate depending on the Boolean value of a controlling expression. As this is an operator, there will be a resulting value when it is used. It is the presence of a value that distinguishes the conditional operator from the `if-else` construct. Here is the form of the conditional operator:

Boolean-control-expression `?` *result-expression-one* `:` *result-expression-two*

The conditional operator is one of several C++ operators that consist of two symbols that are separated from each other. In this case, the symbols are `?` and `:`. The control expression is evaluated first to determine which of the two result expressions should then be evaluated. If the control expression evaluates as `true`, the value of the overall expression is the result of evaluating the first result expression. If it evaluates as `false`, the value of the overall expression is the value of the second result expression. If there are side effects from the evaluations, only those for evaluating the control expression and the appropriate choice of the result expressions will occur.

Language Note: C programmers should be particularly careful, because C++ has extended the potential use of this operator, so that, for example:

```
i < j ? i = 0 : j = 0;
```

compiles and works (it sets the smaller of **i** and **j** to zero). More controversially, the following compiles in C++:

```
(i < j ? i : j) = 0;
```

In other words, where both the alternatives provide objects of the same type (presumably *int* in this case), a conditional expression in parentheses can appear on the left of an assignment. It is generally a poor idea to use this facility.

Here is a small snippet of code demonstrating a simple use of the conditional operator (it assumes that `count` is a number of oranges):

```
std::cout << "There " << ((count == 1) ? "is" : "are" ) << count
    << " orange" << ((count != 1) ? "s" : "") << ".\n";
```

It deals with providing the correct version for a single object. It even deals with that quirk of English that treats zero objects as plural. (Note that the operator-precedence rules make the parentheses around `count == 1` and `count != 1` redundant. I have used the parentheses to assist your reading of the statements.)

TRY THIS

Go back to the numbers program (page 52) and:

1. change the `if` statement that includes an exit by `return 0` to an `if-else` statement to handle the two cases as alternatives;
2. change the output statement to deal with the case where the user inputs only one value before ending with −999.

Looping

C++ has three major constructs to deal with repetition. It also has a way to roll your own; however, good programmers normally avoid that option.

> Language Note: Some languages, particularly the functional languages, use recursion as their main tool for repetition. It is possible to use this mechanism in C++, but the resulting code will generally be inferior to that written using C++'s native looping mechanisms. C++ compilers are not tuned to produce good object code when recursion is used as a looping mechanism. The use of recursion for looping will also make your code harder for C++ programmers to understand, because you will be writing code in a way that is strange to them.

The do-while Loop

We have already been using this in a highly specialized form so that we can repeat some action until an internal condition results in breaking out. The general form of the do-while loop is:

```
do{
     action-one
     action-two
     etc.
} while(Boolean-expression)
```

In pseudocode, the do-while loop has this effect:

A: action-one
action-two
etc.
if Boolean-expression **evaluates as true then go to A**

This always executes the actions section at least once. Then the program checks to see whether it should go back and repeat the section. We keep repeating the actions until one of two things happens: either the Boolean expression in the while clause evaluates as false, or one of the internal actions forces a breakout. The first option is the usual one, though we have not used that form so far in this book. For example, the following code fragment displays the numbers from 0 to 9 together with their squares:

```
int i(0);
do{
  std::cout << i << "   " << i*i << '\n';
} while(++i < 10);
```

 TRY THIS

Write a short program that incorporates the above code snippet. Compile, link, and execute it to check that the output is as predicted. Now change the ++i to i++, and compile and execute the result. Did the different results surprise you? Do you understand the difference? Note that we sometimes need to be careful about whether we use pre- or post-increment.

The `while` *Loop*

A straight `while` loop tests at the start and is probably commoner than `do-while`. The major difference is that `do-while` loops always run at least once, whereas `while` loops test immediately and the actions section is only executed if the test evaluates as `true`. The form of a `while` loop in C++ is:

`while`(*Boolean-expression*)`{`
    action-one
    action-two
    etc.
`}`

In pseudocode, the `while` loop has this effect (compare this with the pseudocode for the `do-while` loop):

go to B
A: *action-one*
action-two
etc.
B: if *Boolean-expression* ***evaluates as true then go to A***

I could have used straightforward `while(true)` loops everywhere that I have so far used `do-while(true)` in this book. Indeed, it is probably better to use this form for loops that rely on internal breakouts because it warns a reader of the code to watch for an internal **break** statement or **return** statement. The reason that I chose otherwise is partly so that I could write this here. There is not a lot between the choices but giving the marginally better one second may help you to remember that C++ often gives you a choice.

We can write the snippet of code above as:

```
int i(0);
while(i++ < 10){
   std::cout << i << "   " << i*i << '\n';
}
```

However, the results are not exactly the same.

WARNING!

Resist the temptation to write:

```
int i(0);
while(i < 10) {
   std::cout << i++ << "   " << i*i << '\n';
}
```

There is a potential for something very nasty happening if you write code that both increments a variable and uses that variable a second time all within the same statement. Notice that I wrote 'potential'. Such statements have what is called 'undefined behavior' (which I will address directly in Chapter 6). This means that the C++ Standard makes no requirements on such code. It can do what you expected; or it can do something different, even something disastrous. I once had a program that reprogrammed the BIOS of an expensive graphics card because of undefined behavior. What makes it hard to learn about undefined behavior is that the program is allowed to do what you expected; it just isn't required to.

I will point out other potential for undefined behavior as I go. However, you should note that this is not unique to C++: all programming languages have cases of undefined behavior; C++ is more up-front about it than some.

Experienced C++ programmers use a simple guideline: "Do not use increment and decrement operators in expressions with other variables." This is just a guideline, so there are places where expert programmers will ignore it. However, you need a good reason for doing so. The absolute rule is: "Never use a second instance of a variable that is being incremented or decremented within the same full expression." For now, you can think of a full expression as something such as the control expression in a decision or loop, or any expression that ends with a semicolon.

TRY THIS

Modify the previous program by replacing the do-while with a while. Check the results and decide how to modify the program so that you get the same results as before.

The for Loop

The third and most commonly used loop construct in C++ is the for loop. It is easy to use once you get the feel of it, but it can be a little strange at first. The form of the for loop is:

for (*initialization-expression* ; *Boolean-control-expression* ; *termination-expression*) *action*

In pseudocode, the for loop has this effect:

initialization-expression
go to B
A: *action*
termination-expression
B: if *Boolean-control-expression* **evaluates as true then go to A**

Let me take each of those parts separately.

Initialization
The initialization part is executed exactly once. It states what must be done before entry to the loop for the first time. It can be empty (i.e. do nothing); it can set a number of variables to initial values before the loop starts; it can also be used to define one or more variables of a single type. The commonest option in C++ is the last one, defining a single variable that will control the loop.

Control expression
The control expression is always executed immediately before each execution of the action statement to determine whether it should be executed again (or the first time, whether it should be executed even once). The loop ends immediately this expression evaluates as false. This part can also be empty, but if it is, the loop will have to use an internal breakout – just as we have been using for do-while(true) loops. In other words, leaving out a control expression is equivalent to writing true at that point.

Termination
The termination part is an optional action that will be executed at the end of every pass through the loop and immediately before the next test of the control expression. Note that this happens at the end of a pass so is not executed before the first pass.

Action

The action, or controlled statement, can be a simple statement but is more often a compound statement (a block of statements contained within braces). It provides the actions that will be executed during each pass through the loop. This statement can be a null one (empty), in which case the only actions taken will be those provided by the control and termination expressions. For example, the following is valid (though not generally advocated as good code):

```
for(int i(0); i < 10;
    std::cout << ++i << '\n');
```

Putting it together

Here is the equivalent to the earlier snippets but using a `for` loop instead of a `while` loop:

```
for(int i(0); i != 10; ++i)
    std::cout << i << " "
        << i*i << '\n';
```

Defining the control variable of a `for` loop in the initialization clause is the normal idiom in C++. The control expression for a counted case such as this one is usually expressed using the `!=` (not-equals) operator. This may be strange if you have come from a language such as C that uses a different idiom (such as the less-than operator), but comparing for inequality works in C++ even when the control variable is a user-defined type that does not support a strict ordering (we will eventually make extensive use of types called iterators that exhibit this property). The C++ idiom works just as well when we are using an integer variable as we are here.

It is also normal to use pre-increment in C++ when we are dealing with freestanding increment expressions. For integer objects it makes no difference whether we use pre- or post-increment, but later on we will be using other types of iterator (objects that are

Recursion

I refer to recursion several times in this chapter. Some programmers may not be familiar with the concept, and others may be puzzled as to how it could be used as a substitute for looping. Here is a short program to illustrate both recursion and its use for looping.

```cpp
#include <iostream>
#include <ostream>

void print_square(int i){
    if(i != 10){
        std::cout  << i << " "
            << i*i << '\n';
        return print_square(i+1);
    }
}

int main(){
    print_square(0);
}
```

This code works perfectly satisfactorily, and some compilers may even compile it efficiently, but as recursion is not normally used this way in C++ we do not expect a C++ compiler to handle this code efficiently. As far as the compiler is concerned, it will need ten instances of `print_square`'s parameter as opposed to the single control variable used by our normal C++ versions of the program. From the functional-programming perspective, the recursive form is cleaner because it does not use any variable, just pure values. However, C++ compilers have not been tuned to handle pure values and recursion.

If you are still mystified, the term recursion is used to refer to cases where a function calls itself as `print_square` does in the above example. Just like a loop, a recursive function needs some way to stop. Unlike a loop, when it runs out of control it can quickly consume all the available resources on your computer.

used to control repetition and identify members of collections), and for those pre-increment is often more efficient. Therefore, we adopt a style that works well in all cases. We call such automatic choices 'idioms'. Knowing the idioms of a language makes it easier both to write your own code and to read other programmers' code.

Language Note: One of the problems with idioms is that newcomers often try to recycle the idioms of their previous language. Sometimes these work well; sometimes they seem to work but there are hidden traps; and sometimes they either work badly in C++ (e.g. using recursion for looping) or do not work at all (e.g. using the Python form of for loop, which is a very powerful one, but not one that C++ currently provides). Most C idioms will work in C++, but every one of them needs to be re-examined in the context of C++, because not all of them are the preferred option in C++.

break, continue, and goto

There are several ways of varying from the normal flow of code in a construct. I am leaving the details of `return` until Chapter 5, when I deal with functions. You will also have noted that throwing an exception exits from the normal flow. I am also leaving details of that for a later chapter.

I have already made extensive use of `break` without going into much detail as to what it does. `break` causes an immediate exit from any of the above loop constructs (`for`, `while`, and `do-while`) as well as forcing an exit from a `switch` statement (and an `if` statement, but you should generally avoid its use there). The statement immediately after the construct in question will be the next one executed after a `break` statement.

It is good practice to avoid using `break` for exiting loops, though we have seen one of the exceptions to this in its use for exiting an otherwise infinite loop. It is often possible to change the source code so that `break` is unnecessary. The resulting code is often simpler even if it was not so obvious in the first place. If you find yourself writing more complicated code in order to avoid an early exit from a loop, you are probably heading in the wrong direction. Often programmers are still using a mental model that involves early exit while trying to abide by a coding guideline that prohibits the use of `break`. Try to design your code so that an early exit from a loop is unnecessary. Then you will reduce your use of `break` for all the right reasons, and your code will likely become simpler and more elegant.

Sometimes we find that we need to abandon the current pass of a loop and go immediately to the next one. C++ provides a special mechanism for that: the keyword `continue`. Here is a small code snippet to demonstrate its use (however, this is only a demonstration of use and not an illustration of good coding practice):

```
std::cout << "The following digits are not divisible by 5:\n";
for(int i(1); i != 10; ++i) {
  if(i == 5) continue;
  std::cout << i << '\n';
}
```

In this case it would have been easy to eliminate the `continue` by replacing the above code with:

```
std::cout << "The following digits are not divisible by 5:\n";
for(int i(1); i != 10; ++i) {
  if(i != 5) std::cout << i << '\n';
}
```

However, I might argue that the first form is clearer because it makes the exceptional case explicit whereas the second one buries it. In this simple case, I do not think there is much in it, but the decision whether or not to use `continue` should be based on which alternative makes the resulting code clearer.

I am going to say much about `goto`. I have never found it useful in over a decade of programming in C++. I have no great philosophical objection to `goto`; I just find that any code that uses it can be rewritten in a simpler form without it. Its continued presence in C++ is one of those holdovers from the past when long functions were common. These days we tend to write many shorter functions and rely on good compilers to reduce the number of actual function calls. goto is not generally useful in modern C++ programming. You need to know it exists because you might come across it in someone else's code, but you do not need to use it.

> Language Note: One of the problems for programmers used to languages such as BASIC is that they are accustomed to using goto. Some of the idioms they are used to use goto and they just import those into C++. The biggest problem with the use of goto is that it usually results in code that lacks clarity. Such code is hard to maintain and is prone to bugs.

In theory you can roll your own loops by using goto and if (witness the use of these in the pseudocode above). In practice, no C++ programmer would do that.

WALKTHROUGH

The Number-Sorting Program

Here are the important lines of that program again, to save you having to turn back and forth between the source code (page 52) and my commentary. I have highlighted the lines that I am going to write about.

```
 7 int main() {
 8   try{
 9     std::vector<int> numbers;
10     do {
11       std::cout << "Next whole number (-999 to stop): ";
12       int next;
13       std::cin >> next;
14       if(next == -999) break;
15       numbers.push_back(next);
16     } while(true);
17     if(numbers.size() == 0){
18       std::cout << "There were no numbers input.\n";
19       return 0;  // exit program
20     }
21     std::sort(numbers.begin(), numbers.end());
22     std::cout << "Here are the " << numbers.size()
23         << " numbers you typed in ascending numerical order:\n";
24     for(int i(0); i != numbers.size(); ++i){
25       std::cout << numbers[i] << ", ";
26     }
27     std::cout << '\n';
28   }
29   catch(...){
30     std::cerr << "***An exception was thrown.***\n";
31   }
32 }
```

Line 9 defines **numbers** as the name of an object that encapsulates a contiguous sequence of **int**s. The use of **std::vector** specifies that it will be a contiguous sequence. The **<int>** specifies that it is a sequence of **int**s. Because I have provided no extra information in the definition, **numbers** will start out as an empty sequence. C++ **std::vector** sequences have a growth strategy that allows them to expand as needed in a way that provides optimum general performance. They are the C++ programmer's first-choice container for sequences of objects of the same type.

Line 12 defines the variable **next** directly before its point of first use. Strictly speaking, as we have defined **next** within a block of source code, the code recreates it every time the block repeats. However, any respectable compiler will avoid adding extra code. I have not initialized **next** because I am going to obtain a value from the **std::cin** in the next line. This is one of the special cases where we may reasonably leave out the initialization of a variable of a fundamental type. Nonetheless, many programmers insist on initialization even in this instance, because they worry about someone later on separating the point of definition from the point where the variable is first written to, thereby leaving the gate open for someone else to add code that uses the variable before it has been written to.

If you thought carefully about line 13 in the context of the comment I made about assumptions, you will have noted that the code assumes that the user always types in a valid integer. Even such trivial errors as trying to input a number with a decimal point will send the program into an infinite loop. We are not yet ready to deal with that issue other than by sending a message to **std::cerr** and then giving up by throwing an exception.

TRY THIS

If you have not already done so, go back and amend the program so that it tests **std::cin** immediately after its use and throws an exception if it has failed.

WALKTHROUGH

Continued

Line 14 tests for end of input. If the user has entered the specified value, the program skips forward to start executing from line 17. Otherwise, it executes line 15. This line uses the mechanism provided by **std::vector** for adding a new object to the end of the sequence it is holding. If there is not enough space for the new object, **push_back()** will trigger the internal behavior that provides a larger amount of space and, if necessary, copies the existing values into that space so that the objects in the sequence remain contiguous. In other words, **std::vector** automatically maintains its contents as a contiguous sequence.

Lines 17−20 deal with the possibility that no numbers were provided. They make use of the mechanism provided by **std::vector** that reports the current number of objects in the sequence. **numbers.size()** always evaluates to the number of objects in the sequence that we are calling **numbers**. Line 19, **return 0** is the mechanism for leaving **main** (i.e. the program) early. We could have avoided the need for an early exit by putting the remainder of the normal processing in a block controlled by **else**.

TRY THIS

Modify the program to eliminate the **return 0** and make the rest of normal processing a block controlled by **else**. When you have done this, consider the two versions and decide which seems clearer to you. I prefer the early return, but some coding guidelines prohibit use of early returns. Try to come up with an alternative design that avoids making the normal processing the **else** part of an **if-else**.

WALKTHROUGH

Continued

Line 21 uses one of the more powerful features of modern C++, the concept of applying 'algorithms' to sequences. The **#include <algorithm>** line provides access to the somewhat misnamed 'algorithm' part of the Library. **std::sort** is one of roughly 80 algorithms provided by the Library. The default version of it requires two arguments. The first argument specifies where the sequence starts, and the second one specifies how to determine that the sequence has finished. By default **std::sort()** sorts a sequence into the natural ascending order for the type of objects in the sequence – it uses the < (less-than) operator for the type of objects stored in the sequence.

numbers.begin() uses the mechanism of **std::vector** that supplies the value (called an iterator) that identifies the start of the sequence. **numbers.end()** supplies the iterator that signifies that the sequence has ended (we will discuss the details of iterators another time, but for now just know that they generally identify the location of objects). Note that **end()** does not identify the last object: it is a special iterator that determines whether the sequence has ended (in other words, unlike most iterators, this one does not identify the location of an object). This representation of the end of a sequence may seem strange at first, but it has many advantages, and as you get used to it you will find it strange that you ever expected the end of a sequence to be the last element rather than after the last one.

Now if you look at line 21 again you will see that it results in the rearranging of the sequence called **numbers** into ascending order.

Lines 24–26 output the sorted sequence in **numbers** as a comma-separated list. The control expression of the **for** loop keeps going until it has counted all the elements of **numbers**. Notice that along with many other languages, C++ starts counting at zero, with the consequence that you have finished when the count reaches the number of the elements in the container (given by **numbers.size()**).

Line 25 uses the feature of **std::vector** that allows access to elements by using a subscript or index. That means that we can treat **std::vector** objects as if they are arrays, but arrays with a lot of added functionality. How surprising you find this depends on your prior programming experience.

On Magic Numbers

Programmers often refer to numerical literals as 'magic numbers'. Sometimes the significance of a literal number is obvious from the context in which it is used, as is the case for the factor used for converting hours to minutes in the following code snippet:

```
int hours;
std::cin >> hours;
int minutes(hours * 60);
```

I see nothing wrong with using the literal **60** in this context. But there are cases where even though the context makes the use clear we might still prefer to use a named value. For example:

```
double radius;
std::cin >> radius;
double circumference(2 * radius * 3.14159625);
```

You probably recognize the literal as an approximation for the mathematical constant π, but are you sure I typed the figures correctly? (I did not.) In addition, if π turns up in a program it will probably do so more than once.

Readability and correctness are just two reasons for replacing the literal with a name. In C++, we do that by defining a **const**-qualified name for the literal. The above code now becomes:

```
double const pi(3.14159265);   // corrected
double radius;
std::cin >> radius;
double circumference(2 * pi * radius);
```

That final statement becomes instantly recognizable by anyone with even the smallest amount of domain knowledge. The use of a named constant means that we only have to type the value in once – carefully – and after that, we write readable code. Should I mistype the value of π or want to provide more significant figures I have a single point at which to make the change.

Where magic numbers become a matter for more concern is where the values are essentially arbitrary. In the number-sorting program, the choice of −999 to flag end of input is entirely arbitrary. It signifies termination of input because I decided that that is what it would mean. A stranger looking at the code can legitimately ask what is special about −999. The answer is that it is a magic number whose property is neither more nor less than what I choose it to be. We should always replace such numeric literals with named values. In C++, we do that by providing an appropriate name for a **const**-qualified object of a suitable type. In the number-sorting program, I might provide:

```
int const end_input(-999);
```

Now I replace line 11 with

```
std::cout << "Next whole number (" << end_input << " to stop): ";
```

and line 14 with:

```
if(next == end_input) break;
```

I hope you think the result is clearer and easier to maintain. You can easily change the termination value to something else by changing the definition of **end_input**. In addition, the source code should need less commentary because the named values communicate my intention.

From now onwards, look at literals with a degree of suspicion, and ask yourself if their use is sensible in context, or do they have smell of 'magic'? You will get back the cost of a little extra typing many times over in reduced maintenance time.

The names **fgw::red1** etc. for the bits in the color-coding in the default palette of colors used by **fgw::playpen** objects are an example of removing magic numbers. In this case the names stop being useful (actually, they become positively misleading) when we move away from the default palette. Named values do not solve all our problems. We have to choose names carefully.

EXERCISES

1. Write a program that asks the user how many words they are going to input, and then collects those words into a `std::vector<std::string>`. When the input has completed, sort the words alphabetically and print them out in a column.

2. Write a program that collects words from the keyboard until 'END' is typed in. It should then sort the words and output them in a column. Try to avoid the magic use of 'END' by using a suitably named constant object.

3. Write a program that displays a column of 20 black pixels in the Playpen window. Check carefully that it is a column of 20, not 19 or 21. I suggest that you do not use the default Playpen scale but set the scale to something larger. You might like to think about a way that will allow you to count the pixels as they are plotted.

4. Write a program that prompts the user for two whole numbers and then displays a cross in the Playpen window whose height is the first number and whose width is the second. Modify this program so that the user can select a color other than black. For example, you might ask the user for the amount of red (0 to 7), the amount of green (0 to 7) and the amount of blue (0 to 7). You know enough C++ and enough about the default Playpen palette to achieve this, but it will be hard if you are not already a fluent programmer in some other language.

5. Write a program that covers the Playpen with 256 colored tiles, one of each of the 256 colors in the default palette. If you use a scale of 32, 16 rows of 16 logical pixels will exactly cover the Playpen. The only hint I will give you is to consider using nested `for` loops. You may have to experiment quite a bit. (Don't forget that you can change the origin if that helps you.)

6. Write a program that draws the diagonals of the Playpen.

7. The median of a collection of values is the one in the middle when they are arranged in numerical order. If there are two middle ones (because there are an even number of values in the collection) the median is the arithmetic mean of the middle pair. Write a program that collects numbers from input and then outputs their median.

8. An examination is graded on the basis that the top 20% of the candidates get 'A', the next 20% get 'B', and so on to the bottom 20%, who get 'E'. Write a program that collects the marks for 20 candidates and then outputs the grade boundaries. Note that you do not need to know the maximum possible mark. For a perfect solution you will need to resolve issues concerning multiple candidates on a grade boundary.

STRETCHING EXERCISES

These exercises give experienced programmers a greater challenge. If you found the above exercises tough, leave these ones for now. You can always come back to them later. As always, answers should be limited to using only C++ that I have introduced so far.

9. The triangular numbers are those resulting from the sum of the first *n* whole numbers. So the first four are: 1; 3 (= 1 + 2); 6 (= 1 + 2 + 3) and 10 (= 1 + 2 + 3 + 4). Write a program that displays triangular numbers of pixels as triangles in the Playpen. It should start by displaying a single pixel in a color of your choice and

wait till the user presses the Enter key. At that point it should add a row of two pixels with the existing one above and central. This process should be repeated until the screen displays the tenth triangular number.

10. Write a program that separates the whole numbers from 1 to 100 into two sets so that the sum of the square roots of the numbers in each set are equal, to six significant figures. Be careful: you are dealing with floating-point numbers, and the concept of equality will need careful handling. You may use the Library function `std::sqrt`. You will need to include the `<cmath>` header.

11. Write a program that takes a number of words as input and outputs their average (arithmetic mean) length and the overall ratio of vowels to consonants. You may use the fact that objects of the `std::string` type, like those of a `std::vector` type can report their size (number of characters) by using `size( )`.

12. Write a program that will take in pairs of words and then output 'anagram' or 'not anagram' depending on whether they are or are not composed of the same letters. `std::string` objects can be sorted in exactly the same way that we sorted a `std::vector` object. You can also compare strings for equality using `==` between them. That should be enough help.

13. Write a program that accepts integer values in the range −100 to 100 and outputs their names in text. So if the input were 27, the output should be 'twenty-seven'. If the input were −39 the output would be 'minus thirty-nine' or 'negative thirty-nine'. If you feel up to it, try converting your program to work with some other natural language such as French. Even harder, try writing a program where the user types in the text and the output is the number.

REFERENCE SECTION

Decisions

C++ provides three primary mechanisms for making decisions:

1. `if-else`, for an essentially two-way decision. The `else` is optional, but if it is present it must be the next statement after the one controlled by the `if`. The controlled statement may be either a simple statement or a compound one (a block of statements in braces).
2. `switch`, allowing a multi-way selection controlled by an integer value. The selections are identified by the **case** keyword followed by a constant integer value and a colon. Execution of a selection is terminated by the next **break** or **return** statement or by the closing brace of the `switch` statement. A `switch` statement may include a single catch-all option identified by the **default** keyword.
3. A conditional operator that selects which of two expressions to evaluate depending on a control expression.
   The form is: *control-expression ? expression-for-true : expression-for-false*.
      The difference between mechanisms 1 and 3 is that in the former we have controlled **statements**, and in the latter we have controlled **expressions**. Expressions are evaluated to provide values that may be used as part of larger expressions within the same statement. Statements are complete and do not have values. The following code snippets (intended to be part of the exit from a function) demonstrate the difference in use:

```
std::string response;
std::cout << "Yes or no? ";
std::cin >> response;
if(response[0] == 'n') return 0;
```

```
else return 1;
```

or

```
std::string response;
std::cout << "Yes or no? ";
std::cin >> response;
return (response[0] == 'n') ? 0 : 1;
```

The first case uses two `return` statements selected by the `if-else` construct; the second case returns a value selected by a conditional expression.

Looping, Repetition, and Iteration

These are just three terms with very similar meanings. C++ provides three main mechanisms for looping.

1. `while`(*control-expression*) *action*. The action statement (usually a compound statement enclosed in braces) is repeated so long as the control expression evaluates as `true` (or non-zero). The control expression is evaluated before every repetition including the first. If it evaluates to `false` (or zero) the action statement is not executed and processing resumes with the next statement. Note that this means that the action part of the statement may sometimes not be executed even once.

2. `do`{*actions*} `while`(*control-expression*)`;` This variant tests for repetition after each execution of the action block. It is used when the actions must always be executed at least once. Otherwise, it is similar to the `while` loop..

3. `for`(*initialization*; *test*; *termination*) *action*. This form of looping is largely equivalent to writing:

   initialization;
   `while`(*test*)`{`
       action
       termination;
   `}`

We never need to use a `for` statement (or alternatively we can always write a `while` statement as a `for` statement). However, using both constructs allows us to provide idioms that help other programmers follow our intentions. It is generally idiomatic to use a `for` statement when the number of repeats is determined by some value (e.g. when we want to count through a number of cases). We use a `while` statement when we expect the end of repetition will result from some other condition such as reaching the end of a file that we are processing.

The most common use of `do-while` is for cases where some form of data must be obtained and processed with an option to get more data depending on the result of the current repetition.

C++ provides several ways to terminate processing of a loop. The `continue` keyword allows the program to abort the current iteration and go directly to the test for the next repetition. In the case of a `for` loop, `continue` immediately resumes execution with the *termination* statement before testing for another repetition.

The `break` statement is used to exit the loop altogether. In other words, `break` forces execution to resume with the statement immediately after the current loop construct.

There are other statements such as `return` statements that will result in early termination of a loop, but those are consequences of their designed behavior rather than behavior designed to get out of a loop.

Standard C++ Library Types

`std::string`

This type provides text type behavior. It also provides suitable behavior for a sequence of `char` values. It includes the functionality we expect for text such as supporting appending text and comparing text for equality. As a sequence type, it provides the functionality of a C++ sequence. Sequence objects know their length or size, they know where they start and end, they can usually be indexed and they can be sorted. We will learn more of the functionality of **std::string** in later chapters.

`std::vector`*<type>*

std::vector is an instance of what C++ calls a class template. It provides the functionality we expect for a dynamically resizable array of something. Because the functionality of a sequence is largely independent of the type of object in the sequence, we want a way to specify that functionality independent of the type of object being stored in the sequence. One of the major uses of a class template is providing such generic functionality. We can plug in an extensive range of types at the point of use. Only relatively few types will fail to work correctly with **std::vector**. The basic criterion for a type to be usable to instantiate a **std::vector** is that objects of the type must be copiable and assignable. In other words, you must be able to pass objects of the type by value, and you must be able to assign a value of the type to an object of the same type. At this stage in your study of C++, those restrictions are not likely to mean much, but they will by the time you have finished using the tutorial part of this book.

CHAPTER (4)

Namespaces and the C++ Standard Library

I will be introducing several services provided by the C++ Standard Library. I will explain namespaces and how to avoid having to type such things as `std::` and `fgw::` over and over again.

The Library is a substantial resource for any C++ programmer and one that it pays to know about. Nicolai Josuttis took almost 800 pages to cover it his excellent tutorial and reference, *The C++ Standard Library* [Josuttis 1999] and there will shortly be a volume by Dietmar Küel detailing a substantial set of recent additions. I will be limiting my coverage to those parts that I use in this book. However, you should get used to checking whether the Library provides what you need for a program before spending time writing your own code. The easiest way to check is to ask. Usenet newsgroups such as `comp.lang.c++.moderated` and `alt.comp.lang.learn.c-c++` are invaluable resources for asking questions about what C++ provides that might help with solving a problem.

Wide Versus Narrow Character Set Support

C++ provides full support for two kinds of character set: narrow and wide. We can represent characters in the C++ narrow character sets with 8-bit values. These character sets are fine for Standard English and even have room for values representing the more common accented letters. However, 8 bits (256 values) are insufficient for representing the character sets used elsewhere in the world. Even 16 bits (65536 values) are insufficient for a simple encoding of all the characters used somewhere in the world.

For more than a decade the Unicode Consortium has been working at providing a universal encoding for all character sets being used anywhere in the world. The latest Unicode Standard (version 4) requires 20 bits for a flat encoding (i.e. one that does not involve special codes to shift from one character set to another). Unicode is effectively equivalent to the ISO 10646 character-encoding standard.

C++ provides the `wchar_t` type to support extended character encoding, i.e. characters that belong to some extended character representation. C++ does not require that the values for `wchar_t` represent Unicode. However, C++ provides a standard representation for Unicode literals.

C++ also provides support for all types and objects based on `wchar_t` that are analogs of the types and objects based on `char`. I will confine myself, in this book, to the narrow character set and its support through `char`-based objects and types. The current release of the MDS implementation at the time of writing does not provide full support for the wide-character alternatives of `std::string` and the console I/O objects. In the context of learning C++, that is not a serious handicap. When you have learned to use the narrow versions correctly, you will find it easy to switch to the wide ones when you need them.

Namespaces

In the early '90s it became clear that C++ programmers would make extensive use of third-party libraries. In addition, the Standard Library was itself likely to grow. Names in different libraries were likely to clash. Worse, compilers would not always be able to identify such cases as being errors. As we will see in the next chapter, it is possible to use a single name with several meanings visible in the same scope (it is called overloading). Devising a mechanism that would distinguish names from different libraries seemed useful. The namespace mechanism was designed to deal with these problems.

> *Definition: A scope, sometimes called a declarative scope, is a region of source code in which declared names retain the meaning given to them by the declaration. The smallest normal scope is that provided by a matched pair of braces inside a function definition. A try block is an example of such a scope. The largest scope is that called 'the global scope' and includes all names that are declared outside of any more restrictive scope. The concept of scope is important but one that is best acquired by giving examples in relevant contexts as and when they occur. Names in inner scopes can hide the same names in outer ones.*

We can provide a scope for a library or part of a library using the following syntax:

namespace X**{**
    declarations-and-definitions
}

The effect of this construct is to prefix all the names declared/defined between the braces with X:: to provide a fully elaborated name. Within a namespace scope, the names declared in that namespace can be used without any elaboration, but the default outside the braces requires the full elaboration by prefixing the namespace name and a double colon. For example:

```
namespace example{
  int i(0);
  int j(i);  // initialize j from i
}
int k(i);  // error, no i in scope
int k(example::i);  // OK, use the i found in namespace example
```

All blocks that are qualified by the same namespace name are part of the same scope. So

```
namespace example{
  int m(i);  // initialize a new int, m, with the value of the i
             // that was declared in namespace example above
}
```

extends the namespace **example** by adding a new name, **m**, and initializing it with the current value stored in **example::i**. Perhaps you wonder about code such as

```
namespace example{
  int i(0);
}
int i(1);
int n(i);
```

(in other words, code where a name declared inside a namespace matches one declared outside the namespace). Declaring the same name in different scopes creates different instances of the name and so they name different objects: n will be initialized with 1, not 0.

WARNING!

Reusing names in different scopes is a constant cause of confusion and is best avoided.

It is useful to know where a function or other entity has been declared, but that is sometimes information that we do not need to make explicit. I would never call an object cout because that, to both me and every other C++ programmer, is the name of the console output object. In just about every context, we expect it to be synonymous with std::cout. Indeed many older books on C++ just use cout; many of them were written before namespaces were invented and the full name was adjusted to std::cout.

The designers of C++ did not invent namespaces to force programmers to type more symbols but to provide a mechanism for disambiguation when two programmers pick on the same name for a non-local entity such as a function or a user-defined type. How can we regain the simplicity of unelaborated names?

C++ provides two main mechanisms and a way to shorten long namespace names.

using Directives

A using directive is a mechanism to allow a programmer to use all the names from a namespace without explicitly prefixing them with the namespace name. We should use such a crude tool with care. Nonetheless, using directives are frequent in books because they save space and reduce the need to write source-code statements over two or more lines. On the other hand, we normally avoid using directives in production-quality code.

The form of a using directive is simply:

```
using namespace X;
```

From that point, the compiler will check for declarations in visible parts of namespace X when it is searching for a name's declaration. The reason that I specified visible parts is that a using directive is not some magical incantation that allows the compiler to see names declared elsewhere or at some future place such as in files that have not been included into the present one. A using directive is not an instruction to the compiler to search for all the places that declare names in that namespace. It simply tells the compiler that when looking for a name it must look inside any currently visible blocks belonging to that namespace. Note that source code is not visible until the compiler has passed through it. Declarations are not visible until after the point of declaration. C++ treats declarations in the strict order in which they appear in a translation unit (the technical term for a file of source code after all the included files have been processed into it).

using Declarations

A using declaration is a mechanism that allows the compiler to use simple names (names without namespace qualification) from any visible declarations of a specific fully elaborated name. This use is 'as if' we had declared the name at the point of the using declaration without the elaboration of the namespace prefix. Superficially, a using declaration may seem to do the same thing as a using directive, just confined to a single name. Far from it, it does something quite different: a using declaration brings a name into the current scope, whereas a using directive tells a compiler another place to look for names that it has not yet found.

When I write

```
using std::cout;
```

I tell the compiler to find all the declarations of **cout** in currently visible blocks for namespace **std** and treat those declarations as if they replace the **using** declaration.

Example

In the next chapter, we will be looking at some aspects of C++ functions. That will include demonstrating that two functions can share a name (called function overloading) as long as the types of their parameters allow them to be distinguished. However, I want to clarify the difference between **using** declarations and **using** directives. Please compile and execute the following two programs and note the difference in output:

Program 1

```
   #include <iostream>

   namespace x{
      void foo(int){std::cout << "int case";}
   }

A  using namespace x;

   namespace x{
      void foo(double){std::cout << "double case";}
   }

   int main(){
      foo(1.3);
   }
```

Program 2

```
   #include <iostream>

   namespace x{
      void foo(int){std::cout << "int case";}
   }

B  using x::foo;

   namespace x{
      void foo(double){std::cout << "double case";}
   }

   int main(){
      foo(1.3);
   }
```

Commentary

In the first case the compiler is told at line A that it can look for names in namespace **x** if it does not find the name in the current scope. When it comes to **foo(1.3)** it does not find a candidate outside namespace **x** but finds two candidates inside; it chooses the one that uses a **double** because that exactly matches the type of the argument.

In the second case, line B instructs the compiler that all the declarations of `x::foo` that it has so far seen should be treated as if they had been declared at line B (without the elaboration of `x::`). However, it has no impact on any subsequent declarations of `foo` in namespace `x`. When it comes to `foo(1.3)` the only declaration available is `void foo(int)`, so that is the one it uses by implicitly converting `1.3` to `1`, which is then ignored because `foo` does not actually make any further use of the value passed to its parameter.

Do not worry about how function calls and function overloading work: we will tackle that in the next chapter. For now, I want you to keep focused on the different behaviors provided by a `using` **declaration** and a `using` **directive** as shown by the above code.

Namespace *std* and Namespace *fgw*

All those places where you have had to type `std::` are examples of the using fully elaborated names from the Standard Library. There are advantages to using fully elaborated names. In the early chapters of this book it is always clear which names come from the Standard Library, because they always start with `std::`. That tells you where you can look for documentation.

In contrast, I have always prefixed the names from my support library with `fgw::`, which tells you that you need to refer to any documentation that I have provided for my library if you want to learn more about such names.

In this book, I will generally use `using` declarations for names from the C++ Standard Library. Otherwise, I will use the fully elaborated names (as I have been doing up to now). I will do much the same for names from my library except that I will sometimes use a `using` **directive**. In particular, I will do this when using the color names such as `fgw::red1`. There are a lot of them and it gets tedious to bring them in with `using` declarations. Using fully elaborated names can also be tiresome if there is no actual conflict with another library.

 TRY THIS

Choose some of the code you typed in for the earlier chapters and modify it so that it no longer uses fully elaborated names. It is your choice whether you use `using` directives, `using` declarations, or a mixture. Experiment until you feel reasonably confident with both.

Fully Elaborated Global Names

One advantage of namespaces is that we have a mechanism to distinguish identically spelled names from different namespaces; we can use their fully elaborated names even when the short versions of the names collide. However, how should we tackle the problem of collisions that involve a global name, i.e. a name that has been declared outside of any namespace or other limited scope?

The answer is simple once you know it: just prefix the global name with a pair of colons. C++ calls the double colon the scope operator, though I think it is pushing the concept of an operator by using that terminology. Here is a silly program that demonstrates the use of a fully elaborated global name:

```
1 #include <iostream>
2 using namespace std;
3
4 int cout(1);
5
6 int main(){
7   std::cout << ::cout;
8 }
```

TRY THIS

Type in and execute that program. It should work and result in outputting 1 to the console window. Now try replacing either or both of the fully elaborated names in line 7 by the simple name. When you try to compile, you will receive an 'ambiguity' error: the compiler cannot tell which declaration of cout you meant it to use.

Now go back to the original code and replace line 2 with

```
using std::cout;
```

Try to compile the code. You get a quite different error, because the compiler considers that you tried to declare the same name but with a different type in the same scope. You can have functions sharing a name in the same scope but that does not extend to variables.

With **using** directives, there is no collision of declared names because they are each in their own scope, and we can use full elaboration to resolve any ambiguity; with **using** declarations, we import declarations and so get an irresolvable conflict. We have to either remove the **using** declaration or change the name of one of the objects.

Namespace Aliases

Both **std** and **fgw** are very short names for namespaces. There is a real risk that using short names will result in a collision of the names of namespaces used by different library writers. The designers of C++ wanted to encourage the use of long names for namespaces while allowing users to provide shorter alternatives. This led to the idea of a namespace alias. Here is an example of both the idea and its use:

```
namespace Company_with_very_long_name{
   int data;
}
namespace cwvln = Company_with_very_long_name;
```

Now

```
cwvln::data = 1;
```

means exactly the same as:

```
Company_with_very_long_name::data = 1;
```

WARNING!

The idea was fine but there are some unfortunate surprises when it comes to using namespace aliases that have resulted in them not being widely used. This may change in the future if those responsible for the design of C++ can remove the causes of the surprises.

Input from std::cin

The Library provides various mechanisms for extracting data from an input object. We are currently limited to using **std::cin** for input, and I am going to tackle three ways of extracting data from it.

The first – using get( ) – extracts the next character and returns its value as a char. So we can write

```
char c;
c = std::cin.get( );
```

and c will now contain the value for the next character in the input. If we wanted to, we could extract a whole line of input with this code fragment:

```
std::string input_line;
char c(0);
while(true){
  c = std::cin.get( );
  if(c == '\n') break;
  input_line += c;
}
```

TRY THIS

Write a short program to use that fragment and write out the result to the console window. Try to produce an alternative formulation that uses while(c != '\') rather than the conditional break statement. Your solution should do exactly the same: read input up to the first newline, saving the input up to the newline but discarding the actual newline character.

Reading an entire line of input is quite a common requirement, so C++ provides a way to do it directly with a function called getline( ). Here is a code snippet that demonstrates using getline( ) to read a whole line of input into a std::string object:

```
std::string input_line;
std::getline(std::cin, input_line);
```

It does precisely the same as the previous code, but it is shorter, and the use of a suitably named function documents what we are doing. The resulting code is both shorter and easier to understand.

Perhaps you are puzzled by the different syntax for using get( ) and getline( ). get( ) is preceded by the name of the object it is getting data from, while getline( ) has the source of data named within the following parentheses. This is not an arbitrary difference but one that represents the different natures of the two methods. Getting characters from input is part of the basic behavior (called semantics) of input objects, and so we use the syntax that represents such behavior in C++ – the source object's name followed by a dot and the name of the function that provides the desired behavior. However, reading whole lines into std::string objects requires the cooperation of two objects, so we use a syntax that reflects the equal status of std::cin and the instance of std::string that we are calling input_line.

TRY THIS

Modify your previous program to use std::getline( ), and check that it gives the same results.

The third way to extract data from std::cin is by using the streaming or extraction operator, >>. We have used this operator in earlier programs. The extraction operator works by identifying the type of the receiving object (the variable on the right) and using appropriate behavior for that type of object. By default, it ignores all leading whitespace characters (spaces, tabs, carriage returns, and newlines) in the source object (`std::cin`). It terminates input at the first unsuitable character. By default, C++ deems trailing whitespace to be unsuitable for all types. This means that when you use `std::cin >> x`, regardless of the type of `x`, all leading whitespace is ignored and input ceases not later than the first trailing whitespace character. Some data types, such as the numerical types, classify other characters (e.g. punctuation marks) as being unsuitable. Unlike `getline( )`, which extracts and discards the terminating character (by default the newline character), the extraction operator leaves the terminating character in the input, ready for the next use of the input object.

Here is a small code snippet using the extraction operator to insert input into a `std::string` object.

```
std::string word;
std::cin >> word;
```

 TRY THIS

Write a program that uses the above code to extract words from `std::cin`. Experiment with this program and the earlier ones until you are sure you understand the different behavior as regards the significance of spaces in your input.

Output with `std::cout`

There are two main C++ ways to output data to an output object such as `std::cout`. The first is by using the `put( )` function to put a single `char` value to the output object. For example,

```
char c('x');
char newline('\n');
std::cout.put(c);
std::cout.put(newline);
```

would display an 'x' in the console window and move to a new line for any subsequent output.

 TRY THIS

Write a program to use the above code and verify that it works as predicted.

The streaming operator is the commoner mechanism for data output. In this case, we use the left-shift operator to represent streaming (or shifting) data into the output object. That is, we use `<<` to insert data into an output stream. We have already made extensive use of this operator to display prompts and results.

Standard Console Output Objects

C++ provides two other standard output objects; `std::cerr` and `std::clog`. C++ uses `std::cerr` for reporting errors. Those coming from a C background will already be familiar with the concept because they have a similar idea implemented by C's `stderr` object. The default destination for `std::cerr` is the monitor. You will eventually learn how to change the connection to a file or to some other sink for data. A second default feature of `std::cerr` is that it is unbuffered. That means that data sent to `std::cerr` is immediately processed and not batched up until it becomes necessary or desirable to deal with it.

The intended use of `std::clog` is for logging events to some suitable data sink. The assumption is that such events will be a normal part of the program's execution and so there will be no hurry to complete the process of dispatching the data to the output object. For that reason, `std::clog` is normally buffered (as is `std::cin`), and completion of processing will be delayed until either it is forced or the buffer is full. Like `std::cerr`, `std::clog` defaults to the monitor.

Even though all three standard console output objects default to the monitor, it is good practice to use the appropriate one for the purpose at hand. If you want to report an error, use `std::cerr`, but if you are logging an event that does not constitute an error (it might be a failure of some process, but not one that the programmer wishes to treat as an error), use `std::clog`. Use `std::cout` for normal program output and interaction with the user. By always using the appropriate output, you will find it simple to modify programs to dispatch the different categories of output to different places when you have learned how to do that.

TRY THIS

Write a program that collects some words from the keyboard, stores them in a `std::vector<std::string>` object (by using `push_back()`), sorts them, and then displays the sorted list on the monitor. The program should also log the start and end of each phase: data acquisition, data processing, and data output. Of course, you will also arrange to catch possible exceptions and send a message to an appropriate output object.

TRY THIS

The `fgw::playpen` type supports four different plotting modes. See the next section for details. Write a program that will help you explore these different plotting modes. To get best advantage you will need to be able to change the origin and the scale as well as the plotting mode. Do not use fully elaborated names. Use `using` declarations for the C++ Standard Library elements and a `using` directive for my library.

Playpen Plotting Modes

`fgw::playpen` supports four different plotting behaviors. The default one, `fgw::direct`, simply replaces the current pixel color with the one designated by the color argument provided by any function used for modifying the Playpen. For example, `paper.plot(3, 4, 23)` will change the pixel (3, 4) (at the current scale and origin) to whatever color 23 maps to in the current palette.

The `fgw::additive` mode combines the plotting color with the background color by adding the two on a bitwise basis (i.e. $0 + 0 = 0$, $0 + 1 = 1$, $1 + 0 = 1$, and $1 + 1 = 0$ – note, no carry in the last case). Given a current color of 21 (binary 00010101) and a plotting color of 49 (00110001) the resulting color will be binary 00110101, which is 53. A bit in the result is 1 if the bit in either the current color or the plotting color is 1; otherwise it is 0. Those familiar with bitwise operations will recognize this as a bitwise *or* operation.

The `fgw::filter` mode results in the pixel taking on the color defined by those color elements shared by the current color and the plotting color. I called it `filter` because its behavior is exactly that of a color filter applied to colored light. Given a current color of 21 (00010101) and a plotting color of 49 (00110001) the result will be 00010001, which is 17. This is equivalent to a bitwise *and* applied to the two colors.

The `fgw::disjoint` mode produces a new color from those elements that are only present in either the current color or the plotting color but not both. So given colors **21** (00010101) and **49** (00110001) the result will be 00100100, which is **36**. This is equivalent to a bitwise *exclusive or* applied to the two colors.

When plotting pixels with a scale factor greater than **1**, the plotting-mode rule is applied at the level of screen pixels. Therefore, except in the case of `fgw::direct`, the different constituent physical pixels making up a logical pixel may result in different colors if they started as different ones.

`fgw::disjoint` has the special property of being reversible. By that, I mean that if you plot the same pixel twice using the same color the resulting color will be the same as the starting color. That property makes `fgw::disjoint` suitable for such purposes as providing a cursor.

The `fgw::playpen::setplotmode()` function is used to change the plotting mode. For example, the following code fragment changes the plotting mode to `fgw::disjoint`:

```
fgw::playpen paper;
paper.setplotmode(fgw::disjoint);
```

Like all functions, `setplotmode()` returns a value. The returned value is the previous plotting mode.

Further Practice

At this point, you may wish to read an alternative description of what we have covered so far. You may also want some more ideas for practice. I have arranged that the text of *You Can Do It!* is on the CD that comes with this book. While that book used somewhat simpler tools and aims at raw programming novices, the text, ideas, and examples are compatible with this one. Please dip into that book for programming ideas and examples of simple solutions using a very limited subset of C++. At this stage in your learning of C++, I recommend that you quickly skim through the first four chapters of *You Can Do It!* and try some of the exercises. I do not think your time will have been wasted.

REFERENCE SECTION

Standard I/O Objects

Narrow-character support

Fully elaborated name	Purpose
`std::cin`	Provides a source of data. It is connected to the keyboard by default.
`std::cout`	Provides a sink for normal data produced by the program. By default it is connected, buffered, to the monitor.
`std::cerr`	Provides a sink for error reporting by the program. By default it is connected, unbuffered, to the monitor.
`std::clog`	Provides a sink for logging messages produced by the program. By default it is connected, buffered, to the monitor.

Wide-character support

Fully elaborated name	Purpose
std::wcin	Provides a source of data. It is connected to the keyboard by default.
std::wcout	Provides a sink for normal data produced by the program. By default it is connected, buffered, to the monitor.
std::wcerr	Provides a sink for error reporting by the program. By default it is connected, unbuffered, to the monitor.
std::wclog	Provides a sink for logging messages produced by the program. By default it is connected, buffered, to the monitor.

Note that these are not available in the default installation of MDS.

Namespace Support

Namespaces in C++ provide a mechanism for partitioning global declarations and definitions into distinct, named scopes (declarative regions). The principle objective is to avoid name clashes between source code (particularly for libraries) provided by different programmers, teams, or companies. We can further partition namespaces with nested namespaces.

Elaborated names are ones that identify the full context of their declarations by including the relevant namespace names. The context of a declaration includes both namespaces (maybe nested) and, possibly, the name of a user-defined type. For example, std::cin is a fully elaborated name that refers to an input object that is declared as part of the C++ Standard Library. fgw::playpen::setplotmode( ) is the fully elaborated name for the setplotmode( ) function that is part of the playpen type that is defined in namespace fgw.

A name is declared in a namespace by placing its declaration in a block that is prefixed with namespace *name*. For example,

```
namespace fgw{
  int counter(0);
}
```

creates an int variable whose fully elaborated name is fgw::counter and initializes it to zero.

C++ allows us to import declarations of names from a namespace with a using declaration. So

```
using std::cout;
```

allows us to use the unelaborated name cout from there onwards within the scope where the using declaration occurs, as if the name had been declared at the point of the using declaration.

C++ allows the programmer to instruct the compiler to look for names in another namespace. The mechanism is the using directive and takes the form:

```
using namespace fgw;
```

This tells the compiler that in the current scope it must also look in any visible namespace fgw blocks for any names used by the programmer in the subsequent source code.

Finally, C++ provides a mechanism for aliasing for a namespace:

```
namespace short = long_namespace_name;
```

Currently this last mechanism is not widely used.

The :: symbol is called the scope operator in C++ and separates the context part of a fully elaborated name from the simple name. We provide the fully elaborated version of a name that is declared outside any named namespace, function, or part of the definition of a user-defined type by prefixing the name with ::. That is, the fully elaborated name is the simple name preceded by the scope operator.

Scope

We introduce names into a program by declarations. A declaration always has a scope, which limits the region of source code in which that declaration of the name applies. C++ provides the following categories of scope:

global scope: the scope of names that are declared outside any block or other scope and have not been restricted to file scope. Global scope is little used in modern C++, though some companies, such as Microsoft, still make extensive use of global scope in their libraries.

file scope: the scope of declarations that have been restricted to the current file by the use of the keyword **static**. This is less used today, because an alternative mechanism using an unnamed namespace (which will be described later in this book) is usually preferred.

function scope: largely of academic interest, because the only kind of name that can have function scope is a label used as a destination of a **goto** statement.

prototype scope: the scope used for names of parameters that are provided in a declaration of a function that is not also a definition of the function. The only practical significance of this scope is that such names have no significance anywhere else.

block scope: any region enclosed in a pair of braces that is part of the definition of a function.

namespace scope: the regions enclosed in braces whose opening brace is prefixed with the **namespace** keyword, usually followed with a name for the namespace.

class scope: the region from the opening to the closing brace of a class definition together with the scopes of any definitions of names declared in the definition of a class.

Note that at this stage you probably do not know enough about C++ to appreciate the above list fully. I have provided the list for your future reference. The most important aspect of scope is the concept that names have limited regions in which they have any meaning.

Characters and Strings

I have already mentioned that C++ provides types for characters. The **char** type is designed to handle the native narrow character type for the platform that your program is being compiled for. It is usually an 8-bit type but does not have to be. The C++ Standard only requires that it be at least 8 bits wide.

C++ provides the **wchar_t** type for use with wide character sets. The commonest widths for **wchar_t** are 16 bits and 32 bits, though the only requirement is that **wchar_t** must be able to represent all the values of the **char** type on the same platform.

The character types are treated as integer types in C++. The C++ Standard requires implementations to specify whether the character types will be treated as **signed** or **unsigned** types when used in a numerical context. It is usually better to avoid any need for such knowledge by never using a character type in a numerical context.

Strings are sequences of characters. In C++, the library provides a general abstraction for the concept of a string; that abstraction is a template called **basic_string**. We will see more detail of what that means later on.

In particular, the C++ Standard Library also provides two specializations of the string abstraction, called `std::string` and `std::wstring`. The former is a string of `char` and the latter is a string of `wchar_t`. The string abstraction in C++ has numerous features including the ability to customize behavior for specific national character sets. Most of the features are beyond the scope of this book. However, we will be using the following (which we will apply to `std::string` but which are available for all specializations of the `basic_string` abstraction).

Two string objects can be compared for order, e.g. `str1 < str2` evaluates as `true` if the character sequence stored in `str1` would come before that in `str2` in a dictionary ordering.

A string object is expandable, i.e. we can append characters to it. If there is insufficient free space adjacent to the memory being used to store the previous values, the string object will acquire sufficient contiguous memory, copy the old values into it, add the extra values, and release the memory used for the previous representation. String types include the ability to reserve contiguous memory for later use. That reduces the amount of copying when we repeatedly append extra characters.

A string object knows its current size, i.e. how many characters currently make up the sequence.

We can sort a string object, i.e. we can reorder the characters in it according to a rule optionally provided by the programmer. The default for ordering is the numerical order of the codes representing the characters.

We can copy a string object. That is important because copying values is a requirement for the use of C++ types in some contexts. For example, when we use a `std::vector<std::string>` to provide a sequence of `std::string` we are implicitly relying on the guarantee that we can copy `std::string` objects.

We can read and write `std::string` values to and from streams that use `char` data. Likewise we can read and write `std::wstring` values directly to and from streams that use `wchar_t` data.

CHAPTER 5

Writing Functions in C++

So far, we have been using functions from the C++ Standard Library or from my library. The time has come for us to look at writing functions for ourselves. In this chapter, I will deal with writing what C++ calls free functions. In a later chapter, I will tackle member functions. Some other programming languages call the latter methods or messages.

We distinguish member functions from free functions by the syntax we use to call them. A call of a member function starts with the name of an object followed by a dot (.) operator. Alternatively, it starts with the address of an object followed by an arrow (->) operator. We have already used the first of these syntactic forms in numerous places, such as when we used **std::cin.get( )**.

Those coming from a functional-programming background (having used such languages as Haskell) will need to be careful because the function concept in C++ is somewhat wider than that used by functional languages. If you are used to a language such as Pascal that distinguishes between procedures and functions, you will need to note that C++ combines the concept of a procedure and a function into a single concept, which C++ calls a function.

Those coming from strict object-oriented languages may find the concept of a free (i.e. non-member) function strange to start with because they will be used to functions tied to specific types or objects.

Those coming from some backgrounds may find the syntax we use to call functions strange, but the more common problem will be for those who see a familiar syntax and do not notice the slight differences in semantics (behavior) between C++ and the languages with which they are familiar.

Let me first try to tie down the C++ function concept.

The C++ Function Concept

The fundamental idea of a function in C++ is that of a set of actions bundled together and given a name. Sometimes the actions do not require the supply of any data. However, data is usually required. We call the supplied data the *arguments* of a function. *Parameters* are the variables declared to hold the arguments while a function does its work. For example, we used the following statement in one of our earlier programs:

```
std::sort(numbers.begin( ), numbers.end( ));
```

There we were calling the **std::sort** function and passing it two arguments, which told the function what it must sort; **numbers.begin( )** and **numbers.end( )** provide the arguments that **std::sort** needs. We have no need to know how `std::sort()` does its task nor do we need to know what the parameters that will hold the arguments are called. Only the provider of the `std::sort()` function needs those details.

This separation of concerns is a fundamental principle of modern programming languages and their use for writing programs. We try to limit knowledge on a need-to-know basis. Learning how something is done can be very educational, but it can often get in the way of our doing something that is useful. In addition, we should note that a later version of a function might achieve its ends differently. The function declaration is part of a contract between the implementer of the function (the programmer who writes the definition) and the user of the function. It tells us what kind of data will be needed and it tells us what kind of thing will be returned. (In C, the return is always a value or `void`, but in C++ we can also return references.)

Part of the value of functions in C++ is that they allow us to focus our attention on one thing at a time. Indeed, a good function conceptually does exactly one thing, and a good function name completely describes whatever it is that the function does. `std::sort()` is an example of a good name. The first part tells us that it belongs to the C++ Standard Library; the second part tells us that it sorts the data it is given. There are some other similar functions in the C++ Standard Library, such as `std::partial_sort()` and `std::stable_sort()`. The first of those is useful, for example, when you just want the top values in the correct order. In our number-sorting program, if we only wanted the three smallest items to be first, second, and third in the sequence, we could replace the sort instruction with:

```
std::partial_sort(numbers.begin(), numbers.begin() + 3, numbers.end());
```

WARNING!

The choice of required arguments for that function seems somewhat counterintuitive. Intuitively, we might have expected the second argument to be 3 rather than being the value of the first argument incremented by 3. It is an example of how a designer's view can affect the interface of a function. Unfortunately the C++ Standard Library has quite a few cases of unintuitive names and unintuitive data requirements. Only experience and good references can reduce mediocre design choices. We should learn from them that good names and choice of data requirements are important design issues that are sometimes hard to achieve in practice.

TRY THIS

Go back to your source code for getting numbers from the keyboard and then sorting and displaying the result on the screen. Modify the code to display only the three smallest numbers on the screen. You will have to handle the special case of the user supplying fewer than three numbers. I leave it to you to choose how.

Sorting in Other Orders

Unless you are unusual, you will be wondering how you could have got the three largest values instead of the three smallest. The default action for sorting is always smallest-first (defined by implicitly applying the `<` operator). However, we can provide an extra argument that supplies a different rule (often called a 'policy argument', because it supplies the policy to be used in executing a function).

The C++ Standard Library packages up some common policies so that we can use them without writing them for ourselves. The one that is useful for our current needs is `std::greater<type>()`. This will provide whatever rule the specified type uses to select the greater of two values of the specified type.

In general, policy arguments are the final arguments in a function call (we will see why a little later in this chapter). So

```
std::partial_sort(numbers.begin( ), numbers.begin( )+3, numbers.end( ),
    std::greater<int>( ));
```

will place the three highest values in the first three places.

If it seems to you that supplying a policy argument for a Library function would make sense, the chances are very high that the C++ Standard Library functions will allow you to do so. You can sort an entire sequence of ints in descending order by adding std::greater<int>( ) as a third argument when you call std::sort( ). For example, using our existing declarations,

```
std::sort(numbers.begin( ), numbers.end( ), std::greater<int>( ));
```

will sort our sequence of numbers in descending order.

TRY THIS

Modify your previous program so that it collects a list of words from std::cin, sorts them in reverse alphabetical order, and then displays the results as a comma-separated list on the screen.

Designing a Function

Before attempting to design a function, you need a clear idea of what it is that you are trying to do. The basic guideline is that a function should do one thing and do it well. Let me walk you through the process of designing and implementing a function for getting an int value from an input source and returning the value to the caller.

The Interface or Function Declaration

Our function needs a name. get_int seems to be a reasonable name, so let us use that for the time being. We know it will return an int, because that is what it is supposed to do. We also know that we will need to provide an input source as an argument.

In C++, input sources have a general type of std::istream. We call data sources and sinks 'streams' in C++. Those that provide input are objects of type std::istream, and those that provide output are of type std::ostream. C++ also provides types for objects that can both supply input and accept output.

The rules for a function declaration in C++ are that:

- it starts by nominating the type of the returned data (what you get back when you call, i.e. use, the function in your program);
- the name of the function follows;
- the declaration ends with a comma-separated list of parameter types in parentheses.

Optionally the parameters in declarations can include a name as well as a type. However, in the context of a function declaration the parameter names have no significance to the compiler. Any names provided are to help human readers understand what data is required. A good name for a parameter is much better than a comment providing the same information.

When I put these three elements together, I arrive at the following declaration for a function designed to get an int value from a data source:

```
int get_int(std::istream & data_source);
```

*Language Note: You may be puzzled by that use of **&**, particularly if you are already familiar with C. In C++ the ampersand is used for three distinct purposes (we say that it is overloaded); they can always be distinguished by the context. The ampersand is a logical and operator when placed between two values; it is an address-of operator when used before a variable (so **&data** would mean 'use the address of the object that **data** refers to'); and in the context of a declaration it converts the preceding type into a reference type. The special quality of C++ reference types is that the objects they refer to must already exist. In the context of a parameter, this means that the function will use an object supplied by an argument provided by the function call. All other (non-reference) parameters are value parameters. That means that the function will use a copy of the supplied argument.*

It is not normally possible to copy a stream object. Having more than one object connected to a specific data source or data sink would normally be a recipe for chaos. We deal with that problem by passing stream objects around by reference. In this case, the parameter will be a reference to some already existing `std::istream` object. Remember that references do not use new objects; they just provide new names to access already existing objects. When we call `get_int( )`, we will need to provide a suitable `std::istream` object that `get_int( )` can use as a source of data.

The final semicolon limits the above source-code statement to being just a declaration and nothing more. One of the interesting features of function declarations in C++ is that they provide the compiler with enough information for using the function in source code even though they do not provide enough information for the final program. For example, the following code should compile:

```
1 // written by FGW 25/08/04
2 #include <istream>
3 #include <iostream>
4
5 int get_int(std::istream & data_source);
6
7 int main( ){
8    try {
9      int i(0);
10     i = get_int(std::cin);
11     std::cout << "The input was " << i << ".\n";
12   }
13   catch(...){
14     std::cerr << "***An exception was thrown.***\n";
15   }
16 }
```

When you create a project and try this code, you will find that it compiles. If you try to link it or execute the program, the linker will complain that it cannot find a definition of `get_int( )`. C++ allows us to separate declarations from definitions. It is normal to take advantage of this so that we can change the definition if we want to without having to recompile an entire program. We might need to change a definition because we discovered an error in the existing definition. Even if there were no error, we might want to change the definition because we have discovered a way to improve on our earlier efforts.

It would be a mistake to consider that the separation of definition and declaration is unimportant. For example, Java programmers may feel that this C++ mechanism serves little purpose because Java does not make a clear distinction (though Java interfaces are sometimes used as a substitute). Industrial-quality programs can be very large and take many hours to compile from scratch. The C++ (and C) mechanism of separation of declaration and definition allows us to limit recompilation to just those files that have changed. We leave it to the linker to put all the parts together. As a result, missing parts might not be noticed until link time.

In this case, the missing part is the code that specifies how `get_int( )` carries out its task. We used the function at line 10, and the compiler was able to code a call to a function using `std::cin` as the argument for the `std::istream` parameter. The compiler then inserts a request to the linker to find the definition and adjust the code to use it. The linker sees the request and looks among the provided object code (compiled files and libraries). It issues a suitable error message when it does not find a definition for the requested function.

The separation of compiling and linking is one of the ways that compiled programs differ from interpreted ones. Generally, an interpreted language – such as many versions of BASIC – only recognizes that something is missing when the program is running. This may be satisfactory in some cases but it would be a disaster in others. A program controlling a nuclear power station must know before the event that the definition of the function providing an emergency close-down exists.

What happens at each stage of the process differs from implementation to implementation. The latest tools from Microsoft tend to delay much more of the work until link time because that makes it easier to mix pieces of code written in different languages. There is no clear-cut distinction between interpreting and compiling. For example, it is usually possible to interpret C++ source code. By that, I mean, feed your source code in and get immediate action. However, it is not normal to do so, because we did not design C++ to work efficiently as an interpreted language. It is possible to compile languages, such as Python and Perl, that are designed to run through an interpreter. However, doing that may be hard work and not particularly efficient, because those languages are not designed to be compiled.

Here is a simple definition of `get_int( )`:

```cpp
int get_int(std::istream & in){
   int value(0);
   in >> value;
   if(not in) throw std::exception( );
   return value;
}
```

There are two ways out of this function. The first is when the code detects that something went wrong during input. Our current strategy for this is to throw a `std::exception` object. Later we will provide refinements that allow us to handle this problem rather more effectively. The second way out is to return the value from the function. The `return` statement coupled with the return type provided by the declaration and repeated in the definition makes this work.

Note that there are two differences between the declaration and definition of `get_int( )`. First, the definition concludes with a block of statements (called the body of the function), while the pure declaration ends with a semicolon. The second difference is that I changed the name of the parameter. Parameter names in declarations have no purpose other than to document the parameter for programmers using the function. Parameter names in definitions provide a name for the variable used in the definition code. The parameters are initialized with the arguments provided at the point of call. In this case the variable `in` will become a local name for the existing `std::istream` object provided by the caller.

In effect, the declaration of a function provides a name, and specifies what type of data is needed and what type of data will be given back. The compiler uses the declaration by finding the name and checking that the arguments provided by the caller can meet the specified requirements. It then assumes that the result of calling the function will be an object (for a reference return type) or a value of the type specified. Because the compiler knows both the kind of data being provided (the arguments) and the kind of data required (the parameter types), it can often convert the argument type to the parameter type even if they are not the same initially. For example, if the parameter is an `int` but the argument is a `double`, the compiler will insert the code necessary to convert a `double` to an `int`. Note that this kind of matching up may not be possible where the parameters are references, because we cannot normally just convert an object from one type to another even though we can convert values. A region of memory formatted for storing a `double` will probably make no sense as an `int`. We can easily change a `double` value to an `int` value by ignoring the fractional part but that does not generally work for objects (places where values can be stored).

Sometimes the compiler will have to insert code to convert a return value to the type required by the caller of a function. So, for example,

```
double d;
d = get_int(std::cin);
```

will compile, and the compiler will insert code to convert the **int** value returned by **get_int( )** into a **double** value needed for storing in **d**.

The simplest way to provide a function definition is to add it at the end of the file that uses it. That has a serious disadvantage because you would need to duplicate the code in every file that uses the function. There is a second disadvantage in that one of the linker's jobs is to ensure that programmers do not provide two definitions for the same thing. We are not quite ready to tackle this issue, so for the time being either add the definition of **get_int( )** to the end of the file with **main( )** in it or replace the declaration with the definition (single declarations can usually be replaced by the definition because a definition is always a declaration). So either of these should compile, link, and execute:

Program 1

```
 1 // written by FGW 25/08/04 declaration early definition delayed
 2 #include <istream>
 3 #include <iostream>
 4
 5 int get_int(std::istream & data_source);
 6
 7 int main( ){
 8   try {
 9     int i(0);
10     i = get_int(std::cin);
11     std::cout << "The input was " << i << ".\n";
12   }
13   catch(...){
14     std::cerr << "***An exception was thrown.***\n";
15   }
16 }
17
18 int get_int(std::istream & in){
19   int value(0);
20   in >> value;
21   if(not in) throw std::exception( );
22   return value;
23 }
```

Program 2

```
 1 // written by FGW 25/08/04 declaration is definition
 2 #include <istream>
 3 #include <iostream>
 4
5A int get_int(std::istream & in){
5B   int value(0);
5C   in >> value;
5D   if(not in) throw std::exception( );
```

```
5E   return value;
5F }
 6
 7 int main( ){
 8   try {
 9     int i(0);
10     i = get_int(std::cin);
11     std::cout << "The input was " << i << ".\n";
12   }
13   catch(...){
14     std::cerr << "***An exception was thrown.***\n";
15   }
16 }
```

There is not much difference between them, but I prefer Program 1 because it will be easier to convert it to the more conventional form, where we place declarations and definitions into different files.

TRY THIS

Write a get_double( ) function that gets a value of type **double** from an **istream** object and returns the value to the caller. Write a program to test your function. Make sure that you use the resulting executable to test that the program stops with an error message if you input something that is not a **double**. Note that it is not an error to type in an integer value when a **double** is expected: the program will silently add the missing decimal indicator (decimal point in many countries, decimal comma elsewhere) as soon as it hits input that is not a digit.

EXERCISES

1. Implement (i.e. provide a definition of) and test a function whose declaration is:

   ```
   int squared(int);
   ```

   The function should return the square of an integer provided as an argument.

2. Write and test a function that returns the square root of the largest square less than the integer value provided as an argument. Note that you must handle the possibility that the argument is out of range; negative numbers are not suitable input for this function. Handle this case by throwing an exception.

3. Write a function that takes an unsigned integer as an argument and returns half the input value if the value is even. If the input value is odd, it must return three times the input value plus one. Now test your function with a program that prompts the user for a positive number and then repeatedly calls your function to determine the next value. It must output each value until the latest value is 1. For example, given 5 as input the output should be 16, 8, 4, 2, 1. Given 7 as input the output should be 22, 11, 34, 17, 52, 26, 13, 40, 20, 10, 5, 16, 8, 4, 2, 1.

4. Write a function that has four integer parameters in addition to an **fgw::playpen &** parameter. The first two provide the x- and y-coordinates for a Playpen pixel, the third parameter is for the scale to be used, and the fourth one is to provide the plotting color.

5. The function for Exercise 4 can be described as plotting a point of a required size and color at the given coordinates. From that perspective it does a single thing. However, we need the answers to the questions "where?", "how big?", and "what color?" – from which perspective we have three things. Write functions that prompt the user for a color and for a scale (one function for each). The function to get the color should restrict valid responses to the range 0–255; out of range responses should cause the user to be asked to supply another value. Invalid responses should result in an exception being thrown. The function for scale should behave similarly but the valid range of scales is 1–64.

6. Write a function to plot a point at the coordinates given by the arguments passed in to the function, but which calls the functions from Exercise 5 to determine the color and size of the square to be plotted. Note that, as for all free functions that use the Playpen window, you will need to provide a parameter that is a reference to an `fgw::playpen` so that the caller can tell the function which `fgw::playpen` object is being used.

7. Write a function that plots a horizontal line of pixels given the starting point, the number of pixels, and the color as arguments.

8. Write a function that draws a set of parallel horizontal lines given a starting point, a length (number of pixels), a color, the gap between the parallel lines, and the number of lines.

9. By first writing a similar function to that in Exercise 8 but for vertical lines, write a function that will draw a square grid of a given mesh, color, and number of squares per row/column. Write a program that tests this grid function.

C++ Procedures

C++ does not have a separate concept of a procedure – something that acts but has no resulting value. This is not a major problem – we could solve it the way that the earliest versions of C did: simply ignore the returned value from a function whose intended purpose was to package an action.

C fixed this problem by creating a special **void** type that has no values and very little behavior. If we declare the return type of a function as **void**, we are, in effect, saying that the function is a procedure. In other words, it will do something but it will not return any usable value.

For example,

```
void print(std::ostream &, int i);
```

declares **print()** to be a function that does something with an output object and an **int** value. The name suggests that what it will do is print the value of **i** on the output object. However, whatever it does, it does not return a value. In a computer-science sense, it is a procedure.

Pure Functions

Many languages have the concept of a pure function – a function that has no side effects. A pure function takes some values, computes a result, and returns the result as a value. Pure functions deal only with values and do not touch objects. Those familiar with functional programming languages will understand this concept, will know how useful it is, and will be surprised that C++ does not provide a mechanism by which the programmer can tell the compiler that something is a pure function.

It is possible that this may change in the future; for now, you can certainly write pure functions, but the compiler is unlikely to take full advantage of your doing so.

Overloading Functions

C++ allows functions to share names if other details allow the compiler to select the intended function when the programmer uses it. There are two major ways that functions can share their names. First, we can declare functions with the same name in different scopes. For example, we might reuse a name in different namespaces:

```
namespace fgw1{
   int foo( );
}
namespace fgw2{
   int foo( );
}
```

The two declarations of `foo( )` can co-exist because the fully elaborated names are different: `fgw1::foo( )` and `fgw2::foo( )`. Everything will be fine unless you add `using` declarations or `using` directives that allow use of the simple name `foo` without explicitly stating the namespace.

While this is a good motive for using namespaces – we do not have to check the use of names by other programmers – it is uninteresting otherwise. Reused names become interesting when we reuse them in the same scope. The C++ term 'function overloading' refers to this kind of reuse of a name.

The rule for function overloading (in a single scope) is simple: the lists of parameter types must be different. The difference may be that the overloaded functions have different numbers of parameters; or if they have the same number of parameters, at least one of them must be a distinguishable type. Here is a possible set of declarations of an overloaded function:

```
int foo( );
int foo(int);
int foo(int, int);
double foo(double);
```

The compiler will have no immediate difficulty with those four declarations of functions named `foo`. However, if we tried to add

```
int foo(double);
```

it would complain. The only difference between that declaration and the fourth one above is that it has a different return type. A difference in return type is not a sufficient distinction to allow reuse of a function name in C++. There must be a significant difference in the parameter type lists.

Generally, if at least one parameter type is different then the compiler will be happy at the point of declaration, though there may be problems later on. However, adding

```
int foo(int &);
```

to the above overload set will result in a complaint from the compiler because there is no way to distinguish a pass by value from a pass by reference for the same underlying type. If the programmer wrote:

```
int main( ){
   int i(0);
   foo(i);
   return 0;
}
```

the compiler would not know if the programmer intended the version of `foo` that copies the value stored in `i` or the one that uses the `i` object. The language specifies that an overloaded set of functions must not include two declarations that are only different in whether a parameter uses a value or a reference.

Example of Function Overloading

There are a couple of variants on the concept of **get_int( )**. We might want to provide a specific version that always uses **std::cin** as the source of data. A second thing would be to provide a version that dealt with prompting the user for data. For example, given such a function I might rewrite my numbers program as:

```
1 // created on 27/08/04 by FWG
2 #include <algorithm>
3 #include <exception>
4 #include <iostream>
5 #include <vector>
6
7 int main( ){
8   try{
9     std::vector<int> numbers;
10    do{
11      int const next(get_int("Next whole number (-999 to stop): "));
12      if(next == -999) break;
13      numbers.push_back(next);
14    } while(true);
```

(*etc.*)

Given a suitable version of **get_int( )**, line 11 will prompt the user with the supplied text, and use the returned value to initialize the immutable **int** object designated by **next**. What would be a suitable declaration?

```
int get_int(std::string const & prompt);
```

looks about right. Here is a simple definition that we could use:

```
int get_int(std::string prompt){
  std::cout << prompt;
  return get_int(std::cin);
}
```

Notice that this new version of **get_int( )** delegates the actual work to our earlier version. This is another of the fundamental principles of modern programming: reuse what you already have. If you come from a language that uses recursion, note that the above definition is not recursive; the call of **get_int(std::cin)** is to a different function that shares a name.

One of the advantages of delegation is that we only have a single place where we need to make changes if we decide that there are improvements we can make in the basic mechanism.

Let us add another version of **get_int( )**, one that has no parameters because it is implicitly going to use **std::cin** as the data source.

```
int get_int( );
```

Defining that overload is effectively trivial:

```
int get_int( ){
  return get_int(std::cin);
}
```

Note that it delegates everything to our earlier **get_int(std::istream)** version.

The *inline* Keyword

Efficiency-conscious programmers object to such delegation because they are afraid the compiler might add the overhead for a call. There is no need to worry because C++ provides a solution. You declare the function `inline` and provide the definition as part of the declaration:

```
inline int get_int(){return get_int(std::cin);}
```

The `inline` keyword has two effects. The more important one is that it allows the function definition to exist more than once in the program. We can declare a function many times in a program, but normally we may only define it once per program; the `inline` keyword allows multiple definitions. The second effect of using `inline` is to request (note: request, not instruct) the compiler to avoid a function call by replacing the call by the body of the function.

Modern compilers can often do a much better job of optimizing code than programmers can, so do not use `inline` qualification of functions unless you are very certain of what you are doing. In many cases excessive use of `inline` results in a program that is both larger and slower than would have resulted if the programmer had never used `inline`.

Pass by Value or by Reference

Look back at the version of `get_int()` that has a `std::string` parameter. Notice that this is a value parameter (there is no & after the `std::string`). Passing around values that have a complex structure can be expensive in resources. It is worth considering whether we could use an original object instead. We could just as easily have written:

```
int get_int(std::string & prompt);
```

so that `get_int()` will use an existing `std::string` object. Unfortunately, that will not work unless there is an actual existing string object. It may seem odd, but a string literal (text in double quotes) is not a `std::string` object in C++. The compiler is quite capable of creating a temporary unnamed `std::string` from a string literal. It can then use that temporary as the object used by a reference. However, we come up against a C++ safety rule: C++ forbids the use of a temporary via an unqualified reference; we must promise not to change the temporary object by using a reference to `const`. Extracting values from a temporary object is fine; trying to modify one is not. For this reason, we have to use:

```
int get_int(std::string const & prompt);
```

That extra `const` qualification assures the compiler that the definition of the function will only use `prompt` but not try to modify the object it references. The compiler will be happy to allow you to use `get_int(std::string const&)` with a string-literal argument. It will create a temporary `std::string` object from the literal and use that for the reference-to-`const` parameter.

Note that a reference to `const` is colloquially called a `const` reference by many C++ programmers though this is not strictly accurate. As C++ does not have any `const` reference types, there is no danger of confusion.

 TRY THIS

Write a program that uses all the varieties of `get_int()`. Provide suitable definitions and test that the program works as expected. Now test the three alternative versions of `get_int()` that provide a prompt. Check that both the pass-by-value version and the pass-by-reference-to-`const` version compile and work as expected. Also, note that the pass-by-reference **without** the `const` qualification does not compile if called using a string literal, but works if the argument provided by the call is a `std::string`. In other words,

```
int const number(get_int("Next number"));
```

fails to compile if we declare the overload as

```
int get_int(std::string &);
```

but

```
std::string prompt("Next number");
int const number(get_int(prompt));
```

works fine. However, it is verbose and many programmers do not like excessive use of mutable strings (ones that have not been declared to be **const**).

Resetting istream and ostream Objects

C++ stream types include a number of internal flags that allow them to keep track of various events that may happen during their use. The most important state we need to track is when an I/O operation fails. There is no point in continuing if we did not get the data we requested, and we need to address an output failure before the program loses data. It is important to note that I/O objects keep track of what has happened to them but, in general, they do not attempt to predict what will happen in their future. For example, an object using a file as a source of data will only set itself into an end-of-file state when it has actually read an end-of-file marker.

When a C++ I/O object fails, it puts itself in a dormant state. **std::istream** objects ignore all further attempts at extracting data until the program deals with the problem. **std::ostream** objects do nothing with any subsequent data sent to them until the program deals with an output failure.

By design, an I/O object that has failed does nothing more until the program deals with the failure. In effect, the program skips all attempts to use a stream object that is in a failed state.

TRY THIS

Type in, compile, and execute the following short program. After you have checked that it runs as expected when you correctly respond to the prompt with integer values, try responding with a floating-point value. You should see the effect of the bad input. Make sure you understand what happens.

```
#include <iostream>

using std::cin;
using std::cout;

int main(){
  try{
    for(int i(0); i != 10; ++i){
      int j(0);
      cout << "next integer value";
      cin >> j;
      cout << i << "  " << j << '\n';
    }
```

```
    }
    catch(...){std::cerr << "Caught an exception" << '\n'; }
    return 0;
}
```

Now we understand what happens and why it happens, it is time to see how we can fix it. C++ stream objects have a member function **clear( )**, which resets the object to a working state (member functions use the dot syntax to call the function for the object in question). That is all **clear( )** does. It deliberately does not do anything with the data that is waiting for processing. In other words, it does not attempt to cure the cause of the problem but simply restores the object to a working condition. However, the program still has to identify and deal with the cause of the failure.

In this case, we will know that the cause of the failure is inappropriate data blocking the input. We need to remove it. There are several ways to do this, but here is a simple function that will do for now:

```
void clear_cin( ){
  std::cin.clear( );
  std::string garbage;
  std::getline(std::cin, garbage);
}
```

This procedure (it has a **void** return type) clears out the current input line from **std::cin**.

TRY THIS

Add the definition of **clear_cin( )** to your source code for the previous task (place it before **main( )** so that the definition will double up as a declaration). Add **clear_cin( );** between the prompt and the **cin >> j;** statement. Now test the code and check that it handles incorrect input satisfactorily.

EXERCISES

In the following exercises, you are expected to write complete test programs even when you have not been explicitly asked to do so.

10. Adapt the program above so that it only calls **clear_cin( )** if **std::cin** has failed.

11. Rewrite the definition of **get_int( )** so that it allows three attempts at correct input before it gives up and throws an exception.

12. In the case of a general **std::istream** object a prompt is normally inappropriate, as is ruthlessly dumping all the rest of a line of input. Write a **reset_istream(std::istream & data_source)** function that resets the stream object and discards only the next character. Why is this function of only marginal utility?

13. Write a definition for:

    ```
    int get_int(std::istream data_source, int number_of_retries);
    ```

14. Write an overloaded set of functions to get a double from a `std::istream` object, from `std::cin` both with and without a prompt, and in each case with and without a specified number of retries. How are these different from the set of overloaded functions for getting an `int` value?

Default Arguments

Consider the following function declaration:

```
void plot_square(fgw::playpen &, int x, int y, int size, fgw::hue);
```

This function always requires that the caller explicitly provide a color as an argument for the last parameter. In some circumstances, you might find it reasonable to allow the color to default to black. We can do that with a forwarding function that overloads the above declaration:

```
inline void plot_square(fgw::playpen & paper, int x, int y, int size){
  return plot_square(paper, x, y, size, fgw::black);
}
```

> Language Note: C does not allow programmers to return a *void*. C++ specifically allows a return of a *void* so that programmers can use a single consistent idiom for forwarding functions such as the above. Without that provision, we would have to omit the *return* and just write a call to the function to which we are delegating the work. This might not seem to be a great burden, but when we cover writing generic functions in a later chapter, we will see that distinguishing a *void* return type from all other types is an irritant or worse.

Notice that the forwarding function is provided as a definition. This is the normal way to do that but it has two costs. First, we probably want to make that definition available to the compiler wherever we call the function, so that it can replace the call with a call to the function to which we are delegating the work. To allow such potential multiple definitions we need to qualify the function as `inline`. The fact that that also advises the compiler to replace the actual call with a call to the delegated function is not important – good compilers will do that anyway. What is important is that `inline` overrides redefinition issues.

The second point is that I have to name all the parameters. In the earlier pure declaration, I could skip naming the first parameter because there is no documentary advantage (well I do not think there is). I do not have the same freedom when it comes to a declaration that is also a definition.

One disadvantage of using a forwarding function is that it may not be immediately clear what is being provided and why. At the very least, the definition should be preceded by a suitable comment that explains the what and the why. However, C++ provides another option if the default (special-case) value is the argument for the final parameter. The method is to provide a default argument. Using a default argument we could rewrite the original declaration of `plot_square()` as:

```
void plot_square(fgw::playpen &, int x, int y, int size,
    fgw::hue = fgw::black);
```

When we do that, we tell the compiler that if the function is called without an explicitly provided final argument, it is to use the one provided in the declaration. Default arguments must be provided in declarations:

the compiler needs to know what the defaults are so that it can add them to a call when the programmer omits one or more of them.

We are not limited to using a default for the final argument. However, we cannot use defaults for earlier arguments unless we also use defaults for all the subsequent ones. Once we start relying on a default argument for a function call we must use the defaults for all the remaining arguments. For example, we could declare `plot_square( )` as:

```
void plot_square(fgw::playpen & = paper, int x = 0, int y = 0,
    int size = 1, fgw::hue = fgw::black);
```

(Note that default arguments are always provided by the syntax = *default*, which comes after the parameter name if one is provided.)

If I provided this declaration and then wrote the statement

```
plot_square( );
```

in my source code the compiler would behave as if I had actually written:

```
plot_square(paper, 0, 0, 1, fgw::black);
```

In this case providing defaults for all the arguments is unlikely to be useful. As C++ does not allow me to write

```
plot_square(, 10, 10, , fgw::black);
```

as shorthand for:

```
plot_square(paper, 10, 10, 1, fgw::black);
```

there is little value in this case to having defaults for all the parameters.

The problem with using default arguments is that once we start using defaults we are stuck with them for all the remaining parameters. For example, suppose that I want the size of the square to default to the currently used scale. I could do that by making `size` default to `0`, because the way the scale feature of Playpen is designed is to ignore out-of-range scales. However, which is more likely? That I want to use black? Or that I want to use the current scale? The way I have designed the `plot_square( )` function, I can only make the color default to black, or make the size default to the current scale **and** the color to black. I cannot specify the color but use the default value for the size.

This is a limitation to default arguments, which makes them less powerful than forwarding functions. For example, I can write

```
inline void plot_square(fgw::playpen & paper, int x, int y, fgw::hue
shade = fgw::black){
   return plot_square(paper, x, y, 0, shade);
}
```

to provide a version of `plot_square` that uses the current scale as the size of the plotted square.

Example of an Overloaded Set of Functions

Here I bring together the ideas we have explored in the preceding section so that we can focus on their use and possible consequences. Consider these three function declarations:

```
void plot_square(fgw::playpen &, int x, int y, int size,
    fgw::hue = fgw::black);

inline void plot_square(fgw::playpen & paper, int x, int y,
    fgw::hue shade = fgw::black){
  return plot_square(paper, x, y, 0, shade);
}

inline void plot_square(fgw::playpen & paper, int size,
    fgw::hue shade = fgw::black){
  return plot_square(paper, 0, 0, size, shade);
}
```

The first thing we must do is check that all the combinations of using default arguments and overloaded alternatives result in distinguishable calls. In other words, the compiler must be able to tell from the call which of the overloaded functions to use and which default arguments will complete the chosen call. I find that the most useful way to do this check is to list all the variations of the type lists. Here they are for the above set of overloaded functions:

- Using the first declaration with all five arguments:

  ```
  void plot_square(fgw::playpen &, int, int, int, fgw::hue);
  ```

- Using the first declaration with the default fgw::hue:

  ```
  void plot_square(fgw::playpen &, int, int, int);
  ```

- Using the second declaration with all four arguments:

  ```
  void plot_square(fgw::playpen &, int, int, fgw::hue);
  ```

- Using the second declaration with the default fgw::hue:

  ```
  void plot_square(fgw::playpen &, int, int);
  ```

- Using the third declaration with all three arguments:

  ```
  void plot_square(fgw::playpen &, int, fgw::hue);
  ```

- Using the third declaration with the default fgw::hue:

  ```
  void plot_square(fgw::playpen &, int);
  ```

Check this list carefully. Every one of the possible sets of explicitly provided argument types is different. That means the compiler can distinguish the various choices as long as we provide exactly the right types of arguments.

We are not quite finished. What if we do not provide exactly the correct types? For example, suppose we write:

```
plot_square(paper, 1.12, 1.4, 13)
```

Now the compiler will go through a routine looking for a best match. Effectively it creates a list of candidates such as the one above. It discards any that have the wrong number of parameters. In this case, it is left with just two possibilities:

```
void plot_square(fgw::playpen &, int, int, int);   // default fgw::hue
void plot_square(fgw::playpen &, int, int, fgw::hue);   // first inline
```

Next, it takes each argument in turn and categorizes it as an exact match, or some level of mismatch all the way up to "no implicit conversion makes the argument match the parameter type". In this case, the first argument is an exact match for both candidates. The second and third arguments can be converted to **int** by the standard conversion of **double** to **int**. That applies for both the candidates. Finally, the last argument (**13**) is an exact match for an **int** but requires a conversion to make it a value for an **fgw::hue**. (That is one reason that I made the color codes a user-defined type in my Playpen library instead of lazily using an **int**. I wanted to be able to distinguish between colors and **int**s even though colors were coded with integer values.)

The first of the two candidates is as good as the second for three of the arguments and better for the fourth. That allows the compiler to make an unambiguous choice.

Do not worry too much about 'best match' problems when using overloaded functions, possibly combined with default arguments. The compiler will make a choice, tell you that there is no viable choice, or tell you that there is no single best choice. Later we will see how to resolve the last of these.

However, when overloading functions you should be careful to ensure that all the overloads conceptually do the same thing. Do not overload a **draw( )** function so that when the argument passed to it is a gun type the result will be a shooting whilst an argument of a pencil type results in a sketch.

Enough theory. Time for some more practical work. Here is a first (faulty) definition of the general **plot_square( )** function:

```
void plot_square(fgw::playpen & paper, int x, int y, int size,
    fgw::hue shade){
  paper.scale(size);
  paper.plot(x, y, shade);
}
```

Note that a definition does not generally include declarations of default arguments unless it is also doubling up as a function declaration.

Here is a small program to test that function definition:

```
int main( ){
  try{
    fgw::playpen paper;
    plot_square(paper, 5, 5, 16, fgw::red1);
    paper.display( );
    std::cin.get( );
  }
  catch(...){std::cerr << "An exception was thrown.\n";}
}
```

TRY THIS

Create a new project for a Playpen-based program. Create a source-code file. Add a suitable opening comment. Add the necessary headers. Type in the declaration of the general **plot_square( )** function followed by the inline definitions of the two specialized overloads. Now type in the test program followed by the definition of the general **plot_square( )** function. Compile and run the result.

TRY THIS

Go back to the previous task and modify the test program so that it tests all six possible ways of calling plot_square( ). Now try changing some of the arguments so that they do not exactly match the parameter types. Some changes may result in code that will not compile; some may result in the compiler issuing a warning (it can do what you asked, but it wants to tell you that what you provided was not exactly what it expected). Try to get a feel for what is happening.

Something Is Not Right

Perhaps you have noticed that calls to plot_square( ) have a side effect. Not only do they plot a square, but they also change the scale of subsequent uses of the fgw::playpen object. Fortunately, we can fix this problem, because the fgw::playpen type has a function that tells you what the current scale is. It is an overload of fgw::playpen's scale( ) function. It is also an exception to the guideline that overloads should conceptually do the same thing. If I write paper.scale( ) I will get an int value returned that represents the current scale of paper. In other words, if I do not provide a value for scale( ), the call tells me what the current value is, but if I do provide a value it changes the scale to the value provided.

I can use this to ensure that plot_square( ) does not change the scale of the fgw::playpen object it is using, or more correctly, that it restores the previous scale before it finishes. Here is the corrected version:

```
void plot_square(fgw::playpen & paper, int x, int y, int size,
    fgw::hue shade){
  int const old_scale(paper.scale());  // save prior scale
  paper.scale(size);
  paper.plot(x, y, shade);
  paper.scale(old_scale);  // restore to prior scale
}
```

I only have to make that change in a single place because the overloaded, specialized versions use the general version to do the real work. It is important to get into the habit of saving any state that you are going to change temporarily and restoring it at the end.

This example should also have emphasized the value of reusing code by calling a single function that does the real work from specialized overloads.

TRY THIS

Test your code from the previous task to check that it works with the corrected version of plot_square( ).

EXERCISES

Some of the following will require you to reuse earlier functions such as get_int( ). In other cases, you should consider writing auxiliary functions that might be used in future exercises. Many of these functions may be very

15. Write a program that repetitively prompts the user for the arguments for a call to `draw_square( )` and then uses them to draw a square in the Playpen window. The program should repeat the process until the user signifies that they want to stop. Part of this exercise is for you to decide how the user will signify the end of the program.

16. The `fgw::playpen` function `setplotmode( )` handles the problem of restoring a previous state differently from the way that the overloaded `scale( )` functions do. `setplotmode( )` returns a value of type `fgw::plotmode`, which represents the previous plotting mode. So, for example,

    `fgw::plotmode old(pad.setplotmode(fgw::disjoint));`

    simultaneously sets `pad`'s plotting mode to `fgw::disjoin` and saves the previous state in `old`. When you have finished you can restore the previous plotting mode with:

    `pad.setplotmode(old);`

    Write and test a definition for:

    `void plot_square(fgw::playpen & paper, fgw::plotmode pm, int x, int y,`
    `    int size, fgw::hue shade);`

    If you think carefully about the ideas behind forwarding functions, you should be able to do this with very little extra code by delegating most of the extra work to the already written general `plot_square( )` function. This is an example of using forwarding functions to extend a generalization.

17. Overload `plot_square( )` so that for each of the original ways that we could plot a square there is a corresponding version to plot a square in a selected plotting mode. Write a program to test all 12 possible ways of calling `plot_square( )`.

18. Extend Exercise 15 to include selection of the plotting mode. Note that this is not a trivial extension, because you are going to have to decide how to obtain the choice of plotting mode from the user of the program.

Unnamed Parameters

There is one final feature of functions in C++, and that is an allowance for parameters to remain unused in a function's definition. It may seem odd that we would ever want to write a function that will be provided with an argument that is not used. You will have to wait some time before I can give you a good example of the utility of this feature, but this chapter on functions would not be complete if I did not mention unnamed parameters.

Good compilers warn you about variables and parameters that do not seem to have been used in the source code. For example,

```
int foo(){
  int i(10);
  return 1;
}
```

looks to be deeply suspicious. Did the programmer really intend not to use `i`? Such warnings are helpful and we do not want to turn them off, because more often than not, the compiler is correct to be suspicious, and the warning helps us to debug our code. However, in the case of parameters there are times when we genuinely do not want to use the argument provided by the function call.

Suppose you are writing a function to open a window and you want it to be portable across several operating systems. That almost certainly means that you will need to provide a different definition of the function for each of the systems. The declarations will be the same regardless, but we need to provide definitions tailored to specific systems. Now imagine that one system allows you to place a colored frame around the window, but another does not. That means that the function declaration must allow for data about the color of the frame. The system that does not provide colored frames cannot use that information and will simply have to ignore it.

To avoid the warning for an unused parameter, C++ allows the programmer to omit a name for any parameter that is unused in the definition. This omission is in the **definition** of the function (parameter names may always be omitted in function declarations), and its only effect is to suppress the warnings that most compilers would otherwise generate.

In high-quality development environments, where code is required to compile warning-free even at the severest warning level, this is a greatly appreciated feature of C++.

Separate Compilation and Header Files

Until now, I have asked you to place all your source code in a single file. That is not generally good C++ coding practice. We want to be able to reuse code as well as reduce build times.

Programmers coming from such languages as Java find the idea of separate compilation strange, because they are used to a somewhat different strategy wherein libraries are loaded at execution time. They actually do have a kind of separate compilation but not the kind that C++ uses.

C++ (like C) packages declarations and other items (such as inline definitions) into special source-code files called *header files*. The concept of a header file is to provide the compiler with exactly the information it needs to use functions, types, and other material whose definitions will be provided either by another file of source code or by a library. We limit the compiler's knowledge to what it needs in order to do its job, and postpone the rest of the process of producing a program to two other tools: a linker and a loader. The job of the linker is to combine code from different places into a single executable. The job of the loader is to fix up a specific execution of a program by providing suitable resources and ensuring that the executable knows the locations of those resources.

All those header files you have been including into your programs are files of declarations and other material such as some inline definitions that the compiler needs to compile your source code. When you then build your executable, the linker takes all the compiled code nominated by your project together with the general C++ libraries, some system libraries, and any special libraries specified in the project (for example, the `gdi32` and `fgw` libraries you have to add to your project when using `fgw::playpen` objects).

When you use `#include` in your source code, you are telling the compiler where to look for supplementary information it may need. When you add libraries to your project, you are telling the linker where to find supplementary object code (the result of compiling source code) that will be needed to produce a complete program.

It is not only library writers who can limit the exposure of their work at compile time; you can as well. Indeed, you are encouraged to do so.

In order to use separate compilation you need to separate your code into distinct though meaningful files. One part of this separation is to create pairs of header and implementation files. To see how this works carry out the following task.

TRY THIS

Create a new project in MDS. Now create a header file called `plot_square.h`. Note that creating a header file is one of the options for creating new files. Now type the following into that header file (mostly you can cut and paste from your earlier use of the overloaded `plot_square( )` functions):

```
#include "playpen.h"

// declarations
void plot_square(fgw::playpen &, int x, int y, int size,
    fgw::hue = fgw::black);

// inline forwarding functions
inline void plot_square(fgw::playpen & paper, int x, int y,
    fgw::hue shade = fgw::black){
  return plot_square(paper, x, y, 0, shade);
}
inline void plot_square(fgw::playpen & paper, int size,
    fgw::hue shade = fgw::black){
  return plot_square(paper, 0, 0, size, shade);
}
```

The first line is because the subsequent code needs to know the declarations of such things as `fgw::playpen` and `fgw::black`. Header files, particularly user-written ones such as this one, often include other header files. Those included header files provide information for the compiler, but they also provide information for the programmer: the list of inclusions tells the programmer about the way this header depends on other facilities. In this case, we can see that the rest of the file only depends on fundamental C++ and facilities provided by `playpen`.

Now go back to your test program. Remove the above material from it and replace it with `#include "plot_square.h"`. Next cut out the definition of the general `plot_square( )` function and paste it into a new C++ source file called `plot_square.cpp` (note that the IDE adds the correct extensions for you, as it did for the header file). Add `#include "plot_square.h"` to the beginning of this file. (This is not strictly necessary in this case – `#include "playpen.h"` would have been enough. However, later we will need to include headers into implementation files, so there is no harm in developing good habits now.)

Finally add this source-code file to the project, along with the modified source-code file with the version of `main( )` that tests the code. The latter file now contains just the necessary `#include`s and the definition of `main( )`. Everything else has been separated out into a header file, containing the material the compiler needs to compile the file with `main( )` in it, and an implementation file, which, when compiled, provides the linker with the material it needs in order to complete the executable.

EXERCISES

19. Rework Exercise 18 so that all your function declarations are in header files and their definitions are in implementation files. The material for the overloaded `plot_square( )` functions should be in one pair of header file and implementation file. Any other functions that you wrote to assist with the program (and there should be several) should be in a distinct header/implementation file pair. Learn to keep separate material in separate files.

20. Extract all the declarations and inline definitions for `get_int( )` and `get_double( )` into a suitably named header file. Extract the non-inline definitions into an implementation file. Now create a project and write a program that tests all the variations of your `get_int( )` and `get_double( )` overload sets.

REFERENCE SECTION

Function Declaration Syntax

All functions are declared (i.e. their names are provided to the compiler) with the following syntax:

return-type function-name(*comma-separated-parameter-type-list*);

The return type is almost always required (we will find that there are a couple of exceptions for some special member functions). The use of the special **void** type signifies that there is no return value and so the function is effectively a procedure.

The function name has the same restrictions as all other names in C++ and must be present.

The parameter type list is a (possibly empty) list of types. Each of the declared parameters may be followed be a name. The parameter names in pure declarations (ones that are not also definitions) have no significance anywhere else; they merely serve to document the purpose of the parameters in question.

A semicolon terminates a function declaration unless it is also a function definition. In that case the body of the definition terminates the declaration part of the definition.

```
namespace my_library {
  double sales_tax(double cost, double percentage_sales_tax_rate);
}
```

Function Definition Syntax

The syntax for a function definition is very similar to that for a function declaration except that:

- The body of the definition, which consists of zero or more statements enclosed in a pair of braces, replaces the terminal semicolon of the pure declaration. If the function has a return type other than **void** those statements must include a **return** statement providing a suitable value or object that will be returned to the point where the function is called.

- Each parameter that is used in the definition body must be named (the name is how the object or value provided by the caller of the function is used in the body of the function).

- One or more namespace or class names followed by scope operators may precede the function name.

```
double my_library::sales_tax(double c, double rate){
  return c * rate / 100;
}

namespace my_library {
  double sales_tax(double c, double rate){
    return c * rate / 100;
  }
}
```

Function Call Syntax

A free function is called by using the function name (possibly fully elaborated with namespace names) followed by a comma-separated list of arguments in parentheses. The parameters provided in the definition are initialized with the arguments provided by the call.

A member function (dealt with in Chapter 9) is called using the dot (.) operator, with its left operand being the name of a class object and its right operand being the function name; a comma-separated list of arguments in parentheses follows. A member function may also be called by using a pointer to an object of the class type. In that case the arrow (->) operator takes the pointer as its left operand and the function name as its right operand; again a comma-separated list of arguments in parentheses follows.

```
double tax(0);
tax = my_library::sales_tax(27.50, 6.25);
```

The above (free) function call might be used to calculate a 6.25% sales tax on an item costing 27.50 monetary units (dollars, pounds, euros, etc.).

```
fgw::playpen paper;
paper.plot(12, 23, red1);
```

The above (member) function call plots a dim red pixel at the coordinates (12, 23) in the Playpen window that is the output device used by the `fgw::playpen` object named `paper`.

Function Overloading

Functions declared in the same scope may have the same name as long as they have distinct parameter type lists. The difference in the parameter types must be sufficient for the compiler to select one solely based on the types of the arguments provided by a function call using the name. Differences in return type are not significant for selecting which of an overloaded set of functions is used.

If there is a function whose parameter types exactly match the types of the arguments in the function call, it will be selected. If there is no such function, the compiler will invoke a number of 'best match' rules. The details of these are complicated. However, in general, if it matters which function is called then the overload set is poorly designed. The intention of providing overloaded function names is to allow programmers to achieve essentially the same objective from possibly different types of data.

One of the more useful forms of function overloading is to deal with the special case where one of the arguments is implicit. The special case can be defined by forwarding the explicit arguments to the general version with the implicit argument or arguments added in.

Given a function whose declaration is

```
void drawline(fgw::playpen &, point start, point end, fgw::hue);
```

(with `point` being some type that represents a point on a plane), the following defines an overload that draws black lines:

```
void drawline(fgw::playpen & p, point start, point end){
  return drawline(p, start, end, fgw::black);
}
```

This one would draw a line from the origin (assuming that the correct way to create a `point` object identifying the origin is `point(0, 0)`):

```
void drawline(fgw::playpen & p, point end, fgw::hue shade){
  return drawline(p, point(0, 0), end, shade);
}
```

Default Arguments

Instead of using function overloading and delegation (as in the example above) it is sometimes convenient to provide a default value for the argument of one or more of the right-hand parameters in a function declaration. Such arguments are provided by appending an equals sign followed by the desired default to the parameter (after the name if one is provided). Once a parameter is provided with a default argument, all the subsequent parameters must also have default arguments. Once a default argument is used by a caller (by omitting an explicit argument in the call) no further explicit arguments can be provided.

Consider:

```
void drawline(fgw::playpen &, point start, point end, fgw::hue = black);
```

This declaration has substantially the same effect as the first of the specialized versions above. Indeed, they are so similar that the compiler will not allow the two declarations to co-exist.

However, the declaration

```
void drawline(fgw::playpen &, point start = point(0, 0), point end,
    fgw::hue);
```

is **not** allowed, because we are not allowed to provide default arguments for parameters unless we provide defaults for all the subsequent parameters.

Unnamed Parameters

In some cases, a parameter that has been included in a function declaration has no practical use in the specific definition provided for some special context. C++ specifies that it is not an error for a parameter to remain unnamed in the definition of a function. In addition, implementers are strongly encouraged to refrain from issuing any form of diagnostic if a parameter is unnamed in a function definition.

This feature of C++ is useful because it allows user code to be more portable. Libraries can be tailored to the needs of specific platforms, and data that has no use on a platform (though provided by users because it would be useful on other platforms) can be silently ignored.

`inline`

The superficial use of this keyword in C++ is to encourage the compiler to substitute the function's definition for calls to the function. The motive for allowing programmers to make this request is to stop the performance enthusiasts from fretting about the many small functions that C++ encourages.

In practice, the valuable feature of defining a function with an explicit inline qualification is that the program is then allowed to contain multiple identical definitions of a function. If the linker finds that a function is redefined because of its appearance in different source-code files, it is required to issue a redefinition error. That requirement is switched off if all the definitions are qualified as `inline`.

In general, there is a tendency for new programmers to overuse `inline`. Modern compilers and linkers can cooperate to do a good job even without programmers hinting that they want the definition of a function to be used inline.

CHAPTER (6)

Behavior, Sequence Points, and Order of Evaluation

This is a short chapter but an important one. It covers a group of related topics that are essential for correct use of C++ for writing robust and reliable programs. There is no reference section because the whole chapter acts as both a reference and a tutorial. However, this chapter concludes with a set of guidelines to help you avoid most of the pitfalls that sequence points and order of evaluation can cause. The guidelines are sufficient for practical purposes, but the rest of the chapter gives you the necessary basics if you wish to understand the guidelines, or wish to ignore them at times.

Those writing C++ for others to use need to be familiar with this material. There are no exercises because the topics do not readily lend themselves to practice. The 'Try This' items are only to help you check on those aspects that are checkable rather than being unpredictable.

Types of Behavior

C++ classifies the expected behavior for source code into four categories: fully defined, implementation-defined, undefined, and unspecified.

Fully Defined Behavior

This is behavior that is completely specified by the C++ Standard; a compiler that does not compile source code with fully defined behavior to do what the C++ Standard says it should do is, at best, buggy. For example, the C++ Standard requires that the following source code compile and result in a program whose output is 2:

```
#include <iostream>
#include <istream>

int main(){
  std::cout << 2 * sizeof('a');
}
```

Note that we need the `#include <istream>` because the Standard does not specify (though many experts thinks it should have) that `<iostream>` provide the full behavior for input and output objects. The

Standard simply requires that <iostream> declare the names cout, cerr, clog, cin, wcout, wcerr, wclog, and wcin in namespace std. Most implementations include <istream> and <ostream> in <iostream>. Though the Standard allows this, it does not require it.

I chose the above example because the equivalent C program

```c
#include <stdio.h>

int main( ){
  printf("%d", 2 * sizeof('a'));
}
```

has an identical requirement if compiled with a C++ compiler, but a different one if compiled by an old C compiler. The first issue is that C++ specifies the behavior of a program whose main( ) function lacks a return statement (as being equivalent to return 0; at the point where there is no more code to execute). C did not, and so the lack of a return statement would be an error in old C. The most recent version of C (often called C99 to distinguish it from the still widely used version standardized in 1989/90 and corrected in 1994) has the same behavior as C++: falling off the end of main is equivalent to return 0;.

The second issue is that in C the type of a literal character is int, not char. The size of an int is implementation-defined and on most systems is either 2 or 4. However, the following variation of the above code is required to output 2 regardless of whether you use a C or C++ compiler.

```c
#include <stdio.h>

int main( ){
  printf("%d", 2 * sizeof(char));
  return 0;
}
```

That is because sizeof char is defined as 1 by both the C and C++ Standards; a char occupies the smallest amount of memory that either language allows to be directly addressed.

Implementation-Defined Behavior

This is behavior that is allowed to vary from one implementation to another, but the implementer is required to document the details. We had an example of this above: the ratio of the amount of memory used by an int object to that used by a char object is implementation-defined. In other words, the output resulting from

```cpp
std::cout << sizeof(int);
```

is implementation-defined.

Another example of implementation-defined behavior is whether a plain char behaves like a small, signed integer (i.e. signed char) or a small, unsigned integer (unsigned char). Many compilers allow the programmer to choose which behavior they want for char.

TRY THIS

Try the following code with the compiler and IDE you are using to discover which form of char it is providing in the configuration you are using.

```
#include <iostream>

int main(){
  char c(-1);
  if(c < 200) std::cout << "signed \n";
  else std::cout << "unsigned \n";
  return 0;
}
```

I have not bothered with exception-handling because this is a tiny program to be used once and thrown away. How we initialize c with -1 depends on whether char is treated as a signed or unsigned integer type. If char is a signed type then -1 is stored as is (in whatever way the system represents negative one – exactly how depends on whether signed integers are represented in two's complement, one's complement or sign and magnitude). If char is being treated as an unsigned type, -1 will wrap around to the largest value available for a char. Note that for any unsigned representation of char the largest possible value is certainly larger than 200.

Unspecified Behavior

This covers cases where the compiler is free to select any one of a number of reasonable actions, and the implementer is not required to document which one the compiler will select. This is usually because all the possible choices will usually have identical results. However, it is often possible to construct code that will behave differently according to the choice the compiler makes.

An example of unspecified behavior is that C++ (unlike some other languages such as Java) does not specify the order of evaluation of subexpressions that are parts of a larger expression. Look at the following source code:

```
#include <iostream>

int global(0);
int add1_to_global(){
  return ++global;
}

int add2_to_global(){
  return (global += 2);
}

int main(){
  std::cout << add1_to_global() + add2_to_global() << '\n';
}
```

The C++ Standard requires that the calls of add1_to_global() and add2_to_global() be done sequentially (i.e. it cannot send the two calls to different CPUs in parallel), but it does not specify which will be evaluated first. In this case, the result will depend on which choice the compiler makes. If it makes the two function calls in a left-to-right order the result will be 4, but if it calls them in reverse order the result will be 5. Whichever order it chooses, the final value stored in global will be 3.

Because the order of evaluation of subexpressions (in this case two function calls) is unspecified by the C++ Standard, both 4 and 5 are correct output for the above program. In fact, the compiler you are using (assuming it is the same version that I have) will produce a program whose output is 5. That tells me that the compiler is creating code that calls add2_to_global() before calling add1_to_global().

WARNING!

If you did not already know that global variables can cause serious problems, this example should demonstrate one of the reasons good programmers avoid them.

While C++ provides rules for the order in which operators are applied during the evaluation of an expression, it provides very few requirements for the order in which subexpressions are evaluated: a subexpression is evaluated before its value is needed by an operator. Many programmers miss the full implications of this rule. For example, using the above functions,

```cpp
int main( ){
  std::cout << add1_to_global( ) << add2_to_global( ) << '\n';
}
```

also has unspecified behavior. The output can be '13' or '23' depending on the order in which the two functions are called. Furthermore the order in which the subexpressions (function calls in this case) are evaluated can vary from one place to another.

WARNING!

It is unsafe to assume that subexpressions will be evaluated in any specific order. Running test code will not tell you anything more than the order in which the subexpressions were evaluated in the test code. If the order matters you must do something to enforce an order, such as evaluating the pieces in separate statements. For example,

```cpp
int main( ){
  std::cout << add1_to_global( );
  std::cout << add2_to_global( ) << '\n';
}
```

must result in the output of '13', because there is no liberty to reorder entire statements.

Undefined Behavior

This is the big problem and one that lurks in far too much code written by people who think they know what they are doing. Any time you do something for which the C++ Standard provides no requirements, you are in the land of undefined behavior. I often see programmers excuse themselves on the basis that they have tested the code and it does what they expected it to. That is the most vicious aspect of undefined behavior; it can hide for years because nothing triggers the problem. There are a number of classic examples of undefined behavior that can cause damage to real systems. For example, I once reprogrammed the EPROM on a very expensive graphics card with a program that effectively did this:

```cpp
void NEVER_RUN_THIS(bool q){
  char message[ ] = "No";
  if(q) strcpy(message, "yes");
}
```

I have stripped out all the other code and named the function in a way that I hope will persuade even the most casual reader never to use it. C programmers will recognize what the code does, and it does the same in C++. In simple terms, it allocates enough local storage to store the text 'No' and then proceeds to try to write 'yes' in the same space. It will not fit so the last character overflows. On many systems, that overflow might not actually do damage. On the system I was using it wrote data on top of the return address for the function. As a result, the function did not return to the caller but returned somewhere else. It was just my bad luck that the place it returned to was executable code that did the damage. Of course, modern operating systems will often spot such wild behavior and simply kick the program off. But:

WARNING!

A programmer must not rely on an operating system to intervene to protect itself and other programs from abuse caused by code with undefined behavior. A program that includes undefined behavior is an accident waiting to happen.

Sequence Points

Sequence points are islands of stability in a C++ program where we can be certain that some actions are completed and that other actions will not have started. All computer languages implicitly have such points, but in C++ (as in C) they are made explicit by the Standard, and good programming requires either strict adherence to a set of guidelines or a good deal of understanding of what can happen between sequence points.

Most of a program consists of evaluating expressions. The evaluation of an expression results in a value. In addition, many expressions also have side effects. The more obvious side effects are such things as opening and closing files, extracting data from files, inserting data into files, and other forms of input and output.

One of the more insidious side effects is that of changing the state of the program itself. By that, I mean writing something to the program's memory. The most obvious example of this is the use of assignment to store a result. It comes as a surprise to many programmers that this process of storing a result is far from being a universally good thing. Those whose prior experience of programming has been with functional languages such as Haskell may even have learned that assignment is a dangerous and highly suspect operation.

A C++ statement such as

```
i = j * k;
```

consists of two distinct elements. The first is the evaluation of the expression i = j * k. We almost always throw away the result, but nonetheless there is a result that can be used in some circumstances. For example,

```
int foo(int & result, int lhs, int rhs){
  return result = lhs * rhs;
}
```

returns the value of the expression result = lhs * rhs. In general, we are usually more interested in the fact that evaluating an assignment expression results in storing a value in the object designated by the left-hand operand of the assignment operator. The function foo( ) does two things. It returns a value, but it also has the side effect of storing the result of evaluating lhs * rhs in the object designated by result. Notice how this is different from:

```
int bar(int lhs, int rhs){
  return lhs * rhs;
}
```

The function bar( ) has no side effects; it works out and returns the result of lhs * rhs. In computer-science terms bar( ) is a *pure function*, because calling it has no permanent effects on either external objects such as printers, or on the program's internal resources such as memory.

One problem with side effects is deciding when they happen. Storing results in memory is a relatively slow process on most machines. In addition, some hardware requires a stabilization time after a memory write before the program accesses that memory again. The solution that C++ uses (one inherited from C) is to specify something called a *sequence point*, where, if necessary, the program must wait while memory stabilizes. That is one of the motives for the concept of a sequence point; however, as programmers, we are more concerned with the practical implications.

Between two sequence points, we are free to read any memory representing objects as often as we like, providing that we do not write to any of that memory. However, if we write to a piece of memory between sequence points, we must only write to it once. Furthermore, we must only read that memory as part of the process of determining what the program will write to it. Breaking either of those rules results in undefined behavior.

Most programmers are happy with the first part of the rule: only write once to a piece of memory between sequence points. Many do not understand the second restriction. That restriction ensures that if memory is both read and written between sequence points then the read will have been completed before the write starts. In the context of C++'s unspecified order of evaluation of subexpressions, that is the only rule that could ensure safety.

Now you can see why it is important to know where the sequence points are in your code. Here is a complete list:

full expression: There is a sequence point at the end of evaluating a full expression. A full expression is one whose value is not directly used as part of evaluating some other expression. For example, in the function **bar( )** above, **lhs * rhs** is a full expression; however, in the function **foo( )**, **lhs * rhs** is not a full expression, because the result is used in evaluating the assignment to **result**.

Note that a single statement can involve more than one full expression. For example, the statement

```
if(a < b) i++;
```

contains two full expressions: **a < b** and **i++**.

function call: Two sequence points protect a function call. There is a sequence point immediately after the evaluation of all the arguments, so the body of the function can proceed on the assumption that all the side effects of initializing the parameters are complete. There is a second sequence point at the point of return, which ensures that any side effects of providing the return value are complete before the code that called the function resumes.

Few programmers write code that has a problem with the return sequence point, but the entry one is sometimes misunderstood. For example,

```
int bar(int lhs, int rhs);
int main( ){
  int i(0);
  std::cout << bar(i, i++);
}
```

may seem fine until you examine the call of **bar( )** more carefully. Two expressions, **i** and **i++**, have to be evaluated in order to call **bar( )**. Those expressions are not full expressions, because the results will be used as arguments to initialize the parameters of **bar( )**. That means that there is no sequence point between the evaluation of **i** and **i++**. However, evaluating the first of those requires that the value stored in the object designated by **i** be read, but not for determining what will be written to it as a side effect of incrementing it during the process of evaluating the second argument. In other words, we have broken the rules about reading and writing to the same object between sequence points. That means that we are in the realms of undefined behavior and anything can happen. In practice, the usual manifestation of the problem is that the two orders of evaluation result in different values for the first argument. That should not lull you into a false sense of security: this is not unspecified behavior but **undefined** behavior. Please learn the difference, because one day it will matter.

comma operator: A comma (,) is, in some contexts, simply punctuation that separates a list of items. In other contexts, it is the C++ sequence operator. Knowing which is which is largely a matter of experience.

Unfortunately, which it is can have a profound effect on your program. When a comma is a sequence operator it injects a sequence point into the code, which means that the expression to the left of the comma is fully evaluated and all side effects complete before the expression on the right is touched.

Even worse, C++ allows programmers to redefine the comma operator if at least one of its operands has a user-defined type. In those circumstances, it is no longer a sequence operator, and the left and right operands (expressions) can be evaluated in either order. The upshot is that it is probably better to assume that a comma is not a sequence operator unless you definitely know that it is.

conditional operator: There is a sequence point between the evaluation of the left-hand operand of the conditional operator and the evaluation of whichever of the other two operands is selected. So

```
int bar(int value){
   value ? value++ : value--;
    ...
   return value;
}
```

is fine in so far as the first statement is concerned. I cannot imagine why I might write such a statement but there is no undefined behavior. The first read of **value** is protected from the later write to the same storage by a sequence point at the **?**.

the | | and && operators: There is a sequence point after the evaluation of the left-hand operand (expression) for the built-in versions of each of these operators. That means that the left-hand operand is fully evaluated and all consequential side effects completed before the right-hand operand is evaluated. Note that the right-hand operand is only evaluated if necessary to determine the result. That means that any side effects of evaluating the right-hand operand are conditional on the value of the left-hand operand.

Multiple Sequence Points

Expressions often contain multiple sequence points, and a programmer must be careful not to assume that sequence points force an order of evaluation. The sequence (comma) operator, the conditional operator, and the | | and && operators force an order of evaluation on their operands but that is as far as it goes. If you write

i = (*expr1* **| |** *expr2*) + (*expr3* **&&** *expr4*)**;**

any evaluation sequence that fully evaluates (including side effects) *expr1* before *expr2* and *expr3* before *expr4* is within the rules. There is no requirement that, for example, *expr1* be evaluated before *expr4*.

Order of Evaluation

There is not much more to say. Between sequence points, subexpressions can be evaluated in any order that is consistent with the associativity and precedence of the operators involved. Most importantly, parentheses do not change order of evaluation, only precedence. For example, the rules for operators require that in

double d;
d = *expr1* **/** *expr2* ***** *expr3***;**

the division must be completed before the multiplication, and both those must be completed before the assignment to **d**. However, *expr1*, *expr2*, *expr3*, and the address of the object designated by **d** can be evaluated in any order. Adding some parentheses cannot change the latter allowance. So

double d;
d = *expr1* **/** (*expr2* ***** *expr3*)**;**

forces execution of the multiplication to occur before the division but has no other impact.

Guidelines

Note that the following guidelines give you a set of safe programming practices with regard to order of evaluation and sequence points. Ignoring a guideline is fine as long as you are willing to spend time checking that you have not introduced undefined behavior into your code. You should also check that any unspecified behavior would not result in erroneous results. In addition, you should document any implementation-defined behavior on which you are relying. For example, if your program relies on `int` using a 32-bit representation, that should be clearly documented.

> Rule 1: *Only use increment and decrement operators as full expressions. Do not have more than one assignment or compound assignment operator in a full expression.*

If you follow this rule, you will not fall foul of the rule restricting reading and writing to the same storage between sequence points.

> Rule 2: *Avoid writing functions that modify a global object.*

There are exceptions to this rule such as using `std::cout`, which is a global object (in namespace `std`), but even here you need some care. For example, consider:

```cpp
#include <iostream>

int hello(){
  std::cout << "Hello ";
  return 1;
}
int world(){
  std::cout << "World ";
  return 2;
}

int main(){
  std::cout << hello() + world() << '\n';
}
```

Try that code. Then try replacing

```cpp
  std::cout << hello() + world() << '\n';
```

with

```cpp
  std::cout << hello() << world() << '\n';
```

or:

```cpp
  std::cout << hello(), world() << '\n';
```

Do not try to explain the results because in the first two cases we have unspecified behavior. There are other orderings available to the compiler. In the third case the compiler must call `hello()` first and then call `world()` but there is something far stranger happening. The program first executes everything to the left of the comma. It then executes everything to the right of the comma. The latter only seems to work. Here is why. The expression `world() << '\n'` is evaluated as the value returned from `world()` shifted left by the number of places that `'\n'` represents as a number.

Try changing the `'\n'` to `"\n"`. In the first two cases it produces the same result, but in the third case you get a compile time error because `"\n"` is a string literal and cannot be converted into an integer value. Alternatively, try changing the return type of `world()` to `double`. Again, the first two examples compile and execute as before (though that is because the decimal indicator is suppressed for output of `double` values that are exact whole numbers). However, you again get a compile time error in the third case because the left-shift operator cannot be applied to a floating-point type.

> Rule 3: *Do not pass the same object to two functions by reference unless there is an intervening sequence point or both functions take the argument by* const *reference.*

Remember that passing a reference (rather than a **const** reference) allows the function to change the object being referenced. If at least one of two function calls can change the object, the unspecified order of evaluation between sequence points means that there may be more than one possible result for your code. For example, consider:

```
int foo(int const & i){
   return i;
}

int bar(int & i){
   return i++;
}

int main(){
   int i(0);
   std::cout << bar(i) << foo(i) << '\n';
}
```

If `bar()` is called first the output will be '01', but if `foo()` is called first then it will be '00'. The sequence points in the function call and return only remove the potential for undefined behavior; they do not influence the order of evaluation of the various bits needed to execute the output statement.

> Rule 4: *Do not call functions with arguments provided by expressions unless you are certain that the order of evaluation of the arguments will not matter.*

Remember that the comma used to separate arguments in a function call is just punctuation and is not a sequence operator.

CHAPTER 7

Generic Functions

C++ provides some very useful mechanisms for writing code that is independent of the data types used. We have already been using them when, for example, we created vectors to contain a specified type. `std::vector<int>`, `std::vector<long>`, `std::vector<std::string>`, and even `std::vector<std::vector<int>>` are all examples of using the general C++ concept of a vector container as a sequence of objects of a specified type.

The fundamental mechanism is the C++ template. In this chapter, I am going to focus on C++ function templates. We most commonly simply use functions generated from function templates provided by libraries (either the Standard C++ Library or third-party ones). However, this chapter will also cover writing simple function templates. The primary intention is to help you understand the template concept.

Some readers may wish to delay learning the details of writing function templates. If you are one of them, please at least skim this chapter so that you will know what they are and how to use them. You can come back later to study writing them in more detail.

> Language Note: *Much of this chapter may seem surprising if your previous programming experience has been with a dynamically typed language such as Python. C++ is a statically typed language. That means that the types of objects and expressions must be determined at compile time. We will see later that C++ also supports a limited amount of dynamic typing, but only for names; objects must have a static type, i.e. a type that the compiler can identify.*

Which Is Larger

Choosing the larger of two values is a common problem – so common that you probably want to make it a function. The following short function returns the larger of two `int` values supplied to it as arguments:

```
int max(int first, int second){
  return first > second ? first : second;
}
```

That function is so simple – it is just a wrapper for using the conditional operator – that you may wonder why we should make it into a function. One reason is that good programming not only avoids 'magic numbers' but also avoids 'magic expressions'; we try to name things to help the human reader follow what our code is doing. In general, self-expressive code is worth the risk of a possible slight degradation in performance, because it saves a great deal of maintenance time. C++ also provides tools to tackle the issue of efficiency when it matters.

TRY THIS

Here is a small program that uses the above function to select the largest of a set of integer values input via the console (i.e. keyboard):

```cpp
1 #include <iostream>
2 #include <vector>
3
4 int max(int first, int second){
5   return first > second ? first : second;
6 }
7
8 int main( ){
9   try{
10     std::vector<int> data;
11     std::cout << "Type in some integers. End input with -9999.\n\n";
12     int value(0);
13     do{
14       std::cin >> value;
15       data.push_back(value);
16     } while(value != -9999);
17     int maximum(-9999);
18     for(size_t i(0); i != data.size( ); ++i){
19       maximum = max(maximum, data[i]);
20     }
21     std::cout << "The largest input value was " << maximum << ".\n";
22   }
23   catch(...){ std::cerr << "\n***An exception was thrown***\n";}
24 }
```

Create a project, type in the program, and try it.

WALKTHROUGH

Most of the above code should be familiar to you by now. Lines 10 to 16 create a container called **data**, which is a sequence of **int** values, stored in a **std::vector<int>** object. Data provided by the keyboard is stored in it. Note that we have to define **value** outside the data-capture loop because it is used in the **while**-clause that checks to see if input has finished. (Try moving the definition of **value** inside the **do-while** loop to see that the compiler then rejects the code.) Storing the terminating value gives us a small benefit in that it ensures that there will always be at least one value stored in **data**.

The design also assumes that only valid data will be supplied – it does not check for input failure. We will deal with that problem later in this chapter.

Line 18 uses the Standard-defined name, **size_t**, for the unsigned integer type used to measure the size of objects in C++. Which unsigned integer type is used for **size_t** is implementation-defined (i.e. the compiler implementer must document which choice was made from the available unsigned types).

Line 19 uses the function `max()` to go through the supplied data to find the largest value. If no data was provided, apart from the terminating value, the original value of maximum (-9999 in the above code) will be used.

Getting the Largest

Suppose that we now want to select the largest value from a sequence of values of type `double`. If you look at the above code you will realize that very little has to change in `main()`. We will need to change all the instances of `int` in the body of `main()` to `double`. We will also need to change the end of data test – remember that it is unsafe to compare floating-point values for equality. We might change the test to check that the input value is greater than `-9999.0`.

 TRY THIS

Try making those changes. Be careful that you do not change the definition of `max()`. Also make sure that you did not change the return type of `main()`; that must always be `int`.

When you come to compile the result you will get a number of warnings. Ignore them for now; build and execute the program. You should notice that the program gets the answers **slightly wrong** if the largest value is **not** an exact integer value. Think about why that should be.

The problem is that the values are being converted (rounded) to `int` values on the way into `max()`. To avoid that, we need to add a new version of `max()`, one that takes two `double`s. In the short term we might just edit our current version of `max()` by replacing `int` by `double` throughout its declaration and definition, including its return type.

The short-term measure of replacing `int max(int, int)` with `double max(double, double)` only works if we do not want to use both versions within a single program.

Getting the Largest Using a `typedef`

In practice, there are many different types of values for which we may want to choose the bigger of two (or the one that comes second when the values are arranged in order). Here is a way that works as long as there is only a single relevant type in the program. It uses the C++ device (inherited from C) for giving an existing type a new name. The mechanism is a `typedef` declaration. This works like any other declaration of a name, but the name becomes a synonym for a type rather than a variable or function name. The following code demonstrates its use for providing some support for writing generic (type-independent) code:

```
1 #include <iostream>
2 #include <vector>
3 typedef int value_t;
4 value_t max(value_t first, value_t second){
5   return first > second ? first : second;
6 }
7
```

```
 8 int main( ){
 9   try{
10     std::vector<value_t> data;
11     std::cout << "Type in some integers. End input with -9999\n\n";
12     value_t value;
13     do{
14       std::cin >> value;
15       data.push_back(value);
16     } while(value > -9999);
17     value_t maximum(-9999);
18     for(size_t i(0); i != data.size( ); ++i){
19       maximum = max(maximum, data[i]);
20     }
21     std::cout << "The largest input value was " << maximum << ".\n";
22   }
23   catch(...){ std::cerr << "\n***An exception was thrown***\n"; }
24 }
```

Yes, that is the code from the previous program with two changes: line 3 now contains a **typedef** declaration that makes **value_t** a synonym for **int**, and all the relevant uses of **int** have been changed to **value_t**. Notice how our code now distinguishes between the uses of **int** to represent the kind of data we wish to process and other uses of **int** such as the return from **main( )**. This is another example of removing 'magic' from our code.

Before you try it, it is time to remove those magic uses of **-9999**. You will appreciate why in a few moments. Change line 7 to:

```
value_t const limit(-9999);
```

Now modify line 11 so that it outputs the message but uses **limit** instead of **-9999**. You will have to reorganize the statement because you cannot use variables, even **const** qualified ones, inside quotation marks.

Finally replace the other two uses of **-9999** with **limit**.

TRY THIS

The resulting program should work exactly as the earlier one did. However, we now have the ability to reuse **main( )** for other types, by making a couple of simple changes to the source code.

Try changing the **typedef** so that **value_t** is a synonym for **double**, and change **limit**'s initializer to **-9999.0**. Now build and execute the program. How well the message at line 11 fits with the new version depends on how general you managed to make it. You could have pulled the message into a **std::string** and placed that out front along with the other pieces that need changing for different types. However, I am sure you get the idea: write code so that is easily adjusted from a general case to a specific one.

Now for a final demonstration of the power of writing code this way. Try changing line 3 to

```
typedef std::string value_t;
```

and line 7 to:

```
value_t limit("@");
```

You will need to add #include <string> so that the compiler can find the declarations relating to the std::string type. You will probably also need to tweak the message asking for data input.

Build and execute the resulting program. Note that 'largest' in this context will mean the word, or string of characters, that would be last when the data is sorted into lexical (alphabetical) order.

EXERCISES

1. Tidy up the above program by declaring a suitable std::string const prompt and modifying line 11 to use it. Arrange the code so that the three things that need modifying for different types are declared/defined as three consecutive statements.

2. Change the output so that it also lists the input values a comma-separated list. The output should be something like the 'The largest value in (...) was ...' with the dots replaced by the correct data.

3. Write a program that outputs the second-largest value from a sequence of values. You must not modify the order of the sequence, so using std::sort( ) and then selecting the second from the end is not a valid solution to this problem.

Getting the Largest Using a Template

Choosing the greater of two values uses exactly the same basic code for any type for which the > operator can be used. The only thing we need to change is the type of the data. The C++ function-template mechanism is designed to deal with this. It allows us to create type parameters to which we can pass type arguments. Here is a function template for creating max( ) functions:

```
template <typename value_type>
value_type max(value_type first, value_type second){
  return first > second ? first : second;
}
```

Let us focus on the first line of that code. The template keyword tells the compiler that what follows is generic code. The code between the angle brackets tells the compiler the generic parameters. These are provided as a list (comma-separated if there is more than one parameter). There are three kinds of generic parameter: type, value, and template. For the time being I am going to deal only with type parameters – the other two are expert territory and best left alone until you have more substantial experience of writing C++. Type parameters are identified by the keyword typename (class can also be used, but I prefer to use the more descriptive option), followed by a parameter name. As you can see above, the parameter name behaves in a similar fashion to a typedef name as far as the function-template code is concerned.

The big difference is in the way we use a function template. I can explicitly provide the relevant type argument(s) at the point where I want to call a function generated from the function template. I can rewrite my example program as:

```
1 #include <iostream>
2 #include <vector>
```

```
 3 #include <string>
 4
 5 template <typename value_type>
 6 value_type max(value_type first, value_type second){
 7   return first > second ? first : second;
 8 }
 9 typedef int value_t;
10 value_t limit(-9999);
11 std::string type("integers");
12
13 int main( ){
14  try{
15    std::vector<value_t> data;
16    std::cout << "Type in some " << type <<
17        ". End input with " << limit << ".\n\n";
18    int value;
19    do{
20      std::cin >> value;
21      data.push_back(value);
22    } while(value > -9999);
23    value_t maximum(-9999);
24    for(size_t i(0); i != data.size( ); ++i){
25      maximum = max<value_t>(maximum, data[i]);
26    }
27    std::cout << "The largest input value was " << maximum << ".\n";
28  }
29  catch(...){std::cerr << "\n***An exception was thrown***\n";}
30 }
```

I have tidied up the code but the critical change is at line 25: **max<value_t>** specifies that the version of max( ) generated for the type of **value_t** must be used. **value_t** is the type argument passed to the function template parameter, **value_type**. Your first reaction may be that we seem to have gained very little over just using a **typedef**. If we were only interested in this single program, you would be right. Indeed if you try this code with **value_t** being some type from the Standard C++ Library such as **std::string** it will no longer compile. Put that to one side for now because I will deal with that issue later in this chapter.

The advantage of using a template is a longer-term one: we can use the function template for **max( )** whenever we want to select the larger of two values. There are two conditions required for using a function template. The first is that the compiler must see the actual definition of the template function (though a new mechanism – using the keyword **export** – for allowing the compiler to go ahead with only a declaration of the template function is beginning to become available in some compilers). The second condition is that the generated code must be valid for the template arguments. In this case the type must have a useable **>** operator with the correct behavior. We will shortly see that the latter requirement is an important one.

In most cases we can omit the explicit template type arguments (the type or types in the angle brackets used when the function is called) for a function template, because the compiler will be able to deduce the relevant type(s) from the argument(s) supplied for the generated function. Here is an example for you to try.

 TRY THIS

```
1 #include <iostream>
2 #include <string>
```

```
 3
 4 template<typename value_type>
 5 value_type max(value_type first, value_type second){
 6   return first > second ? first : second;
 7 }
 8
 9 int main( ){
10   try{
11     std::cout << max(12, 24) << '\n';
12     std::cout << max(12.3, -1.4) << '\n';
13     std::cout << max('a', 'b') << '\n';
14   }
15   catch(...){std::cerr << "\n***An exception was thrown***\n";}
16 }
```

Create a project and try out that short program. Notice that the results are correct for each of the three calls of **max( )**. The compiler has worked out that the first one is comparing two **int**s, the second compares two **double**s and the third compares two **char**s.

Now change line 13 to

```
std::cout << max('b', 'a') << '\n';
```

and check that the result is still 'b'. Next change that line to:

```
std::cout << max("b", "a") << '\n';
```

On my system the result is still 'b'. However, when you try

```
std::cout << max("a", "b") << '\n';
```

you should get a surprise – the result is 'a'. (Some systems may reverse the last two results.) Something odd is happening here, and it is an example of the kind of problem you may have to deal with. **'a'** and **'b'** are **char** literals. In other words, they are values of type **char**. When we ask that they be compared the compiler generates code that treats them as small integers. The code representing **'a'** has a lower value than the code that represents **'b'** (they are actually 97 and 98 respectively if the system is using ASCII).

However, when we use double quotes we create a string literal. The program uses some special storage it has available to store the codes for the specific string of **char**s that we have specified. It then adds one more location in which it stores a zero as an end-of-string marker. The upshot is that **"a"** and **"b"** are not any kind of integer (they are actually arrays of **char**, but do not worry if your previous programming experience has not covered this idea). There are no comparison operators between string literals (that may come as a surprise if you previously used languages that do provide comparisons between string literals), so the compiler looks for an alternative. What it does is compare the addresses where the string literals are stored. The answers you get from the last two versions of the program depend on where the string literals are stored, not on what letters are used. On the compiler I am using it stores earlier string literals at higher (larger) addresses than later ones.

We fix the problem by telling the compiler what we want to compare by writing:

```
std::cout << max<std::string>("b", "a") << '\n';
```

There are other ways to fix it but this works fine so there is no reason to add complications.

Ambiguity

Try replacing one of the lines using **max( )** in the program we are currently studying with:

```
std::cout << max(12.2, 24) << '\n';
```

In other words, make the first argument have a different type to the second. As human beings, we have no difficulty in recognizing that we are implicitly dealing with floating-point values even though the second one is written as an **int** value. The compiler is more restricted. It tries to deduce the type that must be passed to the **value_type** template parameter and comes up with two different answers. The C++ rule for type deduction for template parameters is that only exact matches count, and that all choices for deduction must result in exactly the same type.

We can easily fix this example in one of two ways. We can change the type of the second parameter by writing it as **24.0**, or we can explicitly provide the template type parameter by writing:

```
std::cout << max<double>(12.2, 24) << '\n';
```

Both ways will resolve the ambiguity and direct the compiler to make an appropriate choice. As to which is the better solution, that depends on the context. It is up to the programmer to choose an appropriate solution from the available options.

Overloading

A function template can co-exist with a function of the same name. If both the function template and the plain function can exactly match the types of the arguments in a call using implicit type deduction, the plain one is preferred. If the function template cannot provide an exact match but the plain one can be called by converting the type of the arguments then the plain one will be used. Here is some code for you to experiment with to help understand these rules:

 TRY THIS

```
 1 #include <iostream>
 2 #include <string>
 3
 4 template<typename value_type>
 5 value_type max(value_type first, value_type second){
 6   return first > second ? first : second;
 7 }
 8
 9 int max(int first, int second){
10   return first > second ? first : second;
11 }
12
13 int main( ){
14   try{
15     std::cout << max(1, 2.5) << '\n';
16   }
17   catch(...){std::cerr << "\n***An exception was thrown***\n";}
18 }
```

When you try to compile this, the compiler issues a warning (at least it will if you have not turned the warning off). Notice the nature of the warning; it is telling you that it has to narrow a floating-point value to an int. Why is that? At line 15, it looks for a version of max( ) that it can use. Because the types of the two arguments are different, it abandons the function template (because that requires that the deduced types for the template parameter be the same for both the function arguments – they aren't: the first is an int and the second is a double). However, I have also provided a plain (non-template) version of max( ). In this case, the arguments still do not exactly match, but the compiler spots that it can convert the second argument to an int value by rounding it to 2. Therefore, it chooses that option and warns the programmer that it narrowed a value from a double to an int.

In this case, we should probably take this warning seriously, because the value we get back is not actually the maximum of the values we supplied.

Instrumenting Code

Sometimes, when we are testing code, we want some extra information during the execution of a program that we would not want if we were producing a finished product. We call the process of adding source code to provide such extra information 'instrumenting the code'. Suppose we want to check that the compiler chooses the plain version of max( ) in preference to generating a function from the function template if both are exact matches. We could modify the two definitions so that each reports on its use:

```cpp
template<typename value_type>
value_type max(value_type first, value_type second){
  std::cout << "Template used.\n";
  return first > second ? first : second;
}

int max(int first, int second){
  std::cout << "Plain function used.\n";
  return first > second ? first : second;
}
```

 TRY THIS

Use those two definitions with the following version of main( ):

```cpp
1 int main(){
2   try{
3     int i(3);
4     int j(5);
5     std::cout << max(i, j);
6   }
7   catch(...){std::cerr << "\n***An exception was thrown***\n";}
8 }
```

I have added some variables to the program just to make it clear that they are allowed. Indeed we could call max( ) with expressions; for example, max(i * 2, j + 6). I hope you noticed that as long as both the expressions result in int values we get the message 'Plain function used.'

Now try replacing line 5 with:

```
std::cout << max(i * 1.5, j + 2.3);
```

Notice that now we get the function-template definition used, because both those expressions are doubles.

Please experiment with other choices until you are happy you understand how a function template interacts with a plain function of the same name.

Function Templates Can Be Specialized

Suppose we try the following version of **main( )**:

```
int main( ){
  try{
    std::string s1("help");
    std::string s2("me");
    std::cout << max(s1, s2);
  }
  catch(...){ }
}
```

You may be surprised that it does not compile, because we used something similar earlier on without any problems when we were writing code with a **typedef**. However, what may surprise you even more is the reason the compiler gives for rejecting the code: it complains of ambiguity. Remember that when I introduced a program that used the template, I warned you to avoid types from the Standard C++ Library. The compiler has found a second template called **max**; this one is hidden away in namespace **std**. Why has it now found this one and added it to the potential candidates? The first thing to notice is that the compiler has called an ambiguity error, not a redefinition error. That tells us that it is all right to overload function templates, but that the problem was that it could not choose one as better than the other. However, how did it find the second one? The answer lies in something called *argument-dependent lookup* (ADL). When looking for a function name, the compiler will also look in the namespaces of the arguments provided in the function call; we call that ADL. In this case, the argument type is **std::string**, so it not only searches the obviously visible declarations and finds ours, but it also searches the parts of **std** namespace that it can see. There it finds another declaration of a function template called **max**. ADL is intended to be helpful, and it usually is, but sometimes it springs a surprise. This is such a case where a name hidden away in a namespace gets unexpectedly exposed and causes a conflict.

Fixing ADL Ambiguity

We can easily fix the problem by using the fully qualified name of the function we are using. That disables ADL and causes the compiler to look only in the namespace specified by the qualification. In this case we need to replace **max** with **::max** (i.e. explicitly specify the global version we have provided).

The new code compiles and executes fine. But there is more. We might want to compare words but ignore the case used, so that 'word', 'Word', and 'WORD' will all be treated as equivalent. We need a special version of **max( )** to do that.

Specializing max( )

We could write a plain function that has two **std::string** arguments. However, that enables conversions (i.e. allows use of any type from which a **std::string** can be implicitly created). If we do not want to allow conversions, we must stick with a template. The following code is an example of specialization that specializes our **max( )** function template for **std::string**.

```
1 template<>
2 std::string const & max<std::string const &>(std::string const & first,
3     std::string const & second){
4   std::string s1(first);
5   std::string s2(second);
6   std::transform(s1.begin( ), s1.end( ), s1.begin( ), tolower);
7   std::transform(s2.begin( ), s2.end( ), s2.begin( ), tolower);
8   return s1 > s2 ? first : second;
9 }
```

WALKTHROUGH

Line 1 is the way we tell the compiler that the following code is a special case of a template for which we are providing a new definition. Line 2 declares the original template with the type(s) for the special case replacing the name(s) given in the original function template. That is, we have to provide the type's name (or names if there was more than one template type parameter) as template arguments (the **<std::string>** following **max**).

Lines 4 and 5 simply create copies of the function's arguments, because we are going to change them but still want to be able to return a copy of the original.

Lines 6 and 7 use **std::transform**, one of the Standard C++ Library functions (declared in **<algorithm>**, so we will need to include that header when we try to compile this code). **std::transform** takes four parameters. The first two give the beginning and end of the sequence to be transformed (just as **std::sort( )** did for a sequence to be sorted). The third parameter identifies where the transformed sequence will start – in this case, the transformation is in situ, i.e. the transformed elements will replace the originals. The fourth parameter names the function that is applied to each element of the sequence to create the elements of the transformed sequence.

Line 8 compares the lowercase strings to select which of the originals to return.

TRY THIS

Try including the specialization of **max( )** for **std::string** with the version of **main( )** that compares two **std::string** objects. Experiment with different values stored in the **std::string** objects until you are happy that the resulting code is making a case-independent comparison.

EXERCISES

4. Write a template for squaring numbers. The important issue here is that the value of the square of a number should have the same type as that of the value provided. Your function template should work for any type that supports the multiplication operator.

5. Write a function template that has three parameters of the same type and returns the middle of the three in order of size.

6. Specialize your function template for middle so that it will select the middle of three words in a case-independent way.

Overloading Function Templates

The error message earlier when we tried to use **max( )** for a **std::string** hinted that it might be possible to overload function templates. Not only is it possible but it can also be useful.

The example I am going to give next lacks full generality because I am going to deal with a single type of C++ container – **std::vector** – when there are actually many types of containers in C++ (some of which we will look at in later chapters). The following code declares and defines a function template that returns the maximum value found in a **std::vector<T>** object, where T will be replaced by the exact type when the function is generated from the template.

```
1 template<typename T>
2 T max(std::vector<T> & data){
3   if(not data.size()) throw std::range_error("No data");
4   T maximum(data[0]);
5   for(size_t i(1); i != data.size(); ++i){
6     maximum = ::max(maximum, data[i]);
7   }
8   return maximum;
9 }
```

WALKTHROUGH

The source code uses **std::vector** and **std::range_error**, so the compiler will have had to have seen the contents of the **<vector>** and **<stdexcept>** headers if it is to compile code using this **max( )** function template.

Line 1 declares that the following is some generic code based on a type called T (it is idiomatic to name a template type parameter with T, just as mathematicians use *x*, *y*, and *z* for unknowns but *a*, *b*, and *c* for constants). Line 2 says that this is a function that will be given a reference to **std::vector** of T values as an argument and will return a T value.

Notice that the function parameter declared in line 2 is a reference. The reference is important because we certainly would not normally want to pass containers such as **std::vector<T>** around by value (i.e. copying the container). Containers can contain large numbers of elements. In addition, the elements themselves can be large and expensive to copy.

Line 3 is an example of something that is easy to miss. It is just possible that a programmer hands over an empty vector. With the simple design we are using this will be an error that we need to detect and deal with. In this case, I have borrowed a Standard C++ Library type used to report problems with ranges. It is an imperfect choice but will do for now. The controlling expression in the **if** statement uses the Boolean **not** operator (if you prefer you can use the symbolic operator **!**). If **data.size( )** is zero, **not data.size( )** will be **true**; otherwise the expression will evaluate to **false**.

Line 4 sets the provisional value of **maximum** to the value of **data[0]**. At this stage, we know that **data[0]** exists because we checked that there was at least one value in **data** at line 3.

Lines 5–7 loop through all the values in **data** keeping track of which is the largest so far. Notice that line 6 uses the other **max( )** function template. This is a common technique and demonstrates that the compiler can keep track of what version of an overloaded set of function templates it should use. Also notice that I have used a fully elaborated name to avoid any possible confusion with **std::max( )**. Even if there were no name collision, it is still good practice to use fully elaborated names inside template definitions. We cannot know what names may be dragged in by the function arguments of a specific function generated from a function template by providing the template type arguments.

 ## TRY THIS

Create a project to produce a program from the following version of **main( )**. You will need to add the definitions of the two function templates for **max( )** as well as including suitable headers.

```
int main( ){
  try{
    std::vector<int> data;
    std::cout << max(data);
  }
  catch(std::range_error & error){ std::cerr << error.what( );}
  catch(...){std::cerr << "Caught unknown exception\n";}
}
```

There are two things to notice about this code. Firstly, it tests the bad case where there is no data. Secondly, it demonstrates how we can deal with a specific type of exception. When provided with a list of **catch** clauses the program will use the first one that fits the exception thrown. In this case both **catch(std::range_error & error)** and **catch(...)** could deal with the exception thrown by our call of **max( )** with an empty vector. If you reverse the order, the compiler will give you an error, because **catch(...)** (i.e. catch all exceptions) must be the last **catch** clause. Note that **catch** clauses look a bit like functions with one parameter, and they behave very similarly. The C++ Standard Library exceptions support a **what( )** member function that will regurgitate whatever message was provided at the point where the exception was created.

Now try inserting some values into **data** with a few lines such as:

```
data.push_back(5);
```

Also, try modifying the program so that it has values of some other type stored in a suitable `std::vector`. Make sure you try it for `std::string`. You may notice that, unlike our previous function template for `max()`, there is no problem with ambiguity for that last case. That is because the Standard C++ Library does not provide a function template for `max()` that could be confused with the one we have written using a `std::vector<T>` parameter.

C++ Iterators

The C++ iterator is a type whose values locate another object.

> *Language Note: Most computing languages incorporate some form of implementation of the iterator concept. Some, such as Java, try to keep to minimalist support because general iterators are sources of confusion for many people. Others, such as C, provide extensive arithmetic support for manipulating iterators.*

C++ has an entire hierarchy of iterator categories built on the simple idea of an object that can store values that locate other objects. The following is a summary of the most important types of C++ iterator. Each category includes the functionality of all previously described categories. So, for example, a bidirectional iterator can be used wherever a forward iterator is required.

trivial iterator: The simplest kind of iterator, a trivial iterator, just provides the location of an object and nothing more. It is rather like a URL that we use when locating material on the World Wide Web. Given an iterator, we get the object it locates by preceding it with an * (asterisk). So if `location` is an iterator, `*location` is the object itself. The unary * operator is called the *dereference operator*, because in the context of computer science, 'dereferencing' means getting whatever is identified by a pointer or address.

> *Language Note: A C pointer that points to a single object rather than into an array is an example of a trivial iterator. Function pointers in most languages that support them will be trivial iterators. Languages such as C allow arrays of function pointers, but the individual elements of such an array are trivial pointers. We will eventually deal with pointers in C++ (which are almost identical to pointers in C).*

forward iterator: This kind of iterator can use the following operators:

- unary * to obtain the object that the iterator value locates
- -> to access a member of the object located (this will be covered when we deal with the C++ classes)
- ++ for both pre- and post-increment, to change the value stored in an iterator object to locate the next object of the kind being located by the iterator values

In addition we can compare two iterator values for equality (==) or inequality (!=).

There are two special types of forward iterator – an input iterator and an output iterator. The special feature of these iterators is that they are essentially for traversing data exactly once. The data may come from a transient source (such as a keyboard) or go to a transient destination such as a printer.

bidirectional iterator: These are iterators that add the functionality of going backwards through a sequence by using the pre- and post-decrement operators. So, for example, as long as `iter` does not locate the start of a sequence, `--iter` will locate the previous element of a sequence. There is a requirement that the decrement operation undoes an increment one and vice versa so long as the intermediate iterator values are valid.

random-access iterator: These are bidirectional iterators that also support all the operations that allow going forwards and backwards by any integral number of elements that does not take the iterator outside the sequence.

Random-access iterators support addition (+) and subtraction (-) of an integer to/from an iterator value. They also support += and -= to adjust the stored value. They support [ ] (the subscript or index operator), so `iter[n]` is equivalent to `*(iter + n)`.

Given that `iter` and `jter` are iterators into the same sequence, `n = iter - jter` is required to make the value of n such that `iter == jter + n`.

Finally < (less than) is required to be applicable to operands `iter` and `jter` that are random-access iterators into the same sequence. `iter < jter` returns **true** if and only if `iter` locates an object that is strictly before that located by `jter`. The other logical operators are defined in terms of <. So, for example: `iter > jter` is defined to be equivalent to `jter < iter`; `iter != jter` is equivalent to `((iter < jter) or (jter < iter))`; and `iter == jter` is equivalent to `(not(iter != jter))`. Note that the implication of these definitions is that iterators are only required to provide a weak ordering, and that it is possible that two iterators compare equal even though they do not locate the same object.

> *Language Note: A C++ (or C) pointer into an array — we will be dealing with these later — is an example of a random access iterator.*

Reference material: Chapter 7 of *Generic Programming and the STL* [Austern 1999] provides an in-depth study of C++ iterators.

Version of `max(std::vector)` Using an Iterator

Less experienced programmers may wish to skip this section when reading this book for the first time as it gets into some fairly advanced aspects of C++.

It is more normal in C++ to use iterators rather than values when we are dealing with collections or sequences. Given an iterator, it is easy to extract the value of the object it locates. However, given an iterator, we can do much more, such as changing the value of the object the iterator locates. Iterators generally give us access to objects rather than just values.

Here is a version of `max(std::vector<T>)` that returns an iterator to the object with the largest value.

```
1 template <typename T>
2 typename std::vector<T>::iterator max(std::vector<T> & data){
3    typename std::vector<T>::iterator maximum(data.begin( ));
4    for(typename std::vector<T>::iterator iter(data.begin( ));
5        iter != data.end( ); ++iter){
6      maximum = (*iter > *maximum ? iter : maximum);
7    }
8    return maximum;
9 }
```

WALKTHROUGH

Look carefully at line 2. Now focus on the return type of **max( )** (that is, everything before **max**). We want to return an iterator for an object that is an element of a **std::vector<T>**. The type of an iterator for a **std::vector** is provided by the definition of the **std::vector** class template (do not worry – we will deal with the details of class templates later, but for now that is just the proper name for this kind of type). The name of the type for such an iterator is **std::vector<T>::iterator** with **T** replaced by the exact type the vector contains. However, in the context of templates, the compiler needs to have it confirmed that **std::vector<T>::iterator** is the name of a type and not the name of something else such as a variable or function. That is what the **typename** does here (and why the keyword was introduced into C++ in the first place).

Line 3 just sets up an iterator to hold the location of the largest element of the vector. You may wonder why I no longer check that there are any elements. The mechanism for dealing with empty containers is that the iterator value for their start is the same as that for their end. **data.begin( )** gives the location of the start of the vector's data and **data.end( )** will give a special value that marks that there are no more elements. If the container is empty **data.begin( )** will have that same special value as **data.end( )**. One advantage of this mechanism is that we can often treat empty containers the same way as we treat all the others. As long as we do not try to access an object located by the **.end( )** iterator all will be fine.

Lines 4–7 simply loop through the container from start to finish, updating **maximum** so that it points to the element with the largest value so far. The ***iter** and ***maximum** are used so that we compare the values of the objects, not the values of the iterators. That is why we cannot call our other **max** function template: it would compare the iterators, not the objects that the iterators locate.

TRY THIS

Modify your earlier program so that it uses this function template for **max( )** to find the maximum value of the values stored in a vector. Make sure you try versions for several different types.

The fgw::read Function Templates

The Standard C++ Library has many examples of function templates. We often use them without even realizing that that is what we are doing. In many cases, the compiler can deduce the types from the function arguments used in the call. When I write **std::sort(data.begin( ), data.end( ))** the compiler recognizes that I want a specific instance of the **std::sort( )** function template that uses iterators of the type of the arguments **data.begin( )** and **data.end( )**. This is a major benefit because it provides a great deal of versatility coupled with transparency. The programmer does not have to spend time making things explicit when the compiler can deduce what we mean.

However, there is another powerful use of function templates: we can reuse a function name even when the parameter list is not sufficiently different for ordinary overloading to work. The classic case is when we want to carry out essentially the same process, with the same parameters but with different return types.

Consider the problem of getting data from some form of input; if the data provided does not match the type required the input stream fails. In effect that means that we should always check that data input succeeded. Such checks are tedious and repetitious because they are effectively the same for all types that can get values from input by using the **>>** operator.

Remember the problem of getting an **int** or a **double** from **std::cin**? Now look at the following function template (if it seems too complicated for you to have written, do not worry as you do not need to understand exactly how it does its job in order to use it):

```
1  template<typename in_type>
2  in_type read(std::string const & prompt, unsigned int max_tries = 3){
3    in_type temp(in_type());
4    unsigned int tries(0);
5    while(tries++ != max_tries){
6      std::cout << prompt;
7      std::cin >> temp;
8      if(not std::cin.eof()) eat_ws_to_eol(std::cin);
9      if(not std::cin.fail() or std::cin.eof()) return temp;
10     std::cin.clear();  // if it has failed, reset it to normal
11     std::cin.ignore(INT_MAX, '\n');  // flush cin
12     std::cout << "\n That input was incorrect, try again: \n";
13   }
14   throw fgw::bad_input("Too many attempts to read data.");
15 }
```

WALKTHROUGH

Lines 1 and 2 tell us that this is a generic function (a function template) called **read**. The template type provides the return type. The generated functions have two parameters. The first is a **std::string** that provides a prompt, and the second has a default argument that will be used if the caller does not provide a second argument. As the template type argument is only used for the return type, the compiler cannot deduce the template type argument from a call. That tells us that we will always have to provide it explicitly.

Line 3 defines a default-initialized object of the **in_type**, which we call **temp**. The **in_type()** used as an initializer in the definition of **temp** is a special syntax that tells the compiler to do whatever is appropriate to default-initialize the object. In the case of fundamental types such as **int** and **double**, this results in **temp** being initialized to zero.

Line 4 defines an object that we will use to track retries. Line 5 effectively says we should keep trying until either we succeed or we have exceeded the maximum number of tries (**3** by default).

Line 6 outputs the provided prompt to the console, and line 7 attempts to extract a suitable value from the console.

The rest of the function gets complicated and demonstrates the value of a template solution. One possibility is that input succeeded but was terminated by the user explicitly providing an end-of-file character (Ctrl+Z on a Microsoft Windows machine and Ctrl+D on a UNIX-based one). Usually users do not terminate input that way but do so by pressing the Enter key. However, users sometimes type ahead when they are familiar with a program, or add redundant spaces at the end of a response. The purpose of line 8 is to call a special function (from my library) that removes such redundant input.

Line 9 effectively says that as long as the input succeeded, the current value of **temp** (i.e. whatever was read at line 7, or possibly if the user hit the end-of-file key immediately, the default value) is returned to the caller.

We can only get to line 10 if input failed. In this case we first reset **std::cin** by calling the **clear()** function, which clears the failure flags. Next line 11 clears out all the input from the failure (that is what the call of **ignore(INT_MAX, '\n')** achieves). Line 12 provides a generic message explaining why the input was rejected. As long as the maximum number of retries has not been exceeded, the code loops back to try again.

If the maximum number of retries is exceeded, the function exits by throwing an exception of a type provided by my library.

Using read<>

The above source code is a slightly modified version of a function template that is provided in the **fgw_text.h** header file. This is one of a set of overloaded function templates to provide support in extracting data from input (the overload set includes provision for extraction from other sources, such as files). The only restriction on the type for which these function templates can be used is that they must be able to use the **>>** operator to extract data from an input source.

Eventually you will be able to write such templates, and probably improve on mine, but the important point is to be able to use them, and by doing so appreciate how templates can help with your programming. For example here is a small program to determine the biggest positive value input with **std::cin** using **fgw::read<>** function templates.

```
1 // created on 15/10/2004
2 #include "fgw_text.h"
3 #include <iostream>
4
5 int main( ){
6   try {
7     int biggest(0);
8     std::string const prompt(
9         "Type in an integer (zero or a negative value to end): "));
10    do{
11     int const i(fgw::read<int>(prompt));
12     if(i < 1) break;
13     if(biggest < i) biggest = i;
14    } while(true);
15    std::cout << "The largest number input was " << biggest << '\n';
16  }
17  catch(fgw::bad_input & except){
18    std::cerr << except.report( );
19  }
20  catch(...){
21    std::cerr << "***An exception was thrown.***\n";
22  }
23 }
```

WALKTHROUGH

By now, most of the above code should be standard. Lines 8 and 9 just move the prompt used for input outside the loop. Line 10 is the interesting line because it not only demonstrates the use of **fgw::read<>** but shows how it can be used to initialize a **const** object at run time. Line 16 is another example of catching a specific exception and dealing with it appropriately. Line 19 then provides for dealing with any other exceptions that happen even though we were not explicitly expecting them. **fgw::bad_input** objects support a function called **report( )**, which provides access to the message provided by the creation of the exception object.

Using read<> With the Default Prompt

If you call `fgw::read<>( )` without supplying any arguments, the compiler will use an overload of the function template that supplies a default prompt. Here is the definition of that function template:

```
template<typename in_type>
in_type read( ){
  return read<in_type>(": ");
}
```

Notice how easy it is to write such a definition, which simply delegates all the real work to the already-written general version. Another advantage of this is that function templates such as this one automatically acquire any improvements, bug fixes, etc. that may be acquired by the general version.

Here is the program from the start of this chapter modified to use **fgw::read<>** to get the data:

```
 1 #include "fgw_text.h"
 2 #include <iostream>
 3 #include <vector>
 4
 5 int max(int first, int second){
 6   return first > second ? first : second;
 7 }
 8
 9 int main( ){
10   try{
11     std::vector<int> data;
12     int value(0);
13     std::cout << "Type in some integers. End input with -9999\\";
14     do{
15       value = read<int>( );
16       data.push_back(value);
17     } while(value != -9999);
18     int maximum(-9999);
19     for(size_t i(0); i != data.size( ); ++i){
20       maximum = max(maximum, data[i]);
21     }
22     std::cout << "The largest input value was " << maximum << ".\";
23   }
24   catch(fgw::bad_input & except)std::cerr << except.report( );
25   catch(...)std::cerr << "\***An exception was thrown***\";
26 }
```

I have highlighted the added or modified lines. Line 1 provides the compiler with access to the definitions of the function templates for **fgw::read<>**. Line 24 explicitly deals with the exception that might result from the user repeatedly failing to supply appropriate input (perhaps their pet cat is trying a little computer use). The valuable line is line 15, which now handles invalid input almost transparently.

EXERCISES

7. Modify the above code so that you can output a sorted list of `double` values that have been supplied by keyboard input.

8. Write a program that collects a list of words from the keyboard using `fgw::read<>()` and then outputs the words in alphabetical order.

9. Modify the previous program to list the words input in reverse alphabetical order.

10. Write a program that prompts the user for two integer values and a basic arithmetical operation (+, −, *, or /) and outputs the correct answer. You will probably find a `switch` statement useful for this program as well as using `fgw::read<>` for input.

STRETCHING EXERCISES

11. The header file `line_drawing.h` for my library provides various functions for drawing lines in the Playpen window. One of the provided functions can be used as if we had declared:

```
void drawline(fgw::playpen & p,
    int beginx, int beginy, int endx, int endy);
```

(There is a defaulted parameter, of which we will learn more much later.) If `paper` is an `fgw::playpen` object, then the statement

```
fgw::drawline(paper, -10, -5, 20, 30);
```

will draw a black line from (−10, −5) to (20, 30).

Remembering that the Playpen is only updated when the display function is applied to the `fgw::playpen` object, write a program that will prompt you for coordinates (pairs of integer values) and then join each new pair (after the first one) to the previous one. Choose some suitable way to end the program.

12. If you want other colors for lines you will need to use the version of `fgw::drawline()` that can accept an `fgw::hue` argument after the coordinates. For example,

```
fgw::drawline(paper, -30, -12, 50, 13, fgw::red4);
```

will create a medium red line from (−30, −12) to (50, 13).

Modify your program from Exercise 11 so that the user is prompted for a color value (range 0 to 255) as well as for the next point. It should then draw the line from the previous point in the specified color.

Note that you will need to use `fgw::read<int>` to get the color because `fgw::read<fgw::hue>` does not work as you might expect.

REFERENCE SECTION

Function templates provide a mechanism for providing type-independent solutions to problems. A function template has two distinct sets of parameters. The first one is a non-empty list of template parameters. The second is an ordinary, perhaps empty, list of function parameters whose types may be determined by the arguments supplied to the template parameters. The return type of a function template may also depend on the template parameters.

A template parameter may be of one of three types:

template type parameter: This is specified by using either **typename** or **class** followed by the name that will be a synonym for the type argument in the remainder of the template declaration.

template value parameter: A limited number of types (mainly integer types) may be used as template value parameters. I have not covered these in this chapter, but we will see examples of such template parameters in later chapters.

template template parameter: These are way out of the scope of an introductory C++ book and are only mentioned here for completeness.

Sometimes a type that depends on a template type will be needed. In such cases the compiler requires notification by prefixing the relevant use of a type with the **typename** keyword. We had an example of this when we used iterators; the iterator type for a vector is a dependent type because it is a type that is defined as part of the definition of a vector. This concept will become clearer when we deal with user-defined types (i.e. types that are neither fundamental C++ types nor derivatives of those types).

The standard form for a function template declaration is:

> **template**<*parameter-list*>
> *return-type* **function-name**(*parameter-list*)**;**

And the form for a function template definition is:

> *return-type* **function-name**(*parameter-list*)**{**
> *body-of-function-template*
> **}**

It is usual to provide the function template definition in a header, because the compiler will need the definition to generate code for the specific template arguments used in the programmer's code. There are advanced uses of templates where bare declarations are useful.

Template Type Argument Deduction

It is often possible for the compiler to deduce the template type arguments from the function arguments when a template is used for a function call. When the compiler is left to deduce the template arguments the deduction must not be ambiguous. For example, if two function arguments have the same template type they must have the same exact type in the function call. We had examples of this restriction in the **max( )** example.

However, if the programmer elects to explicitly specify the template arguments, the normal process of conversions and promotions will be applied to the function arguments. For this reason, explicit specification of template type arguments should be done with care: the compiler will try to comply with the programmer's choice even if that was unwise.

Specialization

Sometimes it is necessary to provide special handling for a type. For example, we might have a function template that needs to handle the **std::string** type differently from other types. We had an example of this when we specialized the **max( )** function template so that we could select the 'larger' of two **std::string** values disregarding the case of the letters.

The syntax for a function-template specialization is:

```
template<>
return-type  function-name<argument-list>(parameter-list){
        code-for-this-special-case
}
```

Note that a specialization is identified by the use of an empty template parameter list and the provision of an explicit template argument list after the function name.

Overloading

More than one function template can share a name (just as more than one function can share a name) as long as the template parameter lists are different. If there is more than one function template with the same name visible to the compiler, it will attempt to determine from the context which one the programmer intends to use. If the compiler cannot determine a unique choice it will issue an ambiguity error and pass the problem back to the programmer, who will now have to resolve the ambiguity. In our example we could resolve the ambiguity by providing a fully elaborated name (i.e. by saying which namespace we want the compiler to use).

Function templates can also share their name with ordinary functions. In such cases the compiler will select an ordinary function whose parameter types exactly match the argument types provided by the call in preference to a function generated from a template.

If the template parameters have been made explicit, then only a function template can be selected. In the case where two function templates can generate code from the given explicit template arguments, the compiler will attempt to resolve the conflict by using a set of rules defined by the C++ Standard. These rules are notoriously difficult to understand and so I will not attempt to describe them here. If such code becomes important to you, you will need to study an advanced text on templates such as *C++ Templates* [Vandevoorde & Josuttis 2002].

Templated Return Type

Sometimes we want to overload a function on its return type. In general the language does not support this, because it is not possible to select from a set of candidate functions based only on a return type. However, we do sometimes want to use the same name for functions that only differ in their return type. In such cases we can use a function template coupled with explicit provision of the template arguments.

The **read<>** function templates from my library are an example of this kind of use of function templates.

Function Templates and the Standard C++ Library

Function templates are pervasive in the Standard C++ Library. The extensive use of type deduction and default arguments makes their use almost transparent to the ordinary programmer. The 80+ items in the algorithm part of the library depend on function-template technology, but you can write a great deal of C++ without realizing that it is the magic of templates that is making your code work.

Language Note: Readers with a background in dynamic and scripting languages may be surprised that I consider templates to be anything special. Many scripting and dynamically bound languages such as Perl and Python have a good deal of genericity built in. What C++ offers is the ability to write extensive code in a type-independent way. C++ was the first mainstream language to offer this facility. It has resulted in a great deal of innovation. Some of this has stretched the syntax of templates in C++ to breaking point. Even Bjarne Stroustrup, the original designer of C++, has been surprised by some of the things that templates have achieved.

CHAPTER 8

User-Defined Types, Part 1: typedef and enum

C++ provides a number of mechanisms for declaring and defining new types and new type names. These range from a simple mechanism (**typedef**) for declaring a name to be an alternative name for an existing type to mechanisms for defining entirely new types and the ways that the existing C++ operators will work with those types. In this and the next couple of chapters, I will be introducing you to these mechanisms, showing you how you have already been using them and how you can provide your own type names and types.

typedef: New Names for Old

The **typedef** keyword allows us to provide a new name for an existing type. That is all it does. The new name is a pure synonym for the old one. There are three primary reasons for wanting a new name for an existing type: opaqueness (wanting to hide what type is being used); using a more descriptive name (i.e. avoiding 'magic' types); and simplification (reducing types with several parts to their name to a single name).

I will now deal with each of these three uses of **typedef** declarations.

Opaque Type Names

Sometimes we want to be able to change the actual type used without having to modify large parts of our code. We have already had examples of that in the code earlier in this book. The Library makes extensive use of **typedef** for this purpose. For example, you will frequently come across **size_t** as the name of a type; in general, we do not need to know the exact type for which it is a synonym. The C++ Standard requires that it is one of the unsigned integer types. The exact type must be suitable for representing the count in bytes (**unsigned char**s) of any object that the implementation will support. The size of the largest possible object is implementation-defined. **unsigned long** is the most common underlying type for **size_t**, though some systems choose **unsigned int**. We will not have any problems as long as we use **size_t** in the way that the designers of C++ (and C) intend. However, we should note that **size_t** is intended for representing the amount of storage allocated for an object. Nothing in the language will prevent us from using it for other things, and, as far as the compiler is concerned, it is just another way of writing whatever the **typedef** provided by the implementation has declared it to mean.

When the implementer of the Library puts

```
typedef unsigned int size_t;
```

in a header file, the result is that `size_t` is just another name for **unsigned int** wherever it is used in code being compiled by the implementation. If you move your source code to another compiler with

```
typedef unsigned long size\_t;
```

in the header file, uses of `size_t` in your code will now be treated as meaning **unsigned long**. It is your responsibility as a programmer to ensure that your code does not depend on the precise type. As long as you use `size_t` in the intended way, there will be no problems.

    `time_t` and `clock_t` are two other opaque types from the C++ Standard. They are specifically for dealing with certain aspects of measuring time. They can be any fundamental arithmetic type – integral or floating point. The wide range of possible types that those type names can alias makes it particularly important that the programmer only use the names for the exact purpose for which they were intended. Careless or ignorant usage can result in surprises when porting code between implementations. This is a general problem with using **typedef** to create an opaque type name: it places a burden on the programmer to avoid abuse.

    In the last chapter, we had another variant of the idea of an opaque type. If you look back, you will see that I used a **typedef** to provide a single place where I could change a type used in a program. The introduction of generic programming tools into C++ has made that use much rarer. We use templates if we want to reuse the same basic code with only a type change.

Descriptive Type Names

Look at this small program:

```
#include <iostream>
#include <istream>
#include <ostream>

int main(){
  std::cout << "How old are you? ";
  int age;
  std::cin >> age;
  std::cout << "In five years you will be " << age + 5 << " years old.\n";
}
```

    Why is **int** the type of **age**? Think about that, because there are quite a few hidden assumptions floating around. For example, I never said that I wanted the user's age as an integer value. Yes, most adults would give their age in years, but children will not always do so.

    Just as experienced programmers avoid using magic numbers they also avoid using magic type names. Their reasons are much the same; they want to write code that is more self-documenting, or they want to avoid repetitive writing of complicated expressions. We prefer **pi** to **3.14159265** because the first is simpler and far less prone to error. We also prefer it because it makes it clear that we are using a specific mathematical constant rather than some arbitrary decimal value.

    We do not gain very much from writing:

```
typedef int years;
years age;
```

    Indeed, in a program as brief as the one above we gain nothing of value, but there are cases that are more complicated where there can be some benefit.

Dealing with Complicated Type Names

The names of many types used in C++ are composed of several tokens. For example, `unsigned int const *` is a four-token name for a type. There are several problems with multi-token names: they are often hard to read; given two instances, it takes time to check that they are the same type; and worst of all, C++ often allows the tokens to be reordered. In the example I have just given, all six possible orderings of `unsigned`, `int`, and `const` are allowed and are equivalent. Using a `typedef` name alleviates most of those problems.

There are also cases where a type name is just plain complicated. For example, C++ inherits the C library, and in that there is a function called `qsort( )`. `qsort( )` is intended for sorting arrays. We do not make much use of `qsort( )` in C++ because, as we have seen, C++ has a more powerful set of generic tools provided by the Library. However, it can be useful to know about such pure C functions when writing code to work in a mixed C and C++ context. The problem is that `qsort( )` needs to know what function it can use to compare members of the array. That information is provided by a function pointer passed as an argument (we will learn about function pointers in a later chapter after we have spent time on pointers). However, what is the type of the parameter that will receive that function pointer? If I told you that it was `int (*)(void const *, void const *)`, I doubt that you would be much the wiser. Such a type name is both hard to remember and useless for documentation purposes, even if you are fluent with C++ declarations. If I write the correct `typedef`, I can replace the declaration of `qsort( )` as

```
void qsort(void * base, size_t elements, size_t size,
    int (*compare)(void const *, void const *));
```

(which says that `qsort` needs four arguments: where the array starts, how many elements there are in the array, how big each element is, and something to compare them with) with:

```
void qsort(void * base, size_t elements, size_t size,
    compare_function_t compare);
```

The type of the fourth parameter in the first case is pure magic, but the second form is, I believe, much more helpful to the reader. Of course, if you need to know the details of the type of a comparison function you will have to look at the `typedef`, which is:

```
typedef int (* compare_function_t)(void const *, void const *);
```

However, you only consider that declaration when you need to, and do not have to unpick the complicated type name the rest of the time. Unpicking complicated declarations takes time and experience, so do not worry about how the above works

We will come back to `typedef`s in a later chapter, but for now you know all you need to know about them.

On Reading Declarations

C++ shares an overly complicated declaration syntax with C. Bjarne Stroustrup, the original designer of C++, has described it as an interesting experiment that failed. C++ retained the C declaration syntax for backward-compatibility with C. The cost of that compatibility is that every C++ programmer has to learn how to read these declarations, as well as how to write them when the need arises.

The secret to reading a declaration is to determine what name is being declared. This can sometimes be less than simple. However, the first step is to recognize which statements are declarations. A declaration usually starts with a type name, a type modifier (`const` or `volatile`) or a storage-class specifier (`extern`, `auto`, `static`, or `typedef`). C++ also has some special cases such as the declaration of a type name with `class`, struct, union, or enum. However, those special cases are not generally part of complicated declarations, so we do not need to consider them here.

Once you have decided that you are looking at a declaration, the next step is to determine what name is being declared. Look for the first thing that is neither a keyword nor the name of a type. Once you have found the principal name being declared, look to the right until you find an unmatched closing parenthesis. Read everything between the name and that parenthesis (we will see how in a moment). Next move to the left of the name until you find an opening parenthesis and interpret everything between the name and that parenthesis, reading from right to left. Now repeat that process by first looking to the right of the closing parenthesis found earlier and then to the left of the opening parenthesis just found. Repeat that process as often as necessary.

Here are a few examples:

- `int const * volatile ivc;`
  There is nothing to the right of `ivc`, so traverse the tokens to its left in right-to-left order. That gives us: "`ivc` is a `volatile` pointer to a `const int`."
- `double * const data[5];`
  The name being declared must be `data`. Immediately to its right is a pair of square brackets. That is read as 'array of'. The `5` tells us that the array has five elements. We have run out of items to the right of `data`, so we now read from the left of it (in a right-to-left direction) giving `const` pointers to `double`. Therefore, the whole declares that `data` is an array of five `const` pointers to `double`s.
- `double (* const data)[5];`
  Now I have inserted a pair of parentheses, which will change what we are declaring. There is a closing parenthesis directly after `data`, so we must first read what is on its left as far back as the opening parenthesis before reading the `[5]` and concluding with the `double`. That gives us: "`data` is a `const` pointer to an array of five `double`s."

If while we are searching to the right we come to an opening parenthesis, that will be the function operator, and the material from there to the corresponding closing parenthesis will be a parameter list.

- `double & (* data)(int, double, void (*)(int));`
  When we unpick that, we get: "`data` is a pointer (that is the `(* data)` part) to a function with three parameters: `int`, `double`, and a pointer to a function with one parameter of type `int` that returns a `void`. (That last parameter is the `void (*)(int)`.) The function pointed to by `data` returns a reference to a `double` (that is the initial `double &`)."

That last example is ugly. We can get even uglier if we want to declare a name for an array of pointers to functions. Fortunately, we do not need these things for most of our programming. When we do, a judicious use of `typedef` to create readable names for bits of the declaration makes it much easier both to write and to read complicated declarations. For example, if I need to declare an array of 10 pointers to functions taking an `int` and returning a `double`, I start by declaring a type name for the function pointers:

```
typedef double (* func_ptr)(int);
```

This declares `func_ptr` to be a pointer to a function that has an `int` parameter and returns a `double`. Now I can use that as a stepping stone for the declaration of the array:

```
func_ptr data[10];
```

This declares data to be an array of 10 `func_ptr`s. In other words, `data` is an array of 10 pointers to functions that have an `int` parameter and return a `double`. It is usually better to break down complicated declarations by careful uses of `typedef`.

enum

C++ has inherited a curious form of user-defined type from C. These types are created by using the keyword **enum**. If you are a C programmer, you need to be careful, because C++ has modified the rules. You should not assume that you know all the details just because you are confident of the use of **enum** in C.

We use **enum** to create a user-defined type that is restricted to integral values, and to provide (usually) one or more named enumerated values. Those named enumerators are part of the definition of an **enum** type – we cannot add them later. Any value of any **enum** type implicitly converts to an integer value. However, there is no implicit conversion in the other direction.

Suppose that I want to write a program that is concerned with different types of cloth. I might want to categorize the cloth by the type of yarn used in its manufacture. I could create a type to represent the yarns with:

```
enum yarn {cotton, linen, silk, nylon, other};
```

That definition declares **yarn** as a type name for an integer type with the five named values (or enumeration constants) **cotton**, **linen**, **silk**, **nylon**, and **other**.

I have said that an **enum** is a type with only integer values, so it makes sense to ask what the values of the enumeration constants will be. C++ provides some simple rules:

1. The value can be provided by explicitly 'assigning' it within the definition.
2. If there is no provided value for the first enumeration constant it takes the default value of zero.
3. Any other enumeration constant that is not explicitly assigned a value implicitly takes the value of the immediately preceding enumeration constant plus one.
4. Two or more enumeration constants can share a value.

When we apply those rules to the above case, we get that **cotton** is 0, **linen** is 1, **silk** is 2, **nylon** is 3, and **other** is 4. Do not just take my word for it, but try this little program to check that my assertion is correct (yes, please do so, because we will be adding things to this program over the next few paragraphs).

```
#include <iostream>
#include <ostream>

enum yarn {cotton, linen, silk, nylon, other};

int main(){
  std::cout << "cotton is " << cotton << '\n';
  std::cout << "linen is " << linen << '\n';
  std::cout << "silk is " << silk << '\n';
  std::cout << "nylon is " << nylon << '\n';
  std::cout << "other is " << other << '\n';
}
```

At this stage it might not seem very surprising that the compiler accepts this program. However, we have just asked **std::cout** to output five values of a type of which it had no prior knowledge. Behind the scenes, the compiler hunted for some way to fulfill your request. What it found was that it was allowed to convert a value of an **enum** type into the value of an **int**. It knows how to make **std::cout** handle **int** values, so the compiler went ahead and carried out the implicit conversion from **yarn** to **int**.

Now modify the definition of **yarn** to

```
enum yarn {cotton = 1, linen, silk, nylon = 3, other};
```

and run the program again. Making silk and nylon have the same value is probably not sensible in practice, but I have done so here to demonstrate that from the compiler's point of view it does not constitute a problem.

TASK 8.1

Try adding other enumeration values (e.g. for wool, rayon, satin, etc.). Experiment with both allowing complete default values (i.e. not specifying any values in the definition) and choosing values. Make sure that you try negative integral values as well as positive ones. Continue until you are happy that you understand how the values of enumeration constants are acquired.

We often find that we want to change the definition of an **enum** type by adding extra enumeration constants. When we do this, we generally do not want to disturb the values that have already been provided. Adding the new enumerators after the existing ones accomplishes that. However, there is often a catchall enumerator, such as **other** in the **yarn** example. Such catchall enumerators usually have either the smallest or the largest specified value. It is common practice to specify the value of such enumerators and insert new enumerators just before them in the definition. For example, suppose we define:

```
enum yarn {cotton, linen, silk, nylon, other = 127};
```

Now we can add a few enumerators without disturbing any of the existing values:

```
enum yarn  {cotton, linen, silk, nylon, wool, satin, other = 127};
```

The reason I chose 127 for **other** is that it gives plenty of room for extra yarns but keeps within the values that can be provided by an 8-bit **signed char**. The significance of that design decision is that it allows the compiler to use that type as the underlying type if it is optimizing for space. (Unlike C, C++ allows the compiler to choose the underlying type used to store the **enum**'s values.)

Arithmetic and enum

C++ does not provide arithmetic operators for **enum** types, though it allows programmers to provide them. Their absence is often overlooked because the implicit conversion from an **enum** type to an integer makes it appear that they exist.

TASK 8.2

Try running this program:

```
#include <iostream>
#include <ostream>

enum yarn  {cotton, linen, silk, nylon, other = 127};

int main(){
  std::cout << cotton + linen << '\n';
  std::cout << silk * nylon << '\n';
  std::cout << other / nylon << '\n';
  std::cout << silk * 4 << '\n';
}
```

Please experiment until you feel confident that C++ will evaluate expressions involving enumerators (i.e. enumeration constants).

It is not obvious at this stage that the compiler is not doing arithmetic with the enumerators but is instead converting them to some kind of integer. We need a tool to investigate what is actually happening. C++ provides such a tool via the keyword **typeid**. That keyword needs some support from the C++ Standard

Library, so we need to #include <typeinfo> when we want to use it. Applying typeid to an expression results in a type_info object. The type_info type has a member function called name() that provides a std::string value that indicates the type of the expression. The std::string value provided by calling name() on a type_info object does not necessarily result in the same name that the programmer provided for the type, but in practice it often does. However, more importantly, it does provide the same result for expressions of the same type.

Try the following program:

```
#include <iostream>
#include <ostream>
#include <typeinfo>

enum yarn {cotton, linen, silk, nylon, other = 127};

int main(){
  std::cout << "The type of 'yarn' is "
       << typeid(yarn).name() << '\n';
  std::cout << "The type of 'cotton' is "
       << typeid(cotton).name() << '\n';
  std::cout << "The type of 'cotton + linen' is "
       << typeid(cotton + linen).name() << '\n';
  std::cout << "The type of 'int' is "
       << typeid(int).name() << '\n';
  std::cout << "The type of 'cotton || linen' is "
       << typeid(cotton || linen).name() << '\n';
}
```

Once again, experiment with other expressions until you feel able to predict the results. However, note that as soon as you attempt to do arithmetic with enumerators you get expressions whose type is not that of the enumerator.

The results of using enumerators for arithmetic are clearly reasonable. Trying to add two yarns together or multiplying a yarn by an integer makes no immediate sense (as a yarn). In other circumstances, some arithmetic operations might make sense for an enum type. We will see shortly that there are various ways to provide arithmetic with enum values.

We already know that enumerators implicitly convert to integer values when we use them in contexts where the numerical value can help. The following short program demonstrates that C++ does not allow conversions in the opposite direction.

Try to compile the following program:

```
#include <iostream>
#include <ostream>

enum yarn {cotton, linen, silk, nylon, other = 127};

int main(){
  yarn thread1(cotton);
```

```
        thread1 = nylon;
        yarn thread2(4);
        thread1 = 4;
        thread1 = cotton + silk;
    }
```

Notice which lines generate errors and note the exact nature of the error.

The above task demonstrates that we can have variables of type **yarn**, but we can only initialize those variables with enumerators. In addition, the only assignments we are allowed are ones where the value being assigned has the correct type. We cannot assign an **int** value to a **yarn** variable.

Sometimes we want to be able to overrule the compiler, perhaps because we know that the numerical value correctly represents a value of the **enum**. The programmer can take responsibility for the conversion by using a cast. C++ has a well-designed hierarchy of casts (explicit conversions), but in the case of converting integer values to an **enum** value I find a modification of the C-style cast is sufficiently expressive. Here is the previous code amended so that it will compile and run:

```
int main( ){
  yarn thread1(cotton);
  thread1 = nylon;
  yarn thread2 = yarn(4);
  thread1 = yarn(4);
  thread1 = yarn(cotton + silk);
}
```

The expressions **yarn(4)** and **yarn(cotton + silk)** are examples of function-style casts. They instruct the compiler to treat the value of the expression in the parentheses as a value of the type before the parentheses. In this case, they tell the compiler to treat **4** and **cotton + silk** as **yarn**s. That is clear nonsense, but if the programmer wants to do that, the compiler will allow it, as long as the programmer takes responsibility by using a cast.

In the example code, the expressions I cast to **yarn** give values that are one of the enumerators. However, it is fair to ask what would happen if I wrote something such as:

```
thread1 = yarn(16);
```

The answer is that the compiler must accept such a statement as long as the value is within a permitted range. The rule for determining the permitted range is a little complicated but effectively says that you should first determine how many bits are needed to express all the enumerated values (in the case of **yarn**, that is 7, the number of bits needed to express **127**). Any value expressible with that number of bits is allowed. The compiler is not required to diagnose attempts to use values outside the range; if the programmer uses any such value, the consequences can be anything (i.e. undefined behavior).

Operator Overloading

C++ allows programmers to redefine most operators as long as at least one of the operands is of a user-defined type. In other words, programmers are not allowed to redefine the meaning of an operator for a fundamental type. Not all operators can be redefined, and some of those that can have special conditions placed on the contexts in which they can be redefined. We will be going into those in more detail in later chapters. However, I want to introduce you to the general principles of redefining an operator. C++ calls this process *operator overloading*, because the redefinition adds new meanings to existing operators.

The rules of C++ allow programmers to do completely silly things when overloading operators. However, just because you are allowed to do silly things does not mean that you should do so. The fundamental design guideline for overloading operators is that the new definition should not cause a domain expert any surprises. For example, if you redefine the + operator for your type the result should recognizably be some kind of addition.

We overload operators by writing functions with special names. These special names are composed of two tokens; the first is the keyword **operator**, and the second is the operator symbol.

Very few operators make any sense in the context of our **yarn** type. However, we might want to be able to write something such as

```
for(yarn i(cotton); i != other; ++i){
  // process a type of yarn
}
```

to deal with all the possible values of **yarn** apart from the catchall **other**. If you try to compile code that includes the above loop, the compiler will indicate an error, because there is no available pre-increment operator for **yarn**. This is one of the cases where the implicit conversion of a **yarn** value to an **int** value will not help. The compiler can increment the resulting **int** value, but cannot write that value back to **i** because there is no implicit conversion from **int** to **yarn**.

We could rewrite the loop as:

```
for(yarn i(cotton); i != other; i = yarn(i + 1)){
  // process a type of yarn
}
```

However, that introduces another problem because the loop will iterate over all the values from 0 to 126 inclusive, even though most of those values do not represent actual enumerators of **yarn**. We need a definition of pre-increment for **yarn**. Here is a possible one:

```
yarn & operator++(yarn & y){
  if(y >= nylon) y = other;
  else if(y < cotton) y = other;
  else y = yarn(y + 1);
  return y;
}
```

Study that definition carefully. The first point to note is that it has a reference parameter: **operator++** needs an lvalue for its operand, because it has to modify the stored value. The choice of a reference type for the return value is not essential but ensures that it works the same way that **operator++** works for fundamental types. Unless there are special reasons to do otherwise, it is good practice to make operator overloads work like the built-in versions, as far as possible. Inside the body of the definition, we first check that the value being incremented is neither the value of the largest ordinary enumerator, nor already too big. If it is, we set the value to our catchall enumerator, **other**. Then we check to see that we do not have a value that is less than the smallest provided enumerator. If the provided value is too small, we set the result to the catchall value. In any other case we increment to the next enumerator. We assume that the enumerators are consecutive and do not include repeated values.

TRY THIS

Try the following program that tests out our overloaded `operator++` for `yarn`:

```
#include <iostream>
#include <ostream>

enum yarn {cotton, linen, silk, nylon, other = 127};

yarn & operator++(yarn & y){
  if(y >= nylon) y = other;
  else if(y < cotton) y = other;
  else y = yarn(y + 1);
  return y;
}

int main( ){
  for(yarn i(cotton); i != other; ++i){
    std::cout << i << '\n';
  }
}
```

There are several problems with the above source code. The first is that any time we add a new enumerator to `yarn` we have to change the definition of `operator++(yarn &)`. We should try to avoid this kind of maintenance problem. We can solve that problem by adding an extra enumerator to mark the end of our meaningful enumerators. For example:

```
enum yarn {cotton, linen, silk, nylon, end_of_yarns, other = 127};
```

We insert any extra enumerators directly before `end_of_yarns`; that way, `end_of_yarns` will always have a value that is one more than the largest legitimate value.

We next modify the definition of `operator++(yarn &)` to:

```
yarn & operator++(yarn & y){
  if(y < cotton) y = other;
  else if(y < (end_of_yarns - 1)) y = yarn(y + 1);
  else y = other;
  return y;
}
```

Please note the changed logic of the definition. Make sure you understand how and why it does what we want. Also note that `end_of_yarns` is treated as a special case and is not treated as a `yarn`.

 **TASK 8.5**   **Verify that the modifications produce the same result as for the definition of `main( )` used above. Try adding some more `yarn` enumerators and check that the program provides the correct output without any changes to the definition of `operator++(yarn &)`.**

Another Overloaded Operator

Perhaps you are wondering whether we could get the output to provide a name instead of a number. To do this we need to do two things. First, we need to store the names of the yarns somewhere (the compiler converts the enumerators into binary for the benefit of the program and thereby discards the names we provided). Probably the simplest way to do this is by defining an array of strings to hold the names and initializing it with the names we are using:

```
char const * yarn_names[ ] = {"cotton", "linen", "silk", "nylon"};
```

C programmers will be familiar with how this definition works. For everyone else, the definition declares **yarn_names** as an array (that is the **[ ]**) of pointers to **const char**. The use of empty square brackets is the way we instruct the compiler to use the number of initializers to determine the size of the array. The advantage is that the array size will automatically adjust if we add extra names. Currently we have provided four string literals as initializers (that is the significance of the pair of braces).

The second thing we need to do is to provide a new overload for **operator<<** which works when the left operand is a **std::ostream** (output) object and the right operand is a **yarn**. Here is a suitable definition:

```
std::ostream & operator<< (std::ostream & out, yarn const & y){
  if(y < cotton) out << "unknown value";
  else if(y < (end_of_yarns)) out << yarn_names[y];
  else out << "unknown value";
  return out;
}
```

TASK 8.6 Add the definition of **yarn_names** and the definition of the overload of **operator<<** to the source code for the previous task. Compile and run it to check that the output is now a list of names rather than numbers.

Overloading the Input Operator

This one is rather more difficult because we have to deal with the problems of incorrect input. For example, what will we do if the user starts an otherwise valid name of a **yarn** with an uppercase letter? I am going to provide a bare-minimum implementation that assumes the user always provides valid input. I then invite you to add code to make the implementation more robust.

```
std::istream & operator>> (std::istream & in, yarn & y){
  std::string input;
  in >> input;
  for(int i(cotton); i != end_of_yarns; ++i){
    if(input == yarn_names[i]){
      y=yarn(i);
      return in;
    }
  }
  y=other;
}
```

TASK 8.7   Type in the above definition for `operator>>`. Now use the following definition of `main()` to test that the operator works as expected.

```
int main(){
  yarn y;
  std::cout << "Please type in a yarn name: ";
  std::cin >> y;
  std::cout << y;

}
```

Now use the standard library function `std::tolower` to process the input so that the use of uppercase letters will be handled gracefully.

Note that the way I handled erroneous input means that any code that uses the overloaded `operator>>` can easily check whether the input was or was not a valid yarn name. In this case, we do not need to throw an exception to notify the user of invalid input: we can leave it to the user to check whether the variable being read into now contains the special enumerator value **other**. This is a perfectly reasonable way to handle erroneous input in this case. Do not get fixated on using exceptions as the only way to deal with problems.

EXERCISE

The purpose of the following is to provide you with some practical work that uses the ideas you have encountered in this chapter. It is important for your later progress that you complete this work because we will be building on it in future chapters.

Ordinary playing cards have two principle attributes: each one has a denomination and belongs to a suit. The denomination is one of ace, king, queen, jack, ten, nine, eight, seven, six, five, four, three, and two; the suit is one of club, diamond, heart, and spade. We could use the numbers from 0 to 51 to identify the 52 cards of a standard pack. For the time being, ignore the possibility of jokers. Some games use multiple packs. Either we can allow for repeated numbers in the range 0 to 51, or we can allow the use of higher numbers and reduce them modulo 52. That is, for a game using four full packs, we could either allow each of the values from 0 to 51 to occur four times, or we could make the range of numbers be 0 to 207. In the latter case, the first step in identifying a card will be to apply %52 to a card number to get down to the range 0 to 51.

Focusing on a single pack (i.e. with card values limited to 0 to 51), there are two strategies for determining attributes for a specific card value. We could imagine that the pack has been sorted so that the first 13 cards are the clubs in sequence, the next 13 are the diamonds, and so on. Now the result of dividing a card value by 13 will identify a suit and the result of using %13 (modulo 13) on the card value will identify the denomination.

Alternatively we could imagine sorting a pack so that the four aces are on top (in the order clubs, diamonds, hearts, spades), followed by the four twos in the same order, and so on. With that organization, we divide by 4 to determine the denomination and use %4 to determine the suit.

Of course, there are other logical ways to organize the 52 cards, as well as many illogical ones. I am only giving you some guidance so that you can focus on the main part of this exercise. You might also consider using a **typedef** to make `card_value` a type name for some suitable integer type.

To complete this exercise you need to write code so that the `main()` below takes a number from 0 to 51 as input and outputs the name of the card that that number represents. For example, assuming you elect to organize your pack in suits rather than in denominations, 37 would represent the Queen of Hearts ($37/13 = 2$, 37 modulo $13 = 12$), assuming that each suit is sorted as ace, two, three, ..., jack, queen, king.

To achieve the desired end you will need to define a suitable `enum` for suits and another for denominations. You will need to provide a function that given a card value returns a suit value. You will need a second function that given a card value returns a denomination.

You will also need to overload `operator<<` for both suit and denomination so that the result of sending values of those types to an output stream is the desired word.

```cpp
int main(){
  try{
    int card(
        read<int>("Please input a card value in the range 0 to 51"));
    card %= 52;  // force into correct range
    std::cout << card << " represents the " << get_denomination(card)
        << " of " << get_suit(card) << "s.\n";
  }
  catch(...){std::cerr << "An exception was thrown.\n"; }
}
```

You are free to modify this test program, which is only provided to help you focus on the design and implementation of the two `enums`.

STRETCHING EXERCISE

If you are an experienced programmer who wants to try something rather more difficult, try to add an `operator>>` for each of the two `enums` you provided for the previous exercise. Once you have done that, try to write a `read_card` function that will extract a named card from input and convert that to a card value.

REFERENCE SECTION

typedef

The C++ keyword **typedef** is used to provide a synonym for an existing type. The existing type can be any fundamental type, derived type or user-defined type (including types derived from user-defined types). The main uses of **typedef** are to provide a type name that identifies the way a simple type is being used and to provide a simple name for a complicated type such as the type of a function.

C++ provides a number of **typedef** names in the Standard Library. The most common of these is `size_t`, which is used as the name of whichever unsigned integer type an implementation uses for values representing the size (in bytes, i.e. **unsigned char**) of the memory footprint of a type or variable. Other Standard Library `typedef`s include `time_t` and `clock_t`, which name the types used for values representing time and clock ticks since program start.

There is a POSIX convention that `typedef` names end in `_t`. Unfortunately, for reasons that seemed good to the designers, that convention is not always adhered to in C++. For example, `wchar_t` is provided by a `typedef` in C but is a fundamental type in C++. There are also numerous places where C++ uses `typedef`s to assist with writing generic code where the names provided do not end in `_t`.

The most important point to note about `typedef` is that it does not create a new type, just a new name for an existing type.

enum

C++ uses the keyword `enum` to create new integer types with a specified set of enumerated values. As well as the enumerated values, all values in a range determined by the number of bits needed to represent the enumerators (in binary) are valid values for the `enum`. The language provides for assignment of an `enum` value to a variable of the same `enum` type. It also provides an implicit conversion from an `enum` value to an `int` value. It does not supply any other operators for `enum` types, nor does it allow implicit conversion from an `int` value to an `enum`.

We must provide the enumerators for an `enum` as part of the definition of the `enum`. Unless explicitly stated as part of the definition, the first enumerator in the provided list will have zero as its value and subsequent enumerators will each have a value of one more than the immediately preceding one.

For example,

```
enum x {red, green, blue};
```

would result in **red** having a value of **0**, **green** having a value of **1**, and **blue** being **2**, whereas

```
enum color {red = 1, green, blue = 4};
```

would result in **red** being **1**, **green** being **2**, and **blue** being **4**.

The language allows more than one enumerator to have the same value. For example,

```
enum color {red = 1, crimson = 1, green, blue = 4, azure = 4};
```

is all right as far as the C++ language is concerned.

Note that the final semicolon is required to end a definition of a new type. Strictly speaking, we could declare a variable or function name between the closing brace of the definition and the semicolon that closes the declaration statement. However, no experienced programmer would use that facility today, though C programmers often used it in days gone by.

Because `enum` provides a true type rather than just a type name, C++ allows the programmer to define meanings for most of the language's operators when applied in a context with at least one operand of the `enum` type. Using the ability to overload operators for `enum` types is not very common but, as long as you limit yourself to places where it makes sense, it is a useful tool for writing clearer source code.

CHAPTER 9

User-Defined Types, Part 2: Simple classes (value types)

The class is a key design and development tool in C++. It comes in several forms and, for historical reasons, three keywords are used to provide user-defined class types. These are **struct** (inherited from C), **class** (introduced in the early development of 'C with classes', which was to become C++), and **union** (a restricted form of class used to minimize memory usage on some systems that have very limited resources). **union** user-defined types are rare these days; they are not generally used except in memory-constrained embedded programming and possibly in low-level library design.

The class concept has two major branches: value types and entity types. C++ uses the same mechanisms for both, which burdens the programmer with understanding the difference. A typical value type is one where you would naturally use copies for arguments when calling a function or for returning data from a function. An entity type is one where copying would normally be an error, and the natural usage would be to use references for both parameters and return from a function. We normally talk about the 'state' of an entity rather than its 'value'. We reserve the latter term for value types. Another way of viewing this distinction is that the identity of an instance of an entity type is significant, whereas only the stored representation is significant for a pure value type. If you find these distinctions hard to understand, wait till you have more experience and then come back to them.

Some languages force us to treat everything as an entity; some languages try to provide a clear separation between value types and entity types. In reality, few things are purely values or purely entities; the context of use needs consideration. The major distinction is in how we choose to use them. Java insists that all the fundamental types are value types and fails to provide a mechanism for using an instance of a fundamental type as an entity. Smalltalk insists that everything is an entity, which leaves us with problems for situations where we clearly want a value. C++ leaves it up to programmers to use things the way they want to. That places a heavy burden on the programmer to select the right behavior. We will see in the next chapter that C++ provides a mechanism for switching off copy semantics (behavior), which results in preventing the resulting type from being a value type – value types are inherently copiable. However, it is not wrong for an entity type to have copy semantics.

There is very little technical difference between declaring user-defined types with the **class** keyword as opposed to **struct**. We will see later that it is customary to limit the use of **struct** to highlight a small subgroup of user-defined types whose data is accessible in the scope of the definition of the type.

We already know that a type usually consists of two elements: memory, which can store a bit pattern representing a value or state; and behavior, which specifies how values of the type can be used and modified. In general, it is only the second element that is of concern to the user of a type. You generally have no need to know how values are stored; you only need to know what you can do with them.

In this chapter, I am going to present the design and implementation of two value types. I am writing up each separately so that you can study either or both as and when you want to. Either example provides the basics of designing and implementing a value type. The two types are a representation of ISBNs (International Standard Book Numbers) and a representation of playing cards. The second of these highlights the need to understand the context of a design, because a playing card can be either an entity or a value type depending on the purpose for which you are designing the type.

ISBN as a class Type

I am starting this chapter with example source code before discussing the technical details. If you prefer, you can study this example in parallel with the technical explanation given in the reference section. This class provides a suitable type for dealing with the ISBN-10 numbering of books. ISBN-13 is scheduled to replace this from January 1st, 2007. ISBN-10 is a simple nine-digit code plus a check 'digit' (I have placed that in quotes because 'X' is also used as a check digit). We calculate the check value by multiplying each of the first nine digits by its place in the sequence, adding those results, and calculating the remainder when divided by 11. 'X' represents a remainder of 10.

For example, 0-470-86398-6 is the ISBN of *You Can Do It!* The following computation validates the number as a valid ISBN:

$$0 \times 1 + 4 \times 2 + 7 \times 3 + 0 \times 4 + 8 \times 5 + 6 \times 6 + 3 \times 7 + 9 \times 8 + 8 \times 9$$

$$= 8 + 21 + 40 + 36 + 21 + 72 + 72 = 270$$

270 divided by 11 is 24 remainder 6. The remainder agrees with the check digit.

There are elaborate rules for determining where the hyphens go when displaying an ISBN, but I am going to keep this simple by ignoring the punctuation.

```
1 #include <iostream>
2 #include <istream>
3 #include <ostream>
4 #include <string>
5
6 class isbn10{
7 public:
8    isbn10();
9    explicit isbn10(std::string const &);
10   ~isbn10();
11   bool is_valid()const;
12   void send_to(std::ostream & = std::cout)const;
13   void get_from(std::istream & = std::cin);
14   bool is_equal(isbn10 const &)const;
15 private:
16   std::string isbn_;
17 };
```

Lines 1–4 give the headers that the compiler will need in order to accept the rest of the source code. Line 6 states that the following lines up to the closing semicolon on line 17 are the definition of a type called isbn10. In the context of declaring type names and defining them (for consistency with C) C++ allows the use of **struct** instead of **class**.

The label **public:** on line 7 introduces a section of the definition that declares the behavior that is associated with instances of isbn10. This part is often referred to as the 'public interface' of the class because it specifies how instances of the class interact with code outside the class.

The label **private:** on line 15 introduces a section of the definition (the 'private interface') that consists of declarations of names that are inaccessible outside the implementation of the class. The most common items for the private interface are one or more declarations of data members, i.e. the types of storage for holding the data for a specific instance.

C++ calls the keywords **public** and **private** *access specifiers*, because they determine who has access to (can use) the names declared in the relevant section. Names declared as **public** can be used by anyone, but names declared as **private** can only be used in the context of implementing the class. There is one further access specifier, **protected**, which we will come to in Chapter 11. There is also a keyword, **friend**, used to grant full access to another class or function.

The public interface of **isbn10** consists of declarations of member functions, and the private interface consists of a declaration of a single data member that we will use to store an ISBN. While the interfaces can include other declarations, it is very rare that a well-designed class has any data members in its public interface.

WALKTHROUGH

The **isbn10** Public Interface

Lines 8 and 9 declare two special functions whose purpose is creating **isbn10** instances. They are called constructors, and we identify them by the use of the class name. Constructors do not have return types, because they are essentially procedures for creating new instances of the class (even though C++ still calls them member functions). The first one (line 8) is a default constructor – the term applied to any constructor that can create an instance without any data being provided.

The second constructor, **isbn10(std::string const &)**, will provide the way of creating an **isbn** instance from a **std::string**. We do not want the compiler to hijack this constructor as an implicit way to convert a **std::string** into an **isbn10**. That is the purpose of the **explicit** qualifier. It forbids the compiler to use the constructor as an implicit conversion from the type of the parameter to the class type. Any constructor can be qualified as **explicit**, but the qualification is only significant for constructors that can create an instance from a single argument (i.e. where any parameters after the first have default arguments provided). C++ does not allow **explicit** qualification of anything else (such as conversion operators).

Line 10 provides a declaration of the destructor. Like constructors, the destructor is a procedure (for destroying an instance of the class) and has no return type. We identify the destructor by preceding the class name with a tilde (~). Unlike constructors, there can be only one destructor, i.e. destructors cannot be overloaded.

Line 11 provides a mechanism for validating the data stored in an instance as a well-formed ISBN. We need such functionality unless we are going to forbid an **isbn10** instance from holding an incorrect ISBN.

Lines 12 and 13 declare a pair of functions to deal with output and input of **isbn10** values. I have provided default arguments for convenience.

Finally, we have a function to compare two **isbn10** values to see whether they are the same.

You may wonder why the declarations of **is_equal( )**, **is_valid( )**, and **send_to( )** each end with **const**. When **const** is attached at the end of the declaration of a member function, we are telling the compiler that the function will not change the value stored in an instance that uses it. That declaration has two effects. The first is that we can call such functions for immutable instances (ones we have declared as **const** or references/pointers that have acquired a **const** qualifier). The second effect is that the compiler will check the definition of that member function to ensure that it does not change the value.

In summary, the behavior of an isbn10 object is that one can be created either from nothing or from a std::string (passed as a const reference), we can check that the stored value is a valid ISBN, we can check that two isbn10 values are the same, we can extract data for an isbn10 from a std::istream, and we can write it out to a std::ostream object.

The compiler implicitly supplies two other pieces of public behavior if we do not do so explicitly. These are the copy constructor and the copy-assignment operator. Those two members allow us to create a new instance as a copy of existing one, and to replace the current value of an instance by the value found in a second instance. I will provide examples of copying when we come to write code to test isbn10.

Implementing isbn10

In addition to the lack of a return type, constructors have another piece of special syntax to support the initialization of an instance at the point of creation. The following implementations for the constructors illustrate it better than words:

```
isbn10::isbn10( ):isbn_("0-00-000000-0"){
   std::cout << "Default isbn10 instance constructed.\n";
}

isbn10::isbn10(std::string const & isbn):isbn_(isbn){
   std::cout << "isbn10 instance constructed and initialized with "
       << isbn_ << ".\n";
}
```

Initialization happens before executing the body of a constructor. After the closing parenthesis of the parameter list there may be a colon followed by a comma-separated list of initializers; this is followed by the opening brace of the constructor's body. (In this case, there is only one initializer, so there are no commas.) Other member data is dealt with in accordance with the rules for implicit initialization, in the context of where the constructor is used. There need not be any code in the bodies of these constructors. To help you learn about what is happening, I have provided code that makes uses of constructors visible.

```
isbn10::~isbn10( ){
   std::cout << "isbn10 instance with value " << isbn_ << " destroyed.\n";
}
```

The definition of the destructor is even simpler. Indeed, I would normally leave the compiler to do it for me. Just as for the two functions that provide for copying, the compiler will generate a destructor if I do not explicitly declare one. Once again, I am providing some instrumentation so that you can see when the destructor is used.

```
1 bool isbn10::is_valid( )const{
2    if(isbn_.size( ) < 10) return false;
3    std::string compressed("");
4    int count(0);
5    for(unsigned int i(0); i != isbn_.size( ); ++i){
6       if(std::isdigit(isbn_[i])){
7          compressed += isbn_[i];
8          ++count;
```

```
 9      }
10      else if((count == 9) and (isbn_[i] == 'X')){
11        compressed += isbn_[i];
12        ++count;
13      }
14    }
15    if(count != 10) return false;
16    int total(0);
17    for(int i(0); i != 9; ++i){
18      total += (i + 1) * (compressed[i] - '0');
19    }
20    total %= 11;
21    char check('X');
22    if(total < 10) check = '0' + total;
23    return (check == compressed[9]);
24 }
```

The function that checks an ISBN for validity is by far the most complicated piece of implementation of isbn10. I have written it so that it makes no assumptions about what we have actually stored as an ISBN. Line 2 checks that there are at least 10 characters. As there are 10 symbols in an ISBN, ignoring hyphens and other punctuation, line 2 rejects all cases where there are definitely too few characters.

Lines 3–14 create a new **std::string** called **compressed**, which only includes those characters we use in computing and checking the check digit. Note the special handling (lines 10–13) of the symbol representing the check digit.

Line 15 rejects any case where **compressed** is the wrong length. Lines 16–20 compute the check sum for the first nine digits. Note that line 18 makes use of the requirement in C++ that the **char** codes for the digits are consecutive and in ascending order; subtracting the **char** code for zero from a digit code gives the numerical value of the digit. Line 20 reduces **total** to the remainder when divided by **11**.

Line 21 creates storage for the checksum and pre-initializes it to the special case of **'X'**. Line 22 creates the correct **char** value for the check values that are actually digits.

Finally, line 23 returns the result of comparing the actual check digit with the computed one.

This definition is far from being industrial-strength. It assumes that any characters ignored in creating the compressed version were legitimate characters for an ISBN. It also does not attempt to check that hyphens have been correctly placed according to the full rules for the ISBN format. Finally, the code uses **10** and **9** as magic values. I am leaving it as an option for readers to improve the quality of the code.

```
void isbn10::send_to(std::ostream & out)const{
  out << isbn_;
}

void isbn10::get_from(std::istream & in){
  in >> isbn_;
}

bool isbn10::is_equal(isbn10 const & rhs)const{
  return (isbn_ == rhs.isbn_);
}
```

The output, input and comparison-for-equality functions simply delegate the processes to the corresponding processes for **std::string**.

TRY THIS

First create a new project (call it **isbn**), and add files **isbn_test.cpp** and **isbn10.cpp** to it. In addition, create a header file called **isbn10.h** and write a suitable header guard to it. Add the header includes and the definition of **isbn10** to **isbn10.h**. Next, add the implementation (definitions of member functions) to **isbn10.cpp**, compile it, and correct any typos or omissions. You will discover that the compiler insists on knowing the definition of **isbn10** before it will compile the implementation. You provide that definition by adding **#include "isbn10.h"** to the beginning of **isbn10.cpp**.

Now write the following code into **isbn_test.cpp**:

```
#include "isbn10.h"

int main(){
  try{
    isbn10 book;
    isbn10 book1("0-470-84674-7");
    book.send_to();
    std::cout << '\n';
    book1.send_to(std::cout);
    std::cout << '\n';
  }
  catch(...){std::cerr << "Program terminated with an exception.\n"; }
  return 0;
}
```

Compile this file, then build the program and run the result. Study the output until you understand how it relates to the code you have written. In particular, note the destructors called for the two instances of **isbn10**; destruction happens in reverse order to construction.

Testing Code

Every experienced programmer understands the value of testing code. This is particularly important when developing user-defined types. We keep the tests and rerun them whenever we make changes to the design or implementation. One of the major purposes of these tests is to ensure that such changes do not break existing code.

Now the little test program you have just tried does not test all the public behavior of **isbn10**. Here are a few statements that you can add to extend the tests to give better coverage of **isbn10** behavior:

1. Add the following:

```
std::cout << "book instance is " << std::boolalpha
    << book.is_valid() << '\n';
```

std::boolalpha changes the way **bool** values are output (and input). By default, **bool** values are output as 0 and 1. Sending **std::boolalpha** to the output stream results in **bool** values being displayed as text. The default text versions of the output are 'false' and 'true', but they can be changed by using the locale mechanisms provided to support internationalization. We can force the stream back to numerical output of `bool` values by using `std::noboolalpha`. Entities such as `std::boolalpha` and `std::noboolalpha` are example of `iostream` manipulators. Manipulators change the behavior of a stream. Note that the behavior change is specific to the stream. You can test this assertion by following the above line with:

```
std::cerr << "book instance is " << book.is_valid() << '\n';
```

Numerical (0 or 1) output results from the second statement, because changing the behavior of `std::cout` has no impact on the behavior of `std::cerr`, even though they both default to outputting to the console window.

2. Add this:

```
std::cout << "The assertion that book and book1 are the same is "
    << book.is_equal(book1) << ".\n";
```

Note that as long as this statement comes after the statement for 1 above, `std::cout` remembers that it is to use text for `bool` values.

3. Precede the statement above with:

```
book = book1;
```

Note the change in the output. This statement has used the compiler-generated implementation for `operator=()`. I will write more about operators in a moment.

4. Try this statement:

```
book = "0-304-36686-2";
```

When you add this statement, the compiler issues a diagnostic because you have not provided an implicit conversion from a `std::string` to an `isbn10` value. There are three ways to fix this problem:

(a) Remove the `explicit` qualifier from the second constructor in the definition of `isbn10`, and change the right-hand side to `std::string("0-304-36686-2");`.

(b) Explicitly convert the string literal to an `isbn10` by modifying the right-hand side to `isbn10("0-304-36686-2")`.

(c) Write an overload for the assignment operator that has an `isbn10` object on its left and a string literal on its right.

Try (a) with and without the change to the test statement. My purpose is to demonstrate that without the `explicit` qualifier a constructor can convert implicitly from its parameter type to the type it is constructing. However, such implicit conversions only work through one level of conversion. A string literal is not a `std::string` even though it implicitly converts to one. To go direct from a string literal to an `isbn10` would require an intermediate implicit conversion to a `std::string` and that is not supported by C++. (Well, it is in some cases for fundamental types, but they represent a special case.) The compiler is allowed to use only one level of user-defined conversion implicitly.

Option (b) is a much better option: not only tell the compiler explicitly what you want, but also let others reading our code see what we expect.

We will have a look at option (c) when we look at writing our own overloads of the assignment operator.

5. Insert these two statements:

```
std::cout << "Please type in an ISBN: ";
book.get_from();
```

Build the resulting program and execute it.

EXERCISE

1. Use the ideas and experience of the above tests of `isbn10` to write a program that tests all the current behavior of `isbn10`. Make sure that you test all the different results that may occur when using the member functions. Ideally, we encapsulate each test in a separate function and call these functions from `main( )`.

Overloading Operators

We normally use == when comparing two values for equality. C++ provides a mechanism whereby for many operators we can define how they behave when one of the operands is a user-defined type (such as an **enum** or class type). We first saw that in the last chapter, when we defined the way that a couple of operators worked for an **enum** type.

When we deal with a class type, we will normally have the choice of providing the operator overload either as a member function or as a free function. When we provide an operator overload as a member function, the first operand (or only operand if the operator takes only one) will implicitly be an instance of the class type. Some operators (e.g. assignment) can only be overloaded by member functions, and a few cannot be overloaded at all. Overloading operators is one of the strengths of C++; it allows us to design classes that use the same mechanisms that a domain expert would expect. Avoid the temptation to overload operators if doing so does not result in code that is naturally readable by those working in the problem domain.

I generally avoid writing member functions to overload operators unless there is a compelling reason to do so. My style is to write an ordinary member function that provides the functionality and then write a free operator overload that delegates the work to the member function. So I would provide the equality operator by adding the following (inline) definition to `isbn10.h`:

```
inline bool operator==(isbn10 const & lhs, isbn10 const & rhs){+
  return lhs.is_equal(rhs);
}
```

I leave it to the reader to add a suitable definition of `!=` for `isbn10` values.

In the same way, we can easily add suitable streaming operators for `isbn10`. However, this time we do not have an option of providing them as member functions, because the left operand is an instance of a type from the Standard Library. Remember that operators provided by member functions are limited to cases where the left-hand (or only) operand is of the correct class type. Here are the overloads for the streaming operators for `isbn10`:

```
inline std::istream & operator>>(std::istream & in, isbn10 const & val){
  val.get_from(in);
  return in;
}
inline std::ostream & operator<<(std::ostream & out, isbn10 const & val){
  val.send_to(out);
  return out;
}
```

EXERCISES

2. Add the above operator overloads to `isbn10.h` and then write tests for each of them.

3. Write a short program that uses `fgw::read<std::string>()` and `fgw::read<isbn10>()`, and note the differences between the two when they are executed. (You will need to include `fgw_text.h` and you will need to tell the compiler where to look for that by adjusting the project settings to add a suitable include directory into the project. The default location – if you accepted the CD's installation defaults – is `C:\tutorial\fgw_headers`.)

4. Find out about ISBN-13, and design, implement, and test a new type called `isbn13`.

A Value Type for Playing Cards

In the following, I am taking the view of playing cards as values that can be freely copied. This would not be a suitable view if I were designing, for example, a program to play poker, where a card needs to have a unique existence. Then I would view a playing card as an entity (which we will do in the next chapter). Here is my initial definition of **card_value**:

```cpp
#include <iostream>
#include <ostream>

class card_value{
public:
  card_value();
  explicit card_value(int);
  card_value(card_value const &);
  ~card_value();
  card_value & operator=(card_value const &);
  std::ostream & send_to(std::ostream &)const;
private:
  int data;
};

int main(){
  try{
    card_value any;
    card_value specific(1);
    card_value another(specific);
    any.send_to(std::cout);
    specific.send_to(std::cout);
    another.send_to(std::cout);
    any = specific;
    any.send_to(std::cout);
  }
  catch(...){
    std::cerr << "An exception was thrown.\n";
  }
}
```

When you try to compile this code (yes, please do enter it to your system and try it), it should compile successfully. However, if you try to link it to produce an executable, you will get a multitude of linker errors. So far, I have declared some member functions as part of the definition of class `card_value`, but I have not provided definitions for those member functions.

Before we tackle that, let us look at the source code above. The section that starts with `class card_value {` and ends with `};` is called a *class definition*. A class definition consists mainly of declarations. We place these in one of two sections designated by the keywords `public` and `private`. These are the public and private interfaces of the class.

public **Versus** private

C++ provides a mechanism for distinguishing between the features of a user-defined type that the user of the type needs to know about and those that only the designer or implementer needs to know about.

> *Language Note: C programmers should note that the `struct` in C++ is almost synonymous with the `class`. Unlike a C `struct`, a C++ `struct` has the same potential for separating features for users from those for designers or implementers. A C++ `struct` has the capacity to provide behavior as well as data storage.*

The public interface provides those parts that are available to users of the type, and it is introduced by the keyword `public`. The private interface consists of the things that are reserved for use by designers and implementers of the type; it is introduced by the keyword `private`.

In the above code, the public interface consists of the declaration of several member functions. Those (member) functions provide the fundamental behavior of instances of the type. The private interface consists of a single declaration that tells the compiler that instances (objects or values) of type `card_value` will have a single block of memory in which to store an `int` value. In the context of a class definition, we declare data members but that declaration is **never** a definition. The declaration of `data` is part of the private interface and so it is inaccessible to code outside the implementation of `card_value`.

> *Language Note: C programmers need to note that things declared as part of a private interface cannot be accessed or referred to outside the class's scope. Member functions have access to all parts of a class's private interface, but functions that are not declared as part of the class will **not** have access to any part of the private interface. That is one of the key developments that makes C++ a better language for a great deal of application development. It enables class designers to change their choices for data storage without affecting client code. (Later we will learn how access can be granted to external functions, using the `friend`.)*

Special Member Functions: Constructors

As there is no way to access the data storage for a `card_value` instance externally, we need a way to create `card_value` objects with provision of a value for `data` (the private member). This is the job of special member functions called *constructors*. We identify a constructor function by reusing the class name – in this case, `card_value`. C++ allows the constructor function to be overloaded, and if you look at the definition of class `card_value`, you will see that it includes three overloads for the constructor.

The first overload, `card_value( )`, is called a default constructor, and will specify how a `card_value` object will be created if the programmer chooses not to provide any information.

The second overload, `explicit card_value(int)`, declares a constructor that requires a single (value) argument of type `int`. The significance of the `explicit` keyword is that it prevents the constructor from being hijacked by the compiler as a way to convert an `int` value into a `card_value` value implicitly. The early design of C++ allowed the use of constructors with single parameters to convert values from the type of the parameter to the type of the constructor implicitly. By the time that that was recognized as a design error it was too late to change the rule. The language designers did the next best thing by providing a mechanism for turning off the use of a constructor for implicit conversion. When writing class definitions, you should usually prefix constructors that only require a single argument with the keyword `explicit`. It is not an error to prefix other constructors with `explicit`; the compiler will simply ignore the keyword, because such constructors cannot be implicit type converters. However, it is often a design error to allow implicit conversion via a constructor.

The third case, `card_value(card_value const &)` is a special constructor; its job is to construct a new instance by copying an existing one. This is the major case where you should not prefix the constructor with `explicit` unless you understand the consequences. I am not going to go into those here, because making a copy constructor explicit is a highly specialist technique and one over which there is a good deal of argument among experts. Until you understand the issues, do not provide explicit copy constructors.

Any time that the compiler decides it needs to copy an object or value, it will use the copy constructor. The commonest cases of this are when you pass an argument by value and when you return a value from a function.

Copy constructors are so fundamental to most code that the compiler will declare one implicitly if you do not do so, and it will attempt to generate code for such an implicitly declared copy constructor. Unfortunately, there are cases where the generated code will be a serious mistake. That is why you need to know about copy constructors. When you gain more understanding, you may elect to leave the compiler to its own devices by not declaring a copy constructor when you know that the compiler will do the right thing. We will also see in the next chapter how we can suppress copy construction in cases where we do not want to allow copying of instances of a type.

Note that a constructor never has a return type. In the computer-science sense, a constructor is a procedure for creating an object. The consequence of executing a constructor is an object of the appropriate type.

Special Member Functions: Destructors

Constructors create new instances (we say that they start the lifetime of an object). Sometimes we need to clean up at the end of an instance's lifetime. That cleanup process (for example, releasing resources acquired during the process of construction) is the task of the destructor. Although a class type can have multiple constructors, it will only have one destructor. However an instance comes into existence, it will be destroyed in exactly the same way. We identify the destructor by placing a tilde (~) before the name of the type.

The declaration of `~card_value( )` in the definition of the class `card_value` shows how to declare a destructor. Like the constructors, the destructor cannot have a return type. A destructor is a procedure that destroys an existing instance of a class type.

Special Member Functions: Copy assignment, operator=

The last of the special member functions is the one that specifies how a value of the class type can be copied into an instance of the same type. This is another of the cases where the compiler will provide a declaration implicitly if you do not. In other words, objects in C++ can be copied unless the programmer takes special action to stop copying. We will see what that special action is in the next chapter, when we deal with types where allowing copying would be a mistake.

`operator=` can only be overloaded in the context of a `class` (or `struct`) type. The left-hand operand of an assignment operation must be an object (lvalue) of the class type. The single parameter specified in the declaration will be the right-hand operand of the = operator (i.e. the expression that comes after the = sign in an assignment expression). By convention, we always return a non-`const` reference to the left-hand operand.

If the parameter in the declaration of `operator=` is a reference to the class (usually a `const` reference because we would not normally expect to change the state/value of an object by copying it), we are declaring a copy assignment operator. That is the way to copy the value/state of one instance to a second instance of the same type. We can, and often do, provide other overloads for the assignment operator, but they are not copy assignments.

Ordinary Member Functions

Ordinary member functions provide much of the behavior of a class. By ordinary member functions, I mean member functions that are not concerned with creating, destroying, or copying class instances or values.

For now, my class **card_value** has just one ordinary member function, called **send_to**. As the name might suggest, this member function provides the behavior of sending the value of a **card_value** to an output stream. During our early development and testing, we will be sending the value of a **card_value** to **std::cout**, but I have designed the **send_to** member function to work with any type of output stream including files.

You are probably curious about the **const** at the end of the declaration. That declares that the member function does not alter the instance using it. Without that qualification, you will get an error if you attempt to output the value of a **const** instance of **card_value** with **send_to( )**. In effect, that terminal **const** promises that the function will not alter the object using it. That promise restricts what you can do in the definition of the function (if you write code that might change the object, the compiler will issue an error message), and it allows you to use the function on all instances of the class including immutable ones. Forgetting the **const** qualification often causes problems long after you thought you had finished designing a class. The problem only surfaces the first time you try to use the function on a **const** instance or a **const**-qualified reference to an instance of the type.

 **TASK 9.1**   **Test my assertion about the significance of the const qualification of a member function: modify the example code by adding const to the definition of specific in the code for main( ) (i.e. make it card_value const specific(1)), and remove the const from the end of the declaration of send_to. You should now get an error message when you try to compile the code.**

Implementing Constructors

There is a special syntax for implementing (defining) a constructor; it includes a facility for initializing the data members. In general, functions have parameters initialized with the arguments provided at the point of call. The special property of a constructor is that it has to initialize the data members of the instance it is creating. We must initialize data members before the process enters the body of the constructor (but after any parameters have been initialized).

The section of the definition of a constructor that provides explicit initialization of the instance's data members is introduced by a colon (:) immediately after the closing parenthesis of the parameter list. Here are possible definitions of the three constructors for the **card_value** type:

```
card_value::card_value( ):data(0){
  std::clog << "Default card_value (ace of clubs) constructed.\n";
}

card_value::card_value(int i):data(i){
```

```
        std::clog << "card_value constructed from " << i << ".\n";
}

card_value::card_value(card_value const & c):data(c.data){
    std::clog << "card_value constructed by copying.\n";
}
```

Notice the syntax for identifying the member function when referring to it outside the class definition. The full name of a member function outside the scope of the class definition requires that you prefix the member function name with the class scope to which it belongs. That is the purpose of the `card_value::` prefix to the constructor identifier in each of the above definitions.

In the copy constructor, we need to identify the version of **data** that belongs to the parameter. We do that using the same dot notation that we used earlier when calling a member function for an object. If you are familiar with languages such as C and Java, you will already be used to this syntax.

Because we are in a learning situation, I have defined the bodies of the three constructors so that each reports on its use. You would not normally do that when you write production code. We call such added code *instrumentation*.

Notice how we initialize the data member (called **data**) in each case. Had I left out the `:data(0)` in the first case, I would have had an uninitialized **int** representing the value of **any** in the code above. We generally try to avoid writing constructors that result in uninitialized data, because accidentally accessing such data (in a member function) results in undefined behavior.

The syntax for initializing a data member of a class is to include the name of the data member in a comma-separated initialization list. This list is placed between a colon following the closing parenthesis of the parameter list and the opening brace of the body of the constructor definition. We place the initializing expression in parentheses directly after the name of the data member we wish to initialize. You should note that data members are always initialized in the order in which we declare them in the class definition, regardless of the order in which we write the initializer list. A good compiler will warn you if it spots different ordering of the two (declaration and initializer list).

Implementing a Destructor

This is trivial in this case because there is nothing to clean up. The **card_value** type does not acquire any extra resources (other than the base memory, and that is released automatically at the end of the object's lifetime). However, because we are learning, I have instrumented the destructor to give you an example of defining one. It will also make its automatic use in your code visible when the program runs. Here is a definition of an instrumented destructor for **card_value** objects:

```
card_value::~card_value(card_value const & c) {
    std::clog << "card_value " << data << " destroyed.\n";
}
```

As we are inside a member function, we can access the private members and do so with their simple names. Therefore, in this case, **data** is the value held by the instance of **card_value** that we are destroying. Notice that we have to qualify the destructor identifier with **card_value::** to tell the compiler the class to which this member function belongs.

Implementing Copy Assignment, operator=

There are two special features of copy assignment. The first is that C++ requires that all overloads of **operator=** are in a class scope. That requirement is a subtle consequence of the second feature: if the programmer does not explicitly declare a copy assignment, the compiler will declare one implicitly. It will then attempt to generate a definition if such an assignment is required by the source code (i.e. if the programmer attempts to assign the value/state of one instance to another instance of the same type). Once you declare a copy-assignment operator, everything else is like any other member function:

```
card_value & card_value::operator=(card_value const & c){
  std::clog << "card_value " << data << " replaced by "
      << c.data << ".\n";
  data = c.data;
  return *this;
}
```

Once again, we have to specify the class to which this definition belongs. The return type comes first, just as it would in the definition of a non-member function. The other point to note is in the return-statement: *this is a special expression that refers to the object that is invoking a member function. In this case, it will be the left-hand operand of the assignment. There is little point in debating whether this is the correct thing to return. The designers of the language say that it is (though the language allows us to have any return type we want), and the way we return the left operand is with the statement return *this;.

This is not the time to tackle exactly why *this is the object using a member function. For now, just think of it as the way C++ spells what some languages call 'self', i.e. the object in use.

If I did not want to instrument this function, there would be no point in declaring and defining it, because the compiler-generated implicit declaration and definition would do the same thing.

Implementing a Member Function

All we need to do now is implement the send_to member function. Here is a simple implementation:

```
std::ostream & card_value::send_to(std::ostream & out)const{
  out << data;
  return out;
}
```

There is not much to say about this definition. We are going to modify it later on, but this is enough to get our example working.

Add the above implementation code at the end of the file you prepared with the original example code. Everything should now work when you try to compile and link. If it does not, you will need to correct your typos.

Now modify the code so that each of the three card_value variables has a different value when the program ends. That will allow you to see that the three instances of card_value are destroyed in the reverse order of their construction. You might also tidy up the code by adding a few extra statements to format the output of send_to reasonably. Do not change the definition of send_to in order to achieve that, but add some code to the definition of main().

Separate Compilation

Programming languages have different ways of handling large quantities of source code. C++ has inherited the mechanism that C uses, which is to place declarations and definitions in different files. The exception to this in C (and therefore in C++) is to treat the definition of a user-defined type, a `struct` (and therefore a C++ `class`), a `union` or an `enum` as a declaration. The added complexity in C++ is that the definitions of `struct/class` and `union` types usually include declarations of member functions. The definitions of those member functions are often referred to as the *implementation* of the type and are placed in a separate definition or implementation file.

The declarations and type definitions are placed in files that are called header files, and traditionally use a `.h` suffix for the file-name extension. Files of implementation code as well as application and library code are often loosely referred to as source files (though, strictly speaking, header files are also source files). For convenience, C++ 'source' files use either `.cpp` or `.cxx` as the file-name extension, to distinguish them from pure C source files, which traditionally use a `.c` extension. None of this will be strange to C programmers, but those coming from other languages have some learning to do.

The purpose of a header file is to provide the information that is essential for a compiler to compile user code. The implementation file largely provides the definitions of the declarations in a header file. The linker will need the compiled result, but the compiler does not need the definition in order to compile code using it. That means that an implementer can change details or correct bugs without triggering a complete recompilation of all the source code in a program. Because complete recompilation of a large program can take a great deal of time, we can save much development time by isolating implementation source code from user code. The header file makes this isolation possible.

Rather than spend time explaining the details, here is the code we have been working on in this chapter reorganized to separate the implementation of `card_value` from code that simply uses the `card_value` type.

The Header File

In your IDE, create a new header file called `card.h` (or anything else you want to call it). Copy and paste the code from your earlier source file to produce:

```
#include <ostream>

class card_value{
public:
  card_value();
  explicit card_value(int);
  card_value(card_value const &);
  ~card_value();
  card_value & operator=(card_value const &);
  std::ostream & send_to(std::ostream &)const;
private:
  int data;
};
```

Strictly speaking, for the current case that is enough, but multiple inclusions of the same header file (often indirectly) into a single source code file can result in redefinition errors, so it is normal to provide what are called header guards. These consist of three lines of code, two at the start of the header file and one at the end. The idea behind a header guard is to provide a way that the compiler can identify when it has already read a header file and does not need to read it again. The initial two lines have the form:

```
#ifndef unique-id
#define unique-id
```

where *unique-id* is some name that uniquely identifies the header file. For the simple code that we will be using in this book, it is usually enough to use the name of the header file spelt in uppercase, with the dot separating the file-name extension replaced with an underscore. Therefore, I would start `card.h` with these two lines:

```
#ifndef CARD_H
#define CARD_H
```

In plain English, those lines say: "If you have not yet had a definition of `CARD_H`, continue and first define it (as nothing)." The result is that the first time the compiler sees a `#include "card.h"` it will continue to read in the file. However, if the code results in a subsequent attempt to include `card.h` it will skip the contents of the file until it reaches a line that stops it skipping. The line that stops the 'skipping' is:

```
#endif
```

That line matches the opening `#ifndef` and should be the last line of the header file. So `card.h` becomes:

```
#ifndef CARD_H
#define CARD_H
#include <ostream>

class card{
public:
  card_value();
  explicit card_value(int);
  card_value(card_value const &);
  ~card_value();
  card_value & operator=(card_value const &);
  std::ostream & send_to(std::ostream &)const;
private:
  int data;
};
```

```
#endif
```

Finally notice that `card.h` does not `#include <iostream>`. That is because the definition of `card_value` does not make any use of standard stream objects. Always limit included files and headers to those needed by the code in the file. Including extra unnecessary headers and files adds clutter and can result in unnecessary recompilation of source-code files.

The Implementation File

This file contains implementation details for items declared in the corresponding header file. It only needs to be recompiled if we make changes to the implementation source code. Any project that uses the resulting compiled code (called object code) will only need it when the linker creates the executable.

Move the definitions of the member functions of `card_value` into a file called `card.cpp`. (Use the IDE to create a new C++ source-code file.) The compiler will need to know the definition of the `card_value` type before it will compile definitions of its member functions. We provide that information by including `card.h` at the start of `card.cpp`. Your implementation file for `card_value` should look like this:

```
#include "card.h"
#include <iostream>  // needed for std::clog
```

```
card_value::card_value( ):data(0){
  std::clog << "Default card_value constructed.\n";
}

card_value::card_value(int i):data(i){
  std::clog << "card_value constructed from " << i << ".\n";
}

card_value::card_value(card_value const & c):data(c.data){
  std::clog << "card_value constructed by copying.\n";
}

card_value::~card_value( ){
  std::clog << "card_value with value " << data << " destroyed.\n";
}

card_value & card_value::operator=(card_value const & c){
  std::clog << "card value " << data << " replaced by "
      << c.data << ".\n";
  data = c.data;
  return *this;
}

std::ostream & card_value::send_to(std::ostream & out)const{
  out << data;
  return out;
}
```

TASK 9.3 → Create a new project and place `card.cpp` in it. Note that you do not need to put `card.h` into the project, as the IDE will find it as a dependency (because `card.cpp` includes `card.h`).

Compile `card.cpp`. Correct any typos. If you try to build an executable, the linker will complain that it cannot find `main( )`. Remember that every program needs a single function called `main( )` that acts as the start point for the program.

The Application File

In production-level projects there are usually several (even hundreds of) application files that consist of user code that builds on top of libraries and other lower-level code. Indeed code usually consists of many layers with a single simple file containing `main( )` sitting on top. That will not normally be the case in this book, because such code is usually too complicated for learning purposes.

For our current project you need to create a second C++ source-code file (call it `testcard.cpp`) and place this source code in it:

```
#include "card.h"
#include <iostream>

int main( ) {
```

```
try{
    card_value any;
    card_value specific(1);
    card_value another(specific);
    any.send_to(std::cout);
    specific.send_to(std::cout);
    another.send_to(std::cout);
    any = specific;
    any.send_to(std::cout);
}
catch(...){
    std::cerr << "An exception was thrown.\n";
}
}
```

Notice that you now need to include `iostream` because our definition of `main()` uses both `std::cout` and `std::cerr`. Yes, I could have included `iostream` as part of `card.h` rather than include it in each of `testmain.cpp` and `card.cpp`. However, that would result in the inclusion of `iostream` every time you needed a definition of `card_value`. That would not always be necessary. Get in the habit of limiting visibility by including only essential header files. This is particularly true when you include one header file in another.

 **TASK 9.4** Compile `testmain.cpp` and build the project (create an executable). Run the resulting program. You will find that the resulting output is rather messy; a few extra line breaks would help, as would some more text. Please take time to tidy up the output by enhancing the code in `testcard.cpp`.

Comment

At first sight, we have gone to a lot of trouble to get back where we started. The benefit is that we have decoupled the implementation details of `card_value` from users of `card_value`. Many projects can use the `card_value` type, while the implementers of the type can refine, debug, and improve it. The header file acts as the mediator that allows both to work separately. It allows there to be many different users of the `card_value` type; all they need is the header file for `card_value` and the latest compiled form (called an object file) of the implementation of `card_value`. The users have no need to concern themselves with the internals of the `card_value` class's implementation. We often store object code in archives called *libraries*. Indeed that is what we normally mean by the term 'library' in a programming context.

Developing the `card_value` Type

So far, our `card_value` type is using a non-idiomatic mechanism for output to a stream. In C++, we expect to provide output by using `<<` (in this context, the insertion operator). We can provide a new overload for `operator<<` that will do this, but we cannot do so within the scope of the `card_value` class because overloading operators in class scope only works if the first (left-hand) operand of the operator is of the relevant class type. The first operand of `operator<<` (used as an inserter to a stream) has to be an `ostream` object. This means that we have to provide the overload we want outside the class. However, this is very simple to do because `send_to()` already provides the functionality we need. Just add

```
inline std::ostream & operator<<(std::ostream & out, card_value const & c){
  return c.send_to(out);
}
```

after the definition of **card_value** in **card.h**. The **inline** keyword asks the compiler to substitute the body of this definition for any call of the function. Although **inline** is only a request, a compiler that did not honor the request in this case would be a very poor one. If you examine the code, you will see that it tells the compiler that it can send the value of a **card_value** to an output stream by calling **send_to( )** on the **card_value** value (the right operand) and passing in the left operand.

We call functions like this one *forwarding* or *delegating* functions. C++ programmers often make extensive use of such functions, particularly for cases such as this, where they need to reorder the arguments of a function.

There is a small extra, but essential, feature of using **inline**: it requires that the compiler cooperate with the linker, so that it is not an error if the linker finds the definition of the function in more than one file of object code. Without the **inline** qualification, we may get redefinition errors if we use the header file in more than one implementation file in a project. If you get redefinition errors at link time, check that all the header files have header guards (see above) and that any functions defined in a header file have been qualified as **inline**.

TASK 9.5 Add the above definition to your **card.h** and modify **main( )** so that it uses **operator<<** rather than direct calls to **send_to( )**. Compile, link, and test the resulting code. I think you will find that one consequence of providing support for **operator<<** for **card_value** is that it is now simpler to provide tidy output.

Adding get_from( )

Given that we can write a **card_value** value to an output stream, it seems natural that we should also be able to get a **card_value** value from an input stream. However, this reverse operation is plagued by the problem that the source of the input might be a human being (or worse still, a cat walking over a keyboard). Input will always be from a fallible source; the problems are how to handle erroneous input and whether to prompt for the input. Input from a console is usually preceded by a prompt; if the input fails validation, we normally have some mechanism for retrying. Input from a file, serial port, etc. does not normally have a prompt, and if it fails validation, we have to retreat to an error-recovery mechanism.

When faced with this kind of issue in C++, the mind should turn to function overloading to deal with the different kinds of behavior. Here is a pair of versions of a member function called **get_from( )** to deal with the problem.

```
bool get_from();  // deal with input from std::cin
std::istream & get_from(std::istream &);  // deal with general input
```

Add those declarations to the public part of the definition of **card_value**. You will also need to add **#include <istream>** as a header in **card.h** because of the use of **std::istream** in the second declaration.

Next, let us look at defining those functions. Let me take the general case first:

```
std::istream & card_value::get_from(std::istream & in){
  in >> data;
  if(not in) throw std::exception();
  return in;
}
```

When you add this definition to `card.cpp` you may also need to add `#include <exception>` to provide the declaration of `std::exception`. Eventually we will want to provide our own exception type tailored to the needs of `card_value`, but for now, I am just using the Standard Library default exception type.

This version of `get_from()` tries to read a value from the designated input. If it fails to get a value, it simply gives up and throws an exception. However, it is still not doing full validation, because it assumes that any valid `int` will be a valid `card_value` value. There are two ways to deal with this issue. We can accept any `int` value and then reduce it to the required range. Alternatively, we can check that the supplied value is in range and throw an exception if it is not. Here is one way to implement the first option:

```cpp
std::istream & card_value::get_from(std::istream & in){
  unsigned int temp;
  in >> temp;
  if(not in) throw std::exception();
  data = temp % 52;
  return in;
}
```

I could have done one of two things to improve that further. I could have used the `read<>` function from my `fgwlib` library to get automatic validation of the input being appropriate to the `unsigned int` type. I could, and normally should, remove that magic `52`. The reason that I am being a little lazy is that I know that I am going to be changing the handling of `card_value` values in a way that makes such changes unnecessary.

Now let me deal with the special case. Here is one possible implementation:

```cpp
bool card_value::get_from(){
  std::cout << "Please input a value for a card "
      << "(an integer in the range 0-51 inclusive): ";
  try{
    get_from(std::cin);
  }
  catch(...){return false;}
  return true;
}
```

I am not claiming this is the only way, or even the best way, to deal with this problem. I have chosen this particular solution to illustrate a number of implementation mechanisms that are available to you. The `bool` return is another way to handle functions that can fail; instead of throwing an exception, we use the return from the function to report success or failure. This is a good way to deal with problems that we are likely to handle locally. In this case, we do not care why `get_from(std::cin)` failed: if calling it results in an exception, then this version of `get_from()` failed. Another implementation point is that we can implement this version in terms of the general one by first issuing the prompt and then calling the general version. This is a common way of dealing with special cases.

Another question that arises is this: should I reset the input stream in `get_from()` if it fails, and should I do so in the `get_from(std::istream&)` version? I think that no is usually the better answer in both cases. You do not know why it failed and so it is not your responsibility to act, particularly as doing so would hide the cause (possibly reading the end-of-file marker) from the caller of the function. The caller may want that information in order to decide how to proceed.

Implementing operator>> for card_value

Now that we have the functionality of reading a `card_value` value from an input stream, we can support `operator>>` to extract a value from a `std::istream`. We have to be careful to handle the special case of extraction from `std::cin`. Here is a possible implementation:

```
inline std::istream & operator>>(std::istream & in, card_value & c){
  if(&in == &std::cin) c.get_from( );
  else c.get_from(in);
  return in;
}
```

In this context the &s in the `if` statement are the address-of operator. The controlling expression in the `if` statement asks whether the left operand of this use of `operator>>` is `std::cin`. If it is, use the version of `get_from( )` tailored for `std::cin` as a source of data; otherwise, use the general form.

Note that when you add the inline definition of `operator>>` to `card.h`, you will also need to add `#include <iostream>` to provide the declaration of `std::cin`. Strictly speaking, for portability to other compilers you also need to add `#include <istream>`.

Language Note: *Unlike C programmers, C++ programmers make relatively little use of the address-of operator. In many of the places where it would be used in C, we would instead use a reference in C++.*

 **TASK 9.6** Add the declarations of `get_from( )` and `get_from(std::istream)` to the definition of `card_value` in `card.h`. Add the definitions of those functions to `card.cpp`. Add the inline definition of `operator>>(std::istream &, card_value &)` to `card.h`.

Now modify `cardmain.cpp` to test that the input functions work as designed. Note that you do not need to test the general version of `get_from( )` explicitly, because the special version (for `std::cin`) tests it indirectly. Make sure you include use of `operator>>` for a `card_value`.

Changing the Implementation

We have a working version of `card_value` with support for the simple things we might do with it. There is more functionality that we could add, such as comparing two `card_value` values to see if they are the same (`operator==`) or to see which comes first in some ordering of our choice (`operator<` and `operator>`), but I am going to put those aside for now.

In this section, I am going to focus on changing the implementation so that we deal with the attributes of a `card_value` rather than the raw value we have used internally. To do this I am going to use the ideas from the previous chapter and add an `enum suit` and an `enum denomination` to the public interface of `card_value`. I will also need to deal with the string literals that provide names for the values of those attributes. Only the implementations of the input and output functions need these names; they are data and so should be part of the private interface of `card_value`. They are very special data because they are a property of the class as a whole, so I will be showing you how to provide such data in a `class` context.

Using enums to Represent Attributes

The first step is to add the following two `enum` definitions to the public interface of `card_value`:

```
enum suit{club, diamond, heart, spade};
enum denomination {ace, two, three, four, five, six, seven, eight,
    nine, ten, jack, queen, king};
```

Now that we have provided these two `enum`s as local types for a `card_value`, it makes sense to provide a constructor that will work with them. Note that the definitions of `suit` and `denomination` need to occur before any use of them. It is usually a good idea to place the definitions of such nested types near the beginning of the class definition. Here is one possible constructor declaration:

```
card_value(denomination, suit);
```

Here is a possible definition of the extra constructor:

```
card_value::card_value(denomination d, suit s):data(s*13 + d){
  std::clog << "card_value constructed from attributes: "
      << d << " of " << s << "s.\n";
}
```

One question that class designers need to consider is to what extent they should protect the user from stupidity. Should we check that the **denomination** and **suit** values provided as arguments are valid ones? I have not done so here, but if you think there should be checks, you need to add checks that **s** and **d** are within the relevant ranges and throw an exception if they are not. Throwing an exception is about the only way of reporting a problem from within a constructor.

You might be tempted to remove one or more of our earlier constructors from the definition of **card_value**. In general, you should not remove or modify a declaration in a class definition: doing so would very likely break existing code that uses the class.

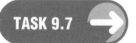

TASK 9.7

Add the **enums** and the declaration of the new constructor to the definition of card_value in **card.h**. Add the definition of the new constructor to **card.cpp**. Make sure that **card.cpp** still compiles. Now add this line to the definition of **main** in **cardmain.cpp**:

```
card_value yac(5, 2);
```

Try to compile **cardmain.cpp**. You now get an error because there are no implicit conversions from the **int** literals of 5 and 2 to **card_value::denomination** and **card_value::suit**. (Note that you have to qualify local types with the enclosing class type when you refer to them outside class scope. Local types are members and subject to the same rules as other members.)

Replace 5 and 2 by **five** and **heart** respectively. You still get an error, though a different one. This time the compiler does not recognize **five** and **heart** as enumerators. We are outside the scope of **card_value**, and so we must qualify the enumerators with the enclosing class name. When we edit our code so that we have

```
card_value yac(card_value::five, card_value::heart);
```

it compiles.

Names for Values

The problem with the output of our program is that it is just a **card_value** value; we really would hope to be able to get the output to use human readable names. To do this we need to do two things: we need to provide the names (as we did in the last chapter); and we need to modify our output to use them.

We provide the names by defining **static** data members. **static** members of a class are data or functions that are for the class as a whole rather than for individual instances of a class. Here is how we provide the literal names for the enumerators. In the private part of the definition of **card_value**, add the following two declarations:

```
static char const * suit_names[4];
static char const * denomination_names[13];
```

We need to add definitions of those two variables. The place to do that is in the implementation file, so add the following to **card.cpp**:

```
char const * card_value::suit_names[4]
    = {"club", "diamond", "heart", "spade"};
char const * card_value::denomination_names[13]
    = {"ace", "2", "3", "4", "5", "6", "7", "8",
    "9", "10", "jack", "queen", "king"};
```

Notice that we drop the **static** but add **card_value::** when we provide the definitions. The keyword **static** has the wrong meaning outside a class definition (the alternative meaning of **static** will be explained elsewhere), but the compiler needs to know that what we are defining here belongs to **card_value**.

Pointers and Arrays

C++ has inherited C's collection type, which is a linear array of the collected type. C++ also provides a rich selection of other collection facilities such as the **std::vector<>** that we have already used. In general, we prefer to use C++ collections rather than arrays because the former have a much richer structure and range of facilities. However, there are times when the simplicity of the array is useful.

As a general rule, you might use an array when:

- the size is known and fixed at the time the source code is written;
- suitable initialization can be provided.

One strong motive for using an array is that we know what the stored values should be but there is no way to compute them. The **static** data members **suit_names** and **denomination_names** in **card_value** are excellent examples; we know what they should be because they are a fact rather than something that is computable.

We declare an array in C++ by specifying the type of the object held in the array and adding a pair of square brackets after the name being declared. We generally place the size of the array in the square brackets, but if we leave the brackets empty, the compiler determines the size by counting the provided initializers.

Initializers are provided in the declaration/definition of an array as a comma-separated list enclosed in curly braces 'assigned' to the array.

I do not want to spend much time on C++ pointers at this stage, but you do need a minimal amount of information in order to make sense of some of the source code in this chapter. We saw earlier that appending an asterisk to a type name creates a new type that is a pointer to the named type. A pointer value is effectively the address of the storage for the object. A pointer variable provides storage for a pointer value. Generations of programmers have been confused by pointers, which is a good reason for keeping their use to the minimum.

In most circumstances when you refer to an array in your source code, the compiler will use the address of the start of the array, and if you need to store that address you will need storage for a suitable pointer type.

For historical reasons, string literals are implicitly arrays of **char**, and we pass them around in source code by using the address of the place where the compiler has placed the actual string. Fortunately, the new programmer does not need a deep understanding of pointers and plain arrays in C++ in order to use them in introductory code.

Look at the definition of **card_value::suit_names**. The **[4]** tells us that we are defining an array of four elements. The **char const *** tells us that the elements are storage for the addresses of immutable **char**s (which includes the start addresses of immutable arrays of **char** because of the way that C++ uses such addresses when asked to handle an array). The = sign tells the computer that we are about to provide explicit initialization for the array. The initializer list (provided in the curly braces) consists of four string literals. As the compiler needs addresses to initialize the elements of `card_value::suit_names`, it uses the addresses of where the string literals are stored (addresses that it provides by the internal mechanism it uses for string literals).

In any context where an array of `char` is needed (i.e. when working with simple C-style strings rather than C++ `std::string`), `card_value::suit_names[0]` will be treated as an array containing the characters `'c'`, `'l'`, `'u'`, `'b'`, and a final `'\0'` to mark the end of the string.

The biggest problem with pointers and arrays is that a pointer used to refer to an array (through its start address) is indistinguishable from a pointer used to reference a single object.

I will be tackling pointers in more detail in Chapter 11.

> *Language Note: C programmers are likely to have the biggest problem with learning the C++ idioms for using pointers, because they will have a good understanding of their idiomatic use in C. However, such idioms are often dangerous in a C++ context.*

Those two definitions use the special syntax for initializing a fixed-size array at the point of definition. We are also using the special support that C++ has inherited from C to handle string literals as arrays of `char`. When the compiler deals with the above code it will provide space to store the actual literals and then place the address of each into the relevant point of the array. The `char const *` specifies that we are using addresses (that is the meaning of the asterisk in this context) of `char`s that cannot be changed through this address value. The `[4]` and `[13]` specify the number of elements in each of the arrays.

Now we have the names available, we can go back and change the implementation of `send_to` so that it sends named values of the attributes to the output. Here is one way to do it:

```
std::ostream & card_value::send_to(std::ostream & out)const{
    out << denomination_names[data % 13] << " of " << suit_names[data/13];
    return out;
}
```

TASK 9.8 Add all the above code to the relevant files. Note that you do not need to touch `cardmain.cpp`; users should not have to change their code because a class implementer has changed the implementation. Build the new version and execute it. Notice that you get the new behavior for output.

Tidying Up

If you look at the output from your last task, you will realize that the instrumentation that we added to the constructors, destructor, and copy assignment is still outputting numbers. We can clean that up very easily. Here is the cleaned-up copy assignment as an example:

```
card_value & card_value::operator=(card_value const & c){
    std::clog << "card value " << *this << " replaced by " << c << ".\n";
    data = c.data;
    return *this;
}
```

The key is that we can now send a `card_value` value to output, rather than using the internal representation (the member called `data`). The other essential is that `*this` always represents the object using a function (being created, destroyed, etc.).

TASK 9.9 Clean up all the instrumentation in our implementation of `card_value` so that output always refers to a `card_value` value in the form '*x* of *y*' (e.g. 'three of spades'). In particular, tidy up the instrumentation in the constructors and the destructor. Build and execute the resulting code.

TRY THIS

Instrumenting code is all very well, but we do not want all those messages when we use our work to produce a program to play a card game that we intend sharing with our friends. The messages help us kept track of what is happening but are invasive in the context of a 'release' product.

Save a copy of `card.cpp` but call the copy `card1.cpp`. Now edit `card1.cpp` to remove all the instrumentation. Replace `card.cpp` in your project with `card1.cpp`. Rebuild the project. Voila, uninstrumented code.

This is just one of the payoffs for keeping implementation separate and using a header file to provide the compiler with what it needs to compile user code. In fact, all you need to do is link your application with the appropriate object file for the implementation you wish to use.

Add comparison operators for `card_value` as members of the class. For example, you can declare and implement `operator==` for `card_value` with

```
bool operator==(card_value const &)const;
```

added to the public interface of `card_value`, and define it in the implementation as:

```
bool operator==(card_value const & c)const{
  return data == c.data;
}
```

Add that along with declarations and definitions of `operator<` and `operator>` for `card_value`. Note that in all cases the parameter should be a `const` reference (or value), and the member function should be qualified as `const` (that `const` just after the closing parenthesis of the parameter list). Comparing instances should not change them.

You should find those additions straightforward. The next task is a bit more demanding: you need to update the `get_from(std::istream &)` function so that it reads the output of `send_to()` correctly. The reason is that `send_to()` may be used to store data in a file, and you want to be able to read that data back from the file by using `get_from(std::istream &)`.

As a hint, you can input a single word into a temporary variable of type `std::string`. The `c_str()` member of `std::string` allows you to view a `std::string` object as an array of `char`. The `strcmp()` library function (inherited from C) takes two null-terminated arrays of `char` (C-style strings) and returns zero if they are identical.

For example, `strcmp(temp.c_str, card_value::suit_names[club])` returns zero if and only if the string stored in temp is `"club"`.

At this point, you may want to reimplement the special version of `get_from()` that uses `std::cin` so that the user is prompted for each of the attributes of a `card_value`. Note that this change means that you can no longer forward to the general function.

If you are hopelessly stuck when trying this, check the answer I give at the end of this book.

Consolidation – a Point Class

Read chapters 5 and 6 of *You Can Do It!* from the CD to get an alternative presentation of designing a class (a 2D point class for use with my Playpen library). Then try one or more of the following exercises.

EXERCISES

I have worked through the development of the `card_value` class. At this point, you need to stop and work on a couple of classes for yourself. Here are some possibilities for you to work on. Please note that these classes are far from trivial, and so you should expect to take some time to provide complete implementations of the definitions provided. You should also plan to work incrementally rather than trying to do the whole job at once.

5. Here is the start of a class for calendar dates within a single year. You will find that it uses most of the things we have covered in designing and developing `card_value`. You may modify the private interface if you think you have a better way to structure the data.

```
class date{
public:
  date();
  explicit date(int day_number, bool leap_year = false);
  date(std::string month, int day, bool leap_year = false);
  date(date const &);
  ~date();
  date & operator=(date const &);
  ostream & send_to(ostream &)const;
  istream & get_from();  // uses std::cin
  istream & get_from(std::istream &);
  bool leap_year();
private:
  bool leap;
  unsigned int day;  // counted from January 1st as 0
  static signed char const
      days_in_month[12];  // uses signed char as a small int
  static char const * month_names[12];
};
```

Create a suitable header file and place the `date` definition in it. Create a suitable implementation file and implement the `date` class. Now create an application file that consists of a definition of `main()` that tests all the functionality of `date`. You might find it easier to implement the class without managing the differences required for a leap year, then go back to add the modifications necessary to handle leap years. The provision of default arguments in the constructors should make that easier. You will also find it easier to implement date bit by bit; do not try to do it all at once but tackle it by incremental refinement and improvement (as I did for `card_value`).

Note that I have only declared the first constructor as `explicit`. Because we can call that constructor with a single argument by using the default argument for `leap_year`, we need to protect against accidental use of the constructor by the compiler as a conversion operator between an `int` and a `date`. The second constructor does not suffer from this problem, because it always needs at least two arguments.

Several functions will need to validate the data provided, to ensure that they are legitimate dates (e.g. there is no January 32nd). You will need to decide what to do with an invalid date. For example, an invalid date passed as an argument to a constructor will probably need to be handled by throwing an exception.

When you have the specified interface implemented and working correctly, spend some time on enhancements such as providing streaming operators, and increment and decrement operators (add the declarations `date operator++();` and `date operator--();` to the class definition).

Note that it makes no sense to add two dates together, but you can subtract one date from another to find the interval between them. So add `int operator-(date const&)const;` to the definition of `date` and provide an implementation. It also makes sense to add an integer value to a date. Add `date operator+(int);` to the definition of date and implement it.

There is a great deal more you could add to this class if you wanted to flesh it out to be a robust general-purpose type for use in your code. Remember that you can always add to a class and modify its implementation and private interface. However, you should not change the public interface in any way that might break existing code, e.g. by removing a public declaration or by changing the return type or the type of a parameter. You can add extra overloads of a function to handle alternative parameter types.

6. Use the `date` class from Exercise 5 as a basis for designing and implementing a more general date class that deals with dates across a range of years. One interesting function to include in this is one to output the day of the week of the currently stored date value.

7. Here is a skeleton definition for a class to represent color values with the primary colors (red, green, and blue – for light) treated as attributes.

```cpp
class rgbcolor{
public:
  rgbcolor();
  rgbcolor(int red, int green, int blue);
  rgbcolor(rgbcolor const &);
  ~rgbcolor();
  rgbcolor & operator=(rgbcolor const &);
  ostream & send_to(ostream &);
  istream & get_from();  // use std::cin as source
  istream & get_from(istream &);
  int red();  // returns current value of red component
  int blue();  // returns current value of blue component
  int green();  // returns current value of green component
  void red(int newval);
  void blue(int newval);
  void green(int newval);
private:
  int red_;
  int blue_;
  int green_;
};
```

Create a header file for the class definition and the declaration of support functions. Create files for the implementation and test source code. Note the overloading of the `red()`, `blue()`, and `green()` functions: the versions with an empty parameter list return the current value of the relevant attribute; the versions with an `int` parameter change the stored value of the parameter. It happens that the three attributes are stored separately, but there is no reason for a user to assume that, and if the class designer decides to store the information in some other way, they are free to do so as long as they maintain the public interface.

Though this class could form the basis for redefining the palette for Playpen, actually making the change will require more knowledge of the `playpen` interface than you currently have.

You can expand the functionality of `rgbcolor` in many ways. Please take the time to add at least one extra feature to `rgbcolor`.

Defining Member Functions in a Class Definition

You may wonder about the efficiency of many of the simple member functions that either return or modify an attribute, for example, the `red( )`, `blue( )`, and `green( )` functions in the `rgbcolor` type in Exercise 7.

You can define a member function in the class definition. Doing so makes the definition implicitly inline. Most experts advise that defining member functions in a class definition is generally a poor idea. However, where no computation is involved it is more acceptable. So we could replace

```
int red( );  // returns current value of red component
```

and

```
void red(int newval);
```

with

```
int red( ){return red_;}
```

and

```
void red(int newval){red_ = newval;}
```

respectively.

However, if I change the way that the data is stored so that computation is required to extract or modify the red attribute, such definitions of members functions inside a class definition would become more suspect. Making a function inline is an optimization, and you should generally avoid hand-optimization unless the code has inadequate performance. Modern compilers are generally good (and are getting better with each release) at inlining small functions at link time even when the programmer has not suggested it.

I will generally avoid in-class definitions in the code I provide in this book, but you need to know it is possible and understand its significance when you see it in other code.

REFERENCE SECTION

The class is an important mechanism for adding user-defined types in C++. We use the keywords `class` and `struct` to declare and define class types. With a single difference, described later, the two keywords are interchangeable. We use a third keyword, `union`, to declare and define a very restricted user-defined type that is used to allow sharing of raw memory for different types of objects during its existence.

Declaration of a Class Name

We can declare the name of a class with one of the following forms:

```
class name;
struct name;
```

There should be no difference between those two declarations, and they do not commit the programmer to using the same keyword in the corresponding definition. I say "should be no difference" because some compilers (e.g. some versions of Visual C++) do treat them differently, so it is probably wise to be consistent even though C++ does not require you to be.

Once a declaration of a class type is visible to the compiler, you may use references and pointers to the type declared. So given the declaration

```
class foo;
```

the definition

```
foo * ptr_foo(0);
```

is fine and defines `ptr_foo` as a pointer, initialized as a null pointer, to a `foo`. However, because references need to be initialized at the point of definition, you can only use a reference in the context of a declaration that is not a definition. The main cases covered by this are parameter and return types of functions (including member functions) and the declaration of reference members of a class type.

Many people call the declaration of a class name a 'forward declaration' to emphasize that it is only a declaration.

Definition of a Class

The definition of a class type (with either keyword) consists of declarations of data members and member functions. It can also include the definitions of nested user-defined types (including **enum** and **union** types) and the declaration of new type names using **typedef**. Finally, a class definition can include declarations of external types and functions as friends of the class. We write the definition of a class in the form:

```
class name {
    // declarations of class members
};
```

We can replace **class** with **struct**. Note that the final semicolon is essential and must not be omitted.

The declarations in a class definition belong to one of three interfaces: public, private, and protected. Each declaration or definition of a nested type is assigned to one of those three interfaces depending on which of three access specifiers has been used most recently. If no access specifier has so far been used in the definition of a class then classes defined with the **class** keyword default to private access and those defined using the **struct** keyword default to public access. That is the only language difference between using **struct** and using **class** to define a class type.

We use the keywords **public**, **private**, and **protected** to identify sections of a class definition that belong to each of the interfaces. A class definition can have more than one section for a given interface. In other words, we can use any of these keywords more than once in a class definition.

The public interface consists of those members of a class that can be used outside the scope of the class. It usually consists of the declarations of member functions that provide the public behavior for instances of the class. It sometimes includes the definitions of nested types and the use of **typedef** to provide local names for types. It is normally poor practice to place data members in a public interface.

The private interface contains declarations and definitions of those things that the class designer wishes to control. Generally, the private interface contains the declarations of all the data members, as well as any utility functions that the class implementer wants to use but which do not constitute part of the published behavior of the class.

The protected interface is a specialist interface to support certain needs of class designers who intend that the class will be used as the basis for other class designs. You will learn more about this in Chapter 12. In general, the protected interface should not include declarations of data members. However, many people ignore that design guideline.

In addition to providing the behavior and state/value of instances of a class, it is sometimes desirable to provide some behavior and state/value for the class as a whole. Such features of a class definition are identified by the use of the keyword **static**. This is quite different from uses of that keyword in other places in C++.

Ordinary member functions must have an instance as part of their use. Inside an ordinary member function the instance that invoked it is called ***this**. The reason for the asterisk is that, for historical reasons, **this** is a pointer value not an object. Prefixing a pointer with an asterisk refers to the object whose address is provided by the pointer.

It is usual to consider ***this** (or **this**) as an extra parameter that every ordinary member function has. The argument that provides the initialization for this implicit parameter is the instance that precedes the dot in the syntax for using member functions. When a member function is called from within the implementation of another member function for the class, there is an implicit ***this.** prefixing the member-function call. For example, given the class definition

```
struct example(){
  void foo();
  void bar();
// other members
};
```

the code

```
void example::foo(){
  bar();
}
```

is equivalent to:

```
void example::foo(){
  *this.bar();
}
```

static Members

Class member functions (identified by using **static** in their declaration) do not have access to an implicit ***this** parameter. They cannot make use of instance data or ordinary member functions. Suppose we wanted to keep track of how many **card_value** instances a process is using. We can do that by adding

```
static int count;
```

to the private interface of **card_value**. We can then modify all the constructors so that they increment **count** (using **++count;**). We also need to modify the destructor by including the statement **--count;**. Now every time a new **card_value** instance is created, **count** goes up by one, and every time an instance is destroyed, it goes down by one. Remember that we only declare data in a class definition – it still has to be defined and initialized somewhere. The place to do that, in this case, is in **card_value**'s implementation file, by adding the line:

```
int card_value::count(0);
```

That statement will create a single **int** object for use by the **card_value** type and set it to zero.

We now need a way to ask what the current **count** is. To do this we provide a public **static** member function:

```
static int get_count();
```

The **static** tells the compiler that this member function has no hidden ***this** parameter and so is restricted to other **static** members of the class. Its implementation is:

```
int card_value::get_count(){return count;}
```

If we want to call that function in our code, we use its full name, **card_value::count()**. The language also allows us to use an instance and dot notation, so

```
int main(){
  card_value any;
  std::cout << any.get_count();
}
```

will work, but it is generally better style to emphasize that we are using a **static** member function with:

```
int main(){
  card_value any;
  std::cout << card_value::get_count();
}
```

If you do not have an instance of **card_value** to use, that is your only option.

There is a special case where **static** members can be initialized in the class definition. This is the case where the **static** member is a **const**-qualified instance of some integer type. All three properties must be true: it must be a **static** member; it must be an integer member; and it must be **const**-qualified. The purpose of this special license is to allow the removal of magic integer values from class definitions by allowing integer literal values to be named in the class definition. We will see examples later in this book.

Constructors and Destructors

The job of a constructor function is to create a new instance of a class type by acquiring the necessary resources (including the base memory for the data) and initializing data members. In general, a well-designed constructor will place an instance into a safe state for use in a program. An instance of a class starts its lifetime when its constructor has finished running. We identify a constructor by using the class name. A class can have (and usually does have) multiple constructors to allow instances to be created from different initial data.

Every class has a single destructor, whose task is to release the resources used by an instance when its lifetime ends. The lifetime of an instance of a class ends when its destructor is called (not completed, just called). Generally, a destructor is called implicitly when a variable goes out of scope. Explicitly calling a destructor is uncommon. We identify a destructor by prefixing the class name with a tilde (~).

Neither constructors nor destructors can have a return type. It is normal to report a failure to construct an instance by throwing an exception. It is usually a serious design fault if a destructor can fail. Throwing an exception from a destructor is never the right answer to a destruction failure, though the language allows you to do so.

Initializer Lists

C++ has a special syntax to provide for initializing data members. When defining a constructor, a colon after the closing parenthesis of the parameter list for a constructor introduces a list of initializers. This list ends at the opening brace of the body of the definition. We place the individual members that are to be initialized explicitly in a comma-separated list; each data member name is followed by the initializing expression in parentheses.

Members are always initialized in their order of declaration in the class; there is no significance to changing the order of the initializer list.

Some data members must be initialized (reference members, `const` members, and members that do not have a default initializer); these must be explicitly provided for in an initializer list. In a few cases, members cannot be fully initialized, and the final values must be assigned from within the body of the constructor. The main example of this is where a data member is a raw C-style array.

Unless you know that the member in question has a default initializer that will do a correct job, it is good practice to initialize data (where possible) in an initializer list.

Special Members

The C++ standard specifies four special member functions that will be implicitly declared unless some action of the programmer inhibits this behavior. These are:

default constructor: the function that specifies how to create a new instance without any provided data. The explicit declaration of any constructor in a class definition suppresses implicit declaration of a default constructor.

copy constructor: the function that specifies how to create a new instance of a class as a copy of an existing instance. The compiler implicitly declares a copy constructor unless the programmer explicitly declares a copy constructor in the class definition.

destructor: The compiler will implicitly declare a destructor unless the programmer explicitly declares one in the class definition.

copy-assignment operator: This is an overload of `operator=` that specifies how the state/value of an instance of the class appearing as the right-hand operand of an = is used to replace the state/value of the left-hand operand of the same type. The compiler will implicitly declare a copy assignment operator unless the programmer explicitly declares one. Note that declaring some other overload of `operator=` does not suppress implicit declaration and compiler generation of a copy-assignment version.

Implementation

We call the choice of data members and the definitions of the member functions the *implementation* of a class. Wherever possible, we place the implementation of a class in a separate file of source code. As the compiler needs to know about memory requirements for class instances, the data members have to be visible to the compiler when dealing with application-level source code, and so the declarations of data members are part of the class definition. Though the data members are visible, we usually make them inaccessible by placing the relevant declarations in the private interface of the class.

Elaborated Versus Simple Names

When you are inside the scope of a class, either because you are in the definition of the class itself or because you are defining a class member, the simple name as declared in the class definition is enough. However, outside the scope of a class, you need to identify what class is using the name. When defining member functions or `static` class data, that requires that you prefix the simple name with the class name and scope operator (`::`).

CHAPTER (10)

User-Defined Types, Part 3: Simple classes (homogeneous entity types)

In the last chapter, we focused on using a class to provide a new user-defined value type. That is a type whose instances we would freely copy, for example, to provide arguments for function calls and returns from functions. In this chapter, we are going to look at using classes to provide types where we would want to use the same instance in most of our code – a copy will not do.

Another way of looking at the difference between a value type and an entity type is by considering what we mean when we ask whether two instances are the same. When we are thinking in terms of values, we can fairly say that two distinct instances (in the programming sense that they occupy different memory or have different addresses) are the same if they can be used interchangeably without affecting a program. When we are thinking in terms of entities, we only regard two 'instances' as the same if they actually occupy the same memory (i.e. have the same address).

Many people refer to 'entity' types as 'object' types. This leads to confusion in the context of C++, where the term 'object' is much closer in meaning to 'instance'. When I use the term 'object' in this book, I am referring to a specific instance of a type, regardless of whether it is semantically a value, an entity, or something else.

Examples of Value and Entity Types

Many people have difficulty with the dichotomy between value and entity types. In the last chapter, the `isbn10` type was a clear example of a value type. So too the title of a book, the publisher's name, and the copyright date would be represented by value types. An actual book would normally be an entity. Contrast telling a friend the ISBN, title, authorship, and publisher of a book with lending them a book. I also wrote about playing cards, and developed a `card_value` type to handle the values of playing cards. You would be surprised if you were dealt two aces of spades when playing poker (the cards are entities), but there is no problem in several people recording a hand of cards (they are only interested in the values, not the actual cards).

Here are a few other examples of value−entity pairs:

• A credit card number versus a credit card. The credit card number is one of several attributes of a credit card, one that is often copied for use when purchasing items by mail order. However, copying credit cards themselves is normally a criminal activity.

• A car number versus a car number plate. A car number is something that we can, for example, note down when we witness an accident. A car number plate is something that is normally one of a pair, and further copying would be suspect.

- An address versus a house. Houses have addresses (some other things do as well). We can easily pass copies of an address around, but copying a house is hard.

One of the properties of an entity is that it is something that has some form of existence. That existence has some significance that makes copies distinct from the original. On the other hand, a value is something where any copy is as good as (and indistinguishable from) any other.

A Simple Playing-Card Entity

This example uses the `card_value` type from the last chapter to provide a `card` type that represents playing cards as entities. Here is my definition for `card`:

```
class card{
public:
  explicit card(card_value);
  explicit card(std::istream &);
  ~card( );
  void send_to(std::ostream &)const;
  bool is_same(card const &)const;
  card_value get_value( )const;
private:
  card(card const &);  // disable copy constructor
  void operator=(card const &);  // disable assignment
  card_value const value_;
};
```

I have not provided a default constructor (i.e. one that does not need arguments). The compiler will not generate one for me because I have declared at least one other constructor (in fact I have declared three). Compiler-generation of the default constructor only happens if no constructors are declared explicitly.

I have provided two public ways to create a `card` instance. The first is to create a `card` with a specific value, which means that there are no 'blank' cards. The second one allows us to create a `card` from data provided by an input stream. As I am not allowing a card to change its value magically, I need to provide a way to create a card from data provided externally.

This type does not need an explicit destructor, but I am providing one for the time being. This will allow me to instrument it so that its use is visible during the execution of programs.

The next three member functions provide for sending a `card`'s data to an output stream, checking to see whether two names refer to the same `card` instance, and extracting the value of a `card`. The last of those will allow us to check whether two `card`s have the same value as distinct from checking whether two names refer to the same `card`.

There are various alternative declarations that would provide us with the same abilities; however, we should try to keep class interfaces lean.

The first two declarations in the private interface are the idiomatic way to suppress copy semantics. We declare the two relevant special member functions (the copy constructor and the copy-assignment function) as private members. Consequently, these members are inaccessible to code outside the implementation. We usually do not provide definitions for these members; that protects us against accidental usage within the class implementation.

I have chosen to declare **value_** as **const** because I consider a playing card to have an immutable value. Some compilers may be able to make use of this design choice to produce better-optimized code. However, that is not in itself a reason for making the value immutable, and we will see that such a design choice can have unforeseen consequences (which is a reason for doing it here: you will have a chance to see the consequences).

Implementation of card

Most of the implementation is trivial. When you come to try code, place the class definition in the same header file as **card_value** (but after it) and the implementation in the implementation file for **card_value**.

```
card::card(card_value cv):value_(cv){
  std::clog << "Card instance created from " << cv << ".\n";
}
card::~card( ){
  std::clog << "The " << value_ << " card destroyed.\n";
}
void card::send_to(std::ostream & out)const{
  out << value_;
}
bool card::is_same(card const & c)const{
  return this == &c;
}
card_value card::get_value( )const{
  return value_;
}
```

One of the constructors is problematical, because **const** data members must be initialized in the initializer list. We need to deal with the problem of getting a **card_value** from an input stream. The normal process of using a streaming operator will not work here. We need some help. One of the benefits of the **fgw::read<>** function template from my library is that it supports initialization. You will need to add **#include "fgw_text.h"** to the implementation file and tell the compiler where it can find that header by using the Project Settings dialog box to add the **fgw_headers** subdirectory to the includes path. Here is an implementation of **card(std::istream &)** that uses **fgw::read<>**:

```
card::card(std::istream & in):value_(fgw::read<card_value>(in)){
  std::clog << "Card instance created from " << value_
      << " supplied from input.\n";
}
```

If you did not have access to **fgw_text.h**, you could achieve a similar result by adding a helper function in the implementation file. For example, you could add:

```
card_value get_it(std::istream & in){
  card_value temp;
  in >> temp;
  return temp;
}
```

That implementation requires extra work to make it robust. The helper function allows us to define **card(std::istream &)** as:

```
card::card(std::istream & in):value_(get_it(in)){
  std::clog << "Card instance created from " << value_
      << " supplied from input.\n";
}
```

TRY THIS

Add the above code to the appropriate files, and then compile and execute a program with:

```
int main(){
  card c(card_value(12));
}
```

Make sure you are using instrumented versions of both `card_value` and `card`. Study the resulting output; it will give you some idea as to how much can sometimes be hidden under the hood. Programmers from other languages are sometimes concerned that even a simple C++ program may generate a lot of code. In fact, the code is necessary to achieve our objectives, and all that C++ has done is allow us to reduce the amount of code we write at the application level.

EXERCISES

1. Write a complete test program for `card`.

2. Add an inline overload of `operator<<( )` to output a card to an output stream.

3. Comment on why the current design does not support an `operator>>( )`.

4. Add a constructor to `card` that constructs a card directly from a `card_value::denomination` and a `card_value::suit`.

5. When you checked the output from your test code, you may have noticed that it reported calls of the copy constructor and destructor for `card_value` when we constructed a `card` from a `card_value`. Consider how you might remove that copy. Consider whether this removal would be helpful in the case of uninstrumented code. Hint: `card_value` instances consist of a simple `int` value internally and so should be no more expensive to copy than copying an `int` would be.

Another Entity Type: Deck of Cards

My second example of an entity type is rather different, and we will see that it has some impact on our design for `card_value` and `card`. One of the problems we will need to address is whether we should handle the individual cards in a deck of cards as values (`card_value` instances) or entities (`card` instances). I am going to do my initial design using `card_value` instances and then revisit the design from the more natural perspective where they are `card` instances.

```
class deck{
public:
  deck( );
  ~deck( );
  void shuffle( );
  card_value next( );
  void top( );
  void copy_from(deck const &);
```

```
private:
  deck(deck const &);
  deck & operator=(deck const &);
  static int const cards = 52;
  int position;
  card_value pack[cards];
};
```

Later we will find that there are several flaws in this definition.

Let us look at the members to see how we could implement them. I will start with the data members. The declaration of **cards** introduces a special syntax that C++ allows for a member that is **static** (i.e. belonging to the class as a whole), of an integer type (**int** in this case), and **const** (fixed in value). This special syntax allows provision of the value as part of the declaration. Note that using that provision does not make the declaration into a definition. The definition still has to be provided exactly once in the program. In this case, we need to add the statement

```
int const deck::cards;
```

to the implementation file for **deck** (usually we would name that file **deck.cpp**). Three things to note: there is no **static** in the definition; we have to write **deck::cards**; and we must **not** provide the value again (if you use the facility for providing the value in the class definition, it must not be provided in the member definition). The purpose of the declaration is to name **52** as the number of cards in a pack.

We are going to use the instance variable **position** to keep track of where we are in the deck for such purposes as dealing cards. The last piece of data tells the compiler that a **deck** consists of an array of **card_value** called **pack**. One of the requirements for a dimension of an array is that it must be an integer value known to the compiler. One of the principle motives for the special syntax for providing a value in the declaration of a **static const** integer member was to support declarations of array members with a named value as the dimension.

As we are looking at the private interface of **deck**, I might as well explain those two function declarations. You may recognize them from the previous chapter as being the copy constructor and copy-assignment operator for **deck**. If we did not declare them, the compiler would declare them implicitly as members of the public interface. I want to remove copy semantics from **deck**, because it would almost certainly be an error to pass or return a **deck** by value. The idiomatic way to do that is to declare the two special functions dealing with copying as members of the private interface. That means that if a programmer accidentally tries to copy an instance of **deck** the compiler will report an error (an access violation for attempting to use a private member of a class). As we do not want to use copy semantics, we do not provide a definition for these two functions in the implementation file. That adds an extra safeguard in case we forget and try to copy a **deck** in a member function. In that case, the linker will give us a missing-definition error message.

Having just gone to a lot of trouble to remove accidental copying, you may be surprised by the **copy_from( )** public member function. While we do not want a **deck** passed or returned by value, nor do we want one changed by a copy assignment: we might still want to produce a duplicate explicitly. That is the purpose of **copy_from( )**. Here is a suitable implementation of **copy_from( )**:

```
void deck::copy_from(deck const & source){
  for(int i(0); i != cards; ++i){
    pack[i] = source.pack[i];
    position = source.position;
  }
}
```

Now let us look at the constructor. Here we have to deal with the rule that we must use a default constructor to create the elements of an array – we have no option. That means that we will have to establish the correct cards inside the body of the constructor for **deck**. I am going to opt for a simple implementation even though expert programmers would (legitimately) criticize it as coupling the card_value and deck implementations. However, it is worth noting that the coupling is real because a deck **is** a collection of cards.

```
deck::deck( ):position(0){
  for(int i(0); i != cards; ++i) pack[i] = card_value(i);
}
```

This definition uses the card_value(int) constructor of card_value and the copy-assignment operator for card_value to replace the default created card_value so that our pack has one copy of each possible card.

The destructor for deck has nothing to do (unless you want to instrument it). The array is destroyed automatically after the body of the destructor has run. The process of destruction will destroy each of the elements of the array by calling the card_value destructor for it. The elements of an array are destroyed in the reverse order of their construction. Note that you can (and should) check that assertion by using the instrumented implementation of card_value. When you do so, you will see that quite a lot of construction and destruction happens in the background.

I will come back to shuffle( ) in a moment, but first I will deal with the two other member functions. The purpose of next( ) is to return the value of the card_value currently identified by position, and increment position by one. Here is a simple implementation:

```
card_value deck::next( ){
  card_value value(pack[position]);
  ++position;
  if(position == cards) position = 0;
  return value;
}
```

We deal with going off the end of the pack with the simple solution of returning to the top.

The intention of the top( ) function is to reset position to the top. That makes it simple to define it as:

```
void deck::top( ){position = 0;}
```

Finally, we need to implement a function that will shuffle the deck. Most of the work for such a function can be done by using the Standard C++ Library function random_shuffle( ) (declared in the algorithm header). We can call that function for any sequence of entities if we supply an iterator to the start and an iterator to one past the end as the two arguments. Iterators are generalized location indicators; in the case of arrays they are simple pointers to the elements of the array. We get the start of an array by using the array name, and we get one past the end by adding on the number of elements in the array. Put that all together and we get:

```
void deck::shuffle( ){
  std::random_shuffle(pack, pack + cards);
}
```

TASK 10.1 ➡ Create a new project (in the chapter_10 directory). Copy card.h and card.cpp from the chapter_9 directory. (You will be changing some of the source code, so we want new copies, and it might be wise to rename them so that you do not confuse different versions.) Now create a deck.h file and insert a suitable header guard and the definition of the deck class. In addition to the code above, you will need to include card.h, so that the compiler can see the definition of card_value when we use it in the definition of deck.

Create a file named `deck.cpp`, and copy the implementation of the deck member functions and the static data member into it. You will need to include some headers and header files (I am leaving you to determine which). It is usually good practice to have a way to determine the order in which you write the `#includes`. My rule is to deal with the header files first and the C++ headers second. Within each group, I include them in alphabetical order.

Finally create a file named `testdeck.cpp` and add necessary headers and header files (in future, I will just use the term 'header' to include both Standard headers and user-written/third-party library header files). Add the following minimal version of `main()`:

```
int main(){
  try{
    deck d;
  }
  catch(...){std::cerr
               << "An exception was caught in main\n";}
}
```

Your project will need to include `card.cpp`, `deck.cpp`, and `test-deck.cpp`. When all those files compile successfully, build and execute the program. You will be flooded with messages produced by the instrumentation of the `card_value` class. Modify the implementation of `card_value` by removing the instrumentation and try again. This is now so simple that you will get no output. Add some instrumentation to the constructor and destructor for deck and try again.

It makes sense to keep the instrumented and uninstrumented implementations alongside each other in similarly (but not identically) named files. That way you can select which you use by editing the project to include the version you require. Another option would be to have two subdirectories, one for instrumented code and one for release versions. This option depends on your IDE allowing you to use `.cpp` files from different directories.

Output for deck

Before we test the other public member functions of **deck**, we need a way to examine the deck by printing out the cards. The following function does the job but reveals a design flaw in **deck**. In a moment, we will look at the flaw in the context of this draft definition:

```
std::ostream & operator<<(std::ostream & out, deck const & d){
  d.top();
  for(int i(0); i != 52; ++i) out << d.next() << '\n';
  return out;
}
```

I have chosen to use **operator<<** for output because C++ programmers expect that operator to do output. We would also expect that output of an object's state would not alter the state, which is why the second parameter is a **const** reference rather than a simple reference. At this point, we hit the first problem.

If we want to output the entire **deck** we must make sure we start at the beginning. The only member function we have for getting **card_value** values is **next( )**. That is not a **const** member function, because it changes the value stored in our **position** variable. That means that we cannot use **next( )** on a **const** reference to a **deck**. In addition, we do not know what value is currently stored in **position**. The only way we can access that is by using **top( )** to reset **position** to 0. The consequence is that our **deck** type does not have the functionality that we need, even though it looked OK to start with. Yes, we could remove that **const** qualification from the second parameter of the **operator<<** overload for **deck**. However, that only hides the problem: as currently designed, outputting a **deck** to a stream changes its internals.

There are several ways to fix this problem but let us stick with a simple one. What we need is a way to find which **card_value** value is at a specified point in the **deck**. We can achieve this using a member function with the following declaration:

```
card_value get_card(int pos)const;
```

The definition seems simple:

```
card_value deck::get_card(int pos)const{
   return deck[pos];
}
```

However, do you see the problem? Yes, it is not robust: a user could ask for a card at a position that is not valid for a standard deck (outside the range 0 to 51). Again, let us stick with a simple solution even though it is not up to production quality. Check and throw an exception if the value of **pos** is out of range. (You will need to include the **stdexcept** header so that the compiler can see a declaration of **std::range_error**.)

```
card_value deck::get_card(int pos)const{
   if(pos < 0 or pos > (cards - 1))
       throw std::range_error("No such position in deck");
   return pack[pos];
}
```

Using that in the definition of **operator<<** we get:

```
std::ostream & operator<<(std::ostream & out, deck const & d){
   for(int i(0); i != 52; ++i) out << d.get_card(i) << '\n';
   return out;
}
```

Even this code has a problem – the use of a magic 52. This highlights that the number of cards in a deck is not a private property but a public one. We could just add a **static** member function that returns the value. However, that seems somewhat excessive for such a case, and I would be happy to make the declaration of **cards** part of the public interface of **deck**. I want to keep **cards** within the scope of **deck** because it is specifically a property of **deck** rather than being some global value. We should always declare variables and constants in the smallest scope that supports their use. Once we have moved the declaration of **cards** to the public interface we can write:

```
std::ostream & operator<<(std::ostream & out, deck const & d){
   for(int i(0); i != deck::cards; ++i) out << d.get_card(i) << '\n';
   return out;
}
```

All the changes I have been suggesting have stuck with the design rule that we should avoid invalidating earlier code. Moving something from the private interface to the public interface is fine: old code will continue to work. Similarly, adding a new member function is usually acceptable, though we sometimes need to think before adding a new overload to an existing function. By the way, adding a const qualification is usually acceptable, but removing one almost always has the potential for breaking existing code.

TASK 10.2

Modify deck.h and deck.cpp so that the last version of std::ostream & operator<<(std::ostream & out, deck const & d) compiles satisfactorily. Now modify testdeck.cpp to define main() as:

```
int main(){
  try{
    deck d;
    d.shuffle();
    std::cout << d;
  }
  catch(...){std::cerr
            << "An exception was caught in main.\n";}
}
```

Build the project and run it a couple of times. Do you notice a problem? Each run of the program produces an identical shuffle. That may be fine when we are testing code, but it is not much use if we want to shuffle the deck differently each time. The C++ Standard is silent on this issue of how we can randomize the pseudo-random number generator used by the default version of random_shuffle (perhaps because there is an alternative form of random_shuffle() that uses a user-written pseudo-random number generator). In the case of the version of the Library that ships with this book, using std::srand() (declared in the cstdlib header) to seed the generator used by std::rand() works fine. (Do not worry too much about these little details; I am only including them to prevent false expectations if you later use a different C++ implementation.) Therefore, modify main() to:

```
int main(){
  try{
    std::srand(1);
    deck d;
    d.shuffle();
    std::cout << d;
  }
  catch(...){std::cerr
            << "An exception was caught in main.\n";}
}
```

However, that is no immediate improvement, because we have hardwired the seed used by std::srand(). If we really want different results each time we run the program, we need to remove that hard-coded argument passed to `std::srand()`. Here is a way that we can hand the responsibility to the user:

```cpp
int main(){
  try{
    std::srand(fgw::read<int>(
      "Input a seed for the random number generator: "));
    deck d;
    d.shuffle();
    std::cout << d;
  }
  catch(...){std::cerr
                << "An exception was caught in main.\n";}
}
```

You will need to include the `fgw_text.h` header file in order to use my `read<>` function. You may also need to amend the project settings to tell the compiler where to look for that header file by adding to the includes path.

As an alternative to seeding the random number generator with a user-provided value, you can seed it with a value dependent on the system's best approximation to calendar time by using:

```cpp
std::srand(time(0));
```

That statement is equivalent to `std::srand(-1)` if your system does not have a suitable internal clock. However, the kind of computer you are using for this book should not have that problem.

If you want to learn more about pseudo-random number generators, please read Chapter 10 of *You Can Do It!* (electronic copy on this book's CD).

Creating a deck Instance From a File

We have provided a mechanism for writing out the current order of a **deck** (of cards). It would make sense to provide a mechanism for creating a **deck** instance with that order used for initialization. The terms 'creating' and 'initialization' should suggest using a constructor. Here is a way to do that.

Add the declaration **deck(std::istream &);** to the definition of **deck**. Now add this definition to **deck.cpp**:

```cpp
deck::deck(std::istream & in):position(0){
  for(int i(0); i != cards; ++i) in >> pack[i];
}
```

Note that this definition delegates all the input validation to the **operator>>** provided for **card_value**. It also assumes that the input operator for **card_value** matches the output operator. We should have ensured that that is the case, because programmers reasonably expect that what is written to a stream can be read back from a stream.

One other implicit assumption in the above constructor is that the source of data will be sufficient and correct for a **deck**. It would be a useful exercise to refine the above definition to perform some validation.

The first step might be to recognize that because `card_value` supports the streaming operators (`<<` and `>>`), we can use `fgw::read<card_value>(in)` to extract card values from input. That will ensure that we only use legitimate card values. Incidentally, that will cater for a source that has too few values, because it will fail by throwing an exception when we ask for more values than it has to give. If we want to do a better job, we will also check that all the `card_value` values are different. I will leave it to you to choose a way to do that. (Creating a copy of the `deck` and sorting it might be a good way to start such a check.)

EXERCISES

6. Design a class `hand` to represent a hand of cards. Because we do not know the number of cards in a hand at design time (indeed, the number of cards might vary during the execution of a program concerned with hands of cards), we need a container that can take a variable number of elements. `std::vector` is such a container. We will also need a variable to track the current number of cards in a hand.

   Here is something to get you started:

```
class hand{
public:
  hand();  // create an empty hand
  void add(card_value);  // add a card
  void sort();  // sort hand by suit and denomination
  card_value card_at(int i);  // return card at specified position
  int size();  // return number of cards in the hand
private:
  std::vector<card_value> hand_of_cards;
  int number_of_cards;
}
```

   This is just to get you started. You will need to add more member functions (note that a `hand` is an entity, so you should deal with the problem of copying) and some non-member ones as well. Your test program should allow you to shuffle a deck and deal a specified number of cards from the top of the deck into a hand, display the hand, then sort the hand and display it again. You might like to experiment with `std::reverse()`, which is a standard algorithm that reverses the elements of a sequence, so that the cards are sorted in the order spades, hearts, diamonds, clubs. (`std::reverse(hand_of_cards.begin(), hand_of_cards.end())` will reverse the current order.)

7. Design a function to value a bridge hand. Contract bridge players initially value a hand with something they call 'honor card points' (HCPs). They value every ace as 4, every king as 3, every queen as 2 and every jack (knave) as 1. Write a function that creates a hand of 13 cards by taking the next 13 cards from a `deck` (the `deck::next()` function will help with that). The declaration of this function will be:

```
void bridge_hand(hand &, deck &);
```

   When you define this function, you will need to deal with the possibility that the first parameter is not an empty `hand` object.

   Now define (implement) a function that returns the number of HCPs in the `hand` passed in by reference. Note that valuing a hand does not change it, hence the `const` reference parameter.

```
int hand_value(hand const &);
```

Write a program to deal out four hands from a shuffled deck of cards and output the hands with each suit on a new line (in the order spades, hearts, diamonds, clubs), following each hand with its HCP value. There should be a complete blank line between consecutive hands. So typical output might be:

Hand 1:: S 5
          H AJ962
          D A7
          C A10976
          HCPs: 13

Hand 2:: S 92
          H Q853
          D 962
          C QJ83
          HCPs: 5

Hand 3:: S AKQJ1073
          H 4
          D J54
          C K4
          HCPs: 14

Hand 4:: S 864
          H K107
          D KQ1083
          C 52
          HCPs: 8

While the above is close to an ideal output, it needs quite a bit of extra work to suppress the suit part of a card's name, given the way that the `card` output currently works. Do not feel you have to achieve the above layout, especially as doing so will most likely require augmenting the card type with functions that simply report the value of the `card` rather than its name.

8. Read Chapter 6 of *You Can Do It!* (on CD) and use the ideas in that chapter to create a polygon entity type. Note that if you suppress the copy semantics (by making the copy constructor and copy-assignment operator private) you will need to provide a mechanism for copying polygons, such as a `copy_from( )` member function.

A polygon type is a classic example of a type that can reasonably be viewed as either a value type or an entity type, depending on the context in which you intend to use it.

STRETCHING EXERCISES

You will have noticed that I have kept to using `card_value` *instances throughout this chapter, even though a pack of cards would more normally be considered as a collection of* `cards`. *If you are feeling in an experimental mood, try replacing* `card_value` *with* `card` *throughout the code I have provided in this chapter. However, you will find that it does not work and the fix is not obvious; indeed, it deserves a chapter all to itself. A solution is in the next chapter.*

REFERENCE SECTION

Entity Types

Entity types are ones where the identity of an instance of the type is significant. If I lend you $50, I do not care how you repay the loan as long as you do so. If I lend you an original Rembrandt painting, I care very much that you return the original – a copy just will not do. Money is a value type; original paintings are very definitely entities.

Suppressing Copy Semantics

One distinguishing feature of a value type is that it can be, and often is, passed and returned by value. We are rarely concerned with the identity of an instance of a value type – only with the value it contains. That means that copies are as good as the originals. If we do nothing, a C++ compiler will treat any type we define as a value type by generating a copy constructor and a copy assignment. If you are curious about why that is the case, it is because the ancestor language, C, is a value-based language in which everything is passed and returned by value.

We need to know how to turn off copy semantics when we wish to design a pure entity class (one whose instances cannot be freely copied). The standard way to do that is to add the following declarations to the private interface of the class:

class-name(*class-name* **const &);**
class-name **& operator=(***class-name* **const &) ;**

The consequence of those additions is that any attempt to copy instances of *class-name* outside the scope of class *class-name* will trigger an access-violation error at compile time.

We do not define those member functions, unless we have a reason to want to allow copying within the class implementation. The lack of a definition means that any accidental attempt to copy from within the class scope will trigger a missing-definition error at link time.

CHAPTER (11)

Pointers, Smart Pointers, Iterators, and Dynamic Instances

I have been using pointers in the early part of this book without spending much time explaining them. I have also used iterators. The time has come for us to look at these mechanisms in some detail. While doing so we will also look at the way C++ allows us to extend the pointer concept and how C++ allows us to create objects during the running of a program. We call the latter *dynamic objects*.

We will also see how a combination of pointers and dynamic objects helps to solve the problem of creating and managing a deck of cards, with the cards treated as entities rather than values.

Quite a lot of this chapter is difficult to understand at first reading. Fortunately, we can do a great deal of programming in C++ without ever using pointers. For example, I never mention pointers in my book for newcomers to programming (*You Can Do It!*). Pointers are probably the single most difficult aspect of programming, and C++ stretches their use in low-level programming. That means that C++ programmers must eventually master them if they are to graduate to become experts.

Even more than elsewhere in this book, this chapter relies on your trying many small programs and experimenting until you are confident that you understand them. However, you can continue with an incomplete understanding, and come back to consolidate it later on.

Raw Pointers

C++ inherited the syntax and semantics of raw pointers from C. However, the way we use pointers in C++ is a little different because we have other tools that take over some of the uses of pointers. For that reason, I am going to give a very brief overview of pointers and then limit myself to their idiomatic use in C++.

In essence, a pointer value is the address of something, and a pointer instance is a place to store such an address. We can take the addresses of objects (data), and we can take the addresses of free functions and static member functions. The addresses of non-static member functions are handled differently and I will not be dealing with them in this book.

C++ obtains addresses in the same way that C does. It has an explicit address-of operator, which is an & (ampersand) preceding an object or function name. The name of a function without a parenthetical list of arguments resolves to the address of the function (given that **foo** is the name of a function, both **foo** and **&foo** evaluate to the address of the function). The name of an array usually evaluates as the address of the first element of the array. There are a few exceptions to this even in C, and a few more in C++.

Pointer objects provide storage for addresses of the same type. The type of a pointer is given by appending an * (asterisk) to a type name. So:

- An `int*` is a pointer to an `int` and can store the address of an `int` object.
- A `float*` is a pointer to a `float` and can store the address of a `float` object.
- If `mytype` is a user-defined type (e.g. a `class` or `enum` type), a `mytype*` is a pointer to a `mytype` and can store the address of a `mytype` object.
- A *type* `const*` is a pointer to a *type* object that can only be used to access the value or state of the object addressed. It can store the addresses of both `const` and non-`const` *type* objects. This pointer type can also be written as `const type*`.
- A *type*`* const` is a `const` pointer to a *type* object. This should not be confused with *type* `const*`. We need to distinguish between `const` pointers, where it is the address that is `const`, and pointers to `const`, where it is the object addressed that is `const`.

There is a subtle difference between a `const` qualifier that is not the last part of a pointer type's name and one that is. We refer to the latter as a top-level `const`, and it results in a type whose instances are immutable. Just like `const`-qualified non-pointer types, instances of a type that is top-level `const` are immutable. A pointer to a `const`-qualified type merely limits access to the addressed object to reading. It does not imply that the object is immutable, only that we cannot make use of the address stored in the pointer to write to the object.

Here is a simple program that we can use to explore pointers in practice (note that space before and after * is optional):

```
int main(){
  int i(0);
  int * i_ptr(&i);
  std::cout << "The address of i is " << i_ptr
      << " and the value of the addressed instance is "
      << *i_ptr << ".\n";
}
```

Note the uses of `i_ptr`. When I declared it, I initialized it by explicitly taking the address of `i`. I then output the value stored by streaming `i_ptr` to `std::cout`. However, when I want the value stored in the object addressed by `i_ptr` (in this case the value stored in `i`) I have to use the dereference operator (which is also an asterisk) and stream `*i_ptr` to `std::cout`. Try to get a clear mental distinction between the value stored in a pointer (an address) and the value of the object addressed.

C++ allows us to declare uninitialized pointers, but doing so is usually an error, because the only safe thing we can do with such a pointer is to assign a legal address to it.

TASK 11.1

Please try making the following edits to the above program and note the results:

1. **Change the declaration of i to `int const i(0)`. Note that the program no longer compiles. Make sure you understand why this is the case. Now change the declaration of`i_ptr` to `int const * i_ptr(&i)`. The program now compiles. Finally, remove the `const` qualifier from the declaration of `i`. Note that the program still compiles and runs satisfactorily.**

2. **Edit the original program to:**

   ```
   int main(){
     int i(0);
     int j(1);
   ```

```
    int * i_ptr(&i);
    std::cout << "The address of i is " << i_ptr
        << " and the value of the addressed instance is "
        << *i_ptr << ".\n";
    i_ptr = &j;
    std::cout << "The address of j is " << i_ptr
        << " and the value of the addressed instance is "
        << *i_ptr << ".\n";
}
```

Compile and run the resulting program. Now change the declaration of i_ptr to int * const i_ptr(&). Note that the resulting code will not compile. Make sure you understand the difference between placing const after the asterisk and before it. (Try int const * i_ptr(&i), and note that the program again compiles and runs successfully.)

3. Edit the original program to:

```
int main( ){
  int i(0);
  int * i_ptr(&i);
  std::cout << "The address of i is " << i_ptr
      << " and the value of the addressed instance is "
      << *i_ptr << ".\n";
  *i_ptr = 2;
  std::cout << "The value of i is now " << i << ".\n";
}
```

Compile and run the resulting program. Now change the declaration of i_ptr to int * const i_ptr(&), and note the reason the program now fails to compile. However, if you now change the assignment to i = 2, all is OK again. There is nothing wrong with assigning to i, just that we cannot use a const int* to do so. Finally change the declaration of i_ptr to int * const i_ptr(&), and restore the assignment to *i_ptr = 2.

A Dangerous Special Case

We could replace the int in the above code with just about any type and it would exhibit similar behavior, as long as we provided suitable initializers for the variables. However, there is a special case for char* (a pointer to char) and the streaming operators (<< and >>). C hijacked char* to provide a string type. We will see more details later when we take a brief look at C-style arrays. However, the important feature to note is that the above code becomes dangerous if you replace int by char. The streaming operators do not treat a char* as a simple pointer to a char. If we want the address of a char, we must tell the compiler to treat the pointer as a generic data pointer.

C++ (like C) provides a special type to handle generic data pointers. It is called void*, and the only thing we can do with a void* is store the address of raw memory in it.

```
int main( ){
  char i('A');
  char * i_ptr(&i);
  std::cout << "The address of i is " << static_cast<void*>(i_ptr)
      << " and the value of the addressed instance is "
      << *i_ptr << ".\n";
}
```

Please try that code, but under no circumstances try it without the `static_cast<void*>` unless you are willing to accept the consequences (actually most systems may not show any problems, but that should not lull you into a false sense of security). The `static_cast<void*>` instructs the compiler to handle the address stored in `i_ptr` as a raw memory address and not as a `char*`.

Arrays

We have already used simple arrays in this book, but I have deliberately avoided going into much detail. We declare arrays in C++ the same way that we declare them in C. The syntax is:
   type array-name [*number-of-elements*];
The elements are numbered from zero, so given

```
int array[10];
```

`array[0]` is the first element and `array[9]` is the last one.
      Simple declarations of arrays result in default initialization. If it is an array of a class type, the elements are created with the type's default constructor. In general, you cannot create an array of a class type if the type lacks a default constructor. However, C++ has inherited a special case from C called direct initialization. The syntax for this is:
   type array-name [*number-of-elements+*] = {*initializer-list*};
      The initializer list is a comma-separated list of initializers used to initialize the elements of the array. If there are fewer initializers than elements, the remaining elements are initialized by default. At this point, the rules become extremely complicated (to the extent that most experts will make mistakes). Fortunately, that complexity need not worry us, because experienced C++ programmers limit their use of arrays and avoid getting into the more problematic areas. If you limit yourself to arrays of built-in types and possibly arrays of pointers, you will avoid problems. C++ has alternative mechanisms to handle collections of objects that are not available to the C programmer.
      The final piece of syntax for declaring arrays is:
   type array-name [ ] = {*initializer-list*};
If we omit the number of elements, the compiler will deduce the number from the number of initializers.

TASK 11.2

1. **Create a project and type in the following short program, then compile and execute it:**

```
int main( ){
  const int array_size(5);
  int array[array_size] = {, 2};
  for(int i(0); i != array_size; ++i){
     std::cout << "Element " << i << " is "
         << array[i] << ".\n";
  }
}
```

Note that the output shows that the final three elements of array are set to zero. That is important: once you start initializing an array in its definition, all its elements are initialized. If you want to create an array of a built-in type with all elements zeroed, just provide an empty initialization list. The results of

```
int array[array_size] = { };
```

and

```
int array[array_size];
```

are not the same. The default for creating an int object is to leave it uninitialized. We get undefined behavior (i.e. absolutely anything can happen as a result) if we trying to read an uninitialized object. In other words, replacing the declaration of array in the above program with int array[array_size] = {}; is fine, but leaving out the = {} results in undefined behavior when we try to output the undefined values.

The above program is simple enough that there is very little risk that the undefined behavior will be harmful (and it is small enough that I just tried it after I had saved all my work), but the results may be instructive (they could still be all zeros, as some systems zero the stack before the first use).

2. Now consider this version of our program:

```
int main( ){
  int array[ ] = {1, 2};
  for(int i(0); i != something; ++i){
    std::cout << "Element " << i << " is "
        << array[i] << ".\n";
  }
}
```

What should replace the *something*? Leaving the compiler to work out the number of elements is fine – till we want to do something that requires that we know how many there are. There is a simple C idiom that solves this problem: we divide the amount of storage allocated to the array by the amount required for a single element. Here is how we could write it:

```
int const array_size(sizeof(array) / sizeof(int));
```

Note that we have to insert that statement after we have declared the array, so our program now becomes:

```
int main(){
  int array[] = {1, 3};
  int const array_size(sizeof(array) / sizeof(int));
  for(int i(0); i != array_size; ++i){
    std::cout << "Element " << i << " is "
        << array[i] << ".\n";
  }
}
```

3. **Try arrays of some other types and experiment until you are reasonably happy you understand the results.**

Arrays and Pointers

One of the design decisions for C++ was to make an effort to keep it compatible with C. Arrays cannot be passed around (or returned) by value in C; nor can they be in C++. C++ has an option to pass an array by reference, but that is limited to cases where the exact size of the array is known at the time we declare the function. For example:

```
void foo(int(& a_ref)[2]){
  std::cout << sizeof(a_ref)/sizeof(int) << '\n';
}
```

This declares the parameter `a_ref` as a reference to an array of two `int`s. We can call `foo( )` with an argument that is an array of two `int`s, but not any other size of array of `int`.

This is a big limitation of using arrays. We do not want to have to provide a new version of a function for each possible size of array. C fixed the problem by using pointers. We can, for example, declare:

```
void send_out(std::ostream &, int * a, int array_size);
```

The definition might be:

```
void send_out(std::ostream & out, int * a, int array_size){
  for(int i(0); i != array_size; ++i){
    out << "The value of element " << i << " is " << a[i] << ".\n";
  }
}
```

Here is a simple program that uses that function:

```
int main(){
  int array[] = {1, 3};
  int const array_size(sizeof(array) / sizeof(int));
  send_out(std::cout, array, array_size);
}
```

We have to pass the size of the array as an explicit argument because the function cannot deduce the size of the array. When we use the name of the array without subscripting, we get the address of the first element. C++ allows us to subscript a pointer; in other words, we can use a pointer object as if it is the name of an array. However, that places a great burden on the programmer, who must ensure that the subscript refers to an actual member of the array. This burden is yet another reason that experienced C++ programmers avoid using arrays when they can use an alternative C++ mechanism (the commonest being a `std::vector`).

When a pointer points to an element of an array, we can increment and decrement the pointer (and add and subtract integer values from it) to move through the elements of the array. However, we must be careful about stepping off the ends. Even loading an invalid pointer value (such as attempting to print it out) is undefined behavior in C++. C++ provides two special cases to assist with working with pointers.

One Beyond the End

The address of storage one beyond the end of an object or array is always a valid address, in the sense that you are allowed to use the address. However, you must not attempt to access any object through such an address (pointer value) because there will not normally be a suitable object located at that address. For example:

```
int main( ){
  int array[ ] = {1, 3};
  int const array_size(sizeof(array) / sizeof(int));
  std::cout << "The address beyond the start of array is "
      << array << ".\n";
  std::cout << "The address beyond the end of array is "
      << array + array_size << ".\n";
}
```

However, you must not replace `array + array_size` with `&array[array_size]`. The first expression stays strictly within the limits of pointers and makes use of the special case that the address just beyond the end of an object is a valid address. The second version asks for the address of the object `array[array_size]`; there is no such object, and consequently the code has undefined behavior.

Null Pointers

Because uninitialized pointers are generally accidents waiting to happen, C++ provides a special value that we can use when we do not have any other valid address to store in a pointer object. The actual value is up to the implementation, but whenever we set a pointer to zero (or use `NULL` from the `<cstdlib>` header), the compiler will substitute that special address. I like to think of that address as being equivalent to a safe landing zone on a hard drive; nothing is there, and so landing there does not cause any damage.

C++ adds some extra support to these null pointers by providing that they convert to `false` when our code requires a `bool` value. All other pointer values (addresses) convert to `true`.

Dynamic Instances

If it were not for the need to deal with dynamically created objects (ones explicitly created while the program is running), we could probably have avoided studying pointers in this book and have left them as a topic for an advanced book.

Languages that support object-orientation have more need than most to support objects created in response to runtime decisions. We will see in the next chapter that we sometimes need the ability to select the exact type of an object during the execution of a program. In addition, we may need to control the lifetime of an object rather than leaving such issues to be dealt with because a variable has gone out of scope.

Languages such as C allow the programmer to acquire a block of raw memory from an area called 'the heap' (using the `34malloc( )` family of library functions) and then 'manually' convert that memory into the object they wish to create. Other languages, such as Python, do all the work behind the scenes and leave the programmer little control. C++ provides a mechanism for creating new instances of a type in memory that has been provided from somewhere. The default mechanism for providing memory is from the heap.

That may sound complicated but it is actually easy in practice. All we need to do is write something such as:

```
mytype * mt_ptr(new mytype);
```

The important part above is **new mytype**, which results in two distinct things happening. First, the compiler arranges to get a suitable size and aligned block of memory for an instance of **mytype**. Just to be thoroughly confusing, C++ names this mechanism **operator new** and proceeds to provide ways in which the user can replace and/or overload that operator. We will not go there in this book; just note that it is possible, and that it is what programmers mean when they talk about 'overloading **new**'. The second thing that happens is that an instance of **mytype** is then constructed in the provided memory, and a pointer to the object is returned by the **new** expression. In the above definition, **mt_ptr** captures and stores the returned pointer. Another way of expressing that is to say that *****mt_ptr** is the newly created instance of **mytype**.

The object we just created will continue to exist until we explicitly destroy it. We usually accomplish this by using the **delete** expression, whose action is the reverse of **new**. **delete** first calls the destructor for the object pointed to, and then uses **operator delete** (again, it can be replaced or overloaded) to return the raw memory to its source (usually the heap).

Playing Cards Revisited

Remember that in the last chapter we had a problem because **card** is an entity type without a default constructor. That meant that we could not have an array of **card**, because arrays require a default constructor (unless we can use direct initialization, as shown in the early part of this chapter). The following short program shows you how we can combine pointers and dynamic objects to work our way around this problem:

```
 1 int main( ){
 2   try{
 3     int const cards(5);
 4     card * d[cards] = { };
 5     for(int i(0); i != cards; ++i){
 6       d[i] = new card(card_value(i));
 7     }
 8     std::random_shuffle(d, d + cards);
 9     for(int i(0); i != cards; ++i){
10       d[i]->send_to(std::cout);
11       std::cout << '\n';
12     }
13     for(int i(0); i != cards; ++i){
14       delete d[i];
15     }
16   }
17   catch(...){
18     std::cerr << "An exception occurred.\n";
19   }
20 }
```

WALKTHROUGH

Line 3 allows us to use a small number of cards for our initial development and then replace it with a full pack later on if we want to. Line 4 defines an array of pointers to `card` called `d` and makes it safe by initializing them to null pointers (that is the effect of the `=` when applied to an array of pointers).

Lines 5–7 loop through the array, on each pass creating a dynamic `card`, whose address is stored. Note that we can choose which constructor we use with `new`.

Line 8 uses the library function `random_shuffle()` (declared in the `<algorithm>` header) to shuffle the elements of `d`. The arguments passed to `random_shuffle()` provide a pointer to the first element of the array and a pointer to the one beyond the end of the array. The whole of the design for handling collections of objects (in this case an array of pointers) is based on being able to provide an iterator (a pointer in the case of an array) to the first element and an iterator to one beyond the end. Without the guarantee that the address one beyond the end of an array is valid, we would not have been able to apply the standard algorithms to simple arrays.

Lines 9–12 output the shuffled cards in order of their positions. Line 10 demonstrates how we can use a pointer to access a member function.

We call `->` the arrow operator, and we read it as 'points to'. If you prefer, you could write `(*d[i]).send_to(std::cout)` (that is, get the instance pointed to by `d[i]` and apply `send_to(std::cout)` to it). However, the arrow operator makes the code clearer and so we would normally prefer it in cases like this one.

Lines 13–15 loop through `d`, destroying each of the `card` instances. If we did not do this, the destructors for the instances would not be called. An important guideline when dealing with dynamic objects is that every time you use the `new` expression you must also use the `delete` expression. You should also avoid creating dynamic arrays with `new`, as that is a significantly different operation, involving multiple calls of the constructor. C++ provides a distinct mechanism for handling dynamic arrays, which is largely defunct in high-level code. These days we use `std::vector<>` when we want a dynamic array, and all the fiddly details are handled for us. (Only people such as the implementers of `std::vector<>` need to spend time understanding the subtleties of dynamic arrays in C++.)

Exception Safety

When we create dynamic objects, we face a problem with their destruction if an exception occurs. How do we ensure that the dynamic objects will be destroyed? There are several solutions to this. Before going on to a more general solution, here is one that works in simple cases where we have complete control. Note that it relies on the guarantee that an attempt to delete a null pointer will result in nothing happening.

We need to ensure that if an exception occurs, the `catch` clause releases any dynamically allocated resources (usually memory, but there are other resources we may need to release). As a rule, we use destructors for releasing resources, but sometimes we can avoid that. Here is our program rearranged to handle the dynamically created instances of `card` even if an exception happens:

```
1 int main(){
2   int const cards(5);
3   card * d[cards] = { };
4   try{
5     for(int i(0); i != cards; ++i){
6       d[i] = new card(card_value(i));
```

```
 7     }
 8     std::random_shuffle(d, d + cards);
 9     for(int i(0); i != cards; ++i){
10       d[i]->send_to(std::cout);
11       std::cout << '\n';
12     }
13   }
14   catch(...){
15     std::cerr << "An exception occurred.\n";
16   }
17   for(int i(0); i != cards; ++i){
18     delete d[i];
19   }
20 }
```

This is exactly the same code that we had before except that I have moved some statements outside the try block. Lines 2 and 3 consist of exception-safe definitions: they will not cause an exception. However, we need the declaration of d to be outside the try block, because d must remain in scope after the end of that block. I have moved the loop that deletes the dynamic instances of card to the end of the program (after the catch(...) clause) so that this cleanup code will run even if an exception fires.

TASK 11.3

1. Create a project. Enter, compile, and run the above program. Note that its output is indistinguishable from the previous version.

2. Insert the line

   ```
   throw std::exception();
   ```

   between lines 7 and 8. Test the program and note that the cleanup happens immediately after we finish constructing the dynamic instances of card.

3. Move the insertion of throw std::exception(); back to between lines 4 and 5. Test the resulting program. Note that the destructor for card is never called – which is what we would hope for, because we threw an exception before any instances of card were constructed.

4. Insert the line

   ```
   if(i == 2) throw std::exception;
   ```

   between lines 6 and 7 in the version of the program from step 1. Test the resulting program and note that there is a destructor called for every constructed card.

Redesigning deck

I am going to call the redesigned class pack to avoid confusion, because I am going to change the public interface in ways that are incompatible with my previous design:

```
class pack{
public:
  static int const cards = 52;
  pack( );
  pack(std::istream &);
  ~pack( );
  void shuffle( );
  card & next( );
  void top( );
  void copy_from(pack const &);
  card & get_card(int pos)const;
private:
  pack(pack const &);
  pack & operator=(pack const &);
  int position;
  card * pack_[cards];
};
```

Remember that one of the identifying properties of an entity is its identity. That is why **next( )** and **get_card( )** return a **card&**. Otherwise, the public interface of **pack** is much the same as that for **deck**.

Implementing pack

There are a few trivial bits that we might as well get out of the way before we look at the more complicated pieces:

```
int const pack::cards;  // define the static member
void pack::top( ){
  position = 0;  // reset to top of pack
}
void pack::shuffle( ){
  std::random_shuffle(pack_, pack_ + cards);  // wrapper for
random_shuffle
}
```

Next, we have the two constructors. We have to cater for exceptions happening during construction, and C++ does not, at the time of writing, provide a mechanism for initializing an array of pointers to null pointers as part of a constructor. The method we used in ordinary code is not available for constructor initializer lists. However, we need our pointers to be safe to delete even if the process of creating instances of **card** fails. The first line of the body of each constructor sets all the pointers in the array to null. We then enter a loop to create the cards we need. If that process fails for any reason, we destroy any already-constructed instances of **card** before rethrowing the exception (that is what the **throw** by itself means). If no exception interferes, the constructor completes (and because we are instrumenting our code, the final line of each constructor body reports successful completion).

```
pack::pack( ):position(0), pack_(){
  try{
    for(int i(0); i != cards; ++i){
      pack_[i] = new card(card_value(i));
    }
  }
  catch(...){
```

```
      std::cerr << "An exception occurred.\n";
      for(int i(0); i != cards; ++i) delete pack_[i];
      throw;
    }
    std::clog << "Pack of cards created.\n";
}
```

The **pack_( )** in the constructor initializer list initializes the array to null pointers. It is a special syntax introduced late in the standardization of C++ to provide explicit zero-initialization of an entity.

```
pack::pack(std::istream & in):position(0), pack_(){
  try{
    for(int i(0); i != cards; ++i){
      card_value const val(fgw::read<card_value>(in));
      pack_[i] = new card(val);
    }
  }
  catch(...){
    std::cerr << "An exception occurred.\n";
    for(int i(0); i != cards; ++i) delete pack_[i];
    throw;
  }
  std::clog << "Pack of cards created from input.\n";
}
```

   fgw::read<> relies on an overload of **operator>>( )** for the type we are reading.
   The destructor is straightforward. However, it is no longer a trivial destructor; it has real work to do before reporting that it has run. This is a typical example of using a destructor to release resources acquired during construction:

```
pack::~pack( ){
  for(int i(0); i != cards; ++i) delete pack_[i];
  std::clog << "Pack of cards destroyed.\n";
}
```

   Experienced programmers may recognize that the semantics of the **copy_from( )** function below is copy assignment. I do not want to allow assignment because it is too easy to make a mistake and copy unintentionally. However, we have to consider all the problems of copying. Look at the **for** loop. First, I create a dynamic copy of the next **card** and hang on to it with a **temp**. That action might fail with an exception. However, if it does, the two instances of **pack** are in stable conditions. The destination one may now be an incomplete copy, but it is in a destructible state. Once I have created my copy of the next **card**, I can safely destroy the one it is replacing and transfer the pointer held in **temp** to the now vacated position in the array **pack_**. This is a short function, but work through it carefully, making sure you understand how it works.

```
void pack::copy_from(pack const & source){
  for(int i(0); i != cards; ++i){
    card * temp(new card(source.pack_[i]->get_value( )));
    delete pack_[i];   // remove current item
    pack_[i] = temp;
  }
  position = source.position;
}
```

When I came to implement `pack::next()` I had to first store a reference to the next card before updating the pointer. Notice how I have dereferenced the pointer to get the `card` instance. I chose to do this at the first opportunity because the compiler may be able to do a better job if it can see what I want as early as possible.

```
card & pack::next(){
  card & next_card(*pack_[position]);
  ++position;
  if(position == cards) position = 0;
  return next_card;
}
card & pack::get_card(int pos)const{
  if(pos < 0 or pos > (cards - 1))
      throw std::range_error("No such position in pack");
  return *pack_[pos];
}
```

Finally, I am providing an overload for `operator<<` for `pack` (the corresponding input is by using the second constructor). There is rather more detail to this function, so I would not define it inline. You will need to provide a suitable declaration in `card.h` and add this definition to `card.cpp`.

```
std::ostream & operator<<(std::ostream & out, pack const & d){
  for(int i(0); i != pack::cards; ++i){
    out << d.get_card(i) << '\n';
  }
  return out;
}
```

1. Add the definition of pack to `card.h` and the implementation to `card.cpp`. (You may find it helpful to declare a smaller value for `pack::cards` while you are trying the code out; I used 5 instead of 52). Make sure that `card.cpp` compiles. Now try this simple test program:

```
int main(){
  try{
    pack p;
    pack p1;
    p1.shuffle();
    p1.copy_from(p);
    p.shuffle();
  }
  catch(...){
    std::cerr << "An exception occurred\n";
  }
}
```

Experiment with this code until you are sure you know how it works.

2. Modify the above program to test input from an input stream. As `std::cin` is the only input stream you have available, you will definitely need to reduce `pack::cards` to less than the 52 cards in a complete pack.

Smart Pointers

We often wish that a pointer would do more for us. For example, when a pointer is holding the address of a dynamically created object, it would be nice if the object were automatically destroyed when the pointer goes out of scope.

C++ provides us with the basics to create user-defined types (classes) whose instances have pointer-like semantics. At a minimum, such classes provide an overload for `operator->` (the points-to operator) and `operator*` (the dereference operator, not the multiplication operator). In addition, we can provide overloads for `operator++` (the increment operator) and `operator--` (the decrement operator). We can also support addition and subtraction of integer values.

In general, a smart pointer is any user-defined type that provides overloads for `operator->` and `operator*`. Such types are almost invariably written as class templates, so that they can be used to manage the addresses of a wide variety of types. They are notoriously difficult to write correctly (and so I will not be tackling that issue in this book). The difficulty is exemplified by `std::auto_ptr<>`, which is the only freestanding smart pointer in the current Standard Library; `std::auto_ptr<>` achieves rather less than it was originally designed to do, and the flaws were discovered too late in the standardization process for correction.

`std::auto_ptr<>` was designed to manage the lifetimes of single dynamic objects (`std::vector<>` largely replaces any requirement for dynamic arrays). However, it was also intended for use in collections, to handle dynamic instances (e.g. `pack`'s array of `card*`), so that we would not need to handle destruction of the dynamic instances explicitly. Unfortunately, there is an issue with the semantics of `std::auto_ptr<>` that makes it unsafe to use such 'algorithms' as `sort()` and `random_shuffle()` on a collection of them.

There are other widely available smart pointers, such as `shared_nptr` from Boost (see `http://www.boost.org/libs/smart_ptr/smart_ptr.htm`). Some of these will be added to the Standard Library at its next release (circa 2009). Many of these, such as `counted_ptr<>` and `shared_ptr<>`, will work safely in a standard container.

Here is a simple program to demonstrate the use of `std::auto_ptr<>`:

```
int main(){
  std::auto_ptr<card> ex(new card(card_value(3)));
  std::clog << "Example of using the overloaded ->: ";
  ex->send_to(std::clog);
  std::clog << '\n';
  std::cout << "Example of dereferencing: " << *ex << '\n';
}
```

`std::auto_ptr<>` is declared in the `<memory>` header; this may have been included indirectly with one of the other headers you need for this program, but that will not always be the case.

Note that this program behaves almost the same as one with the first statement replaced by:

```
card * ex(new card(card_value(3)));
```

However, if you look carefully, you will see that the raw-pointer version never destroys the `card` object.

Guidelines for Using `std::auto_ptr<>`

`std::auto_ptr<>` has non-standard copy semantics: it passes the address it holds to the copy. That means that any copying of a `std::auto_ptr<>` (by using its copy constructor or its copy-assignment operator) changes the copied object. The intention was to provide a smart pointer type that would relay responsibility for an object so that only one instance would be responsible for the life of an object at any moment in a program. This seductive idea has unintentional side effects. The following three guidelines will keep you away from them:

- Do not pass it by value. In other words do not write functions that take a `std::auto_ptr<>` by value; always use a reference parameter.
- Be careful about returning a `std::auto_ptr<>`. Return it by reference if it was provided as a reference parameter (ensuring that the original retains responsibility for the address); return it by value if it is a local variable in the current function (transferring the address it contains to the caller).
- Do not use collections (arrays, `std::vector<>`, etc.) of `std::auto_ptr<>`. The algorithms that manipulate collections are designed to work with standard copy semantics (where copying does not change the original).

Iterators

Like so many other terms, the term 'iterator' in C++ has a different meaning from that used in computer science. An iterator in C++ is an object or value that locates another object. Raw pointers and most smart-pointer types are examples of C++ iterators.

C++ has a hierarchy of iterator concepts. All iterators support `operator->` and `operator*`; in other words, an iterator is always a smart pointer (unless it is a raw pointer).

In addition, a forward iterator supports `operator++` (to move from one instance to the next one). Forward iterators can be useful for input and output where we can only move forward through a sequence.

A bidirectional iterator is a forward iterator that also supports `operator--` (to move to the previous instance). The iterators for `std::list<>` (which is a doubly linked list template type) are examples of bidirectional iterators, because they allow stepwise traversal of a list in either direction. However, a singly linked list type would normally only provide forward iterators.

Random-access iterators are bidirectional iterators that also support `operator+(int)` and `operator-(int)`. A raw pointer is a random-access iterator.

In general, it is the responsibility of the programmer to ensure that invalid iterators are not used. This includes knowing such things as the possible consequences of appending new elements to a `std::vector<>`. The designers of `std::vector<>` stipulated that the elements must be held in contiguous storage. The consequence of this requirement is that adding new elements can result in relocating the storage used for the existing elements. Here is a code snippet to demonstrate the problem:

```
1 std::vector<int> v(1);
2 v[0] = 1000;
3 std::vector<int>::iterator iter(v.begin( ));
4 std::cout << *iter << '\n';
5 for(int i(0); i != 100; ++i) v.push_back(i);
6 // at this point iter is no longer valid and must not be dereferenced
```

Line 1 declares v to be a vector of `int` with a single element. Line 2 initializes this single element to 1000. Line 3 declares `iter` as an iterator for a vector of `int` and initializes it to hold the location of the first (and only) element of v. Line 5 loops 100 times to add another 100 elements to the end of v. That process will almost certainly result in moving the location v is using to store its elements. As a result, `iter` will no longer hold the location of the first element of v.

If you want to turn the above code into a program and are willing to accept all responsibility for the consequences, you can replace line 6 with a repeat of line 4. However, if the result is reformatting your hard drive, do not say I did not warn you. As we are dealing with `int`s the result of this 'dangerous' program is relatively risk-free (I saved all my work and tried it myself). However, doing the same with a user-defined type could have bad consequences, so learn not to do it.

This particular kind of invalidation of operators is specific to `std::vector<>` (and `std::string`). The other standard containers, such as `std::deque<>`, do not have the problem of moving their elements to new locations. Nonetheless, it is usually a poor idea to hang on to an iterator value for any length of time. Refresh the values immediately before use.

REFERENCE SECTION

Pointers

These are derivative types whose values are the addresses of instances of a type. We obtain the name of a pointer type by appending an * (asterisk) to the name of the type whose instances we wish to address. So int* is the pointer type for storing addresses of ints, and card* is the pointer type for holding addresses of card objects.

If we want to use the object addressed by a pointer, we obtain it by prefixing the pointer with an asterisk. Therefore, if i_ptr is an int* containing the address of an int, *i_ptr will be an alias for the int. If mt_ptr is a mytype* holding the address of an instance of mytype, mt_ptr->member is equivalent to (*mt_ptr).member. However, we can overload both operator* and operator-> for user-defined types, so that equivalence could be broken if the programmer providing the overloads does so inconsistently.

Like all other non-reference data types, you can append const to a pointer type to mark the variable being declared as immutable. So

```
int i(0);
int* const ic_ptr(&i);
```

makes ic_ptr an immutable pointer to i. In other words, we cannot assign the address of another int to ic_ptr.

We can also const-qualify the type being pointed to. That prevents the program from using the address stored in the pointer to change the addressed object. For example,

```
int i(0);
int const * ci_ptr(&i);
```

restricts uses of *ci_ptr (dereferencing ci_ptr to get the object whose address is stored in it) to reading the value of the object addressed. Even though i is mutable (and so we could write i = 0;), we cannot write *ci_ptr = 1;.

The following is equivalent to the above definition of ci_ptr:

```
const int * ci_ptr(&i);
```

However, for consistency, I prefer to place the const qualifier directly to the right of the type being qualified.

A pointer to an element of an array (strictly speaking, C++ mostly treats single objects as arrays of one element) can be incremented (++) or decremented (--) to locate an immediately succeeding or preceding element of the same type. You may also add or subtract an integer value to move forward or backward that number of elements. It is the responsibility of the programmer to ensure that such an element exists and is part of the same array. Stepping off either end of an array results in undefined behavior. There is one exception to this rule: C++ allows a pointer to hold the address of just beyond an array or object, but any attempt to dereference such a pointer results in undefined behavior.

There is a second special case: assigning (or initializing) 0 (often provided as a manifest constant called NULL) to a pointer results in placing the pointer in a safe state (but one that must not be dereferenced). We call a pointer that results from this a null pointer. A null pointer has the bool value false; all other pointers are treated as true.

C++ provides a special pointer type, void*, which can store the address of any instance of a data type. However, the only thing we can do with such a pointer is convert it back to a correctly typed pointer for the address stored.

C++ also supports pointers to functions.

Arrays

C++ has a primitive (one-dimensional) array mechanism inherited from C. Arrays are always based on zero; in other words, the first element of an array x is x[0]. There are three variants for declaring an array:

- type *array-name* [*number-of-elements*] ;
  Given that *number-of-elements* is a compile-time constant, this declares an array *array-name* of *number-of-elements* instances of *type*.
- type *array-name* [*number-of-elements*] = {*initializer-list*};
  The array *array-name* is said to be directly initialized. If there are fewer initializers than *number-of-elements*, the remaining elements are default-initialized (to zero for fundamental types and pointers).
- type *array-name* [ ] = {*initializer-list*};
  The number of elements in the array *array-name* is implicitly determined from the number of initializers that have been provided.

Using the name of an array in a context where we need a pointer results in the first element of the array being addressed.

We cannot pass or return arrays by value; instead, we use the address of the array (often implicitly).

If we need multi-dimensional arrays we have to create arrays of arrays (of arrays ...). For example, a ten-by-eight array of `int` is declared as:

```
int twoD[10][8];
```

An initialized two-dimensional array of **double** might be declared as

```
double array2d[3][5] = {{0, 1, 2, 3, 4}, {2,4,7}};
```

which would create an array of the following form:

```
0.0 1.0 2.0 3.0 4.0
2.0 4.0 7.0 0.0 0.0
0.0 0.0 0.0 0.0 0.0
```

Note that once you start initializing, any elements without explicit initializers are set to 0.

Only the first dimension can have an implicit size. Therefore:

```
int array[ ][3] = {{2, 3, 4}, {3}};
```

defines an array of two arrays of three `int`s. However,

```
int array[4][ ] = {{2, 3, 4}, {3}};
```

is an error.

Smart Pointers

The term 'smart pointer' refers to a user-defined type that, at a minimum, provides overloads for **operator->** (the arrow operator, which is applied to a pointer or smart pointer to access a member of the instance whose location is provided by the (smart) pointer) and **operator*** (which converts a (smart) pointer into the object it locates, the operation called *dereferencing*).

Smart pointers allow us to add extra behavior to the pointer concept. We often use a smart-pointer type to manage the lifetime of a dynamic object. Such management is important in contexts where exceptions may have to be dealt with; we need to deal with the release of resources.

`std::auto_ptr<>` is the only smart pointer provided by the Standard Library. It is of limited usefulness because of its quirky copy semantics. Other smart-pointer types are available from Boost (`http://www.boost.org/`), which is the official site for a group of highly skilled library developers testing items that might be added to the next full release of C++ (circa 2009), and some of them are in the recently published Library Technical Report.

Iterators

A C++ iterator does not match the computer-science concept of an iterator. In C++, an iterator is any type (or value of such a type) that locates an object (i.e. it is a raw pointer or smart pointer). The various Standard Library collection types such as `std::vector<>`, `std::map<>`, etc. provide nested iterator types to support access to the contained elements.

Generic Programming and the STL [Austern 1999] gives a detailed description of the design and implementation of iterators.

CHAPTER (12)

User-Defined Types, Part 4: Class hierarchies, polymorphism, inheritance, and subtypes

C++ provides a mechanism for deriving a new user-defined class type from an existing one. In the early days of C++, this mechanism was widely used by programmers who wanted to add to or modify the functionality of an existing class. These days, that is less common, because programmers have become more sophisticated in the use of their tools.

C++ provides three ways to use an existing class as the base for a new one: public, protected, and private inheritance. In this book, I will focus on public inheritance, because the correct use of the other two forms is highly specialized. I am also going to stick strictly to the use of inheritance for providing a class hierarchy where different subclasses may have different implementations of the same interface.

The concept of a planar shape is a common example. Every shape should have a function that displays (draws) it on the screen. However, the way we draw a circle is quite different from the way we draw a regular pentagon. If we had a collection of shapes created at run time according to a user's choices, one piece of functionality for the program would be to refresh the display on the monitor. We would want to iterate through the collection, asking each shape to display itself.

This process of providing different implementations for different cases is an example of something that computer science calls polymorphism (literally, 'many behaviors'). C++ supports several types of polymorphism – both overloading and templates are, in some uses, examples of static (compile-time) polymorphism. We are going to use inheritance to provide runtime, or dynamic, polymorphism. In other words, the compiler delays the decision as to which detailed behavior is appropriate until execution time.

For the purposes of introducing you to the concept and implementation of polymorphism, I am going to develop some code to deal with chess pieces. Every chess piece can move, but the details of the move depend on which piece it is. I will deal with the advanced issue where we need an object (chess piece) to be able to change its behavior (the promotion of a pawn to another piece) in a later chapter. In computer-science terminology, a specific chess piece (such as a knight or a bishop) is a *subtype* of the concept of a chess piece.

We use the term 'subtyping' to refer to cases where objects of a derived type are strictly usable wherever we require an object of the base type. An object of a subtype may have extra behavior, but it has all the behavior of the base type even if the implementation details may be different. We often call this relationship between base and derived type the Liskov Substitution Principle (after Barbara Liskov, who first stated it).

Some readers may not be familiar with the basic moves of chess pieces. I did a quick search of the Internet when I started to write this chapter, using the keywords 'chess', 'tutorial', and 'beginners'. I got over a quarter of a million hits. Fortunately, several early hits met my need. At the time of writing, `http://www.intuitor.com/chess/` provides exactly what we need. It might not still be there when you look, which is why I am telling you how I found it.

An Interface for a Chess Piece

Our first step is to decide what the common properties and types of behavior for a chess piece are. Every chess piece has a color (black or white) and a location (its position on the chessboard – or off the chessboard because it has been captured). Every chess piece has the ability to move, but exactly what moves are legal depends on which piece it is, and in the case of rooks (castles) and kings we have to track past behavior (to allow for the combined move of 'castling'). That last piece of behavior is difficult, because it is not a property of an individual piece.

Here is a possible design for a class to represent a general chess piece:

```
class basic_chesspiece{
public:
  struct position{
    unsigned char file;  // location across the board
    unsigned char rank;  // location towards the opponent
  };
  static position const off_board;
  virtual bool move(position const &);
  position where( )const;
  bool is_white( )const;
  explicit basic_chesspiece(bool white = true, bool castle = false);
  explicit basic_chesspiece(position const &, bool white = true,
      bool castle = false);
  virtual ~basic_chesspiece( );
private:
  bool const white_;  // a chess piece is white or not-white
  position location_;
  bool can_castle_;
// disable copying
  basic_chesspiece(basic_chesspiece const &);
  basic_chesspiece & operator=(basic_chesspiece const &);
};
```

WALKTHROUGH

There are several new things in the above definition. The first, though not entirely new (I have mentioned it before), is the nested **struct** definition. Let me answer the simple question first: why did I define it as a **struct** rather than as a **class**? You already know that the two keywords are, apart from one small detail, synonymous. The small detail is that a **struct** has public access by default. I want to emphasize that the **position** type that is a member of **basic_chesspiece** gives public access to its data. Whether or not that is a good design is a different issue, one that we could debate over a beer sometime.

The second question is: why do I have a nested type at all? The location of a chess piece on a chessboard is made up of the rank (or row) and file (or column) of the square that it is on. Those two values are intimately related and I want to encapsulate that relationship into a type. I do not want to provide any special behavior for this type – well, not at the moment, though I might change my mind later on. C++ (like C and many other languages, but unlike Python, for example) restricts returns from functions to a single value or object. The `position` type allows me to package the two values locating a chess piece into a single object or value.

The next thing you will notice is the appearance of a new keyword, `virtual`. The effect of this keyword is to warn the compiler that we are declaring a member function that may have more than one implementation. Yes, read that again. This is not overloading but something else: a single declaration with context-dependent implementations. Please do not panic – you will shortly see how this can work, and how the context for the decision can be delayed until execution time. The technical term for such delayed selection of implementation code is 'dynamic binding.'

Now have a quick look at the end of the definition before we look at the rest of the public interface. The last two declarations are the idiomatic way that C++ programmers use to switch off the copy semantics that class types have by default. Because we have declared them, the compiler is relieved of the responsibility for them. Because they are private, nothing outside the class can call them; any attempt to do so will result in the compiler diagnosing an access violation. Moreover, when we come to write the implementation, we will not define those two functions; that way, an accidental attempt to use one while implementing the class will cause a link-time error ('undefined function' or something equivalent).

Back to the public interface. The member functions `move()` and `where()` are to allow us to instruct a chess piece to move somewhere else, and to ask a chess piece where it is currently (either on a particular square or off the board). The implementation of `move()` will depend on which chess piece we are using, so we declare it as `virtual`. In other words, we do not know what constitutes a legitimate move until we know which piece we are moving. We cannot know that at compile time (statically) and so must delay the choice of implementation until run time (dynamic binding).

It is probably not clear why I have declared the destructor as `virtual`. For the time being, take it as a coding guideline that any class with a `virtual` member function and a public destructor (yes, there are special class designs which incorporate non-public destructors) **must** declare a `virtual` public destructor.

All we have left of the public interface are the two constructors and a `static` data member. I have declared both constructors as `explicit` because we could use either of them with a single argument, and I do not want that possibility to allow the compiler to use a constructor as an implicit conversion operator (in the first case from `bool` to `basic_chesspiece`, and in the second case from `basic_chesspiece::position` to `basic_chesspiece`).

The static data member `off_board` avoids having some sort of magic value for the position of a chess piece that is off the board. How we represent the 'off board' location is unimportant (to the user), but it will help in reading code if we provide a name for that special value for `position`. In addition, it is a value that users of the class may need to refer to.

Testing the Interface

As soon as we have defined a tentative design for a class, we should create a test program that, at a minimum, uses each of the public members of the class. Here is an example of one for `basic_chesspiece`:

```
#include "chess.h"
#include <iostream>
#include <ostream>

int main(){
  try{
```

```
      basic_chesspiece bc;
      basic_chesspiece::position pos;
      pos = bc.where();
      std::cout << "The piece is on rank " << pos.rank
          << ", file " << pos.file << ".\n";
      bc.move(pos);
      std::cout << "The piece is ";
      if(bc.is_white()) std::cout << "white";
      else std::cout << "black";
      std::cout << ".\n";
    }
  catch(...){
      std::cerr << "Caught an exception.\n";
    }
}
```

TRY THIS

Create a new project. Create three files in that project called **test_chess.cpp**, **chess.h** and **chess.cpp**.

Type the above code into **test_chess.cpp** and the class definition into **chess.h**. Remember to add a suitable header guard. For the moment, leave **chess.cpp** empty.

As long as you have typed the source code correctly, you should be able to compile **test_chess.cpp**. However, if you try to build the project you will get a whole bundle of 'undefined reference to' errors. It is time we tackled that.

Implementing basic_chesspiece

The implementation of this class is straightforward, but to keep us all on track here is mine:

```
#include "chess.h"

bool basic_chesspiece::move(position const & loc){
  location_ = loc;
  return true;
}
basic_chesspiece::position basic_chesspiece::where()const{
  return location_;
}
bool basic_chesspiece::is_white()const{return white_;}
basic_chesspiece::basic_chesspiece(bool white, bool castle)
    :white_(white), can_castle_(castle){ }
basic_chesspiece::basic_chesspiece(position const & location, bool white,
    bool castle):white_(white), location_(location), can_castle_(castle){ }
basic_chesspiece::~basic_chesspiece(){ }
basic_chesspiece::position const basic_chesspiece::off_board = {9, 9};
```

Please note that this is very much a bare-bones implementation and we will need to make it robust and reliable. However, there are a couple of things to notice straight away. The first is that we drop the keywords virtual and explicit from definitions. They tell the compiler things it needs to know when using the declarations, but those things have no impact on the definitions. In much the same way, default arguments belong in declarations and not in definitions.

The final source-code issue concerns how we write the return type for where( ). While parameter types are treated as being in the scope of the class that we are implementing, return types are not. This is because C++ treats source code on a strictly sequential basis. When the compiler sees the return type, it has not yet seen the function name, or any qualification applied to that name. Consequently we have to give position its fully elaborated name of basic_chesspiece::position when we use it as the return type for where( ).

TRY THIS

Copy the above source code into chess.cpp and compile it. When you have it compiling without errors, build the project (which should now build without linker errors) and execute the result. Look carefully at the output. Unless you are unlucky, the output will display a couple of strange symbols in the console window. There are two reasons for this.

The first reason is that the rank and file members of position are unsigned chars. When we send such data to an output stream (std::cout in this case), they are interpreted as characters, not numbers. We probably want numbers. (Chess buffs might want to represent files in standard chess notation, but let us keep it simple for now.) We need to tell the compiler that we want the values treated as integers. We need to use a cast to communicate that instruction to the compiler. In this case, the most appropriate cast is static_cast<int>, which instructs the compiler to treat the following value as an int value. Edit the source code of test_chess.cpp so that the output line is:

```
std::cout << "The piece is on rank " << static_cast<int>(pos.rank)
    << ", file " << static_cast<int>(pos.file)<< ".\n";
```

Now build and run the program again. You will see two nonsense values for the rank and file. We never set those values in the constructor, and the rule for fundamental types is that if the programmer does not give them a value they remain uninitialized. In most cases we get undefined behavior (remember, that is not good) if we try to read an uninitialized value. There is an exception to this rule for unsigned char: you can read the value safely but it will be random junk (whatever happens to be currently in that byte of memory). That is not normally acceptable, so we need to address the issue in the constructor.

The easiest way to handle this is to instruct the compiler that you want to zero-initialize location_. C++ has a little technique to force initialization of objects that lack an explicit constructor. It is easier to show you the technique by example than to try to describe it in words. Here is the amended first constructor:

```
basic_chesspiece::basic_chesspiece(bool white, bool castle)
    :white_(white), location_(off_board), can_castle_(castle){ }
```

That makes the position default to off the board.

Try the amended code and you should now get 9 for both rank and file.

Improving the Implementation

The code we have written so far assumes that code using the basic_chesspiece type will only use correct locations. We need to decide how we deal with attempts to move a piece to a non-existent square. Quite separately, and only in the context of a game, we will need to decide how to deal with occupied squares. If you have not already realized, one of the secrets of good programming is to deal with things one problem at a time.

There are two places where a piece's position can be provided from outside. That means that there are two places where a caller can provide invalid position data. Following the principle of avoiding doing things twice, I am going to provide a single function to validate a position. Furthermore, validation of position data is not a concern of the user and so should be done by a private member function (we keep pure implementation details private). The last thing we need to do before completing the validation routine is to decide what we will do with invalid data. When you write production code this becomes a serious design decision. However, if wrong position data is ever supplied, the program is probably in trouble. That leads me to decide that invalid data will result in an exception.

 TRY THIS

Add this declaration to the private interface of the **basic_chesspiece** class:

```
position const & is_valid_position(position);
```

Now add this to the implementation file:

```
basic_chesspiece::position const &
    basic_chesspiece::is_valid_position(position location){
  if((location.rank == off_board.rank) and
      (location.file == off_board.file))
    return location;
  if(location.file > 7) throw std::out_of_range("Invalid file");
  if(location.rank > 7) throw std::out_of_range("Invalid rank");
  return location;
}
```

You will have to **#include <stdexcept>** in **chess.cpp** to get that definition to compile. We do not need to check that **position::rank** and **position::file** are not less than zero (the first rank and file) because we are using **unsigned char** for those members of **position**. Note that the code first checks for the off-board position.

When that compiles correctly, it will be time to use it in **move( )** and in the constructor that has a **position** parameter. When you look at my code using this validation function you may see why I chose that slightly unexpected return. I looked ahead and realized that I would want to validate a position in the context of an initializer list. However, initializers have to be expressions that provide the initialization value. The two altered functions should be:

```
bool basic_chesspiece::move(position const & loc){
  location_ = is_valid_position(loc);
  return true;
}
basic_chesspiece::basic_chesspiece(position const & location,
    bool white, bool castle):white_(white),
    location_(is_valid_position(location)), can_castle_(castle){
}
```

You should get the same output when you recompile and run the test program. Now modify the test program to test that the implementation correctly handles invalid positions. Make sure that the off board position is treated as valid.

Adding Polish

Strictly speaking, a valid location is nothing directly to do with a basic_chesspiece but is a property of where a piece can be, i.e. a property of a basic_chesspiece::position. Furthermore, it is quite reasonable for a user of our code to want to validate a position. That suggests that the validation function should be a member of the position type. Because structs are just classes in C++ (with public access by default), we are free to add member functions to them. Add the following declaration to the definition of position:

```
position const & is_valid( )const;
```

I have simplified the name because the scope of the declaration provides context. I have made it a const member function because we should be able to validate a const position. There are some design issues here, and at some stage you may want to come back to this design and rework it. For example, you might decide that position should have a constructor that validates its arguments.

Add the following definition to the implementation file (chess.cpp):

```
basic_chesspiece::position const &
basic_chesspiece::position::is_valid( )const{
  if((rank == off_board.rank) and (file == off_board.file)) return *this;
  if(rank > 7) throw std::out_of_range("Invalid rank");
  if(file > 7) throw std::out_of_range("Invalid file");
  return *this;
}
```

Alternatively, simply use your text editor to edit the code you put in earlier for basic_chesspiece:: is_valid_position( ). Now we have to decide what to do about the is_valid_position( ) member of basic_chesspiece. In this case, it is easy just to remove it and edit the definitions of the member function and constructor that used it so that they use the is_valid( ) member function of position instead. However, we often do not want to make that kind of change when it means touching lots of tested and working code. All we essentially need to do is make the new function do the work wherever we called the old one.

The quickest way to do that is to change is_valid_position( ) into an in-class forwarding function:

```
basic_chesspiece::position
    basic_chesspiece::is_valid_position(position const & location){
  return location.is_valid( );
}
```

Note that there are some changes. The function now returns a position by value. Actually, it should have done previously because my original code had a subtle error in it: it returned a reference to a value parameter. The lifetime of a value parameter is the duration of the function. When the function returns, the parameter dies and we have a hanging reference (one that refers to a no-longer-existent object).

I decided to leave the flaw in my code because I wanted to give you an example of just how easy it is to mis-manage lifetime issues. Had the parameter been a reference parameter, then we could safely have returned it by reference, because the argument bound to a reference parameter must have a life that exceeds that of the function.

Why did I notice the error now when I was writing the forwarding version of is_valid_position( )? Well, position::is_valid( ) returns a const reference, and I suddenly realized that I had a problem, because my earlier version of is_valid_position( ) returned a plain reference. C++ does not allow us to pass a const reference to a plain reference. When I started to think about how I should deal with this, I realized that the original code was broken. I hope this is a useful lesson for all of us.

Before I go on, there is an even subtler problem with **const** reference parameters; unlike the plain version, these can take a temporary instance as an argument. The problem with a temporary is that it goes away at the end of the expression that created it. There is a real risk that that happens before you finish using the returned reference. Add "Do not return a **const** reference parameter by **const** reference unless you are sure you understand the consequences" to your collection of guidelines. **const** references are like values in this context; it is unsafe to return them by reference, even **const** reference. It is fine to return a **const** reference parameter by value (as I have done in the above code). If copying is either impossible or too expensive, there are other, more complicated, ways of dealing with returns, but they rely on more advanced design methods. Such methods matter when working on a large-scale application, but this is not the place to tackle such design problems.

If you have not already done so, remove the definition of **is_valid_position( )** from the implementation file. If you do not, the in-class definition will cause a conflict and the compiler will issue an error.

TRY THIS

If you have not already done so, make all the above changes to **chess.h** and **chess.cpp**. Rebuild the project, and check that the program still runs as it did before.

TRY THIS

Add extra statements to **main( )** in **test_chess.cpp** to test all the public members of **basic_chesspiece**. Note that we should include tests of any public members of **position**. Testing the public interface will indirectly test most private member functions. However, you should still test that the private declarations intended to lock out copy semantics are working as expected. You may have to comment out some of the tests when producing an executable, but that is not a justification for not including them in the first place.

You may find it helpful to instrument the constructors and destructor for the purposes of initial tests.

Note that every time you change an implementation of a class, you should run a battery of tests to ensure that you have not inadvertently changed the behavior of existing code.

Implementing a Knight

We now have a working abstraction for a chess piece. It is time to learn how we refine such an abstraction to deal with specific pieces. The knight is the simplest piece for our purpose. It has no special moves, and we do not need to consider how we might deal with the positions of other pieces blocking a move. However, notice that we should not be concerning ourselves with blocking pieces, because that is not a consideration until we try to program a game.

C++ uses a mechanism called public inheritance for specializing an abstraction. Note that inheritance can be used for other purposes, some of which I will deal with in later chapters.

Here is the definition for a new class to represent a chess knight:

```
class knight: public basic_chesspiece{
public:
  virtual bool move(position const &);
  explicit knight(bool white = true);
```

```
    explicit knight(position const &, bool white = true);
    virtual ~basic_chesspiece( );
private:
};
```

The first line of the definition states that `knight` is a public example of a `basic_chesspiece`. One of the commonest errors is leaving out the `public` qualifier of the base class (the type named after the colon). Unfortunately, inheritance defaults to `private`; private inheritance is a special technique that we use infrequently and you will not need for this book.

The `knight` type inherits all the behavior of `basic_chesspiece`. However, it does not have any access rights to the private interface of `basic_chesspiece`.

A *derived type* (the term used to refer to classes based on some other class) does not inherit the constructors and destructor from its base. That makes sense because these are special functions designed to deal with the specifics of a type. That is not the whole story; a derived type is constructed on top of an instance of its base type. A constructor for a derived type first 'calls' a constructor for its base type. Either it implicitly uses the base type's default constructor, or the programmer provides an explicit call in the initializer list.

Note that the constructors for `knight` do not need a parameter for castling, because knights cannot castle. Also, we do not need to suppress copy semantics for `knight`, because it effectively inherits that property from `basic_chesspiece`.

Destruction is always carried out in reverse order to construction. Therefore, when we come to destroy a `knight`, its destructor is called first and the base destructor is called afterwards.

It is easier to grasp these technicalities if we instrument our code to report construction and destruction. In addition, while we are learning, we should add instrumentation to other functions, so that we can observe their use in our programs.

Constructors and Destructor for knight

Here are suitable implementations of these three functions:

```
knight::knight(bool white):basic_chesspiece(white){
  std::cout << "knight constructor 1 called.\n";
}
knight::knight(position const & pos, bool white):basic_chesspiece(pos, white){
  std::cout << "knight constructor 2 called.\n";
}
knight::~knight(){
  std::cout << "knight destructor called.\n";
}
```

Notice how we call a base constructor explicitly in the initializer section of the constructor definitions. The base constructors and base destructor do all the real work. We do not need to provide an argument for the `castle` parameters in the constructors for `basic_chesspiece`, because those constructors default to the appropriate value.

Implementation of move( ) for knight

Remember that we declared the `move( )` function as `virtual` in `basic_chesspiece( )`; that has warned the compiler that the derived types may provide their own implementation. Here is a suitable implementation of `move( )` for a `knight`:

```
1 bool knight::move(position const & destination){
2   destination.is_valid();
```

```
 3    position const current(where());
 4    int const rank_dif(std::abs(current.rank - destination.rank));
 5    if(rank_dif > 2 or rank_dif < 1) return false;
 6    int const file_dif(std::abs(current.file - destination.file));
 7    if(file_dif > 2 or file_dif < 1) return false;
 8    if(rank_dif + file_dif != 3) return false;
 9    return basic_chesspiece::move(destination);
10 }
```

WALKTHROUGH

Line 2 validates the supplied **destination** as being a possible one, either a square on the chessboard or our representation for 'off the board.' If **destination** is invalid, **is_valid()** throws an exception, and the rest of this implementation will be abandoned.

Line 3 uses **where()** to get hold of the current position of the knight in question. We have to do it this way because a derived class does not have direct access to the base class's private interface. We do not have to use fully elaborated names for base-class members when in the scope of a derived class; in the scope of **knight**, **position** is fine.

Lines 4–8 check that the new position is a correct knight's move from the current one. There are many ways to do this check, but it is important to do it. My style is to eliminate the impossible ones progressively. Finally, line 9 delegates the work of updating the position to the base-class version of **move()**. Note the syntax for calling a base class implementation of a virtual function; using the fully elaborated name turns off the dynamic behavior and leaves us with the specified behavior.

std::abs() is a function that C++ inherited from C. Its declaration is in **<cstdlib>**. It converts a negative **int** value into the matching positive one. It returns non-negative values unchanged.

Notice that I always declare and initialize variables as **const** if they will not change during their lifetime. It is a small point, but it avoids accidental abuse and gives the compiler a little extra information that it may be able to use to provide code that is more efficient.

→ TRY THIS

Update **chess.h** and **chess.cpp** to include the definition and implementation for **knight**. Make sure that **chess.cpp** compiles (do not forget to **#include** any necessary headers). While you are at it, ensure that you have instrumented the **basic_chesspiece** constructors and destructor.

Now create a new test file called **test_knight.cpp**. Add it to the project, and remove **test_chess.cpp** from the project. Add the following code to **test_knight.cpp**:

```
#include "chess.h"
#include <iostream>
#include <ostream>

int main(){
  try{
    knight k1;
```

```
        basic_chesspiece::position pos = {1, 2};
        if(k1.move(pos)) std::cout << "OK.";
        else std::cout << "Cannot make that move.";
        std::cout << '\n';
    }
    catch(...){ std::cerr << "Caught an exception.\n";}
}
```

Now compile, link, and execute the resulting program. Look carefully at the output. Do you notice anything odd? You should – and it was a genuine error of mine that I only picked up when testing: I forgot to deal with a piece that is off the board.

Note that we are going to have the same check for moves for all types of chess piece. That suggests to me that we should amend `basic::chesspiece::move()` to check for attempts to move an off-board piece.

There is more than one way to handle this. Should we treat a move of a piece that is off the board as representing placing it on the board, or should we treat it as an illegal move? Moreover, what about removing a piece from the board? I think that I would opt for adding two member functions to `basic_chesspiece`: `remove()`, to place a piece in the off-board position; and `put_at(position)`, to place a piece on the board. The first of those is the same for all pieces and so does not need to be virtual, but the second has to deal with the fact that you cannot put pawns on the eighth rank. That means it will have to be `virtual`, though all other pieces can share the same implementation.

Experiment by changing the details of the code in `test_knight.cpp` until you are sure you understand what is happening.

Getting Polymorphic Behavior

So far, the code we have been using does not leave the decision about the implementation detail until the program runs. Before we go on to deal with other chess pieces, we need something that will exhibit this behavior. Add this global inline function to `chess.h`:

```
inline bool make_move(basic_chesspiece & bc_ref,
    basic_chesspiece::position destination){
  return bc_ref.move(destination);
}
```

I used an inline function because `make_move()` delegates all its behavior to the virtual function declared in `basic_chesspiece`.

This function demonstrates the case where (at the point of definition) the compiler has no knowledge of whether the reference parameter of `make_move()` will refer to a `basic_chesspiece` or to a subtype.

You are about to find two interesting properties of inheritance and references. The first is that a reference can bind to a derived type rather than just the type that it references explicitly. The second is that the subsequent code will work correctly with the real (so-called dynamic) type of the object bound to the reference.

Now that you have added `make_move()`, test it from the `main()` used to test `knight` (in `test_knight.cpp`), with the following added code:

```
basic_chesspiece bc(pos);
basic_chesspiece::position pos1 = {3, 4};
if(make_move(bc, pos1)) std::cout << "OK.";
else std::cout << "Cannot make that move.";
std::cout << '\n';
```

Moving a piece from (1, 2) to (3, 4) is perfectly OK for the abstraction we are calling basic_chesspiece. If you try the code you will find that this part of main( ) generates 'OK' as output. Now change the definition of **bc** to:

```
knight bc(pos);   // bc is now a deceptive name
```

Build and execute the resulting program. **make_move( )** now executes the code for moving a **knight** object, and that code spots that the move from (1, 2) to (3, 4) is not allowed for a knight in chess. In other words, **make_move( )** executes the correct code for the exact type of chess piece it is passed by reference.

Finally, change the declaration of **make_move( )** so that its first parameter gets a **basic_chesspiece** by value (i.e. edit out the **&**), and note the different behavior of the program. This is the result of what C++ calls *slicing*: passing a derived type by value to a base type. When you do that, only the base part of the derived type is copied, and we lose the specialized dynamic behavior. In general, using a value parameter for a polymorphic type is a design error.

Getting the Identity

Polymorphic behavior can be quite difficult to grasp, so I am adding another virtual function to basic_chesspiece and providing different implementations for that class and for **knight**. The new function reports the type of the piece. Here is the declaration to go in the public interface of both basic_chesspiece and knight:

```
virtual void what(std::ostream & = std::cout)const;
```

C++ does not require that the declarations in derived classes be explicitly qualified with **virtual**: once a function is **virtual** it will be **virtual** in all derived classes. Now add these two implementations:

```
void basic_chesspiece::what(std::ostream & out)const{
  out << "Abstract chess piece\n";
}
void knight::what(std::ostream & out)const{
  out << "Knight\n";
}
```

As always, we need something to test our new functionality. Add the following global inline function declaration to **chess.h**:

```
inline void what_are_you(basic_chesspiece const & bc_ref){
  bc_ref.what( );
}
```

TRY THIS

Add a suitable statement to **test_knight**; compile, link, and execute the resulting code. Make sure you test both the case when you call **what_are_you( )** with a **basic_chesspiece** and the case when you call it with a **knight**.

(When I first tried this, I forgot to add **#include <iostream>** and **#include <ostream>** to **chess.h** so that the compiler would recognize my use of **std::ostream** and **std::cout**. I spent a very uncomfortable few minutes trying to understand the very unhelpful error messages that resulted from this error. I am mentioning this to illustrate that when things go wrong, a compiler may not diagnose the problem correctly. Whenever you get an error message that makes no sense, check that you have included all the required headers.)

Removing an Irritant

As I have been working on the test code for this chapter, I have become increasingly irritated by the need to create explicit instances of **basic_chesspiece::position**. I would like to be able to write something such as:

```
knight k(basic_chesspiece::position(2, 3));
```

However, that will not work because such syntax requires a constructor. That is easily fixed by adding one to the definition of **position**. Here are the declaration for **chess.h** and the definition for **chess.cpp**:

```
explicit position(unsigned char rank = 0, unsigned char file = 0);
basic_chesspiece::position::position(unsigned char r, unsigned char c)
    : rank(r), file(c){ }
```

The default arguments ensure that our earlier usage of **position( )** will continue to work as it did before. The constructor is very simple: it just initializes the two data members of **position**. Many programmers use in-class definitions for such simple cases. If you want to try that, replace the declaration of the constructor for **position** with:

```
explicit position(unsigned char r, unsigned char c): rank(r), file(c){ }
```

Do not forget to remove the definition of the constructor from **chess.cpp**.

However, when you come to run either of our test programs, you will discover that we have broken our earlier code, because (at the time of writing, though this may changed in the next version of the C++ Standard, due in 2009) once a class type has a user-provided constructor, it loses the facility of initializing instances (called direct initialization) with the = { . . . } syntax. We must fix the broken statements by replacing, for example,

```
basic_chesspiece::position pos = {1, 2};
```

with:

```
basic_chesspiece::position pos(1, 2);
```

This is not a big change to make early in the use of a class, but it becomes increasingly annoying when we have more code written using the previous version. In general, adding member functions has no effect on existing code, but adding a user-written constructor to a class without one can and does break existing code.

Moving to an Occupied Square

One problem with our design is that it is very easy to confuse responsibilities. The potential move of a chess piece has nothing to do with what may be at the other end. That is an issue to do with a game of chess; collaboration between a chessboard object and a game object should handle such problems. We simply do not have to consider them at this stage, where we are dealing with the moves of a single piece.

In a similar way, when we move on to other pieces we will not consider blocking pieces, but leave such consideration to the design and implementation of a game.

Another Piece

Before asking you to deal with the rest of the chess pieces, here is my implementation of a king. First, the definition for **chess.h**:

```
class king: public basic_chesspiece{
public:
  virtual void what(std::ostream & = std::cout)const;
  virtual bool move(position const &);
  explicit king(bool white = true);
  explicit king(position const &, bool white = true);
  virtual ~king();
private:  // not strictly needed but makes code ready for later additions
};
```

Yes, that is the same as the definition of **knight** but with 'king' replacing 'knight'. In fact, all the definitions for the different chess pieces will follow an identical design. This is not an accident. Every chess piece has the same fundamental behavior and only varies in the detail. However, that detail is exactly what we provide via the implementation.

Here is an implementation of **king**:

```
void king::what(std::ostream & out)const{
  out << "King\n";
}
king::king(bool white):basic_chesspiece(white, true){
  std::cout << "king constructor 1 called.\n";
}
king::king(position const & pos, bool white)
    :basic_chesspiece(pos, white, true){
  std::cout << "king constructor 2 called.\n";
}
king::~king(){
  std::cout << "king destructor called.\n";
}
bool king::move(position const & destination){
  destination.is_valid();
  position const current(where());
  int const rank_dif(std::abs(current.rank - destination.rank));
  if(rank_dif > 1) return false;
  int const file_dif(std::abs(current.file - destination.file));
  if(file_dif > 1) return false;
  return basic_chesspiece::move(destination);
}
```

Now look carefully at that implementation of `king::move( )`. It does not consider the king's special castling move. There are two points to deal with. First, once a king makes a move, it loses its ability to castle. Second, we need a way to deal with actual castling.

We would like to be able to add

```
can_castle_ = false;
```

somewhere in the implementation of `move( )`. If we try doing this by adding that line into the definition of `king::move( )` (yes, do so), we get an access-violation error: a derived type does not have access to the private interface of its base type. We do not want to fix that problem by allowing public writing to `can_castle_`; that would be a breach of the concept of data hiding (one of the basic concepts for object-oriented programming).

This is where the protected interface comes into play. If we want to make some behavior of a class available to objects of classes derived from it but not to anything else, we declare it as protected, using the **protected** keyword. We use that keyword in the same way that we use **private** and **public** in a class definition. Go to the definition of **basic_chesspiece** and add this section:

```
protected:
  bool can_castle( );
  void disable_castle( );
```

The implementations are straightforward:

```
bool basic_chesspiece::can_castle( ){
  return can_castle_;
}
void basic_chesspiece::disable_castle( ){
  can_castle_ = false;
}
```

`disable_castle( )` is a bit unusual because it is a one-way switch, but that matches the way the property works in the game of chess. Both these functions are so simple that there would be no harm in moving their definitions into the class definition and thereby making them implicitly inline.

Once we have enhanced the **basic_chesspiece** class definition with these two protected member functions, we can correct our `king::move( )` implementation by adding the lines shown in bold in the following:

```
bool king::move(position const & destination){
  destination.is_valid( );
  position const current(where( ));
  int const rank_dif(std::abs(current.rank - destination.rank));
  if(rank_dif > 1) return false;
  int const file_dif(std::abs(current.file - destination.file));
  if(rank_dif == 0 and file_dif == 2)
    return castle(destination);  // delegate to special function
  if(file_dif > 1) return false;
  disable_castle( );  // lose ability to castle
  return basic_chesspiece::move(destination);
}
```

The first pair of added lines involves calling a special function to handle castling (which we infer from an attempt to move a king two places left or right). We call such functions 'helper functions', and generally, they belong to the private interface of a class. Add the following declaration in the private section of the definition of **king**:

```
bool castle(position const & destination);
```

Add the following (stub) definition in **chess.cpp**:

```
bool king::castle(position const & destination){
  std::cout << "Castling has not been implemented.\n";
  return false;
}
```

EXERCISES

1. Write a program to test all the behavior of a **king**. Make sure that you include tests for bad moves and for castling.

2. Write a definition for a rook, implement it, and test it. Note that although a rook is involved in castling, it is not the primary participant, and so we do not have to provide special code to handle castling. However, we do have to turn off castling potential when a rook moves.

3. Add definitions and implementations for the bishop and queen. Write code that tests each.

4. Write a definition and implementation for a pawn. This is by far the hardest piece to deal with, because it has three special moves, in addition to capturing with a different move from its non-capture move. For the time being, deal with each of the cases the same way that I dealt with castling, i.e. provide a private helper function that we can flesh out later. The three special circumstances are:
   (a) the pawn's initial double move;
   (b) the pawn's capture move including its *en passant* capture;
   (c) promotion on reaching the far side of the board.

STRETCHING EXERCISES

5. Write a program that prints out eight lines of symbols to represent a chessboard. For example, your output might be:

```
& @ & @ & @ & @
@ & @ & @ & @ &
& @ & @ & @ & @
@ & @ & @ & @ &
& @ & @ & @ & @
@ & @ & @ & @ &
& @ & @ & @ & @
@ & @ & @ & @ &
```

If you want something that looks more elegant, you can use my Playpen graphics library to produce a chequered Playpen window. You can even add a border to the board.

6. Write a program that will take the current position of a knight and mark all the squares that it is 'attacking' (i.e. the squares to which it can move directly). For example, given a knight at rank 4, file 1, the output might be:

```
&   @   &   @   &   @   &   @
#   &   #   &   @   &   @   &
&   @   &   #   &   @   &   @
@   N   @   &   @   &   @   &
&   @   &   #   &   @   &   @
#   &   #   &   @   &   @   &
&   @   &   @   &   @   &   @
@   &   @   &   @   &   @   &
```

Note that we are counting files and ranks from zero. You might want to modify your program so that the external data is provided in the range 1 to 8 and converted into the internal representation of 0 to 7. If you produced a chessboard in Playpen, use it as the basis for this program.

7. Write programs to produce diagrams for the other pieces.

8. Write a program that will take input and use it to set up a position on a board.

9. Modify your solutions to Exercise 8 so that it takes into account pieces that 'block' a move.

REFERENCE SECTION

C++ provides a mechanism by which we can use an existing class as the basis for a new class. The simplest form of this mechanism is to use an existing class as a public base for a new one. C++ allows use of existing classes as protected or private bases, but this book does not deal with the details of such usage.

The syntax for deriving a class from another class is:

```
class derived-type: access-specifier base-type {
...
};
```

Here *derived-type* and *base-type* are the names of the type being defined and the type being used as a base; *access-specifier* is one of `public`, `protected`, and `private`. If the access specifier is omitted, it defaults to `private` if the definition is introduced with the `class` keyword. If the `struct` keyword is used then the default access specifier is `public`. One of the commonest errors in writing a derived-class definition is to forget to specify that the base class is a `public` base.

Sometimes programmers use inheritance to change the behavior of an existing type in such a way that objects of the derived type cannot (correctly) be substituted for objects of the base type. In other words, a function that expects an argument of the base type will not work as designed if it receives an argument of a derived type. Although C++ does not forbid programmers to write such definitions, they are generally frowned on by experienced programmers because they are sources of numerous errors. If you need to write such code, you should learn to use private inheritance.

If a class has been designed as a base class, either it should have a non-`public` destructor (a very specialized technique), or its destructor should be qualified as `virtual`. In a later chapter, we will see how such qualification of a destructor changes the behavior of the destruction to make it safe when we are dealing with polymorphism.

We can attach the `virtual` qualifier to the declaration of any normal member function (but not to constructors) of a base class. Any function declared as `virtual` in a base class can be reimplemented in a derived class. We notify the compiler of our intent to provide a new implementation (function definition) by redeclaring the function in the derived class. Note that while it is customary to qualify the redeclaration as `virtual`, it is not necessary to do so: once we have declared a function as `virtual`, all redeclarations in derived classes are automatically `virtual`.

When code calls a `virtual` function, the compiler must delay the choice of the implementation until it knows the exact type using the function. In the case of references (and pointers), the exact type is usually not known until run time. C++ does not specify how implementers should provide this delayed decision, but interested readers can find more information by using their favorite Internet search engine to search for 'virtual function pointer table'.

Any function in a base class that is not redeclared in a derived class will use the base-class implementation. However, it is unwise to redeclare a non-virtual function; doing so can result in subtle program bugs. Apparently, redeclaring a non-virtual function actually declares a new unrelated function that will result in replacement of the base-class function in some circumstances but not in others. When using references or pointers, the compiler will determine which version to use based on the type of the reference or pointer. That contrasts with virtual functions, where the determination is done at execution time, depending on the type of the object referred to or pointed to.

You also need to be careful of declaring an overload for a function declared in a base class, because it will not always overload the way you expect. The solution is to include a class-scope `using` declaration. See Chapter 18 for more details.

CHAPTER (13)

Dynamic Object Creation and Polymorphic Objects

Once we have a polymorphic type, we need to be able to create instances of its subtypes. Sometimes we know exactly what we want at the time we write the source code, but more often we will not know until the program is executing. I am starting this chapter by showing you a way to deal with this problem in C++.

A second issue concerns a special category of polymorphic types, whose instances must be able to replace themselves with a different subtype. The pawn in chess is an example. When it reaches the eighth rank on the board, it must metamorphose into a queen, rook, bishop, or knight. The player usually chooses to convert it into a queen, but it is the player's choice, and we have to deal with that problem when we design our chess type.

Selecting the Subtype at Runtime

Suppose that I want to write a program that will set up a chess problem from user input. I will need a function to create each piece in response to data provided by the program user. Here is a first draft of such a function:

```cpp
basic_chesspiece * make_piece(){
  std::cout << "Is it white? (y/n): ";
  char response;
  std::cin >> response;
  bool white(std::toupper(response) == 'Y');
  std::cout << "Which file is it on? (0-7): ";
  int file;
  std::cin >> file;
  std::cout << "Which rank is it on? (0-7): ";
  int rank;
  std::cin >> rank;
  basic_chesspiece::position p(file, rank);
  display_menu();
  char choice(select_from_menu());
  basic_chesspiece * piece_ptr(0);
  switch(choice){
    case 'N':
      piece_ptr = new knight(p, white);
```

```
          break;
      case 'B':
          piece_ptr = new bishop(p, white);
          break;
      case 'R':
          piece_ptr = new rook(p, white);
          break;
      case 'Q':
          piece_ptr = new queen(p, white);
          break;
      case 'K':
          piece_ptr = new king(p, white);
          break;
      default:
          piece_ptr = new pawn(p, white);
          break;
   }
   return piece_ptr;
}
```

The above is not a robust implementation because it assumes that the user will respond with appropriate data. For example, the code assumes that the response to "Is it white?" will be a single letter that is either 'y' or 'n'. The `std::toupper( )` function (declared in the `<cstdlib>` header) just ensures that the input is treated as uppercase.

The code calls two other functions, `display_menu( )` and `select_from_menu( )`. As these are of no direct concern to the programmer using our chess-piece code, we place their definitions in `chess.cpp` but do not declare them in `chess.h`. Here are my initial definitions of those two functions:

```
namespace{
  void display_menu( ){
    std::cout << "Which chess piece?\n\n";
    std::cout << "   K    King\n";
    std::cout << "   Q    Queen\n";
    std::cout << "   N    kNight\n";
    std::cout << "   B    Bishop\n";
    std::cout << "   R    Rook\n";
    std::cout << "   P    Pawn\n";
    std::cout << "\nPress the chosen key and then Enter.\n";
  }

  char select_from_menu( ){
    char key;
    std::cin >> key;
    key = std::toupper(key);
    return key;
  }
}
```

I have wrapped the definitions in a block labelled with the keyword **namespace** but without providing a name for the namespace. We can encapsulate any block of global declarations and definitions into a named namespace and they will acquire an elaborated name (like the `std::` elaboration we have been using for members of the Standard Library). We can also encapsulate declarations and definitions into an unnamed namespace. That has a special significance: the consequence is that we can use those entities in the file in which they are declared but nowhere else. Effectively, the unnamed namespace hides the names declared in it from anything outside the file. This is stronger than placing something in the private part of a class; we do not know the fully elaborated name of something declared in an unnamed namespace and so we cannot refer to it outside the current file.

Unnamed Namespaces

We covered the original design of namespaces in Chapter 4. The idea for unnamed namespaces came in very soon after the introduction of named ones. Unnamed namespaces were introduced to provide a general mechanism for constraining names to the current file. C's mechanism of qualifying declarations as **static** does not meet all the needs of C++. C++ needs a way to prevent leakage of the names of user-defined types.

Rather more subtly, **static** declarations cannot meet all the requirements for some templates.

The C use of file-scope **static** makes the name invisible outside the file. Unfortunately, that also makes it impossible to use in some template cases, because they require visibility (so called **extern** linkage). The unnamed namespace tackles the problem differently by making the full name secret and unique. When the compiler comes across an unnamed namespace for the first time in a file, it invents a name. In inventing the name, it invents one in such a way that it will be unique. How implementers achieve this magic is outside the scope of this book.

As the programmer does not know the name of the namespace (and it will almost certainly change every time the file is recompiled), they cannot refer to it in some other file of source code. We have replaced the external invisibility provided by **static** qualification with giving an entity a fully qualified name that we do not know and so cannot use. At the same time, C++ makes the unqualified names from an unnamed namespace usable within the file where they are declared.

It is usually good practice to place all type definitions and global declarations (i.e. ones outside functions and class definitions) in an unnamed namespace until you know that you want to use the entities named in other files.

C++ programs often become very large, involving a million or more lines of code. That means that good control of names is vital. We need to keep the scope of a declaration under control. An unnamed namespace is just one more tool for providing that control.

TRY THIS

Experiment 1

Add a declaration of make_piece( ) to chess.h, and add its definition to chess.cpp. Add the two helper functions to chess.cpp. Make sure that you have provided a definition and implementation for all the chess pieces (king, queen, rook, bishop, knight, and pawn). If you do not want to spend time providing full implementations for all the member functions, at least provide stubs for them. For example:

```
bool bishop::move(position const & destination){
  std::cout << "Not implemented.\n";
  return true;
}
```

If you try to compile chess.cpp without definitions for all six types of chess piece, you will get error messages. In addition, you must provide a definition for every virtual function declared in a subtype. For example, what( ) is qualified as virtual in basic_chesspiece, with the result that there must be an implementation of what( ) in any class derived from basic_chesspiece that includes an explicit declaration of what( ). C++ deems that we must provide an implementation of all declared virtual functions. Later we will see that there is a mechanism in C++ to state explicitly that there is no implementation of a virtual function. We call such cases 'pure virtual functions', and they have an impact on the class that declares them. If a derived class does not explicitly redeclare a virtual function from a base class, it uses the base class implementation. For example, the code

```cpp
class rook: public basic_chesspiece{
public:
  // virtual void what(std::ostream & = std::cout)const;
  // virtual bool move(position const &);
  explicit rook(bool white = true);
  explicit rook(position const &, bool white = true);
  virtual ~rook( );
private:
};
```

– where I have commented out the declarations of what( ) and move( ) – will just reuse the implementations from basic_chesspiece. Please experiment until you are confident that you understand what is needed to get make_piece( ) to compile. Some of the error messages are unhelpful: please note them so that they will make more sense next time you see them.

Experiment 2

Write a program to test make_piece( ). For example, this minimal version will do for a start – once you add the necessary #include of headers:

```cpp
int main( ){
  basic_chesspiece * bc(make_piece( ));
}
```

Please study the output carefully and notice that the destructors for the pieces you construct are not called before the program ends. In Chapter 11 we looked at dynamic instances and learned that the programmer is responsible for destroying them. However, there is very little in the top-level code to suggest that we need to use delete. In addition, explicitly deleting dynamic instances is tedious (and error prone). This is where a suitable smart pointer can be brought in, to automate the process of destruction and management of the lifetime of a dynamic object.

Experiment 3

Change the above program to:

```cpp
int main( ){
  std::auto_ptr<basic_chesspiece> bc(make_piece( ));
}
```

Build and execute this new version, and note that the destructors are now correctly called. You may need to include the <memory> header. This is an example of what std::auto_ptr( ) was designed for; when bc goes out of scope at exit from main( ), delete is called on the pointer that has been encapsulated into the auto_ptr variable bc.

Experiment 4

There is a problem with this solution: we want a dynamic object protected from birth (construction) until death (destruction). The chess piece is created dynamically inside `make_piece( )`, so that is where we should first deal with the problem. Here is replacement code that does that:

```
std::auto_ptr<basic_chesspiece> make_piece( ){
  std::cout << "Is it white? (y/n): ";
  char response;
  std::cin >> response;
  bool white(std::toupper(response) == 'Y');
  std::cout << "Which file is it on? (0-7): ";
  int file;
  std::cin >> file;
  std::cout << "Which rank is it on? (0-7): ";
  int rank;
  std::cin >> rank;
  basic_chesspiece::position p(file, rank);
  display_menu( );
  char choice(select_from_menu( ));
  std::auto_ptr<basic_chesspiece> piece_ptr(0);
  switch(choice){
    case 'N':
      piece_ptr =
          std::auto_ptr<basic_chesspiece>(new knight(p, white));
      break;
    case 'B':
      piece_ptr =
          std::auto_ptr<basic_chesspiece>(new bishop(p, white));
      break;
    case 'R':
      piece_ptr = std::auto_ptr<basic_chesspiece>(new rook(p, white));
      break;
    case 'Q':
      piece_ptr = std::auto_ptr<basic_chesspiece>(new queen(p, white));
      break;
    case 'K':
      piece_ptr = std::auto_ptr<basic_chesspiece>(new king(p, white));
      break;
    default:
      piece_ptr = std::auto_ptr<basic_chesspiece>(new pawn(p, white));
      break;
  }
  return piece_ptr;
}
```

You will need to edit the declaration in **chess.h** because we have changed the return type of **make_piece**. This code relies on the designed behavior of **std::auto_ptr<>**, where assignment and return by value transfer responsibility for the encapsulated pointer. This is why **std::auto_ptr<>** has non-standard copy semantics: the instance being copied must be altered so that it relinquishes responsibility for the pointer. For uses such as the above, it works fine, because I have carefully relayed the pointer (to the dynamically created chess piece) from the place where it was created out to wherever **make_piece( )** was called.

A Chess-Piece Type

The following section is important because it shows how many of the ideas and techniques we have seen so far can be used to provide a powerful abstraction of the concept of a chess piece in a way limits the exposure of implementation details to the user of the type. It also shows you a way that you can provide a type that can actively change its behavior from one 'subtype' to another. I have used quotation marks because the user of the type will be completely unaware that subtypes are involved.

This ability to change behavior under cover is important in some problem domains. One reason that I chose to use chess pieces as an example of a polymorphic type is exactly that a complete implementation of a pawn requires this kind of change (so that it can be promoted when it reaches the eighth rank).

Please work through the following with me. I will highlight the important ideas as I go.

Open a new project. I called mine **chess2**, but then I am not very imaginative when it comes to names! Make sure you set it up the same way as we have set up our earlier projects, and then create a file called **chessmain.cpp** with the following short program in it:

```
#include "chess2.h"
#include <iostream>
#include <ostream>

int main(){
  chesspiece p(chesspiece::pawn, chesspiece::position(2, 3));
  std::cout << "The piece is a " << p.what()
      << ", located on file " << (int)p.where().file
      << " at rank " << (int)p.where().rank << ".\n";
  p.transform(chesspiece::bishop);
  std::cout << "The piece is now a " << p.what()
      << ", located on file " << (int)p.where().file
      << " at rank " << (int)p.where().rank << ".\n";
}
```

Our primary task is first to add code that will allow this program to compile, and then to provide an implementation of that code so that it will link and run. The first step is providing a suitable definition of **chesspiece** in the header file **chess2.h**. Here is that header file with the lines numbered so I can walk you through it.

```
 1 #ifndef CHESS2_H
 2 #define CHESS2_H
 3
 4 #include <memory>
 5 #include <string>
 6
 7 class basic_chesspiece;
 8
 9 class chesspiece{
10 public:
11   enum piece{indeterminate, bishop, king, knight, pawn, queen, rook};
12   struct position{
13     unsigned char file;  // location towards the opponent
14     unsigned char rank;  // location across the board
15     position const & is_valid()const;
16     explicit position(unsigned char f = 0, unsigned char r = 0)
17         :file(f), rank(r){ }
```

```
18   };
19   static position const off_board;
20   bool move(position const &);
21   position where( )const;
22   bool is_white( )const;
23   void transform(piece);
24   std::string what( )const;
25   bool can_castle( ) const;  // query ability
26   void can_castle(bool);  // set ability
27   explicit chesspiece(piece = indeterminate, position = off_board,
28       bool white = true, bool castle = false);
29   ~chesspiece( );
30 private:
31   std::auto_ptr<basic_chesspiece> piece_ptr;
32   // disable copying
33   chesspiece(chesspiece const &);
34   chesspiece & operator=(chesspiece const &);
35 };
36
37 #endif
```

Much of this code will look familiar, because most of the public interface of **chesspiece** closely follows that of **basic_chesspiece**. However, you will have noticed that there is no protected interface and there are no virtual functions. Those absences are significant because they warn the knowledgeable reader that the design of this class makes it unsuitable for use as a base class. In other words, users should not be tempted to derive from it.

WALKTHROUGH

Lines 1, 2, and 37 are just standard boilerplate for a header file. The **#include**s (lines 4 and 5) provide declarations of various pieces of the Standard Library that appear in the declarations in the definition of **chesspiece**. Line 7 demonstrates how to declare the name of a class type (including a **struct**, but not an **enum**) when we do not want to provide a complete definition. Once the compiler has seen a declaration of a class name, there are several ways we can use the name. In addition to using pointers and references to the type, we can use the type name in declarations such as that in line 31.

Line 31 is the key to the whole process; we could use a plain pointer or some other kind of smart pointer, but the key is that extra level of indirection provided by using a pointer. This allows us to hide all the details from the user. This is a variant of a C++ idiom called 'the compiler firewall'.

Line 11 defines an **enum** that I use for identifying the subtypes of chess pieces, including the generic case of a piece that we have not identified. Because I have provided it as a member of **chesspiece**, we will need to use the elaborated names (such as **chesspiece::pawn**) for the enumerators when we use them outside the scope of **chesspiece**.

Lines 12–18 define the type that I am using to package up the position of a chess piece on a chessboard. It is the same as the type that I provided in **basic_chesspiece**.

Line 19 provides a named value of **chesspiece::position** to use as a representation of being off the board. The implementation file will provide the actual representation.

Line 23 declares **transform( )**, the only genuinely new member function. Its job is to provide a method to change a chess piece into a different one. It has two main uses: the first is to allow a pawn to be promoted to some other piece, and the second is to allow us to take a generic piece (of indeterminate type) and specify what its type is. It will be up to the implementer to decide what, if any, safeguards will be supplied to prevent arbitrary metamorphosis.

Several other functions have changed. **what( )** now returns the name of the piece as a **std::string** rather than sending it to an output stream. If you feel happier, you can have the new version live alongside the old one, but you will not be able to default the output stream to **std::cout**. That is because overloaded functions must be distinct from each other even when default arguments are invoked.

Lines 25 and 26 allow us to get and set the castling attribute. By making it public, I allow programmers to set that attribute even for pieces that cannot castle. However, there is no real danger here, because any functions providing castling moves will check the correct subtype before checking that the king and rook retain the capacity to castle.

 TRY THIS

Before going on, make sure that you have the correct code and that **chessmain.cpp** will compile. When you are satisfied, it will be time to move on to the implementation.

Implementing chesspiece

Much of the implementation (in **chess2.cpp**) will be in an unnamed namespace. However, those things declared in **chess2.h**, including **basic_chesspiece**, will have to be in the open at file scope. You will be able to copy and paste from earlier projects for most of the code in **chess2.cpp**. Here are the first few lines:

```
#include "chess2.h"
#include <iostream>
#include <ostream>
#include <stdexcept>

typedef chesspiece::position position;
position const chesspiece::off_board(9, 9);
bool instrument(true);  // switch instrumentation on by default

namespace{
  // provide a short local name
  position const & off_board(chesspiece::off_board);
}
```

The **typedef** provides a shortened version of **chesspiece::position**. It is typical of the way we use the tools of C++ to keep local code simple and easy to read. In this file, we know we are dealing with the implementation of **chesspiece**, so we do not need to use it relentlessly. The following line provides the necessary definition of **chesspiece::off_board**. I would like to use a short name instead. We can use **typedef** to alias a type's name, but when we want to provide an alias for a variable, we have to use a reference. I make sure that the alias does not leak out of the file by encapsulating the declaration of off_board (as a reference to chesspiece::off_board) in the unnamed namespace.

Finally, I make use of a relatively crude mechanism for switching instrumentation on and off. I would not do it this way in production code. I can turn off the display of instrumentation messages by setting instrument to false.

I cannot restrict basic_chesspiece to the current file, because I declared its name in chess2.h. However, nothing outside the implementation of chesspiece needs to know any of the details, so both the definition and implementation of basic_chesspiece can reside here. I have modified the definition a little from our earlier version. Here is the new one:

```
class basic_chesspiece{
public:
  virtual bool move(position const &) = 0;
  position where()const{return location_;}
  bool is_white()const{return white_;}
  virtual std::string what()const = 0;
  explicit basic_chesspiece(bool white = true, bool castle = false);
  explicit basic_chesspiece(position const &,
      bool white = true, bool castle = false);
  virtual ~basic_chesspiece();
  bool can_castle()const{return can_castle_;}
  void can_castle(bool cc){can_castle_ = cc;}
protected:

private:
  bool const white_;  // chess pieces are white or not-white
  position location_;
  bool can_castle_;
// disable copying
  basic_chesspiece(basic_chesspiece const &);
  basic_chesspiece & operator=(basic_chesspiece const &);
};
```

Notice that I have removed position as a nested class. However, the typedef I gave above allows me to use position without qualification, even though it is a member of another class. I have changed the functions dealing with ability to castle by making can_castle() public and replacing disable_castle() with a more general public function can_castle(bool), which allows change of the castling status either way.

move() and what() have become pure virtual functions. A pure virtual function is one that must be implemented in a derived class. We declare that a function is pure by appending = 0 to its declaration. That is the exceptional case with regard to implementing virtual functions. However, it has a serious impact on your code: there are no complete instances of a class that contains a pure virtual function. In other words, we are no longer allowed to have an instance whose type is basic_chesspiece. This constraint is inherited by any subtype that has not provided implementations for all the pure virtual functions. Classes with pure virtual members are called abstract base classes (ABCs for short), and their primary purpose is to provide an interface for a polymorphic type. Usually we resort to pure virtual functions when there is no reasonable complete implementation of the function.

However, we are allowed to provide an implementation of a pure virtual function for the class where it is declared as pure; doing so does not remove the constraint that there will be no instances of the type.

You might think that a class that cannot have instances would be useless, but that is not the case, because we can use pointers and references to such types. You may recall that polymorphic behavior is provided by using references or pointers. Therefore, a pointer or reference to an ABC provides exactly the mechanism to manage a hierarchy of subtypes.

Strictly speaking, I had no need to make move( ) a pure virtual function because there is perfectly reasonable behavior for the abstract piece – behavior that every actual piece will have. I made move( ) a pure virtual so that I could demonstrate the provision of an implementation for such a function and show how it is used by the subtypes. I will say more about that when we deal with the subtype implementations of move( ).

I have used what( ) as an example of the commoner form of pure virtual, which is not implemented in the base class. I have also changed what( ) to match the form I am using in chesspiece, one that returns the name of the piece in a string.

The rest of basic_chesspiece is much the same as the earlier version. Here is its implementation, which can be added immediately after the definition:

```
basic_chesspiece::basic_chesspiece(bool white, bool castle)
    :white_(white), location_(off_board), can_castle_(castle){
  if(instrument)
    std::clog << "basic_chesspiece constructor 1 (off-board) called.\n";
}

basic_chesspiece::basic_chesspiece(position const & location,
    bool white, bool castle)
    :white_(white), location_(location.is_valid( )), can_castle_(castle){
  if(instrument)
    std::clog << "basic_chesspiece constructor 2 (with location) called.\n";
}

basic_chesspiece::~basic_chesspiece( ){
  if(instrument) std::clog << "basic chesspiece destructor called.\n";
}

bool basic_chesspiece::move(position const & loc){
  location_ = loc.is_valid( );
  return true;
}
```

I have modified the instrumentation so that it sends messages to std::clog rather than std::cout. That is the kind of thing std::clog was designed for.

Defining and Implementing the Subtypes

The first thing to note is that nothing needs access to the individual subtypes (pawn, bishop, etc.) other than the implementation of chesspiece. That is a broad design hint that we should tuck them away in the unnamed namespace for chess2.cpp. I am not going to waste space giving you the definitions and implementations of all the subtypes. But here are three examples:

```
namespace{
  class knight: public basic_chesspiece{
  public:
    virtual std::string what( )const;
    virtual bool move(position const &);
    explicit knight(bool white = true);
    explicit knight(position const &, bool white = true);
    virtual ~knight( );
  private:
```

```
};

   class pawn: public basic_chesspiece{
   public:
     virtual std::string what( )const;
     virtual bool move(position const &);
     explicit pawn(bool white = true);
     explicit pawn(position const &, bool white = true);
     virtual ~pawn( );
   private:
   };

   class king: public basic_chesspiece{
   public:
     virtual std::string what( )const;
     virtual bool move(position const &);
     explicit king(bool white = true);
     explicit king(position const &, bool can_castle = true,
         bool white = true);
     virtual ~king( );
   private:
     bool castle(position const & destination);
   };

// other effectively identical definitions omitted
}
```

Notice that the second constructor for a king is different from the other two. The subtypes provide their own constructors and destructor, and the two virtual functions. We saw earlier that the king needs an extra helper function to deal with its castling move. You may also have provided extra functionality to cater for the special moves available to a pawn.

Here is an implementation for those subtypes. I have relied largely on stub functions because my emphasis is on the C++ technology, not the fine detail of writing code to provide correct behavior for chess pieces.

```
namespace{
  // implementation of knight subtype

  knight::knight(bool white):basic_chesspiece(white){
    if(instrument) std::clog << "knight constructor 1 called.\n";
  }
  knight::knight(position const & pos, bool white)
      :basic_chesspiece(pos, white){
    if(instrument) std::clog << "knight constructor 2 called.\n";
  }
  knight::~knight( ){
    if(instrument) std::clog << "knight destructor called.\n";
  }

  bool knight::move(position const & destination){
    destination.is_valid( );
    position const current(where( ));
    int const rank_dif(std::abs(current.rank - destination.rank));
    if(rank_dif > 2 or rank_dif < 1) return false;
```

```cpp
  int const file_dif(std::abs(current.file - destination.file));
  if(file_dif > 2 or file_dif < 1) return false;
  if(rank_dif + file_dif != 3) return false;
  return basic_chesspiece::move(destination);
}

std::string knight::what( )const{
  return "knight";
}

// implementation of pawn subtype

pawn::pawn(bool white):basic_chesspiece(white, true){
  if(instrument) std::clog << "pawn constructor 1 called.\n";
}
pawn::pawn(position const & pos, bool white)
    :basic_chesspiece(pos, white, true){
  if(instrument) std::clog << "pawn constructor 2 called.\n";
}
pawn::~pawn( ){
  if(instrument) std::clog << "pawn destructor called.\n";
}

bool pawn::move(position const & destination){
  std::cout << "Not implemented.\n";
  return true;
}

std::string pawn::what( )const{
  return "pawn";
}

// implementation of king subtype

king::king(bool white):basic_chesspiece(white, true){
  if(instrument) std::clog << "king constructor 1 called.\n";
}
king::king(position const & pos, bool cc, bool white)
    :basic_chesspiece(pos, white, cc){
  if(instrument) std::clog << "king constructor 2 called.\n";
}
king::~king( ){
  if(instrument) std::clog << "king destructor called.\n";
}

bool king::move(position const & destination){
  destination.is_valid( );
  position const current(where( ));
  int const rank_dif(std::abs(current.rank - destination.rank));
  if(rank_dif > 1) return false;
  int const file_dif(std::abs(current.file - destination.file));
  if(rank_dif == 0 and file_dif == 2){
```

```
      return castle(destination);  // delegate to special function
    }
    if(file_dif > 1) return false;
    can_castle(false);  // lose ability to castle
    return basic_chesspiece::move(destination);
  }

  std::string king::what( )const{
    return "king";
  }

  bool king::castle(position const & destination){
    std::cout << "Castling has not been implemented.\n";
    return false;
  }

  // plus similar code for the other chess pieces
}
```

Constructing a Specific Chess Piece

The following is a helper function (based on the one we wrote in the last chapter) to construct the right chess piece on demand:

```
namespace{
  // helper function for chesspiece constructor and for transform
  std::auto_ptr<basic_chesspiece> make(chesspiece::piece p,
      chesspiece::position pos1, bool white, bool can_castle = false){
  position pos(pos1.file, pos1.rank);
  std::auto_ptr<basic_chesspiece> piece_ptr(0);
  switch(p){
    case chesspiece::knight:
      piece_ptr = std::auto_ptr<basic_chesspiece>(new knight(pos, white));
      break;
    case chesspiece::bishop:
      piece_ptr = std::auto_ptr<basic_chesspiece>(new bishop(pos, white));
      break;
    case chesspiece::rook:
      piece_ptr =
          std::auto_ptr<basic_chesspiece>(new rook(pos, can_castle, white));
      break;
    case chesspiece::queen:
      piece_ptr = std::auto_ptr<basic_chesspiece>(new queen(pos, white));
      break;
    case chesspiece::king:
      piece_ptr =
          std::auto_ptr<basic_chesspiece>(new king(pos, can_castle, white));
      break;
    case chesspiece::pawn:
      piece_ptr = std::auto_ptr<basic_chesspiece>(new pawn(pos, white));
      break;
```

```
      default:
        piece_ptr =
            std::auto_ptr<basic_chesspiece>(new indeterminate(pos, white));
    }
    return piece_ptr;
  }
}
```

Note how the `std::auto_ptr<>` instances relay the ownership of the dynamic instance back to the caller by returning by value. The local `piece_ptr` goes out of scope and is destroyed, but it has already passed responsibility for the lifetime of the freshly created piece to the return value.

The chesspiece Constructor and transform( )

The `chesspiece` constructor knows which piece it needs, and calls `make( )` to get the one it needs before storing the address of the new piece safely in its `piece_ptr` data member. This magic of looking after the lifetime of a dynamic object, even one of a polymorphic type, is precisely the job for which `std::auto_ptr` was designed. Here is the implementation of `chesspiece`'s constructor:

```
chesspiece::chesspiece(piece p, position pos, bool white, bool castle)
    :piece_ptr(make(p, pos, white)){
  if(instrument) std::clog << "Chesspiece constructed.\n";
}
```

Simple when you know how. One point to notice is that helper functions like `make( )` are particularly useful for ensuring that we do all we can within the constructor initializer list. But it has a second use; here is the implementation of `transform( )`:

```
void chesspiece::transform(piece p){
  piece_ptr = make(p, where( ), is_white( ), piece_ptr -> can_castle( ));
}
```

This function relies on the special characteristic of the assignment operator for `std::auto_ptr<>`: when you assign a `std::auto_ptr<>` to another one, the left-hand one first ends the lifetime of the object it is currently responsible for before taking on the responsibility for the one it is acquiring. Of, course the right-hand `std::auto_ptr<>` has to release its responsibility. Now you know why `std::auto_ptr<>` has a non-standard copy-assignment operator: it needs it to do the job it is designed to do.

Implementing the Rest of chesspiece

There is not much more to do, because `chesspiece` just delegates the work to `basic_chesspiece`, which in turn delegates much of the work to the implementations of the subtypes (the individual types of chess piece).
First, the non-virtual member functions:

```
position chesspiece::where( )const{return piece_ptr -> where( );}
bool chesspiece::is_white( )const{return piece_ptr -> is_white( );}
bool chesspiece::can_castle( )const{return piece_ptr -> can_castle( );}
void chesspiece::can_castle(bool cc){piece_ptr -> can_castle(cc);}
```

Next, the member functions that forward to virtual versions:

```
std::string chesspiece::what( )const{return piece_ptr -> what( );}
bool chesspiece::move(position const & p){return piece_ptr -> move(p);}
```

Finally, we have the destructor:

```
chesspiece::~chesspiece( ){
  if(instrument) std::clog << "Chesspiece destroyed.\n";
}
```

Before we forget, there is still a member function from `chesspiece::position` to deal with:

```
position const & chesspiece::position::is_valid( )const{
  if((file == off_board.file) and (rank == off_board.rank)) return *this;
  if(rank > 7) throw std::out_of_range("Invalid rank");
  if(file > 7) throw std::out_of_range("Invalid file");
  return *this;
}
```

TRY THIS

When you have added the above code to **chess2.cpp**, you will find that our program from 'A Chess-Piece Type' (page 244) will build and run. Try it with the instrumentation on so that you can see all the work that goes on under the hood. When you have done that, add code to the program to test the rest of the public interface of **chesspiece**.

TRY THIS

Experiment 5

Switch the instrumentation on (by setting the value of `instrument` in `chess2.cpp` to `true`), and build and execute this short program:

```
int main( ){
  chesspiece cp;
}
```

Now go to **chess2.cpp** and remove the **virtual** qualifier from the declaration of the destructor for **basic_chesspiece**. Build and execute the program again. Notice that the compiler issues a warning about a class with virtual functions and a non-virtual destructor (well, it does with the compiler shipped with this book when the warning level is set high enough); while C++ allows this, it is usually a design error.

Study the output and you should notice that the destructor for **indeterminate** has not been called. That failure is harmless for this particular polymorphic hierarchy because the subtype destructors do not actually do anything. However, the omission is generally dangerous (C++ categorizes calling a base destructor without first calling the derived destructor as undefined behavior – anything may happen). Just as for any other member function accessed through a pointer or reference, non-virtual destructors will be those for the type of the pointer or reference rather than for the real type of the instance referenced. Please do not forget this; it is an error to destroy an instance without calling the destructor for the exact type.

Experiment 6

Modify the above program to:

```
int main( ){
  chesspiece cp[2];
  std::sort(cp, cp + 2);
}
```

    Now try to compile it. You will get a veritable cascade of errors (143 when I tried it).
If you comment out the attempt to sort the array, the errors disappear, from which we can
deduce that the problem is not with creating the array but with attempting to sort it. Quite
right too – chesspiece is an entity type with copy semantics suppressed. We can confirm
that by temporarily commenting out the private declarations of the copy constructor and copy-
assignment operator in the definition of chesspiece. Try it. However, do not try to execute
the resulting program, because the compiler-generated copy constructor interacts badly with
std::auto_ptr<>. Remember that copying a std::auto_ptr<> transfers ownership. If we
want 'safe' copy semantics for a type like chesspiece, we must decide what we mean by copying
one. Either we must share ownership of the underlying object, or we must be willing to clone
it (i.e. create a new, distinct object with identical value). We get the former by using a different
smart pointer such as Boost's shared_ptr<> (see http://www.boost.org/). If we want the
latter, we have to write our own copy functions to provide 'deep copying'. That term refers to
copying that includes duplicating the underlying objects that are owned through some kind of
pointer.

Experiment 7

Modify the above program to:

```
int main( ){
  chesspiece * cp[2];
  cp[0] = new chesspiece(chesspiece::rook);
  cp[1] = new chesspiece(chesspiece::pawn);
  std::sort(cp, cp + 2);
}
```

Ignore, for now, that we have not destroyed the dynamic instances of chesspiece; instead,
focus on what std::sort is doing. It is just sorting the addresses of those dynamic instances.
That is not likely to be what we intended. We have to provide a function that will provide some
ordering for the instances rather than for their addresses. Here is one (which sorts chesspieces
alphabetically):

```
bool chesspiece_order(chesspiece const * const lhs,
    chesspiece const * const rhs){
  return lhs->what( ) < rhs->what( );
}
```

    Now expand the test program to:

```
int main( ){
  chesspiece * cp[2];
  cp[0] = new chesspiece(chesspiece::rook);
  cp[1] = new chesspiece(chesspiece::pawn);
```

```
    std::sort(cp, cp + 2, chesspiece_order);
    delete cp[0];
    delete cp[1];
}
```

Note that it uses the alternative form of `std::sort( )`, where you provide a predicate (a function returning a `bool`) to define the order. Build and execute that program, and note the order in which the destructors are called (you will need the instrumentation on for this). Now repeat the exercise with the sort commented out, so that you can check that the sort changes the order.

EXERCISES

1. Write a replacement for the `chesspiece_order( )` function, to order the pieces according to their position. For example, order by rank and then by file.

2. Write a program that displays a collection of `chesspiece`s on a chessboard. Note that your solution to Exercise 1 will help with this task. Identify the different chess pieces by a suitable letter, uppercase for white and lowercase for black.

STRETCHING EXERCISES

3. Write a complete hierarchy for checkers (draughts) pieces. This is easier than for chess because there are only two types of piece (plain and kings), but it still has the characteristic that plain pieces can be promoted to kings.

4. Add a board type that tracks where the pieces are. Note that you will need to provide a facility for querying a square to find out whether it is occupied and, if so, by what color of piece.

5. Extend your solution to Exercise 3 so that a piece can determine whether it can make a capture move. It will need to query the board object. If you work systematically, this exercise is not as difficult as it might seem.

Collections of Objects

Experiment 3 above demonstrates one of the major problems with collections of entities. If they cannot be copied, we have a problem with using the Standard Library algorithms for them, because those algorithms largely expect that they can copy the objects they are working with. We have two main choices: we can use containers of a suitable type of smart pointer (one that supports standard copy semantics, such as Boost's `shared_ptr<>`); or we can encapsulate the collection into a class that will look after the lifetime of the entities it holds. The design will largely depend on our intentions.

In this section, I am going to show how we can implement the concept of a collection of chess pieces on a chessboard.

Design and Implementation of a chessboard Type

Here is a suitable class definition:

```
class chessboard{
public:
  chessboard();
  ~chessboard();
  void remove_piece(chesspiece::position);
  void chessboard::insert_piece(chesspiece::piece, chesspiece::position,
      bool white = true, bool can_castle = false)
  void move_piece(chesspiece::position destination,
      chesspiece::position source);
  chesspiece const * contains_piece(chesspiece::position)const;
private:
  chesspiece * board[64];
  // disable copying
  chessboard(chesspiece const &);
  chessboard & operator=(chessboard const &);
};
```

There is very little to the basic design of a **chessboard** type. We need to be able to construct and destroy one. We need to be able to add pieces to the board and remove them from the board. We need to be able to move a piece. Finally, we need to be able to ask what is on a specific square. Notice that **contains_piece()** returns a **chesspiece const ***. You might be tempted to return a **chesspiece const &** instead, but that does not work, because it will not allow us to handle empty squares.

Here is an implementation:

```
chessboard::chessboard():board(){
  if(instrument) std::clog << "Chess board constructed.\n";
}
chessboard::~chessboard(){
  if(instrument) std::clog << "Destroying pieces.\n";
  for(int i(0); i != 64; ++i){
    if(instrument and board[i])
      std::clog << board[i]->what()
          << " at " << i % 8 << ", " << i / 8 << ".\n";
    delete board[i];
  }
  if(instrument) std::clog << "Chess board emptied and destroyed.\n";
}
void chessboard::remove_piece(chesspiece::position p){
  delete board[p.rank * 8 + p.file];
  board[p.rank * 8 + p.file] = 0;
}
void chessboard::insert_piece(chesspiece::piece pc, chesspiece::position p,
    bool white, bool can_castle){
  board[p.rank * 8 + p.file] = new chesspiece(pc, p, white, can_castle);
}
void chessboard::move_piece(chesspiece::position destination,
```

```
      chesspiece::position source){
    board[destination.rank * 8 + destination.file]
        = board[source.rank * 8 + source.file];
    board[source.rank * 8 + source.file] = 0;
}
chesspiece const * chessboard::contains_piece(chesspiece::position p)const{
    return board[p.rank * 8 + p.file];
}
```

As you see, most of the implementation is straightforward. The destructor is the only slightly complicated function. Even there, the complexity is more apparent than real, because most of the code is instrumentation.

 TRY THIS

Add the definition of chessboard to chess2.h, and then add the implementation to chess2.cpp. When chess2.cpp compiles (i.e. you have dealt with any typos), use the following for testing:

```
int main(){
    chessboard b;
    b.insert_piece(chesspiece::pawn, chesspiece::position(2, 3));
    b.insert_piece(chesspiece::king, chesspiece::position(4, 3), false);
    b.insert_piece(chesspiece::rook, chesspiece::position(0, 0),
        true, true);
    b.move_piece(chesspiece::position(3, 3), chesspiece::position(2, 3));
    chesspiece const * p(0);
    p = b.contains_piece(chesspiece::position(4, 3));
    if(p) std::cout << "That square contains a " << p->what() << ".\n";
    else std::cout << "That square is empty.\n";
    b.remove_piece(chesspiece::position(4, 3));
    p = b.contains_piece(chesspiece::position(4, 3));
    if(p) std::cout << "That square contains a " << p->what() << ".\n";
    else std::cout << "That square is empty.\n";
}
```

STRETCHING EXERCISES

6. Add a display function to chessboard that shows the current board, using suitable upper- and lowercase letters for the black and white pieces.

7. My implementation for chessboard assumes that the user always supplies legal values for chesspiece::position data. Add suitable validation code to trap cases where the provided values do not resolve to a square on the board. As you will need this code several times, it is probably best provided as a helper function in the unnamed namespace for chess2.cpp.

8. Write a set of functions that iterates over all the squares of the board and computes how many white pieces currently attack (i.e. can move directly to) each one. Initially, you can ignore pieces blocking the moves of other pieces. However, a complete solution will take that into account. Your code should be able to display the result as an eight-by-eight grid of integer values.

REFERENCE SECTION

Every compilable unit of C++ source code (a `.cpp` file) implicitly has an unnamed namespace. We place source code in it by placing it in a block introduced by the keyword **namespace**, but without providing a name. We can reopen an unnamed namespace within the file. However, unnamed namespaces in different files are always distinct.

In addition, a named namespace can contain an unnamed namespace. Once again, unnamed namespaces in different files are distinct, even if they are contained within the same named namespace.

Names declared in an unnamed namespace are only usable in the immediately containing scope and other scopes nested within that scope. For example, suppose **example.cpp** is:

```
namespace{
  int i(0);
}
namespace x{
  namespace{
    int i(1);
  }
  namespace y{
    foo( ){
      std::cout << i;   // outputs 1, i.e. x::i
      std::cout << ::i;  // outputs 0
    }
  }
}
int foo( ){
  std::cout << i;   // outputs 0
}
```

The second **i** (in the unnamed namespace within namespace **x**) does not conflict with the first. It can be used as **x::i** throughout the file, and as **i** within namespace **x**. Within namespace **x**, the first **i** has to be referred to as **::i**, because the second **i** takes precedence.

The main value of unnamed namespaces is in their use at file scope, where they ensure that internal names do not collide with identical names in other translation units. The compiler gives each unnamed namespace a unique name, which ensures that the linker will be able to keep otherwise identical names distinct. Unnamed namespaces nested in named namespaces are uncommon.

CHAPTER (14)

Streams, Files, and Persistence

We will now look at the general problem of handling input and output. This important area in programming does not fall naturally into any particular place. We could have dealt with it much earlier, but somehow I never got around to it.

The term 'persistence', when applied to data, refers to storage of data so that it is available in other programs or in later invocations of the same program. It is what we do every time we save our work to a file. Without such a facility, we would have to re-enter everything from the keyboard.

In the interests of brevity, in this chapter I have not encapsulated the active body of `main( )` in a `try` block. By now you should be used to ensuring that exceptions are caught in `main( )`, so it serves no good purpose to add that code to every small example program.

The C++ Stream Hierarchy

C++ bases its provision of input and output facilities on the concept of a stream. There are two important parts to this concept: handling the data format and handling the transmission of data. Suppose I want to output the value ten in a human readable form. In other words, I do not want to output the byte whose bit pattern is 00001010, but rather the characters '1' and '0'. This is exactly the problem solved (for standard output) by:

```
std::cout << 10;
```

The format part of the process converts the internal representation of the value ten (as an `int`) into the external representation, '10'. After that, the program dispatches the external representation to the designated sink (by default for `std::cout`, the screen).

Look at the following short program:

```
int main(){
  int i(65);
  char c(65);
  std::cout << "Sixty-five as an integer is " << i << ".\n";
  std::cout << "Sixty-five as a character is " << c << ".\n";
}
```

Look at the output when you build and run that program. The format section of `ostream` instances treats `char` and `int` values differently. It makes no difference where we intend sending the output – the formatting should be the same. Streams delegate the work of actual input and output to instances of the stream buffer classes. I am going to stick with what the Standard Library provides, but if you later want to learn more, you will find all the gory details in *Standard C++ IOStreams and Locales* [Langer & Kreft 2000].

Now suppose we want to send our output to a file. First, we have to create a suitable output stream (an **ofstream** object), and then we have to connect that object to an open file. We often do the two actions together. Here is a short program to demonstrate that:

```cpp
#include <fstream>
#include <iostream>
#include <ostream>

int main( ){
  std::ofstream outfile("testfile.txt");
  outfile << "Hello World!\n";
  outfile << "Three times four is " << 3 * 4 << ".\n";
}
```

When you build and run this program, you will then be able to examine the result by opening **testfile.txt** (you can do that directly from your IDE). Running the program multiple times will not change the contents of **testfile.txt**, because the default behavior of a **std::ofstream** object is to truncate a file before writing to it.

Unfortunately, the current specifications for the file-stream types do not support using **std::string** instances for file names. For example,

```cpp
int main( ){
  std::string filename;
  std::cout << "What file do you wish to create? ";
  std::cin >> filename;
  std::ofstream outfile(filename);
  outfile << "Hello World!\n";
  outfile << "Three times four is " << 3 * 4 << ".\n";
}
```

will not compile. You have to extract an array of **char** from **filename** by using the **c_str( )** member function of **std::string** for the constructor of **outfile**:

```cpp
std::ofstream outfile(filename.c_str( ));
```

We should also check that the constructor successfully connected a file to the **outfile** object. For example, the construction would fail if the chosen file had been marked as 'read only'. The file-stream constructors do not throw exceptions when they fail to open the designated file; instead they place the stream object into a fail state. Our program with checking becomes:

```cpp
int main( ){
  std::string filename;
  std::cout << "What file do you wish to create? ";
  std::cin >> filename;
  std::ofstream outfile(filename.c_str( ));
  if(outfile){  // outfile evaluates as false if it failed to connect
                // to the designated file
    outfile << "Hello World!\n";
    outfile << "Three times four is " << 3 * 4 << ".\n";
  }
  else std::cout << "Failed to open " << filename << ".\n";
}
```

TRY THIS

Run the above program once to create a file called **a.txt**. Now find this file by using 'My Computer'; right-click on it, select Properties, and make it read-only (those are instructions for Windows users). Run the program again and try to create **a.txt**. Note the result.

Instead of opening the file in the constructor, you can use the **open( )** member function of the file-stream types. For example, you can replace

```
std::ofstream outfile(filename.c_str( ));
```

in the above code by:

```
std::ofstream outfile;
outfile.open(filename.c_str( ));
```

You can explicitly close the file attached to a file-stream object by calling **close( )** rather than waiting until the destructor for the file stream closes it automatically. Here is an example that first writes a file and then reads it back:

```
int main( ){
  std::ofstream outfile("data.txt");
  if(outfile){
    std::cout << "Writing out to data.txt.\n";
    outfile << "Hello World!\n";
    outfile << "Three times four is " << 3 * 4 << ".\n";
    outfile.close( );
  }
  else std::cout << "Failed to open data.txt for writing.\n";
  std::ifstream infile("data.txt");
  if(infile){
    std::cout << "Reading in from data.txt.\n";
    std::string line;
    std::getline(infile, line);
    std::cout << line << '\n';
    std::getline(infile, line);
    std::cout << line << '\n';
  }
  else std::cout << "Failed to open data.txt for reading.\n";
}
```

I have used **std::getline( )** to extract input from the file because it reads whole lines from the input source.

As you are already fluent in using the standard console I/O objects, you only need to acquire skill in using the explicit file-handling properties of the file streams. We have already seen how to open and close a file. You need to know the default behavior for those processes. When we create a **std::ifstream** object and open a file (either by using a constructor, or by calling **open( )**), the file will be opened in text mode. Sometimes we want to open a file to read its contents in **binary** mode (raw mode). The simple way to achieve this is by setting the **binary** flag in the object. Here is an example of doing so:

```
1 int main( ){
2   std::ifstream infile("data.txt", std::ios::binary);
```

```
3    if(infile){
4      while(not infile.eof()){
5        std::cout << std::hex << infile.get() << ' ';
6      }
7    }
8    else std::cout << "Failed to open data.txt for reading.\n";
9  }
```

This program opens the file **data.txt** that we prepared earlier in binary mode; that is the significance of the **std::ios::binary** used in the constructor for **ifstream** in line 2. Line 3 checks that the program has successfully opened the file and made it available to the **infile** object. Line 4 starts a loop that repeats until **infile** is in an end-of-file state; **infile** will reach that state when the program reads the end-of-file marker. In some cases, we need to detect that immediately and avoid trying to process the value representing an end of file. It is all right in this program because we do not mind displaying the value of the end-of-file marker on the screen.

I have added a *manipulator* (the technical name for an object that changes the behavior of a stream object) in the output statement at line 5: **std::hex** forces numerical output into hexadecimal format. (The manipulators **std::oct** and **std::dec** force numerical output into octal and decimal format respectively.) **infile.get()** extracts the next character from **infile** as an **int** value. The reason I chose that function to extract data from input is that it preserves the value for the end-of-file marker. That value in C++ is **-1**, regardless of how the OS may represent it.

Try the above program.

EXERCISES

1. Enhance the above program so that the output is in 16 columns. The simplest way to place output in columns is to use the **std::setw(***n***)** manipulator (where *n* is the width of the column). You will need to **#include <iomanip>** to get full access to the manipulators.

2. Modify your program for Exercise 1 so that it displays each value in hexadecimal followed by the decimal equivalent in parentheses. Place eight values per output line. You will probably find it difficult to get neat columns. Do not spend much time trying to achieve that, as we will shortly see a simple way to do it.

Appending Data

C++ provides many tools for handling input and output. If you want to know about them, you need a good reference such as *The C++ Standard Library* [Josuttis 1999]. However, one very common need is to be able to add data to the end of an existing file. To do this, we need to change the default behavior for opening a file for writing. The default behavior, as we found earlier, is to truncate the file if it already exists. In other words, opening an existing file for writing erases all its contents. If we want to add data at the end we must use the append flag, **std::ios::app**. Build and run the following program:

```
int main(){
  std::ofstream outfile("data.txt", std::ios::app);
  if(outfile){
```

```
    std::cout << "Appending data to data.txt.\n";
    outfile << "This is some more data.\n";
    outfile << "Goodbye sad universe.\n ";
    outfile.close( );
  }
}
```

Examine the result in your text editor (i.e. the one provided by MDS).

Consolidation

If you feel you would like to spend some more time on various aspects of using files, you may find it useful to study the material in Chapters 9 and 10 of *You Can Do It!* Some parts of those chapters rely on a degree of fluency with using my Playpen library. However, many people find that fun as well as instructive. I should also mention that in addition to `ifstream` and `ofstream`, there is an `fstream` type. This provides both read and write facilities. I generally avoid using it because I find mixing reading and writing to the same file far too big a source of confusion and error. In general, I either read everything first and then do some writing, or write everything first and then read it back. Either task is, in my experience, better handled by closing the file after the first stage and reopening it for the second.

String Streams

There are times when it is useful to have an internal source and sink for data. C++ originally provided a way by which an array of `char` could be used for that. The design allowed the array to change its size as long as the address of the array was not made visible outside the stream object. As this mechanism was in wide use long before the publication of the C++ Standard, it is still supported, but it should not be used in new code.

The old streams based on arrays of `char` are made available by including the `<strstream>` header. There are three classes: `istrstream` for input (using the object as a source of data), `ostrtream` for output (using the object as a sink for data), and `strstream` (for both reading and writing). The time to study the details of these streams is when you have to maintain old code that uses them.

By the mid '90s, C++ had a robust `std::string`. It is much more versatile than the old C-style array-of-`char` strings. It was obvious to the designers of C++ that it was the logical source and sink for character data. `std::string` does not need any magic to allow expansion to accommodate added data because that is already part of its design. We can extract the data as an array of `char` if and when we need to by using its `c_str( )` member function.

With this in mind, three new classes were added to C++: `istringstream`, `ostringstream`, and `stringstream`. They are made available by including the `<sstream>` header. Unless there are very special reasons to do otherwise, you should choose these in preference to the corresponding `(i/o)strstream` streams.

Here is a small example of using a `stringstream`, which I will walk you through in a moment:

```
int main( ){
  std::stringstream sink;  // you need the <sstream> header for this
  sink << "This is an example.\n";
  sink << "Five times three is " << 5 * 3 << ".\n";
  std::cout << "There are " << sink.str( ).length( )
      << " characters in the data sink.";
  std::cout << "\nand the contents are:\n\n" << sink.str( );
}
```

Note that you will have to include the necessary headers to compile this program successfully.

The program first creates an (empty) `std::stringstream` object called `sink`. It then uses the insertion operator (`<<`) to send some data to it. Note that because this is a stream, the data will be formatted. I then use the member function `str( )` to access the `std::string` in which a `stringstream` stores the data.

I can use a `std::stringstream` constructor that takes a `std::string` by value (i.e. the `std::string` will be copied) to preload the stream object with data. Here is a short program to illustrate that usage:

```cpp
int main( ){
  std::string s("1 2 3");
  std::stringstream source(s);
  int val(0);
  for(int i(0); i != 3; ++i){
    source >> val;
    std::cout << val << ", ";
  }
  std::cout << '\n';
}
```

We can modify that program to use the default constructor by replacing the definition of source with:

```cpp
std::stringstream source;
source.str(s);
```

In other words, the `str( )` member function is overloaded both to provide access to the current `std::string` being used and to assign a new value to it. The usage in the first program above accesses the current value, and the second one copies `s` into the `std::string` used by `source`.

The string streams are useful for several things. The first is that they allow us to get a line of input from a file or from the console (by using `getline( )`) and then parse that line without the problems incurred by sending our source stream into a fail state (because some input data does not match the program's requirements). Here is an example:

```cpp
int main( ){
  while(true){
    std::string data;
    std::cout << "Type in three numbers separated by spaces: ";
    getline(std::cin, data);
    if(data == "END") break;
    std::stringstream s(data);
    int i, j, k;
    s >> i >> j >> k;
    std::cout << i << ", " << j << ", " << k  << '\n';
  }
}
```

That code is not robust because we should check that the input has not failed before we try to output the values of `i`, `j` and `k`. However, because the declarations are inside the `while` loop, we recreate the objects for each pass through the loop and avoid the problem of pushing `std::cin` into a fail state. The program just illustrates a small idea that you can extend to solve some kinds of input problem.

Converting Numerical Values to Strings

One of the commonest requests from new C++ programmers is how to convert a numerical value such as an `int` or **double** into a string. Despite its very extensive interface, `std::string` does not have a conversion from any of the numerical types. The instinctive reaction form programmers coming from languages where such conversions exist is that this is a defect in the `std::string` specification. However, the (o)`stringstream` types solve the problem very simply. Here is an example of using `ostringstream` to handle the problem of placing the output for Exercise 2 above into neat columns:

```cpp
int main(){
  std::ifstream infile("data.txt", std::ios::binary);
  if(infile){
    std::cout << "Reading in from data.txt.\n";
    int count(0);
    while(not infile.eof()){
      int const val(infile.get());
      std::ostringstream item;
      item << std::hex << val << '(' << std::dec << val << ')';
      std::cout << std::setw(10) << item.str();
      if(++count == 8){
        std::cout << '\n';
        count = 0;
      }
    }
  }
  else std::cout << "Failed to open data.txt for reading.\n";
}
```

When you try that program, you may dislike the output format because each item is right-justified in a field of ten characters. C++ output streams provide two manipulators that we can use to determine whether to left- or right-justify an output field, they are `std::left` and `std::right`. Replace the statement that sends an item to `std::cout` with:

```cpp
std::cout << std::setw(10) << std::left << item.str();
```

Now the program generates neatly tabulated results. Well, almost. Unfortunately, it spoils it by attempting to display the end-of-file value; we cannot represent that value by two hex characters. The problem is that we test for end-of-file too late. Here is an alternative formulation of the `while` loop that avoids that problem:

```cpp
while(true){
  int const val(infile.get());
  if(infile.eof()) break;
  std::ostringstream item;
  item << std::hex << val << '(' << std::dec << val << ')';
  std::cout << std::left << std::setw(10) << item.str();
  if(++count == 8){
    std::cout << '\n';
    count = 0;
  }
}
```

The critical changes are changing the test condition of the **while** loop so as to make it into a forever loop, and then providing a test and **break** internally. There are other ways to achieve the same objective, and this one is just my style. Not everyone agrees, but I am happy to use **break** from within a loop so long as it is the only exit from the loop.

EXERCISE

3. Adapt the above program so that it prints out the single-character hexadecimal values as two characters, by inserting a leading zero.

STRETCHING EXERCISE

4. Write a program that outputs the contents of a file as a block with 16 values per line without spaces, with an adjacent block with the values displayed as characters if they are printable and as a dot if not. You may find the `std::isprint( )` function useful: it returns `true` if a character is printable and `false` otherwise.

Persistence

This term is used to describe a mechanism by which we can store data and recover it for later use during another execution of the program or by another program. For example, we might want to write a program that will store the position reached in a chess game and recover it the following day so that you can continue.

Storing data for non-polymorphic types is relatively simple, because you just need to overload the insertion (`<<`) and extraction (`>>`) operators so that whatever you send to a file can be read back. Many application programs such as word-processors are examples of this kind of persistence. There is no great problem that needs solving.

The process gets more difficult when the output is encoded in some way, for example, text that is stored in a compressed form that must be uncompressed on recovery. This is still not much of a challenge.

The final stage is when we need to store and recover polymorphic data. For example, when dealing with a chess piece, we need to store its type, color, and location. When we recover the information, we need to use the type information to create the correct piece. This may not seem to be a serious problem until we decide to make the file human readable. Typically, we might want to create a file whose contents look something like:

white pawn at (1, 2)
black knight at (5, 6)
etc.

Given such a file, we want to be able to read it line by line and create a matching instance dynamically. Here is some pseudocode to illustrate what we want to achieve:

- Create a suitable object encapsulating a container such as the **chessboard** class from the last chapter.
- Recover one line of data from the file.
- Determine the color, type, file, and rank of the piece.
- Insert the piece onto the **chessboard**.

We can recover a line of data (the data for a single piece) from storage by using `std::getline`. We then want to be able to parse the input line to extract the relevant arguments. Something like:

```cpp
void create_piece(std::stringstream & data, chessboard & board){
  bool const color(get_color(data));
  chesspiece::piece const piece(get_piece_type(data));
  chesspiece::position const position(get_position(data));
  bool can_castle(false);
  if(piece == chesspiece::king or piece == chesspiece::rook)
    can_castle == get_can_castle(data);
  board.insert_piece(piece, position, color, can_castle);
}
```

Now let us look at the four functions that extract the data from the `std::stringstream` object. Here are the declarations:

```cpp
bool get_color(std::stringstream &);
chesspiece::piece get_piece_type(std::stringstream &);
chesspiece::position get_position(std::stringstream &);
bool get_can_castle(std::stringstream &);
```

Each of these functions converts some information that had been stored as text into an appropriate internal representation. Here are definitions of the first, third, and fourth functions (I am delaying the second for a moment because that is the interesting one that will illustrate a useful technique):

```cpp
bool get_color(std::stringstream & data){
  std::string color;
  data >> color;
  return color == "white";
}
chesspiece::position get_position(std::stringstream & data){
  int rank, file;
  int digit;
  while(true){  // search for next char
    digit = data.get();
    if(std::isdigit(digit)) break;  // isdigit is declared in <cctype>
  }
  // using guarantee that digits have consecutive representations:
  file = digit - '0';
  while(true){  // search for next char
    digit = data.get();
    if(std::isdigit(digit)) break;
  }
  rank = digit - '0';
  data.get();  // extract the closing parenthesis
  return chesspiece::position(file, rank);
}
bool get_can_castle(std::stringstream & data){
  std::string castle;
  data >> castle;
  return castle == "yes";
}
```

The above definitions are not robust, production-quality ones. For example, if there are not two digits in **data** giving the position of the piece, **get_position( )** will fail, possibly catastrophically. I am leaving it as an exercise for the reader to provide data validation coupled with appropriate action (such as throwing an exception for a corrupt input file).

> Language Note: C programmers should note that the Standard C headers from the C90 standard are valid in C++. However, the preferred option in C++ is to use headers without the .h extension but prefixing the C header name with the letter c. Therefore, for example, the C header <string.h> becomes <cstring> in C++. That particular header is subject to confusion in C++ because <string> is the C++ header in which std::string is declared, while <cstring> provides the declarations of C's <string.h> (but encapsulated in namespace std).

Converting Text to an Enumerator

Our major problem with **get_piece( )** is that we store the data in a human-readable form, where the name of a piece is saved as text. However, we are representing pieces by enumerators of the **chesspiece::piece enum** type. The problem is how to convert from the external textual representation to the internal enumerator. We could write something such as:

```
chesspiece::piece get_enumumerator(std::string const & textname){
  if(textname == "pawn") return chesspiece::pawn;
  if(textname == "rook") return chesspiece::rook;
  // and so on
}
```

That is a perfectly valid option. However, it lacks elegance, and such a method can cause problems with maintenance. Ideally, we would like to be able to look up the name in a suitable table and get the enumerator straight back. The C++ **std::map** container (declared in **<map>**) provides a suitable data structure for this purpose. A map consists of a set of key–value pairs. Like all the Standard Library containers, **std::map** is a template that can be used for any suitable combination of types for the key and value. In this case, we define:

```
std::map<std::string, chesspiece::piece> text_to_enum;
```

We need a function to initialize the table. We also need to decide where we are going to declare the table. As this is to do with our chess-piece concept, I think that both **text_to_enum** and the function that initializes the table should be static members of **chesspiece**.

Here is a suitable initialization function:

```
void chesspiece::init_text_to_enum( ){
  text_to_enum["bishop"] = chesspiece::bishop;
  text_to_enum["king"] = chesspiece::king;
  text_to_enum["knight"] = chesspiece::knight;
  text_to_enum["pawn"] = chesspiece::pawn;
  text_to_enum["queen"] = chesspiece::queen;
  text_to_enum["indeterminate"] = chesspiece::indeterminate;
}
```

That may look strange to you unless you have come across such containers before. We can access a **std::map** object by using a key as a subscript. If the key is already in the map, the corresponding value will be used exactly as if it were a variable. If the key is not found, it will be automatically added to the map. **chesspiece::init_text_to_enum( )** effectively inserts six text keys as instances of **std::string** and pairs them with the corresponding **chesspiece::piece** enumerators. That function must be executed at least once (executing it more than once has no effect other than taking time) before statements such as

```
std::cout << text_to_enum["knight"] << " is the code for a knight.\n";
```

can be executed correctly. Otherwise, the program will compile and execute, but give incorrect output.

 TRY THIS

Add declarations of **text_to_enum** and **init_text_to_enum( )** as static members of **chesspiece**. Add the definitions to the implementation file for **chesspiece** (remember that you have to provide the definitions for static data members). Now build and execute the following:

```
int main(){
    chesspiece::init_text_to_enum();
    std::cout << "The internal representation of a knight is "
        << chesspiece::text_to_enum["knight"] << ".\n";
}
```

Now we are ready to provide a definition of the function to extract the type of chess piece from our `std::stringstream` object holding the specification of a piece:

```
chesspiece::piece get_piece_type(std::stringstream & data){
    std::string pce;
    data >> pce;
    return chesspiece::text_to_enum[pce];
}
```

This is not a robust definition but one that assumes that the data includes the correctly spelled name of a chess piece.

EXERCISES

5. Create a project, and add the declarations of all the functions necessary for implementing `create_piece( )` to a header file. Put the corresponding definitions in an implementation file. The following small program will act as an initial test:

```
int main(){
    std::stringstream source;
    source << "white pawn at (1, 2)";
    chessboard board;
    create_piece(source, board);
}
```

6. Design and implement a function that saves the specification of a piece to a file. Test it, and try using the file as a source of data for Exercise 5.

7. Reorganize your code base so that `create_piece()` and the matching `save_piece()` become implementation details of `chessboard`. Note that the reorganization should include moving as much of the implementation as possible into the appropriate implementation file, and into that file's unnamed namespace.

8. Add `save_board()` and `get_board()` as members of `chessboard`, so that you can save a board position to a file and then recover it from that file.

9. Add a constructor to `chessboard` that loads a position from a stream. Change its destructor so that it offers to save the position before destroying the board.

STRETCHING EXERCISE

10. Enhance the `deck` class so that you can write the cards out to storage and then recover them. The storage should be in human-readable text.

REFERENCE SECTION

Streams

C++ provides several major categories of stream class. Each of them provides facilities for formatting data as well as sending character data to a sink or extracting it from a source. Most of these facilities are provided through templates so that the user can select the character type (by default, either `char` or `wchar_t`). Streams default to handling data as text, though they can be constructed to handle binary data (no conversion to and from text).

Streams are based on stream-buffer classes (which handle the actual input and output operations). This book does not go into the details of those classes.

The high-level programmer is concerned with three types of stream: the standard console streams, the file streams, and the string streams. Each of these has versions based on `char` and `wchar_t`, as well as facilities for extending them to other kinds of character. There is a fourth, legacy stream type that uses an array of `char` as its input/output buffer. This should not normally be used in new code, and I am not providing details of it in this book.

In general, whenever a stream operation fails, the instance is set into some kind of dormant state where all subsequent attempts to use it do nothing until the program resets the stream object by applying the `clear()` member function. A stream in any form of dormant state evaluates as `false` in any context where a `bool` value is expected.

A stream can be in one of four states:

fail: Some operation since the last time it was set to a good state has failed. This condition can be detected by applying the `fail()` member function to the stream object. That returns `true` if the object is in a fail state. For example, an attempt to extract an `int` value from `std::cin` when the next item of data does not represent such a value places `std::cin` into a fail state. All subsequent attempts to extract data from `std::cin` will be ignored (i.e. do nothing) until the stream is reset with `std::cin.clear()`.

bad: Some operation has failed in a way that may involve the loss of data or the corruption of the stream. This is a more severe situation than those flagged by the fail state. Writing data to a full disk might cause a file stream to enter such a state. The `bad()` member function returns `true` if the object is in a bad state.

eof: An end-of-file marker has been read. (This includes input of an end-of-file marker from the keyboard, though what constitutes such a marker depends on the operating system. Ctrl+Z is an EOF for Windows systems; Ctrl+D is an EOF for UNIX-based systems.) The `eof()` member function returns `true` if an end-of-file marker has been read.

good: A stream that is in none of the above states is in a good state, and the member function `good()` returns `true` for an object in this state. Note that `good()` simply reports the current state of an object and has nothing to say about whether the next operation will succeed.

Console Streams

These (at least the narrow versions using `char`) are declared in `<iostream>`. Strictly speaking, the Standard only requires that header to declare the eight standard console stream objects, and the declarations of the functionality are provided by the `<istream>` and `<ostream>` headers. In practice, most implementations include those headers nested in `<iostream>`.

File Streams

The `<fstream>` header provides the necessary declarations for the three subtypes `ifstream` (input only), `ofstream` (output only), and `fstream` (bidirectional). The file-stream subtypes provide all the functionality of the corresponding basic stream types (input stream, output stream, and bidirectional stream) plus facilities for opening and closing files. The destructor of a file-stream object always closes any associated file.

String Streams

The `<sstream>` header provides the necessary declarations for the three subtypes `istringstream` (input only), `ostringstream` (output only), and `stringstream` (bidirectional). Those types use a `std::string` as a source/sink for data. There are also a matching set of `(i/o)wstringstream` types that use a `std::wstring` as a source/sink for data. More advanced facilities are available for the expert specializing in I/O problems.

The special feature of the string-stream types is the provision of an overloaded `str()` member function. When called without arguments, it returns the buffer as a string (useful when using a `stringstream` to convert data to a `std::string` before using it elsewhere in a program). The version of `str()` that takes a `std::string` as an argument replaces the internal buffer with a **copy** of the argument.

char* Streams

The `<strstream>` header provides the necessary declarations for the three subtypes `istrstream` (input only), `ostrstream` (output only), and `strstream` (bidirectional). These use an array of `char` as a buffer. The Standard provides them simply as support for pre-standard code. They are officially deprecated, which means that the Standards Committee reserves the right to remove them from future releases of the C++ Standard.

Manipulators

The C++ Standard provides a number of special objects that change the state of a stream. These are called manipulators. They are used by applying the appropriate insertion/extraction operator. For example,

```
int main( ){
    std::cin >> std::hex;
    int i;
    std::cin >> i;
    std::cout << "\n\n" << i;
}
```

outputs '16' if you type in '10', i.e. it treats '10' as a hexadecimal value.

The commonest manipulators are:

std::endl: adds a newline character to output and flushes the output buffer.
std::setw(n): sets the width of the field for the next output to n.
std::right and std::left: set the justification for the next output in the output field.
std::dec, std::oct, and std::hex: set the base for subsequent use of the stream.

There are a number of others, as well as facilities for writing your own. For further details, refer to a good reference such as *The C++ Standard Library*.

CHAPTER (15)

Exceptions

We have been making use of exceptions from very early in this book but I have said very little about them. It is time that I remedied this, because exceptions have a fundamental impact on C++, way beyond their use for handling errors. The existence of exceptions changes the way we should write code. We cannot simply bolt exceptions on as an afterthought.

Though this is one of the shorter chapters, its contents are very important to your development as a competent C++ practitioner.

What Is an Exception?

Different programmers will give you different answers to this question. The differences between experts are very much a matter of emphasis. Here is my answer.

An exception is a situation that you can anticipate, where continuation of the normal code will fail, possibly catastrophically. For example, a program reading data from a file in which the data does not match the program's requirements clearly cannot continue with anything that depends on the data. We do not expect corrupt files or files in the wrong format, but we know that such things happen.

Most cases where an expectation has not been met require an alternative execution path. Sometimes that alternative may be to abandon the program, but at other times we may be able to recover and continue with the program's work. Even if we have to abandon the program, we may still want to clean up first. The traditional styles of programming interleave error-handling code (i.e. code to deal with broken expectations) with normal code. This leads to fragile code that is often a nightmare to maintain and modify. Consider the following:

```cpp
int main(){
  std::ifstream infile("data.txt");
  if(not infile){
    std::cerr << "Problem with opening data.txt.\n";
    return EXIT_FAILURE;  // declared in cstdlib
  }
  // process the file
  return EXIT_SUCCESS;
}
```

The error-handling code is intrusive, but in this context we can live with it. However, what if that were not `main( )` but some other function? Should we abandon program execution by calling `abort( )`? Should we report the error to the calling function? If the latter, how should we report the failure? The traditional solution is to provide some kind of error return code. However, that preempts at least one return value, and places a requirement on the calling function to check for the error return. What makes this worse is that often the calling function can only relay the failure report to the function that called it. Error return codes are fine when there is a reasonable expectation that the calling function will both check for an error and handle it locally. Once we go much beyond that, using an error return ceases to be a good solution.

Let me rewrite the above program using exceptions, and then consider how the new form works even when the function is not `main( )`:

```cpp
int main( ){
  try{
    std::ifstream infile("data.txt");
    if(not infile) throw "Problem with opening data.txt.\n";
    // process the file
  }
  catch(char const * message){
    std::cerr << message;
    return EXIT_FAILURE;
  }
  return EXIT_SUCCESS;
}
```

You may think that I should reorganize the above code to:

```cpp
int main( ){
  std::ifstream infile("data.txt");
  if(infile){
    // process the file
    return EXIT_SUCCESS;
  }
  else{
    std::cerr << "Problem with opening data.txt.\n";
    return EXIT_FAILURE;
  }
}
```

Yes, I could, but that code relies on the code handling the problem locally. Now let me move the file use out of `main( )`:

```cpp
void process(std::string const & filename){
  std::ifstream infile(filename.c_str( ));
  if(not infile) throw "Problem with opening data file in process( ).";
  // process the file
}
void process_file( ){
  std::string filename;
  std::cout << "Which file contains the data? ";
  std::cin >> filename;
  process(filename);
}
```

```
int main(){
  try{
    process_file();
  }
  catch(char const * message){
    std::cerr << message;
    return EXIT_FAILURE;
  }
  return EXIT_SUCCESS;
}
```

Do you see how throwing an exception disconnects detection of the problem (failure to open a file) from handling it (in this case, just reporting the problem and ending the program)? However, we gain even more, because there might be other problems incurred during the processing of a successfully opened file. Notice that the intermediate function, **process_file()**, has no need to provide any mechanism for reporting errors that may result from its call of **process()**. The C++ exception mechanism provides this separation and thereby provides us with a way to write simpler code. With a little care, we can write code that retries when something fails. Here is a modified version of **main()**:

```
int main(){
  try{
  bool another(true);
  while(another){
    try{
      process_file();
    }
    catch(char const * message){
      std::cerr << message << '\n';
    }
    std::cout << "Do you want to process another file? ";
    std::cin >> another;
  }
  catch(...){
    std::cerr << "Unknown exception caught.\n";
    return EXIT_FAILURE;
  }
  return EXIT_SUCCESS;
}
```

The inner **catch** handles the 'expected' exception and allows the program to continue with trying another file. The outer **catch** will catch all other types of exceptions and terminate the program.

What Can I throw?

C++ places very few restrictions on what we can use as an exception object. As long as the object can be copied (and that is an absolute requirement, because the exception mechanism may need to move the exception object to a safe location while doing the stack cleanup), you can use it as an exception object. However, it is generally good practice to throw objects of types designed to provide exception objects. My use of a string literal in the example code above is poor coding practice. I used string literals because I did not want to get into the design of exception types until I had shown how exceptions simplify code.

The C++ Library provides a hierarchy (based on class **exception**) of exception types for use within the Standard Library. We can use some of these in our own code (as I have in earlier chapters), but it is normally better to design exception types for our own use. Most of these can be very simple. Indeed, we can often use stateless classes (ones with no data members) as exception types. We can use the Standard Library types as bases for our own types when that seems suitable.

We normally nest exception types in the class that will use them. For example, our **chessboard** type has a number of ways in which it can fail. This is particularly true of the constructor that tries to create a **chessboard** object from data provided by a stream. Unlike other functions, constructors can only reliably report failure by throwing an exception. By using the exception mechanism to deal with failed construction (for example, because it has been impossible to place the object into a destructible state), we can assume that defined objects in our code exist in a stable state that meets the class invariants (those properties that class objects are required to have).

```
class chessboard{
public:
  chessboard();
  chessboard(std::istream &);
  ~chessboard();
  struct exception{ };
  struct bad_data: exception{ };
  struct invalid_piece: bad_data{ };
  struct invalid_position: bad_data{ };
  struct corrupt_stream: exception{ };
  // rest elided
private:
  // details elided
};
```

I have added an entire exception hierarchy into **chessboard**. Each of the exception types in that hierarchy is a stateless class. It does not have to be; for example, I could add a (virtual) member function that reports the type of the exception:

```
class chessboard{
public:
  chessboard();
  chessboard(std::istream &);
  ~chessboard();
  struct exception{
    virtual char const * report()const{
      return "Generic chessboard exception.";
    }
  };
  struct bad_data: exception{
    virtual char const * report()const{
      return "Bad data chessboard exception.";
    }
  };
  struct invalid_piece: bad_data{
    virtual char const * report()const{
      return "Invalid piece chessboard exception.";
    }
```

```
  };
  struct invalid_position: bad_data{
    virtual char const * report( )const{
      return "Invalid position chessboard exception.";
    }
  };
  struct corrupt_stream: exception{
    virtual char const * report( )const{
      return "Corrupt stream chessboard exception.";
    }
  };
  // rest elided
private:
  // details elided
};
```

Now you can write:

```
int main( ){
  try{
    std::ifstream data("Chessposition.txt");
    if(not data) throw "No such file.";
    chessboard board(data);
  }
  catch(char const * message){
    std::cerr << message << '\n';
    return EXIT_FAILURE;
  }
  catch(chessboard::exception const & error){
    std::cerr << error.report( ) << '\n';
    return EXIT_FAILURE;
  }
  catch(...){
    std::cerr << "Unknown exception caught.\n";
    return EXIT_FAILURE;
  }
  return EXIT_SUCCESS;
}
```

Note that the above code catches the possible **chessboard** exceptions with a **const** reference to **chessboard::exception**. In general, we should catch exceptions by reference, so that we preserve any polymorphic behavior provided by possible subtypes. It is also common to catch by **const** reference, because we would not normally want to change the data encapsulated in an exception object.

When there is a list of **catch** clauses, the program executes the first one that matches the actual exception (even if that involves a type conversion). Note that this is different from function overloading, where the compiler attempts to determine a unique best match. For example, adding a **catch(chessboard::corrupt_stream const & cs)** handler after the **catch(chessboard::exception const & error)** handler will do nothing, because the latter will grab the exception and process it. More specialized exceptions (i.e. ones that are derived from a base) must be placed earlier in the list of **catch** clauses.

TRY THIS

Here is some code that we are going to use to explore exceptions:

```
void bar( ){
  chessboard::chessboard b(std::cin);
}

void foo( ){
  chessboard board;
  std::stringstream source;
  source << "white king at (1, 2)";
  create_piece(source, board);
  // bar( );
}

int main( ){
  try{
    chesspiece::init_text_to_enum( );
    foo( );
  }
  catch(chessboard::exception const & except){
    std::cerr << except.report( ) << '\n';
  }
}
```

First, implement the constructor for a **chessboard** object from an input stream as:

```
chessboard::chessboard(std::istream &):board( ){
  throw chessboard::corrupt_stream( );
}
```

That stub function throws an exception so that we have an exception to use for test purposes. If you already have a definition for this constructor, you can add the **throw** statement at the beginning of your existing code until you are ready to incorporate data validation into your code.

Experiment 1

Create a suitable project, and copy the header and implementation files for **chesspiece** and **chessboard** across, so that we can modify them without changing the originals. (It would probably be wise to give the copies distinct names, to avoid confusion with the originals.) Edit the implementation of the **chessboard::chessboard(std::istream &)** constructor to the above version. Now build and execute the project, and look carefully at the output to note the calls of the documented constructors and destructors.

Experiment 2

Remove the comment in the definition of **foo( )**, to activate the call to **bar( )**. Build and execute the new version. Check that all the constructors and destructors are called as before, followed by the message generated by the **catch** clause.

Experiment 3

Replace main( ) with:

```
int main( ){
  try{
    chesspiece::init_text_to_enum( );
    chessboard * pointer = new chessboard;
    delete pointer;
  }
  catch(chessboard::exception const & except){
    std::cerr << except.report( ) << '\n';
  }
}
```

Build and execute this program, and note the results.

Experiment 4

Add a call to bar( ) immediately before the delete pointer, so that the new version is:

```
int main( ){
  try{
    chesspiece::init_text_to_enum( );
    chessboard * pointer = new chessboard;
    bar( );
    delete pointer;
  }
  catch(chessboard::exception const & except){
    std::cerr << except.report( ) << '\n';
  }
}
```

Build and execute this program. Note that the program no longer executes the **chessboard** destructor. This is an important feature of exceptions: the program does not execute code subsequent to the exception if an exception occurs. However, handling an exception includes executing all the destructors for stack-based objects created between the catch point and the throw point. We call that process *stack-unwinding*, and it is executed in reverse order, starting at the object most recently constructed before the exception is thrown. We have to ensure the release of all dynamically allocated resources. Destructors are best for that process, because the exception mechanism executes them as control passes to the selected exception handler.

Experiment 5

Try this last version, where we replace the raw pointer by a std::auto_ptr<>:

```
int main( ){
  try{
    chesspiece::init_text_to_enum( );
    std::auto_ptr<chessboard> pointer(new chessboard);
    bar( );
  }
  catch(chessboard::exception const & except){
    std::cerr << except.report( ) << '\n';
  }
}
```

Conclusion

The important point to note is that catching an exception results in a cleanup of the function-call stack between the point of the throw and the point where the exception is caught. Another point we should note is that an exception will drill straight through code, cleaning up on the way, even though there maybe no local indication that this might happen. Therefore, we have to develop sensitivity to where exceptions might interfere, and ensure correct cleanup of all the objects. In programming terminology, we must respect class invariants and maintain them wherever an exception may pass through.

This necessary extra care, coupled with ensuring the release of dynamically executed resources by destructors, has a serious impact on our coding style. We call such a style *exception-safe programming*. The most fundamental element of exception-safe programming is that we only allocate a resource dynamically if there is a destructor that releases the resource. Experiment 4 above demonstrates code that is not exception safe. Experiment 5 demonstrates how to rewrite the code to make it exception safe.

Here is an example to show another aspect of exception-safe programming. Here is a minimalist start for a string class. It uses C-style strings, and functions that handle those. In particular it uses **std::strcpy( )** and **std::strlen( )**. The header **<cstring>** provides all the necessary declarations. I am not going into a great deal of detail, because most readers do not need to know the grisly details of working with C-style strings when **std::string** is so much more robust.

```
class mystr{
public:
  mystr(char const *);
  mystr(mystr const &);   // copy constructor
  ~mystr();
  mystr const & operator=(mystr const &);   // copy assignment
  // rest of public interface
private:
  char * data_ptr;
};
```

Here is an implementation:

```
mystr::mystr(char const * d_ptr):data_ptr(new char[strlen(d_ptr) + 1]){
  std::strcpy(data_ptr, d_ptr);   // copy the array
  data_ptr[strlen(d_ptr)] = 0;   // add null terminator
}
```

This constructor assumes that it receives a pointer to a C-style string (a null-terminated array of **char**). It then obtains enough dynamic storage to hold a copy of the string including the null terminator, and stores the address of that storage in **data_ptr**.

The destructor releases the memory:

```
mystr::~mystr(){delete[ ] data_ptr;}
```

This uses the correct version of **delete** for arrays (I have not gone into detail about creating and destroying dynamic arrays because we usually use **std::vector<>** to handle any requirement for a dynamic array). At first sight, everything is fine. Look again and you might realize that the default copy semantics will copy the pointer rather than the object it points to. Each **mystr** object will need its own copy of the string. We need to deal with the copy semantics of this class.

First the copy constructor:

```
mystr::mystr(mystr const & original)
    :data_ptr(new char[strlen(original.data_ptr) + 1]){
```

```
    std::strcpy(data_ptr, original.data_ptr);  // copy the array
    data_ptr[strlen(original.data_ptr)] = 0;  // add null terminator
}
```

We call this process *deep copying*: we have not copied **data_ptr**; instead we have copied the data it points to. There are no exception problems yet. However, look carefully at this naïve implementation of the assignment operator:

```
mystr const & mystr::operator=(mystr const & rhs){
  // careful not to do anything if the lhs and rhs are the same object:
  if(this != &rhs){
    delete [] data_ptr; // get rid of the current array for the lhs
    // get storage for the copy of the rhs:
    data_ptr = new char[std::strlen(rhs.data_ptr) + 1];
    std::strcpy(data_ptr, rhs.data_ptr);
    data_ptr[std::strlen(rhs.data_ptr)] = 0;  // null-terminate the copy
  }
  return *this;
}
```

This is the classic form for a user-written copy-assignment operator, and you will find it in numerous books. In the days before exceptions, it was acceptable. However, with the introduction of exceptions, it is completely unacceptable. The problem is that we have deleted the memory attached to **data_ptr** before we have something to replace it. You may wonder why that matters. The problem is that something may go wrong with the attempt to get a new block of memory and initialize it with the copied data. If that should happen (yes, I know it is not likely for this simple case), the object you are assigning to is in an unstable state (the result of a **delete** operation is to place the pointer in a state where it must be written to before any further attempts to read it happen). As long as our use of **new** works, we will not have a problem, but if it fails, we have left an object in a state where we cannot safely destroy it. (You must not apply **delete** twice to the same pointer without an intervening call of **new** or some other action that provides a valid deletable pointer value. One such value is the null-pointer constant. Nothing happens if you try to delete a null pointer; the C++ language guarantees that.

The Exception-Safe Copy-Assignment Idiom

Here is **mystr::operator=( )**, rewritten so that it is exception safe:

```
mystr const & mystr::operator=(mystr const & rhs){
  // get the new block of memory:
  char * temp_ptr = new char[strlen(rhs.data_ptr) + 1];
  std::strcpy(temp_ptr, rhs.data_ptr);  // copy the rhs data
  temp_ptr[strlen(rhs.data_ptr)] = 0;  // null-terminate the copy
  delete [] data_ptr;  // get rid of the current array for the lhs
  data_ptr = temp_ptr;  // transfer the ownership of the copy
  return *this;
}
```

We no longer have to check that the left- and right-hand operands of the assignment are different; if they are the same, we will only have wasted a little time with an unnecessary copy, but we get that back by avoiding the time taken for checking in the normal case where the copy assignment has work to do.

Note how the idiom works: first copy; then delete; and then assign the pointer to the copy. Pointer assignment cannot throw an exception. We first do all the work where an exception might occur; then we finish the task. The consequence is that if there is a failure, the left-hand operand (the object we are assigning to) retains its old value.

Attention to exception safety usually results in simpler code because we remove the error-handling from the main flow of the code. However, we do need to be conscious of exceptions, and write code that functions correctly in their presence. Although the design idea in old C++ books may still be useful, the code implementing them is probably flawed and vulnerable to exceptions.

Rethrowing

Sometimes we want to partially process an exception and then relay it on to another handler to complete the task. Here is a rewrite of my earlier **foo( )** function to demonstrate how this is done:

```
void foo( ){
  try{
    chessboard board;
    std::stringstream source;
    source << "white king at (1, 2)";
    create_piece(source, board);
    bar( );
  }
  catch(chessboard::exception const & except){
    std::cerr << "Exception caught in foo( ) and rethrown.\n";
    // you can place any special processing here
    throw;
  }
}
```

The statement consisting of the simple use of **throw** results in the rethrowing of the caught exception for further processing by another handler. Note that you are always allowed to terminate a **catch** clause by throwing an entirely different and possibly unrelated exception. Indeed, there is nothing special about the body of a **catch** clause; the code in it is just C++ code. The single difference is that a bare **throw** can be used only within the body of a **catch** clause.

 TRY THIS

Experiment 6

Edit your code appropriately so that you can try this revised version of **foo( )**. Note the resulting final message that identifies the type of the actual exception object caught in **main( )**.

Experiment 7

Edit your code for Experiment 6 by changing the **catch** clause in **foo( )** to

```
catch(chessboard::exception except){
```

so that the exception object is caught by value. Build and execute the resulting program. Note the change in the final message. This is an example of a process called *slicing*. Any time that you pass, return, or catch a reference or pointer by value, you lose the dynamic type information.

Exception Specifications: An Idea That Failed

It seems reasonable to provide a mechanism for declaring the exceptions that can propagate from a function. Indeed, it is so reasonable that C++ provides such a mechanism via exception specifications. C++ is not alone in this: several other languages, including Java, provide a similar mechanism. However, experience has shown that it is a poor idea, leading to numerous problems.

The idea is that the declaration of a function includes a specification of the exceptions that may propagate from it. The default specification is that any exception can propagate from the function. So when you see

```
void foo();
```

you know that code that calls `foo()` must be prepared for any exception. At the other extreme, we have

```
void bar() throw();
```

which specifies that no exceptions can propagate from `bar()`. Those two extremes are both clear and possibly useful. There is still some argument as to whether the 'throws nothing' specification of `bar()` is useful in optimizing, but it certainly seems to be, at worst, harmless. The problems arise from everything in between, i.e. where there is a list of types in the parentheses following the `throw`. Such a list is supposed to specify the types of exception that may propagate from the function. The original idea was that this should be statically checkable and so enforceable at compile time. Unfortunately, though this was recognized as impossible from very early on, those responsible for the C++ Standard decided to persevere with runtime enforcement of exception specifications. Most experts these days believe that was a mistake.

You need to know what those mysterious `throw()` clauses are in function declarations because you may come across them, but that is about as far as you need to go with them. If you want to use the empty `throw()` specification, please do so. Personally, I do so when writing my own code.

Exceptions and Destructors

There is a small body of experienced programmers who argue that it is OK for an exception to propagate from a destructor. However, the very large majority maintain that a destructor should never propagate an exception.

There are several arguments, but one of the most persuasive is that an object has ceased to exist when its destructor is entered. So what do you have if the destructor does not complete because it throws an exception? Think carefully about that. In essence, whatever you can do should be done before returning from the destructor; return from a destructor should always be a simple `return` statement (possibly implicit).

If you use throw specifications, always add `throw()` to any destructor that you declare. If the compiler complains about the implementation, have a look and see what the problem is.

REFERENCE SECTION

Exceptions

C++ exceptions are based on three keywords: `try`, `throw`, and `catch`. The `try` keyword is used to warn the compiler (and, more to the point, tell human readers of the code) that the following block of code is followed by one or more exception handlers.

We use the `catch` keyword to introduce an exception handler. A single 'parameter' in parentheses follows the `catch`, and that is followed by the body of the handler as a block of code (i.e. enclosed in braces).

If an exception propagates into the `try` block, the program searches for an appropriate handler from those offered immediately after the close of the `try` block. The program executes the first handler whose parameter can accept the type of the exception object. If none of the available handlers can accept the exception object, the program will propagate the exception object to the next-most-recent `try` block and try again. If the program cannot find an acceptable handler, it calls `std::terminate( )`. The exact behavior of `std::terminate( )` is implementation-defined, but all you need to know here is that it ends the program. C++ provides a mechanism for modifying the behavior of `std::terminate( )`.

There is a special-case `catch` clause designed to catch all exceptions. This is introduced by `catch(...)` and can only be used to carry out processing that is independent of the type of the exception object. However, it can use `throw` to rethrow the exception it caught.

Exceptions are raised by using a `throw` statement at the point where the code detects a problem that needs handling elsewhere. A `throw` statement can throw an object of any copiable type. When an exception is raised in a program, normal processing is suspended, and the program uses some implementation-provided mechanism to find the most recent handler for the exception object. When such a handler has been found, the program unwinds the stack back to the location of the handler. The process of stack-unwinding involves calling the destructors for all stack-based objects between the point where the exception is raised and the point where it is handled. If no handler is found, it is implementation-defined whether the stack is completely unwound or left completely alone. An implementation is not allowed to partially unwind the stack and then terminate the program.

Exception Specifications

C++ provides a mechanism for decorating function declarations with a list of the types of exception that may propagate from a call to it. The syntax is simple: add `throw` immediately after the parenthesis that closes the parameter list, and follow it with a list of types in parentheses. For example,

```
void foo( ) throw(std::exception);
```

specifies that only objects whose type is, or is derived from, `std::exception` may propagate from `foo( )`. Such a specification is checked dynamically (i.e. at execution time) in the event of an exception propagating from `foo( )`. If it does not meet the provided specification, `std::unexpected( )` is called. The default action is to call `std::terminate( )`. C++ provides a mechanism for changing this default behavior. However, making such a change requires advanced understanding of C++.

Experience has led most experts to recommend that programmers do not use exception specifications. The special case of an empty specification (no exception can propagate from the function) is generally considered the only exception specification worth providing.

CHAPTER 16

Overloading Operators and Conversion Operators

C++ inherited a large number of operators from C, and then proceeded to identify several other things as operators. For example, C++ treats ( ) as a function operator and [ ] as a subscript operator. C++ allows overloading of most of its operators; whether doing so is useful depends on the context. The overloading of some operators is restricted to class scope, but most of them can be overloaded at global or namespace scope. The single absolute requirement for overloading an operator is that at least one operand must be of a user-defined type.

We have had examples of operator overloading elsewhere, but this chapter provides more examples and more depth. Even so, this will be far from comprehensive, because overloading operators in C++ is rich with potential. For example, C++ allows us to overload **operator new** (the mechanism that **new** uses to acquire memory in which to construct a dynamic object) and **operator delete** (which releases memory after a dynamic object is destroyed). It also provides for overloading the operators used by the array versions of **new** and **delete** (**operator new[ ]** and **operator delete[ ]**). I am leaving such topics for another book.

Overloading Operators for an Arithmetic Type

(Please treat the whole of this section as an extended experiment; in other words, I expect you to work through this with your compiler. Feel free to experiment further until you understand what is happening. If you want to instrument the constructors, you will need to declare a destructor and a copy constructor, so that you can complete the instrumentation in their definitions.)

Suppose that we want to provide a rational-number type (for non-mathematicians, rational numbers are ones that can be written as the ratio of two whole numbers). We would want to provide all the normal arithmetic operations. We would also probably want to provide some form of conversion to a floating-point type. Providing a complete definition and implementation for such a type would be lengthy and of little general interest; however, there is much we can learn from a partial implementation. Here is a starter definition that you can copy into a suitable header file (`rational.h`). Do not forget to add a header guard.

```
class rational{
public:
  rational();
  rational(long numerator, long denominator = 1);
  // compiler-generated copy constructor, copy assignment and destructor OK
  long numerator()const;
```

```
  long denominator( )const;
  // other functions to be added
  struct exception{ };
  struct divide_by_zero: exception{ };
private:
  long d;
  long n;
};
```

I have not qualified the `rational` constructors as `explicit`. That is intentional: implicitly converting a `long int` to a `rational` with a denominator of 1 is reasonable, and most domain experts would expect it.

Here is a simple initial implementation that you can place in `rational.cpp`:

```
#include "rational.h"

rational::rational( ):n(0), d(1){ }
rational::rational(long numer, long denom):n(numer), d(denom){ }
long rational::denominator( )const{return d;}
long rational::numerator( )const{return n;}
```

When I first wrote the implementation, I was plagued by an error message when I tried to compile it. If you want to see it, replace the parameter names in the second constructor with **numerator** and **denominator**. It seems that (at least for this compiler) the member-function names are hiding the parameter names when it comes to the initializers. I mention this because one day you may be baffled by a similar case.

Test Code

Here is a short test program for **testrational.cpp** (or whatever you choose to call it):

```
int main( ){
  try{
    rational r;
    std::cout << r.numerator( ) << "/" << r.denominator( ) << '\n';
    r = 2;
    std::cout << r.numerator( ) << "/" << r.denominator( ) << '\n';
  }
  catch(rational::exception const & r){
    std::cerr << "Exception from rational caught.\n";
  }
}
```

Note that the assignment works because the compiler is doing two things under the covers. First, it generates a copy-assignment operator that copies the data from a right-hand operand of type `rational` to a left-hand operand of that type. Next, it looks to see whether it can convert 2 into a `rational`. Our second constructor does that by allowing a call of `rational(2, 1)`, using the provided default value for **denominator**. Therefore, the compiler creates a temporary `rational` from 2, and then copies it to the left operand of the assignment. We do not need to provide member functions to write the numerator and denominator values to a `rational`. If we want to change the denominator of a rational without changing the numerator, we write something like:

```
r = rational(r.numerator( ), new_denom);
```

You can add member functions to modify the numerator and denominator some time later if you discover that you need the more direct method for efficiency. Changing a rational that way is unusual, so it is unlikely that such member functions will ever be critical to the overall performance of the `rational` type.

Providing a Streaming Operator for Output

The two output lines in the test code suggest a suitable format for an **operator<<**, but we cannot provide that as a class member because the first operand of such an operator is of the wrong type (an **ostream &**). So add

```
std::ostream & send_to(std::ostream &)const;
```

to the class definition, and add this to the class implementation:

```
std::ostream & rational::send_to(std::ostream & out)const{
  out << n << "/" << d;
  return out;
}
```

Now you can add

```
inline std::ostream & operator<<(std::ostream & out, rational const & r){
  return r.send_to(out);
}
```

to **rational.h** and amend the test program to see that it works.

EXERCISE

1. Before reading the next part, please try to declare and implement a corresponding input operator (>>) that will read data in the same format that we have used for output. (A programmer would expect the provision of either both or neither of a pair of operators such as those for input and output. We call this 'the principle of minimal surprise'.)

Providing a Streaming Operator for Input

Add a declaration of **get_from(istream &)** to the definition of **rational** (note that you will need to include **<istream>** for the declaration of **std::istream**):

```
std::istream & get_from(std::istream &);
```

Add the following definition to the implementation of **rational**:

```
std::istream & rational::get_from(std::istream & in){
  in >> n;
  if(in.get() != '/') throw rational::bad_data();
  in >> d;
  if(not in) throw rational::bad_data();
  return in;
}
```

If you have been following the ideas of using exceptions, you will realize that we need to add

```
struct bad_data: exception{ };
```

to the definition of `rational`.

You may want to add polish to the implementation of `get_from( )`; at the very least, it is reasonable to ensure that we do not change the stored value in a `rational` object until we know we have successfully acquired the complete replacement value. Here is a modified version that provides that guarantee:

```
std::istream & rational::get_from(std::istream & in){
  int n1, d1;
  in >> n1;
  if(in.get( ) != '/') throw rational::bad_data( );
  in >> d1;
  if(not in) throw rational::bad_data( );
  n = n1; d = d1;
  return in;
}
```

Now we can provide `operator>>` to extract a rational value from an input source. Add this definition to `rational.h`:

```
inline std::istream & operator>>(std::istream & in, rational & r){
  return r.get_from(in);
}
```

Providing Multiplication for *rational*

We would normally expect to be able to multiply a rational number by an integer as well as by another rational number. We would also expect to be able to multiply an integer by a rational number. For example, we would expect the following code to compile and execute:

```
void test(rational & r, int i){
  rational r1(2, 3);
  std::cout << r << " times " << r1 << " is " << r * r1 << '\n';
  std::cout << r << " times " << i << " is " << r * i << '\n';
  std::cout << i << " times " << r << " is " << i * r << '\n';
}
```

Overloading `operator*` with a member function would deal with the first two cases. However, in the third case the left operand of * is not a `rational` (though it can be converted to one), and so the compiler will not be able to use a member function (the left operand of an operator determines which scope the compiler searches for an overload). This gives us the clue that we have another case where we should provide a global or namespace overload for the operator.

You might choose to use exactly the same mechanism as we did for the streaming operators: provide the functionality through a member function, and then delegate to that when providing the global operator overload. However, there is another option for arithmetic operators: provide an overload for the corresponding compound assignment operator as a class member. There is a sense in which the compound assignment operators are more primitive than the apparently simpler standard ones. Here is how to do it (the same basic design works for all arithmetic operators, for all user-defined arithmetic types).

Add this declaration to the definition of `rational`:

```
rational & operator*=(rational const &);
```

Now add this `inline` definition to the header file:

```
inline rational operator*(rational lhs, rational const & rhs){
  return lhs *= rhs;
}
```

Note that the declaration of **operator*=( )** returns by reference, but the definition of **operator*( )** returns by value. Also, note that, because we do not want to alter the value of the left operand of **operator*( )**, we have to pass it by value.

Finally, add the implementation of *= to `rational.cpp`:

```
rational & rational::operator*=(rational const & r){
  n *= r.n;
  d *= r.d;
  return *this;
}
```

EXERCISES

2. Write a program that uses `test( )` to test that the multiplication works correctly.

3. Implement and test division (`operator/( )`) for `rational`. (If you have forgotten your high-school math, we divide rationals by inverting the numerator and denominator of the right-hand operand and then multiplying.) At this point, you do not need to trap division by zero.

4. Implement and test addition and subtraction for `rational`. (If two rational numbers are represented by n1/d1 and n2/d2, their sum has numerator n1 * d2 + n2 * d1 and denominator d1 * d2.)

Conversion Operators

C++ overloads the **operator** keyword to support outward conversion operators that support implicit conversion from the class type to another type (single-argument constructors that have not been qualified as **explicit** provide inward conversions). These can be useful in some cases but must be treated with great care, because conversion operators (all kinds: built-in ones, single-argument constructors and outward conversion operators) often have surprising and unwanted consequences. For example, it seems reasonable to provide an implicit conversion from **rational** to one or more floating-point types. However, doing so is far from cost free.

Converting to double

Here is a declaration of an operator to provide an implicit conversion from a **rational** value to a **double**:

```
operator double( );
```

Add this definition to the implementation:

```
rational::operator double( ){
  return double(n)/d;
}
```

TRY THIS

Try the above conversion operator with the code we used earlier for testing multiplication.

If you have it right, the code now fails to compile with an ambiguity error for r * i (i.e. multiplying a rational by an int).

What is the problem? Once we provide a user-defined conversion from rational to double, the compiler has two choices for r * i. It can use the converting constructor to convert i to a rational (which is what it was doing before), and then use the operator*( ) we provided for rational. Alternatively, it can convert the rational into a double by using the conversion operator we have just provided, and then use the built-in multiplication for double. As far as the compiler is concerned, both of those conversions are of equal weight, and so it cannot choose between them. We have to resolve that ambiguity by removing one of the causes. We can remove one of the conversions, or explicitly tell the compiler which operand we wish to convert by using a cast. See also 'Another Way to Deal With Ambiguity' below.

As the conversion operator causes problems, we should consider other options. The simplest one is to provide an explicit conversion function such as

```
double to_double( );
```

implemented by:

```
double rational::to_double( ){
   return double(n)/d
}
```

EXERCISE

5. Write a program that tests the use of to_double( ) to convert from rational to double.

Another Way to Deal With Ambiguity

Another option for removing ambiguity is to provide several overloads for the operator in question. This often requires the addition of more overloads than at first seem necessary. For example, we could replace the single overload for rational operator*(rational lhs, rational const & rhs) with:

```
inline rational operator*(rational lhs, rational const & rhs){
   return lhs *= rhs;
}
inline double operator*(double lhs, rational const & rhs){
   return lhs * to_double(rhs);
}
inline double operator*(rational lhs, double rhs);
   return rhs * to_double(lhs);
}
inline rational operator*(long lhs, rational const & rhs)
```

```
    return rational(lhs) * rhs;
}
inline rational operator*(rational lhs, long rhs)
    return lhs * rational(rhs);
}
```

The last two of those ensure that multiplication of a `rational` by an integer value will result in a `rational` value, rather than a `double`.

The moral of all this is that conversion operators are deceptive and often add complexity rather than removing it.

Tidying Up

There is a good deal more to do if we are to provide a robust, industrial-strength implementation of `rational`. For example, we should do something about trapping overflow of the values stored for the numerator and denominator. We should consider how to deal with attempts at constructing a `rational` from a floating-point type such as `double`. We should also consider providing a function to simplify rational values by eliminating common factors from the numerator and denominator. That last function might be a reasonable place to check for a zero denominator.

I am leaving you to deal with these issues because they do not directly concern the subject of this chapter. However, here is an example of how to block the construction of a `rational` from a `double` (assuming you want to block it rather than provide a way to do it); add this declaration to the private interface of `rational`:

```
rational(double);
```

It follows the same idea as we used earlier for blocking copy semantics; if you do not want something, declare it as private.

Function Objects

If you have never come across the idea before, you will probably find the idea that `( )` is an operator a little strange. If you then discover that C++ allows you to overload the `( )` operator, you will probably have a number of reactions – including doubting that it could be useful. While I understand such reactions, overloading `operator( )` is one of the most powerful tools in C++. It is used extensively in that part of the Standard Library that is often referred to as the STL (Standard Template Library), which provides a rich collection of container types and functions to operate on them. We will be looking at some of these in the next chapter. It is also the basis for providing manipulators with arguments for `iostream` objects. (For example, `std::setw( )`, which sets the field width for input/output, uses overloading of `operator( )` to achieve its objective.)

I am going to use a simple mathematical example to demonstrate how we can overload the function operator in a way that will make domain-specific code more approachable to the domain expert. Back in your school days, you would have drawn the graph of a mathematical function $f(x)$. One way of doing this is to plot the points $(x, f(x))$ for a sample of values of x in the range required. We can express that in programming terms as:

```
void draw_graph(double lower, double upper, double interval,
    math_function & f){
  double x(lower);
  do{
```

```
    plot(x, f(x));
  } while((x += interval) < upper);
}
```

Would it not be nice if we could write exactly that? Here is a simple example of how to do that for a quadratic function. First, the class definition to go in **quadratic.h** (do not forget the header guards):

```
class quadratic{
public:
  quadratic(int a, int b, int c);
  double operator( )const(double x);
private:
  int a_, b_, c_;
};
```

And next the implementation (in **quadratic.cpp**):

```
quadratic::quadratic(int a, int b, int c):a_(a), b_(b), c_(c){ }
double quadratic::operator( )const(double x){
  return ((a_*x + b_)*x + c_);
}
```

We are almost done. Add the declaration

```
void draw_graph(double lower, double upper, double interval,
    quadratic const & f);
```

to **quadratic.h**, and add this implementation to **quadratic.cpp**:

```
void draw_graph(double lower, double upper, double interval,
    quadratic const & f){
  double x(lower);
  do{
    plot(x, f(x));
  } while((x += interval) < upper);
}
```

Finally, we have to declare and implement **plot( )**. If you have acquired some fluency with my Playpen library, you might want to exercise it by using the **fgw::plot( )** function provided in that library as a basis for plotting curves. If you do not want to do that, we can provide a version of **plot( )** that writes out the coordinates to the console. As this is an implementation detail, it belongs in the unnamed namespace of **quadratic.cpp**. Here is the code:

```
namespace{
  void plot(double x, double y){
    std::cout << "(" << x << ", " << y << ")\n";
  }
}
```

Now that we have all that done and compiled, here is a short test program:

```
#include "quadratic.h"

int main( ){
  draw_graph(-4, 4, .2, quadratic(1, 3, 2));
}
```

If you are still a little puzzled, quadratic(1, 3, 2) constructs a temporary quadratic object and passes it to the last parameter of draw_graph( ). Because that parameter takes a const reference, it can bind to a temporary.

EXERCISES

6. Enhance the above program so that the arguments for the call of draw_graph( ) are provided at run time.

7. Modify draw_graph( ) so that you can specify the output stream. Then test it with the following program:

```
#include "quadratic.h"
#include <exception>
#include <fstream>

int main( ){
  try{
    ofstream outfile("graph.data");
    if(not outfile) throw "Cannot open graph.data for writing";
    draw_graph(-4, 4, .2, quadratic(1, 3, 2), outfile);
  }
  catch(...){
    std::cerr << "Something went wrong.\n";
  }
}
```

Generalizing

You may feel that this is all very well, but it only works for quadratic functions; what about all the other mathematical functions that you might want to plot? Notice that the draw_graph( ) implementation does not care what the function is. However, we have tied it to quadratic functions by declaring the type of the last parameter as quadratic. We can do with some polymorphic behavior that will fit the computation to the type of the function.

You may be surprised by how little change we need to provide. Add the following abstract base class to quadratic.h (perhaps not that good a name for the header file – change it if you want to)

```
struct math_function{
  virtual double operator( )(double)const = 0;  // pure virtual
};
```

Modify the definition of quadratic so that it inherits (publicly) from math_function. Finally, change the type of the last parameter of draw_graph( ) to math_function &:

```
class quadratic: public math_function{
public:
  quadratic(int a, int b, int c);
  double operator( )const(double x);
```

```
private:
  int a_, b_, c_;
};
void draw_graph(double lower, double upper, double interval,
    math_function & f){
  double x(lower);
  do{
    plot(x, f(x));
  } while((x += interval) < upper);
}
```

That is it. The program you wrote for Exercise 6 should still work and produce the same results. Now you can add in other functions by deriving suitable classes from **math_function**. Notice that **draw_graph( )** is now exactly what we started this section with.

STRETCHING EXERCISE

8. Review the way we encapsulated the idea of a general chess piece into a **chesspiece** type. Now design, implement, and test a function type that encapsulates a selection of mathematical functions. If you are already familiar with the concept of patterns and understand the factory pattern, try to produce a function factory. (Note that the latter is really too advanced for this book, but it is such an obvious development of the theme that I felt it worth mentioning.)

Conclusion

This chapter has only briefly touched on operator overloading, and there are many more aspects of it. The whole of the smart-pointer technology is built on the foundation of overloading **operator*** (the dereference operator, not the multiplication operator) and **operator->**. A great deal of the convenience of the STL containers depends on overloading **operator[ ]** (the subscript operator). Many of the algorithms provided for manipulation of containers depend on the ability to overload **operator( )** (the function operator).

One of the biggest problems you will have with operator overloading is recognizing when it provides a good solution. It is also necessary to learn how to defuse the potential dangers of overloading operators. For example, it is relatively easy to provide a naïve overload of the subscript operator. However, such implementations nearly always break encapsulation or behave in unexpected ways. Getting it right is not that hard, but you are unlikely to do so without guidance or many hours of debugging.

REFERENCE SECTION

Almost all the C++ operators can be overloaded. Some of them, such as assignment (=), subscript ([ ]), and function (( )) can only be overloaded in the context of a class. All of them require that at least one operand is of a user-defined type. When overloading an operator in class scope, the left-hand operand will be of that class type.

When the left-hand operand of an operator will be of a user-defined type whose definition cannot be changed, you have to overload the operator at global or namespace scope. It is usual to overload an operator whose operands are symmetrical (such as **operator+** and **operator==**) at global or namespace scope.

Generally, the functionality for global/namespace overloads can be provided by a named function at class scope. The only time you should consider using the **friend** mechanism to provide access to a class's private data when overloading an operator is if the operator needs access to the private members of two classes for its left and right operands.

You should be careful to restrict overloading of operators to places where you get real benefits. You need a clear understanding of why you are overloading an operator before doing it. Some operators, such as the sequence (comma) operator and the logic operators, where the built-in versions use lazy evaluation, are probably poor candidates for overloading, even though the language allows you to do so.

CHAPTER (17)

Containers, Iterators, and Algorithms

One of the great strengths of C++ is the way that the Standard Library has used template technology to provide generic implementations of some of the basic building blocks of modern programming. Because of its historical origins, many people call the part of the Standard Library that provides these the Standard Template Library (usually just STL). Alex Stepanov and Dave Musser developed the basic ideas and implementation. Once they had proved the concept, they offered their work to the committees who were drafting the C++ Standard. The STL was clearly a great collection of components, and few people had any hesitation about adopting it into the Standard Library and then refining it.

Put simply, the STL has four elements, including: a set of containers (data structures); suitable iterators for those containers; and a set of functions that provide most of the common algorithms that programmers want to apply to containers. The important fourth element is that the C++ Standard specifies how a programmer can add a data structure that will work with the STL algorithms, and how to add algorithms to work with the STL containers. In other words, the STL is designed to be extensible.

The purpose of this chapter is to introduce you to some of the power of the STL, and encourage you to explore it further. The STL has one serious weakness for the newcomer: the names of the various components are sometimes less than intuitive, and the behavior of some components is not what their names imply. In other words, the names sometimes suggest different behavior, and sometimes the behavior you want will be provided by a name you would not guess. This means that a comprehensive reference plus access to experienced users is just about essential if you are to get maximum benefit. The best references are *The Standard C++ Library* [Josuttis 1999] and *Generic Programming and the STL* [Austern 1999]. The former is appropriate if you want to focus on using what is provided by the Standard Library, and the latter if you want to understand the STL well enough to add your own extensions to it.

The Standard provides `std::vector<>` (giving the functionality of a dynamic array), `std::deque<>` (a double-ended queue – another random-access data structure), `std::list<>` (a doubly linked list, a useful data structure for when frequent changes are made by adding or removing elements internally), and `std::basic_string<>` (a sequence of a character type; `std::string` and `std::wstring` are specializations for `char` and `wchar_t`).

In addition, the Standard provides four associative containers: `std::map<>`, `std::multimap<>`, `std::set<>`, and `std::multiset<>`.

Finally, the Standard provides `std::stack<>` and `std::priority_queue<>` as adaptors of other containers to provide those data structures.

Many other data structures are available through third parties (such as Boost) and, recently, via a Technical Report that provides a number of extensions to the Standard Library. Many of the items in the Technical Report are likely to be added to the C++ Standard in its next full release (circa 2009).

Suitable iterators are associated with each container type. Container types usually provide iterator types as nested types. In general, each container type has four iterator types: **iterator**, **reverse_iterator** (allowing iteration from back to front), **const_iterator** (providing read-only access to the elements of a container), and **const_reverse_iterator** (read-only access in reverse order).

The Standard Library has over 80 function templates, which provide the most common forms of manipulation of the elements of a container. They include sorting for sequences (**std::sort**, **std::stable_sort**, and **std::partial_sort**), copying, and searching, as well as functions to add all the elements of a container (**std::accumulate**). If you want to process the elements of a container, always check whether what you want has already been provided as part of the 'algorithm' section of the Standard Library.

I do not have room to cover everything provided by the STL, so I am going to use three small demonstration problems to give you a feel for what you can do with the Standard library.

Working with a Set

Problem 1

Read in a text file and print out a list of the words contained in it.

Here is my solution:

```
1 #include <set>
2 #include <iostream>
3 #include <istream>
4 #include <ostream>
5 #include <fstream>
6
7 int main(){
8   std::ifstream wordfile("main.cpp");
9   std::set<std::string> words;
10   std::string word;
11   while(true){
12     wordfile >> word;
13     if(wordfile.eof()) break;
14     words.insert(word);
15   }
16   std::ofstream wordlist("words.txt");
17   wordlist << "main.cpp contains each of the following at least once:\n";
18   for(std::set<std::string>::iterator i(words.begin());
19       i != words.end(); ++i){
20     wordlist << *i << '\n';
21   }
22 }
```

I have omitted the exception handling and checking that file streams connect to the specified files, because I want to focus on the essentials of this program.

Lines 1−5 include all the necessary headers. In practice, several of them will be redundant, because most implementations include **<istream>** and **<ostream>** automatically with either **<iostream>** or **<fstream>**. **<set>** provides all the declarations we need if we want to use the **std::set<>** container.

Lines 8−10 provide the variables we need. In particular, line 9 provides **words** as a **std::set** of **std::string**s. I initialized **wordfile** to use **main.cpp**, because that is what I called the file in which I saved this program. This is a lazy trick that avoids my taking time to create a specific text file. It will also allow me to highlight a couple of problems with the program as it stands.

Lines 11–15 constitute a standard 'forever' loop with an internal **break** to terminate it. It simply reads in the source file until the end-of-file marker is read.

Line 16 opens a file into which we can write our results. The code in lines 18–21 sends the contents of **words** to the stream **wordlist**, which results in the data being stored in **words.txt**. There are several points worth noting. The first is the usage of **words.begin( )** and **words.end( )**. Every standard container type provides a pair of member functions called **begin( )** and **end( )**. The former returns an iterator to the first element of the container and the latter a special value of the iterator type that designates 'beyond the end of the container'. In the special case that the container is empty, **begin( )** and **end( )** return the same iterator value.

Look carefully at line 18. I have defined **i** to be an object of type **std::set<std::string>:: iterator** and initialized it to locate the first element in the container I have called **words**. Next, **i** is checked against the special termination value (so if **words** is empty, the loop terminates immediately). Then the dereferenced value of **i** (i.e. ***i**) is sent to the **wordlist** stream. **i** is incremented and the process repeated until we reach the end of **words**.

Here is the result (if you use whitespace differently when you type the code in, your results may be slightly different):

```
main.cpp contains each of the following at least once:
!=
#include
'\n'
*i
++i){
<<
<fstream>
<iostream>
...
wordfile
wordfile("main.cpp");
wordlist
wordlist("words.txt");
words.end( );
words.insert(word);
words;
}
```

What do you notice? Well, the first thing is that the program's concept of a word is not ours. If you check the code, you will see that we applied >> (the extraction operator) to get a **std::string** value. By default, the extraction operator uses whitespace as a delimiter. Let me modify my program to use something more akin to my notion of a word. I need a function to extract the next word from input – something like this:

```
std::string get_word(std::istream & in){
  std::string word;
  while(true){
    char const letter(in.get( ));
    if(in.eof( )) return word;
    if(std::isalpha(letter)){  // note this needs <cctype> included
      word += letter;
      break;
    }
  }
  while(true){
    char const letter(in.get( ));
```

```
    if(in.eof()) break;
    if(not std::isalpha(letter)) break;
    word += letter;
  }
  return word;
}
```

If you study this code, you will see that it basically skips over the contents of the input stream until it gets a letter (`std::isalpha()` returns `true` only if its argument is a letter). It then adds that letter to the previously created empty `std::string` called `word`, and then enters a second loop to add letters until it gets a non-letter from the input stream. The code also handles the special case of reaching the end of the file, either by returning an empty word or by returning the last word.

After a little reorganization, our previous program becomes

```
int main(){
  std::ifstream wordfile("main.cpp");
  std::set<std::string> words;
  while(true){
    std::string const word(get_word(wordfile));
    words.insert(word);
    if(wordfile.eof()) break;
  }
  std::ofstream wordlist("words.txt");
  wordlist << "main.cpp contains each of the following at least once:\n";
  for(std::set<std::string>::iterator i(words.begin());
      i != words.end(); ++i){
    wordlist << *i << '\n';
  }
}
```

and we can build the second version of our solution program. This time the output file is:

```
main.cpp contains each of the following at least once:

at
begin
break
cctype
char
const
contains
cpp
...
this
true
txt
while
word
wordfile
wordlist
words
```

Now you can see the other characteristics of a `std::set<>`: the elements are stored in order (alphabetical order by default for `std::string` objects), and no element repeats. We could have provided a predicate function to give an ordering rule, but the default is to use the < (less-than) operator for the element type.

Problem 1a

List all the unique words in a file as a list in reverse alphabetical order.

We only need to change a single line of our previous program, but we need to do so carefully because we can no longer use the values provided by begin( ) and end( ). Starting with end( ) is no use, because that does not locate the last element but the actual end of the container. We need to use the reverse_iterator and the two member functions that provide the values needed to walk the container backwards, which are called rbegin( ) (effectively the last element in the container) and rend( ) (a special value to mark that we are off the start of the container).

Replace

```
for(std::set<std::string>::iterator i(words.begin( ));
    i != words.end( ); ++i){
```

with:

```
for(std::set<std::string>::reverse_iterator i(words.rbegin( ));
    i != words.rend( ); ++i){
```

Build and execute the program.

Problem 1b

List all the words in a text file with multiple copies (so each word occurs as many times as it is used).

This is even simpler once we understand the properties of the containers in the STL. Go back to the final program for Problem 1, and declare words as a std::multiset<std::string>. Build and execute the program.

Problem 1c

List all the words in a text file, with each word followed by the number of times it occurs.

We have to make a rather greater change to our program to achieve the desired result. However, once again, by choosing an appropriate container we get most of the work done without having to write explicit code. This time we need a std::map<> (declared in <map>), using words as keys and counts as values for the (key, value) pairs.

```
 1 int main( ){
 2   std::ifstream wordfile("main.cpp");
 3   std::map<std::string, int> words;
 4   while(true){
 5     std::string const word(get_word(wordfile));
 6     ++words[word];
 7     if(wordfile.eof( )) break;
 8   }
 9   std::ofstream wordlist("words.txt");
10   wordlist << "main.cpp contains each of the following words:\n";
11   for(std::map<std::string, int>::iterator i(words.begin( ));
12       i != words.end( ); ++i){
13     wordlist << i->first << ", " << i->second << '\n';
14   }
15 }
```

We create a suitable container at line 3 – one that maps **std::string** values to numbers. Line 6 uses a special property of **std::map<>** that allows us to access the value of a key by using the subscript operator (note that **operator[ ]** is overloaded for **std::map<>** to allow access by using a key value). In addition, if the index value is not already in the container, it is automatically added as a key and mapped to the default for the value (which is **0** in the case of an **int**). The first time we find a word in the text file, we add it to the container, the count is set to zero, and that is immediately incremented. Subsequent uses of the same word increment the count.

I have edited line 11 so that we will iterate over the **std::map**. Line 13 is a good example of the sometimes counterintuitive naming in parts of the Standard Library. We might expect to find **key( )** and **value( )** member functions to handle the two parts of a mapped element. However, the elements of a map are actually appropriate instances of **std::pair<>**. That template type from the Standard Library is simply a way of associating a pair of values. In that context, it makes sense to refer to **first** and **second**. Remember that iterators are effectively smart pointers and so support **operator->**.

Problem 1d

List all the words in a text file together with the number of times they occur. The list should be in descending order of frequency, with words having the same frequency listed in alphabetical order.

We can achieve our objective if we can sort the (**std::string, int**) pairs in descending order of the second value without disturbing the existing ordering for words with the same frequency. We need to apply **std::stable_sort( )** (declared in **<algorithm>**) to a suitable container. The problem is that associative containers cannot be sorted, because the elements are always ordered by their keys. We would prefer to keep using a **std::map<>** to collect the data, but need some form of sequence container to handle the sorting problem.

The Standard Library containers have constructors that support construction of a container from the elements of another. I am going to use a **std::vector<>** to handle the reorganization problem. I have already mentioned that a **std::map** contains elements of a **std::pair<>** type. Putting this together, we get the following definition for moving our collected data into a sequence container:

```
std::vector<std::pair<std::string, int> >
    seq_of_words(words.begin( ), words.end( ));
```

The space between the two > signs used to end template arguments is currently required by the language, to avoid confusion with **operator>>**.

That statement copies our data from **words** to **seq_of_words**. Next, we want to apply **std::stable_sort( )** to **seq_of_words**. Like most of the algorithms, **std::stable_sort( )** is provided with default behavior if you do not specify the criterion for sorting. That will not do, so we need a small function to provide this criterion (STL experts often manage to find ways of defining such behavior on the fly, but I am going to keep it simple). The requirement for an ordering function is that it takes two instances of the type concerned and returns a **bool** value (functions that return **bool** are called predicates). Here is the one we want:

```
inline bool compare(std::pair<std::string, int> const & lhs,
    std::pair<std::string, int> const & rhs){
  return lhs.second > rhs.second;
}
```

We can use that function to sort **seq_of_words** with:

```
std::stable_sort(seq_of_words.begin( ), seq_of_words.end( ), compare);
```

Notice that we just use the name of the comparison function as the third argument to **std::stable_sort( )**.

Putting all this together, our `main( )` becomes:

```
int main( ){
  std::ifstream wordfile("main.cpp");
  std::map<std::string, int> words;
  while(true){
    std::string const word(get_word(wordfile));
    ++words[word];
    if(wordfile.eof( )) break;
  }
  std::vector<std::pair<std::string, int> >
      seq_of_words(words.begin( ), words.end( ));
  std::stable_sort(seq_of_words.begin( ), seq_of_words.end( ), compare);
  std::ofstream wordlist("words.txt");
  wordlist << "main.cpp contains each of the following at least once:\n";
  for(std::vector<std::pair<std::string, int> >::iterator
      i(seq_of_words.begin( )); i != seq_of_words.end( ); ++i){
    wordlist << i->first << ", " << i->second << '\n';
  }
}
```

Build and execute the resulting program, and check the output file. Now try changing from `std::stable_sort( )` to `std::sort( )` (just edit out the `stable_`). Build and execute the result. When you examine the output file, you will see that words with the same frequency are no longer in alphabetical order.

Working with Numeric Algorithms

Problem 2

Given a data file consisting of names and salaries with one name and one salary per line, separated by a colon, compute the average (arithmetic mean) salary, the average for the top 25%, and the average for the bottom 25%.

You will need to create a short text file containing suitable test data (call it **salary_data.txt**) and save it in the **chapter_17** folder. Here is the bare bones of a program that solves the problem. You will need to include various headers. As well as the ones we have seen before, you will need **<numeric>** to provide a declaration for **std::accumulate<>** (used in lines 13, 18, and 22) and **<functional>** for the declaration of **std::greater<>** (used in line 12).

```
 1 int main( ){
 2   std::ifstream input("salary_data");
 3   std::vector<double> salaries;
 4   double salary;
 5   std::string name;
 6   while(true){
 7     getline(input, name, ':');
 8     input >> salary;
 9     if(input.eof( )) break;
10     salaries.push_back(salary);
11   }
12   std::sort(salaries.begin( ), salaries.end( ), std::greater<double>( ));
13   double const total(std::accumulate(salaries.begin( ),
14       salaries.end( ), 0.0));
```

```
15   std::cout << "\nTotal payroll: " << total;
16   std::cout << "\nThe mean salary is: " << total / salaries.size();
17   int const quartile(salaries.size() / 4);
18   double const top(std::accumulate(salaries.begin(),
19       salaries.begin() + quartile, 0.0));
20   std::cout << "\nThe mean salary of the top 25% is: "
21       << top / quartile;
22   double const bottom(std::accumulate(salaries.end() - quartile,
23       salaries.end(), 0.0));
24   std::cout << "\nThe mean salary of the top 25% is: "
25       << bottom / quartile << '\n';
26 }
```

I have used the three-argument form of `std::getline()` in line 7 to extract the name part of the data (and effectively discard it). This version of `std::getline()` is often useful when extracting data that has delimiters in it. Line 8 extracts the salary value that follows each name. At line 9, we check that we have not hit the end of the data file, and until we have, line 10 copies the last-read salary to the back of `salaries`.

Line 12 uses the three-parameter form of `std::sort()` to sort `salaries` in descending order. Note that when we use such tools as `std::greater<>`, we have to add a pair of parentheses. Such tools are objects created by using an overloaded `operator()`, and so we need to construct a suitable object. `std::greater<double>()` is a constructor for a temporary used to supply the criterion for sorting.

Every Standard Library container type includes a `size()` member function, which reports the number of elements.

The `std::accumulate<>()` numerical algorithm steps through the range of elements provided by the first two arguments and 'accumulates' their values into the value provided by the third argument. It returns the value of the third argument at the end. I have placed 'accumulates' in quotation marks because it has an optional fourth parameter that can replace the default of addition by some other operation. For example, `std::accumulate(salaries.begin(), salaries.end(), 0.0, std::multiplies<double>())` computes and returns the product of all the salaries. So, by replacing lines 13−16 in the above definition of `main()` with

```
double const total(std::accumulate(salaries.begin(), salaries.end(),
    1.0, std::multiplies<double>()));
std::cout << "\nThe geometric mean salary is "
    << std::pow(total, 1.0 / salaries.size());
```

we could compute the geometric mean of the company payroll.

Note that the above code assumes that there are at least four entries; otherwise, the value of `quartile` would be zero and we would get divide-by-zero errors. As a further exercise in writing C++, please edit the code to include suitable checks to ensure that there is enough data for the program to work.

Problem 2a

In the previous version, we ignored the employee's name by just reading it and discarding it. Use the same data, but output the names of the top 25% and bottom 25% earners.

There are many ways to tackle this problem, but here is a simple solution that builds on what we have covered earlier. First, we define a suitable type to hold the data:

```
class pay_data{
public:
  pay_data(std::istream & in){
```

```
      std::getline(in, name_, ':');
      in >> salary_;
      in.ignore(std::numeric_limits<int>::max(), '\n');
    }
    operator double()const{return salary_;}
    bool operator<(pay_data const & rhs)const{
      return salary_ < rhs.salary_ ;
    }
    std::string name()const{return name_;}
    double salary()const{return salary_;}
private:
    std::string name_;
    double salary_;
};
```

Most of that class definition (with everything implemented in the definition to keep this code simple) is straightforward. There is one interesting thing in the **pay_data** constructor, which arose when I was testing the code. The line that starts **in.ignore** is there because otherwise **std::getline()** picks up the terminating newline character from the previous data item in the file. That line is the idiomatic way to ignore everything left on a line of input. You can ignore everything to the delimiter of your choice, but **'\n'** is by far the most common.

The definition of a conversion operator is a rather lazy way to make **pay_data** behave like a **double** (useful for using **std::accumulate**). Defining **operator<** for **pay_data** ensures that the sorting algorithms can be called without the need to add an argument specifying how the data is ordered. The sorting algorithms in the Standard Library default to using **operator<** for the type. If the type does not provide that operator and you do not specify an ordering function, you get a compilation error.

Here is a short program that uses this class definition to solve the problem.

```
int main(){
  std::ifstream input("salary_data");
  std::vector<pay_data> salaries;
  while(true){
    pay_data salary(input);
    if(input.eof()) break;
    salaries.push_back(salary);  // uses compiler-generated copy constructor
  }
  std::sort(salaries.begin(), salaries.end());
  int const quartile(salaries.size() / 4);
  std::cout << "\nThe following " << quartile
      << " employees earned in the bottom 25\%:\n";
  for(int i(0); i != quartile; ++i){
    std::cout << salaries[i].name() << " earned "
        << salaries[i].salary() << '\n';
  }
  std::reverse(salaries.begin(), salaries.end());
  std::cout << "\nThe following " << quartile
      << " employees earned in the top 25\%:\n";
  for(int i(0); i != quartile; ++i){
    std::cout << salaries[i].name() << " earned "
        << salaries[i].salary() << '\n';
  }
```

Note the use of `std::reverse()` to re-sort `salaries` in descending order. I did not have to do it that way, but it saved me from having to work out exactly where to start the output of the high-salary earners. It also places the higher earners in descending order of salary.

Working with a Multimap

Problem 3

Create a dictionary of anagrams so that we can look up all the words spelled with a given selection of letters. The solution should allow the dictionary to be sent to an output stream (such as the console or a file), and provide for lookup of a word (or collection of letters) with output of a list of all the words that are spelled by rearranging the letters.

I have been rather lazy in my earlier problem solutions, because I have packed rather more code into `main()` than I would consider good design. Let me make amends with this problem and provide a reasonably well designed solution (though many readers may consider they can do better).

First, I am going to provide a couple of **typedef**s to avoid repeated use of long type names:

```
typedef std::multimap<std::string, std::string> dictionary;
typedef std::multimap<std::string, std::string>::const_iterator iter;
```

As you see, I am using a `std::multimap<>`. I intend that a key will be a string of letters in alphabetical order. Each corresponding value (the second element of a pair) will be a word that can be spelled with those letters. I have chosen to use **const_iterator** because I do not intend to allow changes to entries in the dictionary.

Now let me deal with the three things the problem requires us to do: create a dictionary of anagrams, send it to an output stream, and look up a string of letters.

```
void make_anagram_dictionary(dictionary & anagrams, std::istream & source){
  while(true){
    std::string word;
    source >> word;
    if(source.eof()) return;
    if(not std::isalpha(word[0]) return;
    std::string letters(word);
    std::sort(letters.begin(), letters.end());
    anagrams.insert(std::make_pair(letters, word));
  }
}
```

We pass a dictionary by reference (note that the dictionary might already have words in it) and a source of words into this function. It repeatedly extracts the next 'word' from **source**. Before continuing, it checks that it was not at the end of the file and that it did not read a string that began with a non-alphabetic symbol. In either of those cases, it returns to the calling function. As long as it has a legitimate word, it creates a working copy, to which it applies `std::sort()` to arrange the letters in ascending alphabetical order. Finally, it uses `std::make_pair()` to compose a single entity of the ordered letters and the original word, which it inserts into the dictionary.

The following function is the simplest solution to the problem of sending the dictionary to an output stream. It prints each entry on a single line – first the sorted letters, then the word they make:

```
void print_anagram_dictionary(dictionary const & anagrams,
    std::ostream & out){
  for(iter i(anagrams.begin()); i != anagrams.end(); ++i){
    out << i->first << ", " << i->second << '\n';
  }
}
```

Here is our lookup function:

```
void find_anagram(dictionary const & anagrams, std::string const & word,
    std::ostream & out = std::cout){
// note default argument allowed if definition doubles as a declaration
  std::string letters(word);
  std::sort(letters.begin( ), letters.end( ));
  iter lower(anagrams.lower_bound(letters));
  iter upper(anagrams.upper_bound(letters));
  if(lower == upper){
    std::cout << "No word using the letters of " << word
        << " found in the anagram dictionary.\n";
    return;
  }
  std::cout << "The following anagrams of " << word
      << " were found in the anagram dictionary:\n";
  for(iter i(lower); i != upper; ++i){
    std::cout << i -> second << ", ";
  }
  std::cout << '\n';
  return;
}
```

By now, most of the definition of this function should be clear. **lower_bound( )** and **upper_bound( )** are member functions of each of the standard associative containers (**std::map, std::multimap, std::set**, and **std::multiset**). **lower_bound( )** returns an **iterator** value (or **const_iterator** value if the container is **const**-qualified) to the first element that matches its argument. **upper_bound( )** returns an **iterator** value (or **const_iterator** value if the container is **const** qualified) to the first element after the last element that matches its argument. Both return the value of **end( )** if the element is not found. In addition, **upper_bound( )** returns the value of **end( )** if the found element is the last in the container.

Finally, here is a short test program that uses a file provided on the CD called **words_data** as a source to test the functions above:

```
int main( ){
  try{
    std::multimap<std::string, std::string> anagrams;
    std::ifstream input("word_data");
    make_anagram_dictionary(anagrams, input);
    print_anagram_dictionary(anagrams, std::cout);
    find_anagram(anagrams, "vile");
    find_anagram(anagrams, "level");
  }
  catch(...){
    std::cerr << "An exception was thrown.\n";
  }
}
```

Preloading a Container

Sometime we want to create a container with a certain number of values loaded into it at the start. The problem we face is how we can do that. If we use an array as a container, we can often write something such as:

```
int primes[ ] = {2, 3, 5, 7, 11};
```

However, we would want to be able to extend a container of primes by adding new ones to it. That suggests that we would like to be able to write:

```
std::vector<int> vec_of_primes(5) = {2, 3, 5, 7, 11};
```

The language does not support such syntax, or anything close to it. All is not lost, because we can use the facility for constructing a container to contain copies of the elements of a different container. It does require an extra line of code, but normally we can live with that. Here is how:

```
int const prime_values[ ] = {2, 3, 5, 7, 11};
// compute the number of elements:
int const provided_values(sizeof(prime_values) / sizeof(int));
std::vector<int>
    vec_of_primes(prime_values, prime_values + provided_values};
```

The line that defines `provided_values` is the idiomatic way of making code robust against changes in the number of elements used in initializing an array. I have `const`-qualified `prime_values` to give a hint to the compiler that it may, if it can, optimize away the storage for `prime_values`, because I am only going to use the values, not change them.

Future versions of C++ may make this mechanism unnecessary.

EXERCISES

1. The above definition of `find_anagram( )` ends its output with a comma. Improve the output so that this is not the case. (There are several ways to do this, but you might find using a `std::stringstream` useful as a way to prepare output.)

2. Change the definition of `print_anagram_dictionary( )` so that it prints each letter selection followed by a colon and then a comma-separated list of the words formed from that selection.

3. While the sorted letters in the anagram dictionary are held in alphabetical order, the words that can be made from a specific selection are not ordered. Modify your solution to Exercise 2 so that the words are listed in alphabetical order.

4. Combine the solutions of Problems 1 and 3 of this chapter to be able to use an ordinary file of text as the source of words for the anagram dictionary. Warning: you will need to be careful that you do not add the same word more than once to the dictionary. It is worth considering a multi-stage solution where you first extract the words from the current anagram dictionary into a set, then add the new words to this set, and finally create a new version of the anagram dictionary. This is only one of several good ways to solve this problem.

Conclusion

I have only given you the briefest of introductions to the STL and similar components. Undoubtedly, template technology is one of the most powerful features of C++. Writing good templates is time-consuming and makes considerable demands on the programmer's C++ skills. However, using well-designed templates such as those in the Standard Library will save a good deal of your programming time.

Other sources of template components include the library extensions provided by the first Standard C++ Library Technical Report. While the Standard C++ Library is nowhere near as extensive as that provided by Java, those components that are in it have been carefully designed and expertly implemented.

REFERENCE SECTION

Containers

There are two major categories of container: sequence containers and associative containers. A sequence container is one where notionally the elements of the container can be arranged in some arbitrary order. An associative container is one in which there is some rule that predetermines the way that the elements will be organized. Rather than try to pin down the differences in words, it is probably easier to describe the principal STL containers.

Each of the Standard Library containers has one or more constructors for construction from another container or sequence (these constructors take two iterator arguments). Although it is not possible to construct a raw array from a Library container (because arrays do not have constructors), it is possible to construct a Library container from an array by using a pointer to the start and one beyond the end of the array.

Note that all the standard containers are value-based and require that the type of the contained elements supports standard copy semantics (i.e. has both a public copy constructor and a copy-assignment operator, each of whose arguments is a `const` reference). The reason that you cannot have a container of `std::auto_ptr<>` is that it does not have standard copy semantics – it changes the instance being copied, to transfer ownership of the object it points to.

Sequence containers

The raw (built-in) array is the simplest sequence container. Unlike the other C++ sequence containers, it has a fixed number of elements. The reason that you need to know that it meets the STL requirements for a sequence container is that we can apply any algorithm to an array as long as it does not attempt to change the number of elements.

The STL provides three other sequence containers: `std::vector`, `std::deque`, and `std::list`.

`std::vector<>` provides all the functionality of a dynamically sized array; the elements are held in a contiguous array. This container type is designed for efficient growth and access. One consequence of supporting growth in a data structure that holds its data in contiguous storage is that the data may be relocated when the amount of it changes, thereby invalidating any iterators or pointers into the prior version. That means that you should be wary of holding on to iterators into a `std::vector<>`, because they may be made invalid by actions that change the size of the container.

Because of the possibility of relocation, which will invalidate iterators, it is usually better to use subscripting to access the elements of a `std::vector<>`. As long as a `std::vector<>` named `vec` has at least `n + 1` elements, `vec[n]` will be valid (and refer to the last element of `vec`).

`std::deque<>` (stands for double-ended queue) uses a different internal structure, which allows growth at both ends and guarantees that the elements are not moved during the lifetime of an instance of a `std::deque<>`. Meeting that design objective requires an extra level of indirection, so access to individual elements is marginally slower, but the benefit is that iterators into a `std::deque<>` are more stable and we can efficiently add new elements at the beginning as well as at the end.

`std::basic_string<>` is also designed as a sequence container, but one for character-like elements. `std::string`, which we have used extensively, is a specialization of `std::basic_string<>` for a `char`.

The above sequence containers are all random-access containers. That means that we can apply `operator[ ]` to any of them to reference a given element. For example, if `cont` is a random-access sequence container with at least six elements, then `cont[5]` would be the sixth element (remember that we always count from `0`, so the first element would be `cont[0]`).

`std::list<>` is a doubly linked list (there are STL-conforming singly linked lists available from such groups as Boost). List data structures have many advantages, but their main drawback is that they are not random-access containers. You have to traverse the list either forwards or backwards, element by element.

Associative Containers

`std::set<>` is a container that holds its elements in an order that is determined by an ordering function provided to its constructors. By default, it uses `operator<` for the type of the elements it contains. An attempt to add an instance that is identical to an existing element (i.e. compares equal to) is ignored. In other words, every element of a `std::set<>` is unique in that set.

`std::multiset<>` is also a container that holds its elements in an order that is determined by an ordering function provided to its constructors. By default, it too uses `operator<` for the type of the elements it contains. However, unlike `std::set<>`, `std::multiset<>` allows multiple copies of its elements.

`std::map<>` is a collection of pairs of objects, each pair containing a *key* and a *value*. With respect to keys, it is like `std::set<>`, in that every key is unique, and the elements are held in order of the keys (the order being determined by an ordering function, which defaults to `operator<` for the type of the key). `operator[ ]` (the subscript operator) is overloaded for `std::map<>`, so that a map can be indexed with a key to obtain a reference to the corresponding value. Indexing a map container on a non-existent key automatically adds that key to the map with the default for the value type.

`std::multimap<>` is also a collection of pairs of objects, each pair containing a *key* and a *value*. With respect to keys, it is like `std::multiset<>`, in that the elements are held in order of the keys (not necessarily unique; the order being determined by an ordering function, which defaults to `operator<` for the type of the key).

Iterators

Each of the standard containers supplies four iterator types as nested types (`iterator`, `reverse_iterator`, `const_iterator`, and `const_reverse_iterator`). The two `const_` versions provide access to elements of a `const`-qualified container. The two `reverse_` versions are to allow traversal of a container from back to front. The iterators are smart pointers, and so support dereferencing (`operator*` and `operator->`) and pre-/post-increment and -decrement (`operator++` and `operator--`).

Those containers that support random access (`std::vector<>`, `std::deque<>`, and `std::basic_string`) have random-access iterators, i.e. ones that provide overloads for `operator(int)=` and `operator-(int)`.

The built-in array types use raw pointers as iterators.

Each of the Standard Library containers provides member functions that locate the beginning and end of the container for forward and reverse iteration. These are called `begin( )`, `rbegin( )`, `end( )`, and `rend( )`. Each is overloaded for use with `const`-qualified containers.

Algorithms

The Standard C++ Library provides a large number of function templates that allow management of containers. The STL decouples these generic functions from the container types. The types of the iterators used in conjunction with them determine any special handling that may be necessary.

Several headers (most importantly `<numeric>`, `<functional>`, and `<algorithm>`) provide these templates.

Further Reference

Both the description and the use of the STL are substantial. *The C++ Standard Library* [Josuttis 1999] is widely acknowledged as the best available tutorial and reference. It is one of the 'must have' books for any serious C++ programmer.

CHAPTER (18)

Something Old, Something New

C++ is probably the largest and most complex computer-programming language in general use. It supports many programming paradigms and styles. That means that it is impossible to write a book of a reasonable size that covers the whole language. It is even less possible (!) to write a book that covers the many ways we can use C++. Indeed, I doubt that there is any single programmer who understands all the ways C++ is being used. Several years ago, during a refreshments break at a meeting of those responsible for the C++ Standard, we were discussing how many people it would take to ensure that we covered all of C++. Eventually we decided that we might manage it with three people if we chose carefully. I think we were being optimistic.

Professor Bjarne Stroustrup, the original designer of C++, has described it as the equivalent of English, a language in wide use, often as a second language. He added that it is a language that many people use successfully even though they only know a (small) part of it. Dennis Ritchie, the original designer of C, was once asked how much of C he used in an average program. His response was 90%. When Bjarne Stroustrup was asked the same question about C++ he is reputed to have answered: 10% to 20%.

In this book, I have tried to introduce you to a good foundation for programming in C++, but there is a great deal more that you can learn. C++ is a living language, and quite apart from the work going on to extend it, there is an amazing amount of development in using what we already have. This means that C++ programmers soon find that they are dealing with code written in an earlier style. Unfortunately, maintaining old (legacy) code is one of the commonest tasks assigned to newcomers. The purpose of this chapter is to try to give you some help when faced with old code that you did not write. There are issues of style, issues of exception safety, and issues of changing idioms.

My coding style is distinct and individualistic. I will try to highlight some of the main issues in this chapter.

Code Layout and Consistency

Programmers spend a horrifying amount of time in arguments about how we should present code. These are very largely 'religious' issues, in that programmers try to defend their choices with 'rational' arguments that, when looked at closely, are nothing more than subjective likes and dislikes.

One of the biggest time wasters is the use of whitespace and newlines to make code more readable. For example, which of the following is best?

```
int * i_ptr;
int* j_ptr;
int *k_ptr;
```

The answer is that it does not matter, but it helps to be consistent and use the style of your colleagues. What does matter is that we initialize pointers in their definitions. Without further context, you do not know whether the above statements are just declarations (as they would be in the scope of a class definition) or definitions (as they would be at block scope).

When you write code for yourself, choose any layout conventions that you are happy with; when you write code in a team, use that which the team uses. However, in both cases be consistent. If you write things differently, it should be because you are trying to highlight a difference.

For example, we can use either **struct** or **class** in defining a class type. In the modern style for C++, the public interface is listed first (i.e. we write things in a need-to-know order), and it makes no difference to the rest of your code whether you write

```
struct example{
public:
  // interface
private:
  // interface
};
```

or:

```
class example{
public:
  // interface
private:
  // interface
};
```

However, we could leave out the use of the **public** access specifier in the first case. No competent C++ programmer that I know would justify using **struct** rather than **class** so that they could save typing **public:**. It is idiomatic in C++ that using the **struct** keyword highlights the fact that we are including public data members.

A slightly less strong idiom concerns the choice of **class** or **typename** for declaring template type parameters. Either pick one and stick with it, or join the growing band that uses **typename** when the parameter can be any type, and **class** when the parameter is essentially restricted to user-defined types.

Where to Put const

The **const** keyword was introduced to C (borrowed from C++ during the 1980s) well after the language was in extensive use. There was no great reason to choose where the keyword went as a qualifier. As a result, C programmers got into the habit of putting it first whenever that was possible. Generally, the only time it was not possible was when qualifying a pointer as **const** rather than qualifying what a pointer was pointing to. C++ is different in that there are more uses of **const**. One of those uses is in qualifying member functions as ones that do not mutate the object data. That meant that there were now two places where **const** had to be to the right of what it qualified.

Then, in the 1990s, Dan Saks noticed that the increasing use of **typedef** applied to pointers was causing another misunderstanding among many programmers (not the expert ones, but many others). Here is a short code snippet that illustrates the problem:

```
typedef int * int_ptr;
int i;
const int_ptr i_ptr(&i);
```

Many programmers think of **typedef** as some form of macro. They think of it as just an alternative to:

```
#define INT_PTR int *
```

So they mistakenly interpret the definition of `i_ptr` above as:

```
const int * i_ptr(&i);
```

In other words, they read it as: `i_ptr` is a pointer granting read-only access to `i`. That is not how **typedef** works. The **const** qualifies the type, and so the definition above is equivalent to:

```
int_ptr const i_ptr(&i);
```

That is equivalent to:

```
int * const i_ptr(&i);
```

In other words, `i_ptr` contains the address of `i` throughout the lifetime of `i_ptr`.

So we now had two places where **const** had to be on the right, and one place where putting it on the left caused confusion in the minds of some programmers. That led Dan to start a movement to make it idiomatic to place **const** to the right of the type being qualified. Changing habits takes a great deal of time, and many programmers are repeatedly exposed to the older 'idiom'. In a way, it does not matter where you place **const** in the cases where you have a choice. However, I favor consistency, and so I always place it to the right of what I am qualifying. If you sometimes see it on the left, you will have to think carefully about exactly what is being qualified as **const**.

If you have a choice, I suggest that consistency should win the day, but it is not something worth fighting over.

Function-Style Versus Assignment-Style Initialization

C programmers had no choice: initialization of variables in their definitions was always done by using an equality sign. For example:

```
struct ex{
  int y;
  int z;
};
int i = 0;
ex x = {1, 0};
```

C++ inherited that mechanism and maintains it to this day, in order to maximize compatibility between C and C++ source code. However, C++ introduced this situation:

```
class mytype{
public:
  mytype(double x, double y):x_(x), y_(y){ }
private:
  double x_;
  double y_;
};
```

Now C++ needed syntax for calling the constructor. The chosen syntax was to 'call' the constructor with a function-like initializer:

```
mytype mt(3.0, 2.1);
```

So far, so good. However, it then seemed to make sense to allow initialization of fundamental types with a similar syntax. So `int i(0);` became a valid alternative to `int i = 0;`. Unfortunately, this was not pursued to the logical conclusion. For example, we cannot write `ex x(1, 0);` as an alternative to `ex x = {1, 0};`. It got worse. Add the default constructor

```
mytype():x_(0.0), y_(0.0){ }
```

and, surprisingly to most newcomers,

```
mytype mt();
```

does not define `mt` to be a default instance of `mytype`. What it does is to declare `mt` to be a function with no parameter that returns an instance of `mytype` by value. You may soon get used to recognizing the empty brackets as the cause of a problem in your code, and quickly learn to write:

```
mytype mt;
```

However, there are other subtler cases where the compiler manages to parse what the programmer intends to be a definition of a variable as a declaration of a function.

Consider the development of this tiny program:

Version 1

```
#include <iostream>
#include <ostream>

int main(){
  double d(3.3);
  int i(d);
  std::cout << i;
}
```

The program compiles and, when built, outputs 3, just as you expect.

Now your teacher comes along and points out that the compiler is giving you a warning for converting a **double** into an **int** (quite sensibly, because such a conversion can lose some data, and, more to the point, not all **double** values can be expressed as **int** values, even approximately.) You try to fix it with a simple function-style cast:

Version 2

```
#include <iostream>
#include <ostream>

int main(){
  double d(3.3);
  int i(int(d));
  std::cout << i;
}
```

Now the compiler gives you this warning:

```
warning: the address of 'int i(int)' will always evaluate as 'true'
```

What is it on about? It is complaining about your output line, but that is not where the problem is. It has parsed the previous line as a declaration of a function i( ) with an int parameter and an int return. Your first instinct may be to think that the compiler is wrong, but you are mistaken. You have fallen foul of the redundant-parentheses rule, inherited from C. int i(int(d)) is the same as int i(int d) as far as the compiler is concerned. In turn, that is just the same as int i(int), because parameter names have no significance in the context of a function declaration.

Yes, we should fix code that compiles with warnings, because the warnings are sometimes more serious than we think. Note that the warning for Version 1 is not that serious in context, but the warning for Version 2 tells us that the compiler is not seeing what we intended to write.

There are many ways to correct Version 2. My preference is to use the new-style C++ casts – a static_cast<int> in this case:

Version 3a

```
int main( ){
   double d(3.3);
   int i(static_cast<int>(d));
   std::cout << i;
}
```

However, you can also get around the problem by adding another pair of parentheses around the whole argument:

Version 3b

```
int main( ){
   double d(3);
   int i((int(d)));
   std::cout << i;
}
```

That form may be more useful if this problem hits you when initializing an object by calling a constructor that has more than one parameter. Try this code to see that problem manifest:

```
#include <iostream>
#include <ostream>

struct ex{
   ex(int i, int j):i_(i), j_(j){ }
   int i_;
   int j_;
};

int main( ){
   double d(3.3);
   ex i(int(d), int(d));
   std::cout << i.i_;
}
```

This time we get an error for the output statement. Once again, the compiler thinks we are declaring a function called i returning an **ex** by value. We can fix the problem by preventing the compiler from being able to parse your intended definition as a declaration. Add parentheses around the first argument to the constructor for **ex**:

```
int main(){
  double d(3);
  ex i((int(d)), int(d));
  std::cout << i.i_;
}
```

There are numerous other ways to deal with the problem of C++'s most vexing parse. However, the biggest problem is identifying that that is the problem that you have. It is a case where the error message never identifies the actual problem.

Why Use Function-Style Initialization?

I prefer it because it is more consistent. I say 'more' consistent, because there are places where you cannot initialize that way, but they are comparatively rare. On the other hand, there are places where this form is the only one that is valid, even when there is only a single argument. For example, the initializers in a constructor initializer list must use function-style syntax.

Using using

I have generally avoided **using** declarations and **using** directives when preparing code examples for this book. In most cases, the little extra typing involved in using fully qualified names (and having a hotkey to insert **std::** can reduce that) avoids some of the issues that can come up when using simple names via a **using** declaration or **using** directive.

It may not have been apparent that compilers make use of their knowledge of the scope in which the types of the arguments of a function are declared in order to extend the place where they look for overloads of the function name. We used to call the process 'Koenig lookup', because Andy Koenig (at that time the editor of the document that was to become the C++ Standard) proposed the idea. Experience has shown that there are some subtle and sometimes serious problems with the idea, which is why we now refer to it as ADL (argument-dependent lookup). For now, all you need to know is that there are some problem areas here, and you should be prepared to investigate further if they bite you. (As it took several years for the experts to identify the problems, they will probably not bite you soon unless you use cutting-edge libraries.)

Mostly, **using** declarations and directives are purely for convenience; they save us typing some code. **using** declarations can be useful when you want to compose an overload set from declarations in two or more namespaces, but that is usually not that good an idea. The technique needs to be used with understanding. However, there is one special case: a **using** declaration at class scope. Consider the following:

```
class base{
public:
  virtual void foo(int);
  virtual void foo(double);
  virtual void foo(base &);
  // other details
};
```

```
class derived: public base{
public:
  void foo(int);
  // other details
};
```

In other words, we want to provide a specific implementation of `foo(int)` for `derived`. Now consider this code:

```
int main( ){
  derived d;
  base & b_ref(d);  // provide access via a base-class reference
  d.foo(3.2);  // what do you think this calls?
  b_ref.foo(3.2);  // and this one?
}
```

The surprise is that `d.foo(3.2)` calls the `foo(int)` provided in `derived`, because in that scope our declaration of `foo(int)` hides all declarations of `foo( )` in `base`, with the result that the compiler converts `3.2` to an `int` with value `3`. `b_ref(3.2)` does what you should expect and calls the `foo(double)` declared in `base`. It is extremely unlikely that we want different overload resolution for the two cases, so we need to know how to inject all the declarations of the name in a base class into a derived class. This is how:

```
class derived: public base{
public:
  using base::foo;  // inject all declarations of foo found in base
  void foo(int);
  // other details
};
```

You cannot do that if any of the declarations of the name (`foo` in this case) in the base class are private. In addition, the access in the derived class will be the access level of the `using` declaration.

These rules apply regardless of whether the functions are virtual; it is just that you are most likely to come across the problem when writing implementations of polymorphic functions in derived classes.

Switching Off Polymorphism

If you need to overrule polymorphic behavior for some reason, so that the function implementation is that of the static (compile-time) type of a pointer or reference, you do so by qualifying the function name with the class name.

For example:

```
class base{
public:
  virtual void foo(int);
  // other details
};
class derived: public base{
public:
  void foo(int);
  // other details
};
```

```
int main( ){
  derived d;
  base & b_ref(d);  // provide access via a base-class reference
  b_ref.foo(3);  // calls the implementation for derived
  b_ref.base::foo(3);  // calls the implementation for base
}
```

Alternative Spellings for Operators

A number of operators have alternative spelled-out tokens. These exist for historical reasons, largely to do with keyboards for Scandinavian character sets. Several of the operators and other symbols used by C are not found on keyboards that conform to an old ISO Standard and that are used in several Scandinavian countries. After several years of argument, C and C++ agreed to alternative spellings for a number of operators. Most of these are just a mild curiosity, but one particular operator repeatedly gets missed, even by fairly experienced programmers; that is the logical not operator symbol (!). In addition, the logical and (**&&**) and or (**||**) are often confused with the bitwise and (**&**) and or (**|**) operators. For that reason I choose to use the spelled-out versions (**not, and,** and **or**) of those three operators.

Again, it is not a big issue, but you might like to consider whether those spelled-out versions make code more readable or not. As always, when we are dealing with this kind of issue, consistency within a team is far more important than being quirkily individualistic. Given a free hand, I choose the spelled-out versions, but I am not going to fight hard for the choice. However, you should know that you have a choice.

Hungarian Notation

If you are unfamiliar with the term, it refers to the custom that propagated from Microsoft of adding a combination of letters to the start of a variable name to identify the type of the variable. There was some sense to the idea when it was first developed for coding in C, though I think that the beginning of the identifier is the wrong place for such secondary information. However, it makes much less sense in C++, with its vast collection of user-defined types and considerably better type safety.

Programmers still like to add some secondary information to identifiers, and many of them just use a modified version of Hungarian Notation. I am not going to argue against decorating names with extras to identify something of their nature or scope. I generally think it is unnecessary, but if it is helpful, I am happy to do it. However, I am very certain that the right place for such extras is at the end of the identifier. You will have noticed me using identifiers such as **something_ptr** and **somethingelse_ref** where I want to emphasize that a variable is either a pointer or a reference. I also often append an underscore (_) to the name of a data member of a class. The names of data members are (or should be) entirely the concern of the implementer of a class. My mechanism ensures that the names of my private data members do not clash with other names elsewhere.

Names for Constants

The preprocessor **#define** directive was the only consistently available way for providing named constants in C. The preprocessor is a blunt instrument with no respect for scope. Because of that, experienced C programmers chose preprocessor names without any lowercase letters and ensured that there was at least one lowercase letter in all other identifiers. That idiom minimized clashes and unwanted damage done to code by preprocessing. However, many programmers simply learned the rule by rote without understanding. As a result, a school of C++ programming grew up where the rule had mutated into: "The names of constants should be in uppercase."

There are two things wrong with this rule. First, it exposes code to interference by the preprocessor when you include header files. Second, and perhaps just a matter of aesthetics, we have the names of constants 'shouted'. We can become accustomed to almost anything, but I have a strong personal dislike of unnecessary use of uppercase. I continue to advocate strict adherence to the original C guideline (even when I mostly write C++) that identifiers without lowercase letters are for the preprocessor.

I would fight this issue a bit harder than the earlier ones because I think that there is a minor safety issue.

Comments and 'Need to Know'

I am a strong believer that code should be readable and rely as little as possible on comments. Whenever I find it necessary to write a comment, I look at the code to decide whether there is some good way to reorganize the code so that it is comprehensible without the comment. That does not mean that my code is comment-free, but it does mean that my comments are important and should not be ignored.

It is useful to place a comment identifying the author and the last revision date at the start of a file; I do not find it useful to place the entire revision history, design description, and documentation there. People most often look at a file of source code because they want to review the source code. In my opinion, documentation belongs at the end of the file; readers can find it there if they need it. I look at comments as being similar to footnotes and endnotes. You do not expect to find such notes at the start of a chapter; they come either at the end of a page or at the end of the chapter. Sometimes we add parenthetical notes when writing text; those are equivalent to the comments at the end of a line of source code.

I hardly ever use /* */ comments in the body of my source code, but use the // form instead. That allows me to use the former when I want to comment out a substantial block of code for some reason. While some compilers do handle nested comments using nested /* */, most do not.

Multiple Exits from Structures

A substantial school of exponents of structured programming uses a very strong guideline (for some it is absolute) that every structure should have a single entry point and a single exit point (SESE). Now, I freely admit to being less than a devotee of SESE. However, I do have certain personal guidelines:

- Loops have one exit point. This may be internal, in which case the loop is written as `while(true){ ... }`.
- A loop iteration may terminate early (`continue`), but with only one use of `continue` per loop. However, I very rarely use `continue`.
- All exits from a `switch` must be to the same place (either all `break`s or all `return`s), and if they are `return`s, there must be a `default` that `return`s as well.
- If a function contains more than a single `return` statement, re-examine its structure to see if you can write it more cleanly with only one.
- Be wary of negative tests: human beings do not handle these well.
- You can often replace nested structures (`if-else`, `switch`, loops, etc.) with function calls (and I make a great deal of use of the unnamed namespace for such functions).

I find that application of these guidelines leads to most of my code being single-exit, but that is a consequence, not a target.

If you work in an environment where SESE is rigidly enforced, there are a couple of techniques that may help you to write good code despite the SESE requirement. However, first let us get to grips with the problem. Here is a short function (artificial, just to demonstrate) written in my style:

```cpp
double do_something(double total, int count){
  if(count < 0) return negative_count(total, count);
  if(count == 0) return zero_count(total);
  if(count == 1) return unit_count(total);
  return normal_count(total, count);
}
```

This function handles three special cases before dealing with whatever the programmer considers normal. The first thing to note is that I would almost invariably use a named function to handle the computation in each case. That keeps the function simple and easy to understand. The second point is that a maintenance programmer wanting to add special handling for some other case will have no difficulty in doing so.

The naïve programmer when faced with a demand that the function has only a single **return** statement writes something like:

```cpp
double do_something(double total, int count){
  double value;
  if(count < 0){
    value = negative_count(total, count);
  }
  else if(count == 0){
    value = zero_count(total);
  }
  else if(count == 1){
    value = unit_count(total);
  }
  else value = normal_count(total, count);
  return value;
}
```

It obeys the rule, but at the cost of added complexity. If you doubt that claim, suppose that you have to add some code for all non-negative values of **count**. You could encapsulate that code into a function called **do_non_negative_count(double,int)**. See how easy it is to add it to my version:

```cpp
double do_something(double total, int count){
  if(count < 0) return negative_count(total, count);
  do_non_negative_count(total, count);
  if(count == 0) return zero_count(total);
  if(count == 1) return unit_count(total);
  return normal_count(total, count);
}
```

Note how careful you have to be in modifying the SESE version. So does C++ provide anything better? Some exponents of SESE advocate the use of the conditional operator (**?:**) to deal with functions like the one above. They write:

```cpp
double do_something(double total, int count){
  return (count < 0) ? negative_count(total, count)
      : (count == 0) ? zero_count(total)
      : (count == 1) ? unit_count(total)
      : normal_count(total, count);
}
```

How do you modify that code to include the call to **do_non_negative_count(double, int)** ? Use the C++ sequence operator (the comma operator):

```
double do_something(double total, int count){
  return (count < 0) ? negative_count(total, count)
     : (do_non_negative_count(total, count), count == 0) ? zero_count(total)
     : (count == 1) ? unit_count(total)
     : normal_count(total, count);
}
```

With experience, code such as the above is easy to read, but almost certainly because you have disciplined your mind to read it in the earlier form. However, it does solve the problem of a rigidly enforced SESE guideline, and so it is worth having in your toolbox ready for the day when you need it.

Programmers often focus on the use of multiple **return** statements when they debate SESE versus SEME. However, in C++ we should remember that the existence of exceptions adds extra, invisible control paths. If the programmer is unaware of these, their code may seem to be robust and written to good standards for producing structured code, while being fragile or positively dangerous in the presence of exceptions.

Refactoring and the Power of Objects

Most programmers have a habit of letting functions grow. Large functions suffer from several problems. First, they are harder to maintain, because the more code you need to read to understand how a function works, the more likely you are to miss something. Second, large functions usually try to do several things rather than focusing on doing one thing well.

In the earlier days of programming, programmers were reluctant to write many small functions rather than a single large one, because they were concerned about the space and time overheads that resulted from such a coding style. These days, good compilers optimize away those overheads. Indeed the latest version of one well-known and widely used compiler delays code generation until link time. That allows both development in multiple languages and whole-program optimization. These days, programmers should generally focus on readability and maintainability rather than the size and speed of the executable. Optimization should not be a concern of the programmer unless they have measured the performance, found it inadequate, and located the bottleneck.

In general, refactoring of code is to improve readability and make it easier to maintain. We should aim to write functions that have a single conceptual purpose. Multiple structures (loops, switches, decisions, etc.) and nested structures are often a sign that the function is trying to do too much. In addition, the presence of a function with many parameters, or several functions with the same arguments, suggests that there is some object trying to make itself visible, and we should consider whether creating a suitable class type might simplify our code. (If you look at the next section, you will see an instance of this. The PortAudio sound library written in C has many functions that have a dozen or more parameters. My **audio_data** class packages much of this into a single coherent whole.)

The unnamed namespace is one of the major tools for refactoring C++ code. Couple that with packaging related data into a suitable class and we can greatly simplify much of our code. Sometimes we may find ourselves writing a bit more, but we get back the time spent in reduced maintenance costs: there will be fewer bugs, and those that there are will be easier to fix.

Here is a small example program that outputs the roots of a quadratic equation, given the coefficients of the three terms as input. This first solution is typical of one produced by a bright but inexperienced student programmer.

```
int main(){
  double a, b, c;
  std::cout << "Please enter the coefficients of the quadratic, linear, and "
     << "constant terms of a quadratic equation in standard form.\n";
  std::cin >> a >> b >> c;
```

```
    double temp = b * b - 4 * a * c;
    if(temp < 0){
      std::cout << "There are no real roots for that set of coefficients.\n";
      return EXIT_FAILURE;
    }
    temp = std::sqrt(temp) / (2 * a);
    if(temp == 0){
      std::cout << "The equation has a pair of identical roots: "
          << -b / (2 * a) << ".\n";
      return EXIT_SUCCESS;
    }
    std::cout<< temp << "The equation has distinct real roots: "
        << -b / (2 * a) + temp << " and "
        << -b / (2 * a) - temp << ".\n";
}
```

Like most simple programs, it can be broken up into three parts: get the data; compute the results; output the results. When you look at the code, you will see that the programmer has interwoven the last two parts. Here is my first refinement of the program:

```
int main( ){
  try{
    double a, b, c;
    get_coefficients(a, b, c);
    std::pair<double, double> roots (compute_roots(a, b, c));
    print_roots(roots);
  }
  catch(not_real){
    return EXIT_FAILURE;
  }
  return EXIT_SUCCESS;
}
```

Note that code results in a, b, and c being passed to two separate functions. That is a clue that they are parts of a greater whole. That suggests to me that I need a type to handle them. Here is my third shot:

```
int main( ){
  try{
    quadratic_equation qe;
    qe.get_coefficients( );
    qe.compute_roots( );
    qe.print_roots( );
  }
  catch(quadratic_equation::not_real){
    return EXIT_FAILURE;
  }
  return EXIT_SUCCESS;
}
```

Now I have to do the real work by designing and implementing quadratic_equation. Nonetheless, I have already gained better control of my program and improved its readability.

Here is a simple definition of `quadratic_equation`:

```cpp
class quadratic_equation{
public:
  void get_coefficients();
  void compute_roots();
  void print_roots()const;
  struct not_real{};  // used as an exception type
private:
 double a, b, c;
 double discriminant;
 double x1, x2;
};
```

Here is an implementation:

```cpp
void quadratic_equation::get_coefficients(){
  std::cout << "What is the coefficient of the quadratic term? ";
  std::cin >> a;
  std::cout << "What is the coefficient of the linear term? ";
  std::cin >> b;
  std::cout << "What is the constant term? ";
  std::cin >> c;
}

void quadratic_equation::compute_roots(){
  discriminant = b * b - 4 * a * c;
  if(discriminant == 0){
    x1 = x2 = -b / (2 * a);
 }
 if(discriminant > 0){
   double temp(std::sqrt(discriminant));
   x1 = (-b + temp) / (2 * a);
   x2 = (-b - temp) / (2 * a);
 }
 if(discriminant < 0){
   std::cout << "This program does not handle complex roots.\n";
   throw not_real();
 }
}

void quadratic_equation::print_roots()const{
  if(discriminant == 0){
    std::cout << "The roots are equal with a value of " << x1 << ".\n";
 }
 else{
   std::cout << "The roots are " << x1 << " and " << x2 << ".\n";
 }
}
```

You may well want to improve the implementation so that, for example, it validates the data on input. However, let me deal with a couple of other issues. Suppose the instructor now demands that the program send the roots to a file as comma-separated pairs, one set of results per line. First, we need to change the print_roots( ) member function so that it takes a std::ostream & argument. We want to do that without breaking our existing program. We simply add an overload to print_roots( ) by adding

```
void print::roots(std::ostream & out)const;
```

to the definition of quadratic_equation and implementing it with:

```
void quadratic_equation::print_roots(std::ostream & out)const{
  out << x1 << ", " << x2 << '\n';
}
```

Now we can replace the output line in main( ) with:

```
std::ofstream outfile("answers");
qe.print_roots(outfile);
```

If we want to append new answers to an existing file, we can change the way we open answers by writing:

```
std::ofstream outfile("answers", std::ios::app);
```

which results in the file being opened in append mode.

Next, the instructor comes along and requires us to write a program that will read the coefficients from a file that provides the data as sets of values separated by white space. Again, this is a small problem to fix. Add

```
void get_coefficients(std::istream &);
```

to the definition of quadratic_equation, and provide this implementation (or improve it so that it validates the data and handles incorrect data appropriately):

```
void quadratic_equation::get_coefficients(std::istream & in){
  in >> a >> b >> c;
}
```

Here is our new program that does more than the instructor asked; it loops so that it extracts multiple sets of data from the file until the file is exhausted.

```
int main( ){
  try{
    std::ifstream infile("problem_data");
    while(true){
      quadratic_equation qe;
      qe.get_coefficients(infile);
      if(not infile) break;
      qe.compute_roots( );
      std::ofstream outfile("answers");
      qe.print_roots(outfile);
    }
  }
  catch(...){
    std::cerr << "An unknown exception terminated the program.\n";
    return EXIT_FAILURE;
  }
  return EXIT_SUCCESS;
}
```

Finally, the instructor asks us to rewrite our programs (all of them) so they can handle quadratic equations with complex roots. Because of the way we have used a class to do the work, we hardly have to change our original programs (actually, if we do not mind having an unused exception handler, we do not need to do anything to the programs). We need to change the implementation of the class, including changing the definition so that the roots are of type `std::complex<double>` (we will need to include `<complex>`). The implementation of `compute_roots()` is all that has to change:

```
void quadratic_equation::compute_roots(){
  discriminant = b * b - 4 * a * c;
  std::complex<double> temp(std::sqrt(std::complex<double>(discriminant)));
  x1 = (-b - temp) / (2 * a);
  x2 = (-b + temp) / (2 * a);
}
```

If you want to, you can refine the two `print_roots()` member functions so that they only use the format for complex numbers when the imaginary part is non-zero.

Our final benefit from taking this approach to the problem is that we finish with a data type (`quadratic_equation`) that we can use in other circumstances where we need to extract the roots of a quadratic equation.

Using a Legacy Library

We all want to avoid having to reinvent wheels when good ones already exist. Not least of the problems of reinvention is that of having to learn details of both a problem domain and multiple hardware platforms. We want to use what already exists, but we also want to use good C++ code to do so. We want to separate the interface provided by a library from the details of the implementation.

Some time ago, I wanted to add a sound facility to my graphics library. This is hard in many ways. I did not want to be able to play sound files, which can be done using the `std::system()` function from the Standard Library. For example, this short program demonstrates the use of `std::system()` to use RealPlayer to play an MP3 clip from a game I currently have on my machine. Note that I have to double up the backslash characters used in providing a path to the MP3 file.

```
int main(){
  std::system("start realplay.exe E:\\BlueByte\\The Settlers IV\\Snd"
      "\\dark_tribe_01.mp3");
  std::cin.get();
}
```

I wanted to create something similar to my graphics library, with which the newcomer can build up pictures by using a number of simple primitives, such as the ability to set a specific pixel to a chosen color. I wanted to be able to play a specified note for a given duration. If possible, I also wanted to be able to provide tools for combining harmonics to produce more than a simple sine wave. However, I did not want to spend months teaching myself enough about sound systems on personal computers so that I could write the code primitives myself.

I poked around on the Internet and eventually found a portable sound library called PortAudio. It was written in C (and some old C at that) and was messy, at least from my perspective. I was faced with the typical task of using a C library in a C++ environment. First, I tried the code out in an attempt to get some understanding of how it worked and what the various functions did.

Next, I tried to define what I wanted to do. This task came down to writing a suitable interface. Here is my first simple attempt:

```
// declarations of functions to play pure notes
void left_note(audio_data & data,
    double frequency, int duration, double volume);
void right_note(audio_data & data,
    double frequency, int duration, double volume);
void stereo_note(audio_data & data,
    double left_frequency, double right_frequency,
    int duration, double left_volume, double right_volume);
```

Put simply, I wanted to be able to play a pure sine wave of a given frequency, duration, and volume on one or both of a pair of stereo speakers. Everything else was implementation. We need an object to manage the audio data. Here is the class definition:

```
class audio_data{
public:
    // WARNING: public data
    float *out;  // definitely easier to keep this public,
                 // as the callbacks have to manage it
    bool (*callback)(audio_data & data);
    // end of public data
    audio_data();
    // init from stream:
    audio_data(std::istream & in, int size = samples::default_size);
    void new_samples(std::istream & in, int size = samples::default_size);
    float const * get_samples(){return data_table.asarray();}
    int const get_sample_count(){return data_table.size();}
    void duration(int d){duration_ = d;}
    int duration(){return duration_;}
 // similar pairs of functions to handle the other attributes of audio data
 // omitted because they add nothing of importance here
private:
    samples data_table;  // default-initialized to a sine table
    double left_phase_;
    double right_phase_;
    int duration_;
    int length_;
    int tempo_;
    double left_frequency_;
    double right_frequency_;
    double left_volume_;
    double right_volume_;
    unsigned long frames_in_buffer_;
    bool busy_;
    bool reset_callback_;
};
```

I am not going to bore you with the details because the purpose of this section is simply to outline how we can implement a high-level interface for an existing legacy library.

The user of the sound library wants to write some simple instructions that will allow them to produce some simple music. They do not want to have to bother with a large amount of complicated low-level code. The task of the library designer is to provide a number of layers so that the user can enter at the level with which they are comfortable. All they need at the top level is to know what note, duration, and loudness they want. They also need an object (an output stream for sound) to which they can send that data. The audio_data class handles that. The high-level user will need to construct an audio_data object. However, they initially need to know nothing about the details of that type, because we hide the details within the implementation of the constructors. The default audio_data constructor initializes a lookup table of sound samples using pure sine waves. A second constructor uses a suitable file as a source of sample data.

When the user wants to dive deeper into the details, they can do so. Several other classes handle various aspects of the system. Users never have to concern themselves with the low-level C code. On the other hand, those that want to can. Note that if I wanted to build my library on top of a different low-level library, I could do so without touching the high-level interface.

My coding for my draft for a library for music code is currently very rough, and, perhaps, one day I will have the time to return to it and improve it. The important feature is that it is usable now, and because of the layers of encapsulation, I can work on it bit by bit, progressively improving the code while testing that it still outwardly behaves as it did before.

In Conclusion

Books have to stop somewhere. I could easily write another 600 pages and still not cover everything that makes C++ into the vibrant language that it is today. Inevitably, you will come across many things that have not been covered in these pages. You may want to learn how to design and implement template classes, what mutable is for, what use is private inheritance, what protected is all about, how we overload or even replace operator new, and so on.

Some of these things are best covered by selecting good books that specialize in some of the more advanced aspects of C++; some of them are small things that can be learned by making good use of newsgroups such as alt.comp.lang.learn.c-c++ and comp.lang.c++.moderated.

If you have diligently studied the material in this book and done the exercises and experimented with the code, you have a solid basic knowledge of C++ and a sound understanding of how it can be used. I have tried to show you how to build bigger programs by focusing on getting the parts right and avoiding trying to do everything at once.

You certainly still have much to learn, but you also have more than enough C++ to write excellent readable and maintainable code. If our paths cross at some time, please do introduce yourself. Tell me what you liked (that will make me feel good), but tell me what you did not like too, because that will help me the next time I sit down to write a book.

APPENDIX Ⓐ

Those Who Went Before

When I started writing this book, I thought it would be interesting to discover what responses contributors to the `comp.lang.c++.moderated` newsgroup would give to the following request:

> I am in the process of writing a book introducing C++ as a second language (i.e. I assume the reader is able to do simple programming in at least one other language). Yes, I do know that there are other books that do this.
>
> In the introductory chapter, I attempt to cover some of the ways that C++ differs from a wide range of other languages that the reader might already know. I would be interested in contributions from people who have learned C++ as a second language. If you have the time and inclination, could you tell us (I think it might be of general interest to the readership here) what significant differences you found in C++, particularly those that caused you difficulty in understanding C++.

Here are the answers I received. I have edited the spelling and I have corrected the English (several contributors are not native English speakers). I have not suppressed anything nor modified them in any other way.

I thank all those who took the time to share their thoughts and experiences with both the newsgroup and the readers of this book. Remember that each of these contributions is just an individual's response to my request. They might write something different today.

From Victor Bazarov

C++ was my first OO language. When I learned C++, I knew Fortran, C, assembly for a couple of processors, PL/I, BASIC, a bit of Prolog. The main 'shock' was to basically undergo that 'paradigm shift' known to accompany switching between a procedural approach and an OO approach. I do not remember actually reading something like 'From now on you will think differently' but that is what C++ did for me. Essentially, I discovered OO through learning the syntax of C++ and reading the examples given.

I cannot say I remember any difficulties. Perhaps it's because too much time has passed since my first foray into C++, perhaps because there were very few of them. I was a C programmer. Going to C++ was quite natural then (not that it has to be for every C programmer; do not get me wrong).

Another reason why there probably were very few difficulties is that I did not attempt to grasp the entire language at once. In fact, if I recall correctly, the first programs I wrote did not have much of OO. C++ was just a 'better C' to me then. Well, I might have written a class or two, but that was the extent of it. Overloading operators, and templates, came later and were more like an evolution of my knowledge of C++ (however small it was) rather than a dramatic change. I had the luxury to 'take it slow'.

Best of luck with your book!
Victor

Matthew Collett adds

Likewise. I knew Fortran, various dialects of BASIC, some Pascal, even a little assembly. Then I read TC++PL (2nd ed.). It was a mind-expanding experience. (In fact, I found it one of the most conceptually difficult texts I have ever read – which, given that I am by profession a theoretical quantum physicist, is I think a fairly strong statement.;-))

Best wishes,
Matthew Collett

From Ali Cehreli

My first language was C, but I think I was at most an intermediate-level programmer in C when I started learning C++.

RAII (resource allocation is initialization, an abbreviation for the idiom of the language where dynamically allocated resources are encapsulated into an object whose destructor releases them) and exception safety:

For me, the single biggest item in switching to thinking in C++ was realizing that RAII is not just a good thing, but also a must in C++. For some reason, years of following the newsgroups were not enough for me to realize the importance of that idiom.

I woke up from my ignorance after reading the exception-safety section in *Exceptional C++* by Herb Sutter.

Of course RAII (and probably even following the guidelines for exception safety) is not very difficult to grasp, but is very important for the learner to understand early on.

Reading:

I am not sure how C++ is different from other languages in this, but it's not a language to master on one's own. The learner is on a long journey full of reading articles, books, and newsgroups. I do not think the reading has an end.

No assumptions please:

C++ is probably more different from C than one might think. Related to the item above, the learner must not make assumptions but read. For example, one of the fundamental expressions in C++ is not known by far too many programmers because they assume that if `malloc` may return null, `new` might too.

(Before anyone objects, I know that the behavior of `new` was different in the past, but I have seen this mistake in fresh C++ code written by new C++ programmers. Moreover, I am not talking about `new` alone here, but 'writing under assumptions' in general.)

Ali

From Peter Koch Larsen

My background is roughly Algol → Pascal → C → C++ (Algol only 'academic'), so I doubt I will be very representative here. I have had very good mentors so I have not had any serious difficulty understanding the language per se, but I remember in particular my initial reluctance to place variables where they are used instead of at the beginning of a function. My biggest revelation was RAII (resource allocation is initialization), which (with templates) is the most important feature of C++.

Peter

From Maciej Sobczak

I've learned C++ as my nth language (having some previous BASIC, C, and Pascal experience). One of the things that I appreciate most is the ability to (ab)use operator overloading and templates in order to 'bend' the language to the extent that it becomes a separate dialect for performing specific tasks – in other words, the ability to create domain-specific sublanguages. It caused me some difficulty in the sense that it was not visible at the beginning, when I was learning the language. Let me explain this issue. The obligatory line

```
cout << "Hello, World!" << endl;
```

was taken (at the beginning) as a way of doing I/O in C++. OK, I knew how to print things in other languages; this one looks different, but still easy enough to remember. Beginners would even use this 'look and feel' to distinguish one language from another. You look at the code, and you immediately know what language it is. It took me some time of active language use to discover that the above code is not the 'C++ way'; it is a dialect, one of many possible ones, and, incidentally, the most popular. I realized then that in the languages that I already knew, all programs are similar. There may be different libraries that provide similar functionality, but the **way** of doing things is always the same: you call functions in C (and no matter who wrote a library, you can only call its functions); you use classes and call their methods in Java (and no matter who wrote a library, you only call methods of some classes); you call procedures in Pascal (and no matter who wrote the library . . .); and so on. The thing that is different with C++ is that the way to do things highly depends (thanks to operator overloading and templates) on the creativity of the library designer. As a result, two C++ programs can be much more different (in 'look and feel') than in other languages. Moreover, I would risk claiming that two C++ 'dialects' can have more perceptual differences than there are between whole languages (say, Java and C#).

One of the flagship examples (and my favorite in any debate including proponents of other mainstream languages) is the Boost Spirit library. It is syntax-oriented to the extent that it becomes a separate C++ dialect. In other languages, a library for making parsers would have the same 'look and feel' as the library for I/O, or whatever else. Just functions all over the place, or just classes and methods all over the place. In C++, the way of using a library is part of its design, which therefore extends far beyond picking function or class names.

To summarize, C++ is different, because it can be **customized**.

Of course, the above may be taken as a disadvantage, especially from the point of view of the beginner. In the long run, however, I find it to be one of the most powerful features that puts C++ high above others.

(Slightly off-topic: as a scripting language, I appreciate Tcl for the same reason – it allows me to redefine its commands or define new ones to the extent that it is possible to provide complete paradigms, not only dialects. The example is the library providing generic object-oriented features.)

Maciej

Frank Birbacher adds

I like this too. However, apart from introducing new dialects, it can be used to make things work differently behind the facade of the regular syntax. It might just change the semantics of regular constructs. For example, `std::auto_ptr<>`. Objects of this class can almost be used like regular pointers with the same 'look and feel', but the semantics are different: the pointed-to object gets deleted automatically.

Proxies are another example. Iterators provide the same look and feel as pointers, but actually they call regular functions on containers or whatever. In my opinion, this is a big advantage of C++.

C++ is a complex language. One has to do a lot of learning for C++. I started learning BASIC first. When I started with C++ in 1998 (I think) I had most difficulties with its syntax. As time went on, I learned the syntax and then structs/classes. I did not have much experience in OO at all, so I did not see how the classes would help me. But when I learned about the separation of concerns, I started using OO. RAII and exception safety followed. At last, I learned about templates. But after doing OO programs, I stopped using BASIC.

I learned the language slowly by asking questions on `borland.public.cppbuilder.language` and `.students`. I did not encounter major jumps during learning, but now I cannot live without classes, operator overloading, and templates. I wonder how I did before. :) This is the most surprising fact to me.

Frank

From Andy Little

I moved onto MSVC1.0 from QuickC – both Microsoft. I remember the weirdest thing was the `::` operator. It appeared all over the place, and this was before namespaces. I didn't understand what it did at all for a long time. There wasn't (and still isn't) anything like it in C.

Regards
Andy Little

From John Hickin

Best of luck for your new book!

Unlike most of the popular computer languages that I have needed to use previously, C++ has managed to keep up with the times, through the introduction of new features (templates are especially useful because of the unification engine that the compiler must have in order to support them). I think, therefore, that this best describes why C++ is different.

My first computer language was Fortran; this was in the days when a big machine had 16 MB of main memory; core really was magnetic cores in those days. It was mostly very useful to me, but I remember spending a lot of time as a student implementing dynamic memory allocation and recursion using a common block and 'hand-crafted stack frames'. Not fun.

I graduated to PL/I when I became gainfully employed. This was wonderful compared to Fortran, but again my language ran out of gas. This time it was inheritance and run-time type identification that we needed (but we used the term 'generics' to describe these concepts and the PL/I pre-processor to implement them).

I was converted to C++ in just 30 minutes when a colleague introduced me to it. I vividly remember his description of constructors, destructors, and virtual functions, knowing that these concepts would provide everything that I had lacked in PL/I. This was in spite of the fact that the syntax looked suspiciously like that of a language that I had rejected as having a syntax that was too ugly to bear and too difficult to figure out. :-)

Regards,
John.

From Thomas Hansen

Probably, many readers of your book will come from either the Java camp, the VB6.0 camp or the .NET camp. Therefore, I think that what you should stress as one of the biggest differences is that you have to take care of memory yourself, and therefore maybe you should stress the RAII parts of the language.

But I think that C++'s biggest difference is that it supports so many different paradigms and ways to solve the same problem. Write out a 'teaser' containing 15 different ways of solving the 'Hello World' application (to demonstrate how rich C++ is). One with a stream taking a string, another with a stream taking an object with an implicit conversion to a `std::string`, another taking an object with a `friend` global stream operator, etc.

And maybe take in this one (which is really weird for all non-C++ coders since it turns the inheritance tree upside down and gives possibilities not even thought of by even most C++ coders):

```cpp
class X { };

template<class T>
class Y : public T { };

int main()
{
   Y<X> myY;
}
```

I think the main difference between C++ and (most) other languages is not one single feature but rather the richness of the language and the many different ways you have of expressing yourself in C++.

'Balog Pal' adds

Hmm, I would guess 11 of those solutions would intimidate . . . a big part of the audience. Moreover, the part impressed will be the ones already experts in C++ and peeking into the book just for fun.

Thus, I would rather use examples fit to the paradigm under consideration, and not playing mind tricks – also avoiding pure showing off. However, it may worth having a pointer to the 99 bottles of beer website.

I strongly agree with the main point. The main strength of C++ is its multi-paradigm nature and the ability to use so many different styles to solve the problem at hand.

After one has learned to use them it can give wings and avoid the mind-shrinking effect that working with single-paradigm languages (or working long on a small set of problems) so often brings.

This same thing causes difficulty to newcomers to the field. As learning the part of the rules that can be used and is worth learning is relatively easy. But when you're given real-world code to work with, knowledge of styles and idioms will be needed, those of today and those of the past – possibly the whole history of two decades. Without those, you just keep wondering why on earth some code looks like this in one file and that in another.

Paul

From Glen Low

My history is BASIC → Pascal → C → C++. Java, C#, and Objective-C have been my post-C++ languages.

Thinking back on the difficulties in transitioning to C++, in no particular order:

1. The exact syntax of declaring member functions outside of the class declaration. Especially when interacting with templates.

2. Subtleties with the Big 3: copy constructor, destructor, and assignment operator. When and why they get automatically defined. When and why they get invoked, e.g. copy constructor in function return, difference between X x = 1; and X x; x = 1; ...

3. From a Pascal background, the inverted way you declare C or C++ variables, e.g. X ^CHAR; vs. char* X;, especially with the convolutions you can get with object-oriented C++ (think pointer-to-member). Lack of sets.

4. Why arrays are treated like pointers and structs are not, i.e. why you don't have a pointer to an array like a pointer to a struct.

Cheers,
Glen Low, Pixelglow Software

From Jean-Marc Bourguet

Well, C++ is not my second programming language. I was already more or less familiar with several variants of BASIC, several variants of Pascal (one of which was OO), several assembly languages, Algol68, Ada83, Fortran, Lisp, C, Prolog, and SmallTalk. This meant that I already had been introduced to all the concepts (often in two incarnations) supported by C++ and I already knew most of the 'C traps and pitfalls'.

Obviously, if you start C++ without that knowledge, the major challenges are the concepts you are not familiar with. I'll not write about that. I'll try to list what surprises I remember (some of them from learning C: 1−6):

1. char and bool are integral types.
2. Some surprising automatic conversions (mainly integral and pointer types → bool; enum → int).
3. Surprising relations between arrays and pointers.
4. typedef does not introduce a new type but synonyms.
5. No separate compilation, but linking of independently compiled units relying on the programmer's discipline and/or other tools to ensure coherence.
6. Use of the macro-processor (the main use being to achieve coherence above, but then there are some others). Most of the other languages do not have macros, and those that have have them more integrated (see Lisp, PL/1, or Forth immediate words).
7. Declarations everywhere in a block.
8. It is the class which handles visibility rules (in Ada, Modula3, and some variants of Pascal, it is the module or equivalent).
9. Constructors and especially the implicitly called destructor (there is some kind of equivalent in Ada95 but I don't remember one in another language), leading to RAII idiom and the possibility of writing exception-safe code without explicit handling of exceptions.
10. Templates need to be 'macro-expanded'. Most other languages mandate a shared implementation (Eiffel, Modula-3; I think the proposal for Java does as well); Ada83 has both kinds of implementation, and it was a goal of Ada95 to allow the two (I think all the implementations are 'macro-expanded'). This choice along with the possibility to do (partial) explicit specialization makes C++ templates the most powerful genericity mechanism I know.
Jean-Marc

From Chris Young

I came to C++ primarily from C. One of the biggest things to have bitten me in the early days was the use of const/volatile qualifiers. (The C compiler I used only warned about const violations, whereas the C++ compiler is a lot stricter. Therefore getting const/volatile qualifiers placed correctly became very important.) `http://www.xs4all.nl/~carlo17/c++/const.qualifier.html` was of great help here.

Using certain bits of the Standard Library caused indecipherable error messages in the early days (before I heard of STLfilt). This is, of course, an implementation issue more than anything else, but can still be a major put-off for a learner, apt to make mistakes, who has been taught to use the standard containers for general work.

The exception-handling mechanism was difficult to get my head around, about when and how the exception object is copied. For the application that an acquaintance and I were discussing years ago, this was a big deal (we needed to be sure we were not left with a dangling reference when we threw a dynamically allocated exception object):

```
std::auto_ptr<std::exception> except;
// ...
if (something_wrong( ))
    except.reset(new some_exception);
else if (something_else_wrong( ))
    except.reset(new other_exception);
// ...
if (except.get( ))
    throw *except;
```

Actually, the above would not work – not because of dangling references, but because the exception object is going to be sliced [clause 15, paragraphs 1–3 of the C++ Standard]. But it was an interesting thought experiment at the time, and just showed (to me, at least) the unintuitive way exceptions are handled. This will be a surprise to, say, Java programmers; they can most certainly throw exceptions of a derived type and expect it not to be sliced:

```
Exception except = null;
// ...
if (something_wrong( ))
    except = new SomeException( );
else if (something_else_wrong( ))
    except = new OtherException( );
// ...
if (except != null)
    throw except;
```

The unintuitive operation of **operator bool** will cane many newcomers, I think, when all they want is to be able to test an object in a Boolean context. Certainly took me a long time to appreciate why the Standard Library has, say, **operator void*** instead. [It is because **bool** has undesired implicit conversions to the fundamental arithmetic types. – Francis]

While we are on **bool**s, there is also **std::vector <bool>**. This will cane C coders who have been advised to 'use a **std::vector** like an array'. [I have not mentioned this issue in this book, but **std::vector <bool>** has some quirky behavior that you should ask about before using it. – Francis]

That is all I've come up with so far. I'll try to think up more.

Cheers,
Chris K.

From Robert Kindred

One of the biggest differences of C++ from other languages is the ability to use the 'Curiously Recurring Template Pattern'. This is not possible in any other language. I have heard of a language called Leda that can do this, but then I heard that it was compiled by C++.

The biggest selling point to cause me to switch from C was constructors and destructors, and the fact that they are invoked automatically. Almost all `main()` functions in C can be written as:

```
int main(int argc, char* argv[]) {
  init();
  run();
  shutdown();
}
```

With constructors and destructors, two-thirds of this can be hidden to allow focus to be placed on the real task, namely what is in `run()`.

From Stefan Heinzmann

Before getting into C++, I had experience with a number of procedural languages, mainly Pascal, but also some BASIC, C and Fortran. I also had some experience in various assembler languages and in Forth. Before getting to use C++ in earnest, I had exposure to the concept of object-oriented programming, and did some reading on this subject, which brought me into contact with other languages for OOP, such as some OO-extensions to Pascal (Modula family of languages and Eiffel), without having written anything substantial in them. So you may say that the OO paradigm had started to influence my programming style before I got into C++.

I was well aware at that time that the language you use has an influence on the way you think about the problem, and this has been a motivation to look at different languages in order to find new ways of thinking about problems. I remember having been particularly fascinated by the example of the **streams** library, where operator overloading was used for something that looked like a language extension, but was implemented as a library. I think to this day that this is the most fascinating aspect of C++: that it offers enough flexibility to the library programmer to tailor the language, in other words to invent your own domain-specific language and implement it as a library, rather than building a new compiler or preprocessor. Library design is language design, indeed!

I think that examples where this is used to good effect are those where C++ shines most. Besides the **streams** library, you could mention things like the Spirit parser library, or some numeric libraries (for matrix math).

On the other hand, it seems that in this very area the shortcomings of C++ are also felt. It makes me wish there were a language that was simplified as much as possible without giving up the possibility of implementing domain-specific languages as a library. It is this old elusive goal of making it as simple as possible, but no simpler.

C++'s ongoing development has continued to influence my programming style. The C++ I wrote at the beginning is quite different from the style I use now. This reflects the development of the C++ community as a whole – let me just mention templates and exceptions, which have required a long time to mature.

So this may be the other thing that sets C++ apart from many other languages: the development that has taken place within the language. I could say that the development of C++ over the years has allowed me to develop my skills without switching to other languages; C++ has grown with me and I grew with it, lately even to include a good deal of functional thinking. C++ has taken a tour starting at procedural programming and went through OO towards functional programming, as exemplified in the STL, and it has taken me with it.

Of course, for someone learning C++ now, it cannot be the same anymore, and maybe it should not be either. You still need to consider the history, however, in order to understand how and why things ended up the way they are now.

I hope that C++ is not going to freeze any time soon, as there remains a lot of scope for improvement, both for me and for the language.

Cheers
Stefan

Chris Marshall adds

In my case, I had programmed in Pascal, C, early C++ (1989–1991), and then Java – where I learned Java's take on OOP and programming in general (namespaces and exceptions) and fell in love with it.

When I first learned Java (in 1997), my feeling was that it fixed the many ways in which C++ had been broken when I tried to make my peace with it and failed.

Shortly thereafter (1999) I had read some article Stroustrup had written on the popularity of Java and how it was being viewed as a panacea for programming ills. Stroustrup demonstrated some of what was possible in C++ then and pointed out that for its problem domain, Java was an OK language, but it had serious shortcomings outside that domain and C++ was more generally useful there. I bought Stroustrup's book and tried to read it for a few months then gave up in disgust.

It wasn't until late 2003, on my third or fourth attempt at the language and Stroustrup's book, that I felt like I had broken through the barriers of understanding that had been blocking me from learning C++.

Stefan: I was well aware at that time that the language you use has an influence ... Library design is language design, indeed!

I also felt that the design of the << and > > streams operators was brilliant.

Being able to overload those operators allowed you to extend the library without having to define subclasses – a beautiful design.

Stefan: I think that examples where this is used to good effect are those where ... elusive goal of making it as simple as possible, but no simpler.

My personal feeling is that the biggest shortcoming of C++ is that certain books need to be written that teach you how to make the transition from other languages quickly by exploring how to write programs in various subsets of the language. I am particularly struck by the Java → C++ transition myself, of course.

Each language feature by itself in C++ is very complex when you consider all of its implications, and too many books try to cover each language feature in isolation from the rest of the language before teaching you how to write any significant programs at all. To my mind, it would require the patience of Job to read such a 1000-page monster.

We need more books written in the style of *The C Programming Language*. Yes, I realize C++ is a vastly more complicated language than C. I am just saying that you do not have to understand anywhere close to the majority of the language or the Standard C++ Library in order to learn enough to write significant and useful programs in C++ in various programming styles. You could have much smaller books that showed you what you needed to know quickly.

Stefan: C++'s ongoing development has continued to influence my programming ... the development that has taken place within the language.

It has been amazing to watch C++ evolve over the years. I think it is a testament to how unique some of C++'s early, and enduring, language features were. It provides a view of programming that is unique among languages, and it has taken much longer for the consequences of its view to be worked out.

I think one of the most fascinating aspects of the language is how it makes it possible to treat class types similarly to intrinsic types (like `int` and `float`), at a time when many other OOP languages were trying to do away with intrinsic types (having an Integer type derived from Object). It was much harder and took much longer to work out the details of how everything should work the way C++ went, and I think C++ was vindicated in the end. The implications of intrinsic-like class objects are much more interesting and generally useful than the implications of attempting to do away with intrinsic types.

Stefan: I could say that the development of C++ over the years has allowed me to ... exemplified in the STL, and it has taken me with it.

In my case, I am grateful for my time with Java, since it allowed me to learn a certain style of OOP that I kept retreating to when I would get confused in C++. Despite its many virtues, C++ has to be one of the worst teaching languages ever conceived. For people with my mindset, learning C by itself, then learning Java, and then learning C++ is a sane path, and I have trouble imagining any other path to learning C++. [My response is that many people have had a happy introduction to programming using my first book. – Francis]

Stefan: Of course, for someone learning C++ now, it cannot be the same anymore, and maybe it should not be either. ... I hope that C++ isn't going to freeze any time soon, as there remains a lot of scope for improvement, both for me and for the language.

I could not agree more. I cannot wait to see where C++ takes us next.

Chris Marshall

From Marcelo Pinto

My path in learning to program was BASIC → Pascal → C → C++. When I went from BASIC to Pascal I enjoyed the compilation process that made my programs run much faster, but I had a big headache with dynamic structures. Then I heard about C and was caught by the array/dynamic-array similarity in indexing and accessing elements. This was the reason I left Pascal behind. When I started using C++ (not long after C), I was amazed by the operator mechanism and the simplicity it allowed in my programs (I was doing numeric simulations in fluid dynamics). And after that I read Barton and Nackman's book and learned about templates and it amazed me more.

So, I believe that operator overloading and template programming were the two features that caught me.

Good luck.

From Mike Capp

At the point I started learning C++, I knew various dialects of BASIC, 68000 assembler, C, and (parts of) Ada. So I was familiar with structs and function pointers and so on, but hadn't been exposed to OO before. At the time I was that dangerous and perpetually annoying thing, a talented hobbyist with little CS education and zero experience of real life in the coding trenches.

The things I remember being particularly puzzled by were inheritance/vtables and exceptions – not so much **how** they worked, which was pretty easy to understand, but **why** you'd want to use them. I'd hear some language mechanism described and think, 'Yes, but you could do that with an array of function pointers and ...', completely missing the point. It didn't really sink in until I came to write a decent-size project (about seventeen thousand lines of code if I recall correctly) and found to my amazement that the bigger the code-base got, the easier it became to modify and extend, just because there was more supporting code around that didn't keep breaking. That was quite a revelation.

Similar thing with exceptions – I could see the 'what' and the 'how' but not the 'why'. (Hey, just found the incriminating evidence – search with Google using 'Mike Capp Exceptions' – ah, callow days.) Similarly, I think it was having to maintain a 0.5 mloc Pascal return-code nightmare that convinced me there had to be a better way.

In short, my experience was that understanding the rationale for the language was harder than understanding the language itself, and I think that only real-world experience on large projects will change that. Also, C++ 'knowledge' is more about idioms than rules, and idioms (for me at least) took a lot longer to learn.

Oh, actually, one mechanical confusion does spring to mind – the inclusion model for template implementation code. It just felt wrong. (Still does, for that matter, but you get used to it.) [That is for another book. – Francis]

Cheers,
Mike

From 'Spuds'

I have programmed in Fortran, COBOL, BASIC, assembler, and C before moving to C++. I consider myself a fairly accomplished C programmer and have had formal training in C. I remember buying a copy of *Computer*

Language Magazine in 1987 because of an article on C++. Knowing that C was a powerful language, I wanted to discover what C++ had to offer. From reading the article, I understood the basic concept of object-oriented programming and got a taste of the power of encapsulation. At the time I remember thinking that C++ will add about twice the power and twice the complexity of C. Looking back on it now, it seems humorous because I have come to realize that C++ is more of an exponential evolution, probably more on the order of 10 times more powerful and 10 times more complex than C. C++ has been a long road for me because no formal courses were offered back then. I am self-taught. I bought a book on C++ and read it from cover to cover without the benefit of a compiler because the large commercial vendors had not yet come out with a version of C++. I remember there were compilers from smaller vendors that were out of reach for the average hobbyist programmer.

I had to unlearn the mindset of procedural programming and learn to design software using the object-oriented features with which C++ empowered me. Coming from C I struggled with references and preferred pointers to references for the longest time. One of the biggest experiences I remember was when I finally understood what polymorphism was about. I was writing a GUI with different types of components displayed on the screen, such as edit boxes, combo boxes, radio buttons, etc., all derived from the same base class called `ViewComponent`. I loaded up an array with the pointers to the base classes in order from left to right, top to bottom, as they would appear on the screen. Then I called the `draw` function for each component through the base-class pointer and watched each component morph itself on the screen. This seemed to be a more practical example than the shape/circle or point/line examples you see in textbooks.

Over the years, I have acquired a library of books devoted to C++. After 17 years studying the language in my spare time and watching it evolve from a language without templates and exceptions, I have come to a point where I feel comfortable that I am at least able to research a practical programming problem and come up with a reasonable solution using the language. During this past year, I feel like I have switched gears and am thinking on a completely new level in terms of idioms and patterns in order to come up with solutions to interesting and practical problems. The language is so vast that occasionally I have come up with solutions that I have never seen published anywhere, which may be undiscovered territory in C++. At any rate, it has been a long journey, with many rewards along the way. C++ makes you work hard, but from my experience it pays you back handsomely. I made up my mind a long time ago that C++ was a necessary language for the serious programmer. I have never wavered from this opinion over the years and feel even more strongly about it today. For anyone that is considering learning C++, my advice would be: 'do it'. I did it and I will never look back.

From Emily Winch

Unusually, I came to C++ from Java. From that perspective, the major difference was almost a cultural issue – C++ programmers routinely considered the lifetimes of all kinds of resources, whereas in Java one tended to just 'new and forget'.

I was not impressed by the overloading of the meaning of * and &, and found them confusing to remember. In addition, people used a lot more C-ish idioms such as

```
*a++ = *b++;
```

that I had never encountered in a Java program. And the idea that 'pointer to `char`' generally means 'string' was very strange – or that a pointer might really be an array.

In addition, I kept accidentally passing things by value when I meant to pass by reference (Java passes by reference automatically for non-built-in types). Finally, in C++ you lose my favorite Java feature – anonymous classes:

```
frame.addWindowListener(
  new WindowAdapter() {
    public void windowClosed( WindowEvent e ) {
```

```
      // whatever
      // access local variables from the surrounding function if necessary
    }
  }
);
```

I was constantly wanting to write code like that and not knowing how to. In fact, there still is not a really neat way to do that.

Emily.

From Burc Arpat

My background is Basic → Pascal → Delphi (object Pascal) → Java and Perl (at the same time) → C++ (for the last 5 years or so). I do not claim to know C as well as I do C++ (mainly because I rarely use C-only stuff such as `printf` family or raw pointers, or dynamic arrays for that matter). I have used Delphi, Java, and Perl pretty much for everything from multimedia apps to database apps, from scientific apps to internet apps. C++ I have used mainly for scientific coding, as that's what I do nowadays. I am a member of ACCU – a big fan of Francis's 'Scribbles' column in C Vu. I am a daily follower of the Boost list. My total coding experience is more than 10 years.

Weird stuff about C++:

The first problem I had, coming from a long Pascal history, was the lack of the `with` keyword. I think the question I posted about that can still be found using Google. The `with` problem frustrated me big time and led me to believe that C++ does not want to make life easier for the programmer. I hated being forced to declare a temporary reference to bind the contained object as a 'shortcut' rather than simply writing `with`. Later, I realized C++ was actually trying to make life safer.

The second thing was, naturally, the whole template stuff. It took me at least a month or so (and several books) to understand and appreciate why on earth we do not use virtual member functions and instead use templates to achieve all this generic wizardry. Today, I think STL and generic programming should not be shown as 'advanced' techniques and should be introduced pretty much at the same time as OO stuff. I started to adjust to template code only after two years with C++, because of my OO background, and I have seen several people who refuse to understand the logic of generic programming even after several months of using template code, just because they are comfortable with OO. (A Java programmer of 5 years called the template stuff 'stupid', 'syntax garbage', and 'completely unnecessary' right in front of me when we asked him to start contributing to the C++ portion of the code.)

Another template revelation came to me when I understood the computational power of templates (thanks to Andrei [Alexandrescu]'s book, Modern C++ Design). Even if the STL is explained in a book, the metaprogramming aspect is typically completely skipped. You would not believe the number of experienced C++ programmers I have seen who had no idea about the whole metaprogramming deal. One such programmer even said he prefers to use macros because they are equivalent to, quote, 'fancy template stuff'. In an introductory book, it is normal not to talk about metaprogramming, but I think it would be cool to give at least one simple example just to show what can be done and then refer to an advanced template book. [I resisted the temptation and you will have to wait for the next book or read someone else's. – Francis]

Argument-dependent Lookup (ADL, a problematic C++ mechanism that extends the search area for looking up unqualified names to the scopes of the types of the provided arguments) stuff and the whole namespace issue: hordes of C++ programmers have never heard of it, even as Koenig lookup, and thus they have no idea how it might affect them. I remember the first time I saw this code:

```
using std::swap;
swap(lhs, rhs);
```

I remember the hour-long Googling session I had to do immediately after seeing that to understand why on earth the dude who wrote that piece of code did not simply say `std::swap(lhs,~rhs);`.

The whole automatic conversions deal. What can I say? They are confusing.

Finally, operator overloading. It is actually not that big a deal if you think about it, but for some reason my brain was fine with function overloading but not with operator overloading when I started learning C++. I have seen other people suffering from the same problem. I guess one reason is, books typically give lots of function overloading examples but not enough operator overloading examples. [Perhaps this book is guilty of giving you too few examples of both. Operator overloading is nice if you want to allow domain experts to use the symbols with which they are familiar. In that sense, operator overloading is very much more useful than function overloading. – Francis]

Hope this helps . . .
Burch

From Greg Schmidt

Many books teach you how to write C++ programs. Many books teach you how to avoid common C++ pitfalls. There are many books that teach you how to transition from the toy programs and object hierarchies you see in other texts to writing code that solves real-world problems in the best possible way (where 'best' depends on the technology or paradigm the book is pushing).

What I haven't seen are any books (not that I've looked too hard, mind you) that teach the other critical parts of C++ programming, which include things like making sense of compiler and linker error messages, recognizing the effects of various types of undefined behavior, and how to effectively use a debugger. I firmly believe that much of my success as a C++ programmer has come not from my ability to design effective hierarchies or write efficient code, but from my ability to quickly diagnose and correct bugs that arise during all phases of testing. In other words, I am an average programmer, but an exceptional debugger. Unfortunately, I am a lousy teacher, so I cannot write the book that fills this niche.

Like many people posting here, I got to C++ after much experience with BASIC, Pascal, and C (and less experience with a variety of others). I will try not to repeat any of the good points made previously in the thread.

I think that the difficulties encountered in learning C++ will vary greatly depending on what language you are coming to it from.

As a C programmer, I found the usefulness of the many new uses of `const` to be elusive, although now I cannot live without them. (Their omission is my biggest problem with Java; how can you create a language where every object is passed by reference, but have no way to disallow changes to the object?)

If I had come to C++ from BASIC or Pascal or Java, then I imagine (based on my experiences learning C) that the biggest difficulty would be the myriad ways in which you can invoke undefined behavior. Other languages do not allow you to do things so stupid as reading past the end of an array, or pretending that a memory location that holds a `float` actually holds an `int`, but C++ knows that sometimes (rarely, but sometimes) you really do need to do it, and it lets you. Of course, C++ gives you ways (vector, string, etc.) to eliminate most such problems, but they are not mandatory, and they are at best 'one-size-fits-most' solutions, so any serious C++ developer will eventually have to write some potentially dangerous code.

The other big difficulty for me, as others have mentioned, was learning to think in the OO way. Of course, I was learning C++ and MFC at the same time, so it was not just OO but event-driven OO, and that is very different from procedural programming.

Templates did not phase me much, although I use them infrequently enough that I still (after maybe 8 years) have to look up how to do certain things with them.

I immediately fell in love with references, default parameters, function and operator overloading, and the basics of the STL (`cout`, `string`, `vector`). I could feel my mind expanding just reading about them. Things that seemed to me just different (not better) ways of doing the same thing (exceptions, C++-style casts, the STL algorithms) took longer for me to realize the usefulness of.

Hmm, I am starting to ramble now, must be late.

Greg Schmidt

From llewelly

Before I learned C++, I had brief encounters with a variety of BASICs and Pascals (I had used both Borland and Apple), Z80 and 68 k assembler, and the HyperCard scripting language. But C++ was the first language I learned well, in part because I was able to find more books, discussion, and documentation about C++. I had read only one or two books for each of the previous languages I learned before C++ (and also for most of the languages I've learned since then), whereas for C++, I found and read many, many books. The first five or six were truly awful, but as soon as I found *The C++ Programming Language* 2nd ed. by Bjarne Stroustrup, I started finding other good ones, like the *Annotated C++ Reference Manual* (I wish there were a 2nd edition as it's now obsolete), books by Coplien, etc.

I think the differences which confused me most were not differences between C++ and other languages, but differences between vintages of C++. Most of these I can no longer describe – suffice it to say I did a lot (relatively) of programming with templates, starting almost as soon as I began to use C++. This should be normal now, but I learned way back in 1994−5, when the Standard Library (and much of the semantics of templates themselves) were inaccessible figments of WG21 discussions. It seemed every compiler – even different versions of the same compiler – had wildly different notions of what template semantics were. (The concretely described differences, like **for**-loop scoping, never caught me off guard, that I recall.)

I realize this is not what you asked for, but I do not recall any confusion that arose from expectations based on previous languages.

From Anthony Williams

I first tried to learn C++ in 1992, knowing only Pascal (of the Borland variety), BASIC, and various assembly languages. It was hard going. I thought I understood it, but I did not. I also had a poor understanding of the available libraries – I did not even have a good grasp of the Standard C Library.

At the time, I remember thinking that templates looked really nifty, as did operator overloading, but I did not really understand either well enough to make proper use of them. I did not have a compiler that could handle templates in anything like a sensible manner either.

Over the next few years, I developed various horrendous OO designs in C++, and learned C properly, along with a smattering of Perl and UNIX shell scripting. I still felt that C++ was fundamentally just C with OO extensions, much like Borland Pascal is standard Pascal plus OO extensions.

Around 1998 I suddenly managed to grok templates, and came across the STL and the rest of the newly standardized C++ Library. It now pained me that the compiler I had to use did not support the STL, and I wrote some simple templates such as a generic list. When g++ 2.95 came out I convinced the company I was working for to switch over to it, and I have never looked back.

I learned Java after I finally grokked C++, and it seems incredibly simple in comparison, and consequently very restrictive. When I write code in Java, I keep trying to do things 'the C++ way', as it is shorter and more direct, and it then pains me to have to write things out longhand (e.g. having to use **try/finally** to get resources cleaned up properly).

So, the features that I really like about C++ are:

- Templates
- The Standard Library
- Deterministic destruction
- Operator overloading

Templates were hard to learn, but maybe because there were not any good examples around. The STL really helps, because it is standard, and because it makes good use of templates.

A key feature I had to learn is that C++ is not just C with OO; it is much, much more powerful than that.

Anthony

From James Kanze

I am not too sure how relevant it is, but I came to C++ from C, and I found it incredibly simpler and easier. Of course, the C++ I first learned (in 1987–88) **was** a bit simpler than that of today. However, I had been using C for some time, and my standard procedure in C was to define a `struct` and a number of functions to manipulate the `struct`, and then to cross my fingers that no one touched it other than through my functions. The moment I encountered `private`, I knew that given a choice, I would always choose C++ over C. (In fact, I did not have access to a C++ implementation until a year or so later, when I purchased the Zortech compiler for my PC. And I did not get a chance to use it professionally until 1992. However, I knew that given the chance, it would be C++ rather than C.)

David Bradley adds

Interesting – I followed much the same path. I was creating `struct`s of function pointers. I was attempting to create an interface in C. It worked well for the task of talking to various database APIs. When I came across C++, it was a natural move. I also dabbled in Borland's Object Pascal, as I had used Pascal in the past as well.

When I jumped into the language I quickly realized there was more I needed to know than just the syntax. Fortunately, I was able to get formal training and read decent books.

The complaints of manual memory management and erroneous memory access are from people who haven't used the newer facilities in the Standard Library; nor have they sought out third-party libraries for smart pointers and the like. I rarely have these problems in my applications. However, I understand some of the frustration. It is a difficult language. It reminds me a little of English. A very expressive language, but very difficult to learn as a second language.

Therefore, while I enjoy the language, I think there is a fair cost to becoming proficient in the language. In addition, people believe they can jump into something like Java and do things quicker without the risks. However, even as safe as something like Java is, projects still die from the standard classic mistakes.

David Bradley

James Kanze adds

Not necessarily. If you come from C, of course, memory management in C++ seems easy. If you are coming from a higher-level language, however, it probably seems like there is still too much burden on the programmer.

I cannot say that I had memory management problems in C either. However, ensuring that I did not meant extra work. It is less work in C++ than in C, but it is even less work in Java or C++ with garbage collection.

From Brooks Moses

I came to C++ from Fortran, and ... well, for a long time, I had been avoiding it, because I looked at the built-into-the-language ways of dealing with multidimensional arrays, and they seemed sorely lacking. (I do numerical analysis work; if I write something more complicated than 'hello world', it has a multidimensional array in it.) In addition, beyond that, it seemed that many other things such as the string implementation were much lower-level than I wanted to deal with.

The crucial realization that I had when I actually started working with C++ was recognizing the paradigm that a lot of the fundamental functionality is in libraries, rather than in the core language spec. In particular, while the standard libraries do not have multidimensional arrays, they do have rather decent string implementations, and it was a matter of a few hours of work to knock together a basic multidimensional array that does everything I need.

I think that is a difference that is well worth spending some time on. The idea of operator overloading should be introduced into this very early on, too, as it is important in making library-defined functionality as easy to program with as the core-language parts are.

Brooks

Beliavsky adds

If one is using the multidimensional arrays in Fortran 90/95, where one

1. has access to intrinsic array functions like SUM and MAXVAL,
2. can broadcast ELEMENTAL functions like SIN to all array elements, and define your own ELEMENTAL functions,
3. can refer to array sections like x(1:2,:,2:10:2), and
4. can use arrays of dimensions up to at least 7 (required by the standard),
   implementing all this in C++, efficiently, could take months or years. Now that I am used to such functionality, I 'need' it, and moving to C++ would seem like a big step backwards.

From Phil A

The main problem I found when moving to C++ was not with learning the language but more in the way some people (still) use it. Looking at a modern C++ text from Koenig, Meyers, or Alexandrescu, you learn the best techniques for programming with the language as it currently stands. However, in real-world projects, I have not seen much use of the Standard Library, exceptions, or namespaces, but I do see reams of arrays and pages of preprocessor macros.

With a language this flexible, the hardest step for me was the leap from modern textbook purity to your next job maintaining an old server application written in '80s style C++!

From Paul Evans

As with many other posters, I came to C++ circa 1992 from an assembler, BASIC, Pascal, and C background, and had a similar revelation regarding RAII, exceptions, and templates. One thing I have not seen mentioned is an early conceptual problem I had. I could imagine classes, types, inheritance, polymorphisms, OO mappings from application domain to design plus implementation, etc., and all of that was a very exciting way to start thinking about program development (I could only imagine, as I was reading TC++PLed2 and had no access to a compiler). However, perhaps I let my imagination go too far, because I envisioned each object as having its own 'life' or thread. It took a few weeks to realize, in the general sense, they were dormant C structs (state) with associated member functions (behavior) that simply had an 'under-the-hood' 'this' pointer (identity) passed in to hook the state. Now with distributed and multi-threaded programming I do indeed have 'live' objects, but I had to work up to that from the 'dormant' object idea. Maybe I am just a geek with an over-active imagination, or maybe this is a more common obstacle for newbies.

In any case: many thanks to Bjarne Stroustrup for 'making programming more fun'!

Paul

Finally from me

A big thank you to all those who contributed to this appendix. I hope that you enjoyed reading it and that these words from those who are ahead of you on the road to mastery of C++ will inspire you to continue. One of the interesting qualities of many C++ programmers is that however much they like C++ they are not language bigots; they enjoy good tools for expressing solutions to problems as computer programs. They share my belief that C++ belongs in every programmer's toolkit alongside other tools and languages.

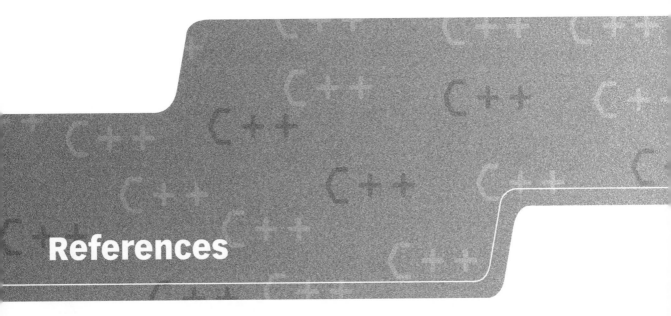

References

Alexandrescu, A. (2001) *Modern C++ Design*. Boston, MA, USA: Addison-Wesley Professional.

Austern, M. (1998) *Generic Programming and the STL*. Boston, MA, USA: Addison-Wesley Professional.

Glassborow, F. (2003) *You Can Do It!* Chichester, UK: John Wiley & Sons.

Josuttis, N. (1999) *The C++ Standard Library*. Boston, MA, USA: Addison-Wesley Professional.

Langer, A., and Kreft, K. (2000) *Standard C++ IOStreams and Locales*. Boston, MA, USA: Addison-Wesley Professional.

Stroustrup, B. (1994) *The Design and Evolution of C++*. Boston, MA, USA: Addison-Wesley Professional.

Vandevoorde, D., and Josuttis, N. (2002) *C++ Templates*. Boston, MA, USA: Addison-Wesley Professional.

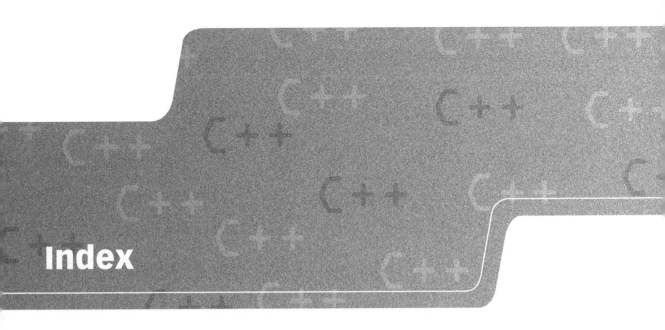

Index